STALIN'S NOMADS

CENTRAL EURASIA IN CONTEXT SERIES

Douglas Northrop, *Editor*

STALIN'S NOMADS

POWER AND FAMINE
IN KAZAKHSTAN

ROBERT KINDLER

TRANSLATED BY CYNTHIA KLOHR

University of Pittsburgh Press

Published by the University of Pittsburgh Press, Pittsburgh, Pa., 15260
Copyright © 2018, University of Pittsburgh Press
Manufactured in the United States of America
Printed on acid-free paper
10 9 8 7 6 5 4 3 2 1

Cataloging-in-Publication data is available from the Library of Congress

ISBN 13: 978-0-8229-6543-5

Cover art: Famine refugees in the region of Pavlodar, 1932, TsGAKFDZ,
5–3569
Cover design: Alex Wolfe

To Bettina

CONTENTS

ACKNOWLEDGMENTS

O VER THE PAST few years I have often felt that my work on Kazakhstan was finished, but each time I did, I quickly found that I was wrong. The topic continues to hold my attention time and again and I find myself fascinated by the dramatic events of the 1920s and 1930s in the steppe of Central Asia.

I had the good fortune of being able to share my interest in this subject with a number of people who not only made good suggestions and provided helpful advice, but who also continued to encourage me at times when I thought that the story would crush me. Foremost among them was Jörg Baberowski, who sponsored my doctoral thesis and gave me every liberty to tell this episode of history in the way I found appropriate.

At the Humboldt University in Berlin's Chair for the History of Eastern Europe I worked together with wonderful colleagues and friends of whom I here wish to mention Felix Schnell, Stefan Wiese, Botakoz Kassymbekova, Mirjam Galley, Christian Teichmann, and Fabian Thunemann as representative of all others. On numerous occasions I was able to present my theses for discussion.

I am grateful for everyone willing to think through Stalinism in Central Asia with me. Always important to me were my conversations with colleagues and friends like Turganbek Allaniiazov, Dietrich Beyrau, Sarah

Cameron, Alexander Frese, Klaus Gestwa, Paul Gregory, Claus Bech Hansen, Jan Hansen, Felix Hermann, Viktor Kondrashin, Maike Lehmann, Martin Lutz, Isabelle Ohayon, Matthew Payne, Niccoló Pianciola, Manuela Putz, Malte Rolf, Walter Sperling, Stephen Wheatcroft, and Manfred Zeller.

The Fritz Thyssen Foundation financially supported the initial years of the project, for which I am very grateful. Adrienne Edgar and Michael Wildt wrote thoughtful opinions of my work. The German edition of this book appeared with Hamburger Edition. I have Jörg Baberowski, Michael Wildt, and Bernd Greiner to thank for it. Without great copyediting by Andrea Boeltken and the work of Birgit Otte my manuscript would never have become a book.

Jürgen Determann and Paula Bradish spared no effort in drawing attention to the book. I owe it to them that it was awarded the Geisteswissenschaften International prize and will now be available in English. I thank the jury for distinguishing my work with that award.

I consider it a great honor to see my book published by Pittsburgh University Press in its series Central Asia in Context. I thank Peter Kracht and Douglas Northrop for that honor. Special thanks to Cynthia Klohr for translating the text into English. Alex Wolfe helped me navigate through the process of editing the manuscript and book production. A special thanks goes to Martin Wagner for his help with proofreading and the index.

No other has been more deeply involved in this project than Bettina. She encouraged me when I thought I had lost sight of the horizon and with one dry remark she could return my thoughts to reality when I became too euphoric. And finally, our daughters Käthe and Friederike influenced this project day in and day out in their own matchless way. And that's what pleases me most.

ABBREVIATIONS

APRF   Arkhiv Prezidenta Rossiiskoi Federatsii (Archive of the President of the Russian Federation)

APRK   Arkhiv Prezidenta Respubliki Kazakhstan (Archive of the President of the Republic of Kazakhstan)

ASSR   Avtonomnaia sovetskaia sotsialisticheskaia Respublika (Autonomous Soviet Socialist Republic)

AZhKRK   Arkhiv Zhokargy Kenesa Respubliki Karakalpakstan (Archive of the Highest Council of the Karakalpakstan Republic)

GANO   Gosudarstvennyi Arkhiv Novosibirskoi Oblasti (National Archive for the Oblast of Novosibirsk)

GARF   Gosudarstvennyi Arkhiv Rossiiskoi Federatsii (State Archive of the Russian Federation)

GASO   Gosudarstvennyi Arkhiv Semipalatiniskoi Oblasti (National Archive for the Oblast of Semipalatinsk)

GAVO   Gosudarstvennyi Arkhiv Vostochno-Kazakhstanskoi Oblasti (National Archive for the Oblast of Eastern Kazakhstan)

KASSR   Kazakhskaia Avtonomnaia Sotsialisticheskaia Sovetskaia Respublika (Kazakh Autonomous Socialist Soviet Republic)

KAZTsIK   Kazakhskii Tsentral'nyi Ispolnitel'nii Komitet (Central Executive Committee of Kazakhstan)

KPK   Komissiia Partiinogo Kontrolia (Party Control Commission)

KSSR   Kazakhskaia Sotsialisticheskaia Sovetskaia Respublika
(Kazakh Socialist Soviet Republic)

MTS   Mashino-traktornaia stantsiia (Machine and tractor station)

NEP   Novaia Ekonomicheskaia Politika (New Economic Policy)

NK RKI   Narodnyi Komissariat Raboche-Krest'ianskaia Inspektsiia
(People's Commissariat of Worker-Peasant Inspection)

NKVD   Narodnyi Komissariat Vnutrennykh Del (People's Commissariat of the Interior, Secret Police as of 1934)

OGPU   Ob'edinennoe Gosudarstvennoe Politicheskoe Upravlenie
(United National Political Administration, National Security until 1934)

PANO   Partiinii Arkhiv Novosibirskogo Obkoma KPSS (Party Archive of the Novosibirsk Oblast Committee of the CPSU)

PP OGPU   Polnomochnyi Predstavitel' OGPU (Authorized Representative of the OGPU)

RGAE   Rossiiskii Gosudarstvennyi Arkhiv Ekonomiki (Russian State Archive of Economics)

RGANI   Rossiiskii Gosudarstvennyi Arkhiv Noveishei Istorii (Russian State Archive of Modern History)

RGASPI   Rossiiskii Gosudarstvennyi Arkhiv Sotsial'no-Politicheskoi Istorii (Russian State Archive of Sociopolitical History)

RGVA   Rossiiskii Gosudarstvennyi Voennyi Arkhiv (Russian State Military Archive)

RKP(B)   Rossiiskaia Kommunisticheskaia Partiia (bol'sheviki) (Russian Communist Party (Bolsheviks), 1918–25

RSFSR   Rossiiskaia Sovetskaia Federativnaia Sotsialisticheskaia Respublika (Russian Soviet Federative Socialist Republic)

SAVO   Sredneaziatskii Voennyi Okrug (Central Asian Military District Commando)

SNK   Sovet Narodnykh Komissarov (Council of People's Commissars)

SSSR   Soiuz Sovetskikh Sotsialisticheskikh Respublik (Union of the Socialist Soviet Republics)

TsA FSB RF Tsentral'nyi Arkhiv Federal'noi Sluzhby Bezopasnosti Rossiiskoi Federatsii (Central Archive of the Federal Secret Service of the Russian Federation)

TsGAKFDZ Tsentral'nyi Gosudarstvennyi Arkhiv Kinofotodokumentov i zvukozapisei Respubliki Kazakhstan (Central State Archive for Kino-photo Documents and Sound Recordings of the Republic of Kazakhstan)

TsGARK Tsentral'nyi Gosudarstvennyi Arkhiv Respubliki Kazakhstan (Central State Archive of the Republic of Kazakhstan)

TsIK Tsentral'nyi Ispolnitel'nyi Komitet (Central Executive Committee)

TsK VKP(B) Tsentral'nyi Komitet VKP(b) (Central Committee of the CPSU [Bolsheviks])

TsKK Tsentral'naia Kontrol'naia Komissiia (Central Control Commission)

VTsIK Vserossiiskii tsentral'nyi ispolnitel'nyi komitet (Central Executive Committee of the RSFSR)

VKP(B) Vsesoiiuznaia Kommunisticheskaia Partiia (bol'shevikov) (All-Russian Communist Party (Bolsheviks) 1925–52)

STALIN'S NOMADS

MAP. 1. Kazakhstan 1933

INTRODUCTION

SULIMBETOV HAD LOST count. When asked how many people had died of starvation, the Soviet deputy chairman of Ushtobe said: "We'll know when the snow melts." In just two days he had recorded more than thirty bodies found at the local train station alone. The dead were strewn all over town. By February 1933 one had no way to bury them. Ditches and pits brimmed over. Mass makeshift graves were blanketed in white. Corpses laced all inbound roads, their eyes lost to the birds.[1]

Ushtobe was not unique. The winter of 1932–33 took countless lives. Soviet Kazakhstan went hungry from 1931 to 1934.[2] About one and a half million people died in that crisis, more than a third of all Kazakhs, or a fourth of Kazakhstan's entire population.[3] People died of hunger or disease, were shot, or slain. Hundreds of thousands were displaced; some turned to begging or banditry. Social nets fell apart. As the nomads' herds were confiscated and depleted, the economy of the steppe collapsed. At the peak of the famine, Kazakhstan was one enormous zone of death. Radical Bolshevik policy had not ushered in socialism, it had brought catastrophe.

In the early 1930s large parts of the Soviet Union, especially Ukraine, the North Caucasus, the Volga region, and Kazakhstan suffered from dearth. Of all these areas, Kazakhstan's loss in proportion to its total population was the greatest.[4] What triggered such devastation? How did the people and Soviet institutions meet the challenge? What mark did famine leave on them? The story of hunger and rule in Kazakhstan remains to be told.

Famine was inseparably linked to the Bolshevik experiment in widespread social reform in Central Asia, namely, the attempt to permanently sedentarize Kazakh nomads. Until the mid-1930s it was the single most important Soviet project for the modernization of Kazakhstan. "Backward" nomads were to become "modern," particularly acquiescent, subjects. Food shortage and permanent settlement were two sides of one coin: the food crisis made forced settlement a catastrophe, yet, in the end, hunger forced most Kazakhs to give up their nomadic way of life and become sedentary.

How did the Kazakh people deal with continued crisis? Little study has focused on how they organized themselves under the conditions of famine and what it meant for them once the crisis subsided. Many of the social networks they devised for survival under the food shortage continued to exist well after scarcity receded. Those networks were not entirely identical to the clans that had ruled society in the past. Clans were replaced by kolkhozes, brigades, and other collectives that produced and distributed indispensable resources. People became dependent on the institutions of the Soviet state. Imbalance brought about by scarcity enabled the Bolsheviks to assert their claim to power and to forge a society of dependents ready for collectivization. It was Sovietization by hunger.

Under Stalin the Soviet Union was built on turmoil, instability, and repeated excessive violence.[5] The attempts to impose rule and transform the country that followed from the collectivization campaign brought social burdens and crises. What the people perceived as a sequence of dramatic trepidations, the men around Stalin saw as an efficient strategy to rule the country. Incessant escalation was their mode of rule. Crises were both method and aim. Early Soviet Kazakhstan is an example of why that was so and how, in the early 1930s, the Communists at times apparently lost control of the dynamics they had unleashed. Their combined efforts to collectivize agriculture and force Kazakh nomads to settle threw the region into chaos, causing mass flight, civil war, and an unprecedented shortage of food. It came to the brink of destroying society. Simultaneously, the catastrophe helped the Bolsheviks implement their power permanently. The tragedy of Kazakhstan's nomads reveals how the assertion of power worked at the periphery of Stalin's Soviet Union, namely, by demanding much too much of the people.

SETTLING NOMADS AND GAINING POWER

Soviet modernity made no provision for pastoralists.[6] Nomadic mobility undermined all attempts to standardize administrative practices. As long as the Kazakhs and their animals wandered the grassy plains, the government could not get a handle on them. Comprehensive rule could not be had as long as the nomads questioned the very notion of modern statehood.[7] To gain real power over the indigenous population, first the Bolsheviks needed to gain control. Authority only took hold where orders were heard, where there was at least some "probability that certain specific commands" would "be obeyed by a given group of persons."[8] People who did not stay put, and, moreover, took their means of production with them wherever they went, were unlikely candidates for submission. Nomads were difficult to tax and difficult to supervise. But pastoralists controlled the steppe's economic resources. They crossed borders as they saw fit, violating the integrity of Soviet territory and eluding any government's monopoly on force.[9] One Soviet official complained: "We can take much from the farmers . . . and give little in return, but not so with the nomads . . . they just move on."[10] These circumstances thwarted the dictatorship of the proletariat. Nomads had to settle down.

James Scott once characterized sedentarization as a method for securing taxation and military recruitment and maintaining stability, which is crucial for materializing the tenets of "highly modern" ideologies seeking to radically change society by reducing complex matters to quantifiable variables. The probability of catastrophe grows when authoritarian leaders use such methods on societies that are unable to ward off radical change.[11] The sedentarization of Kazakhstan's nomads supports Scott's analysis: Bolsheviks knew that they could not break up the long-standing hierarchies of the native population without settling them. But the road from theoretical sedentism to real permanent settlement was long, arduous, and paved with suffering.

The Soviets first responded to conditions in nomadic auls with awareness-raising campaigns, investment, and sometimes with compulsory measures.[12] But when, as part of the Stalinist "revolution from above," the Bolsheviks began settling the nomads, they destroyed more than just the nomadic economy. The end of nomadic mobility meant the collapse of social relationships and networks upheld by annual migration.[13] And yet we shall see that the disastrous consequences of collectivization and sedentarization were not the result of ideological attack alone; scarcity was also the devastating result of various parties applying premodern practices while pursing their own interests in the steppe.

Until the mid-1930s, for Kazakhstan's ethnically and culturally heterogeneous society, state authority had been nothing more than a much-trumpeted fiction. The steppe had its own kind of authority that was not unconditionally willing to submit itself to Communist claims to power.[14] And various groups in Kazakhstan's multiethnic society competed with one another. Collectivization and sedentarization gave them opportunities to advocate their own particular interests. Excessive violence in the drive for collectivization and the subsequent civil war in the steppe reveal that not all party members and Soviet functionaries were willing executioners of orders.[15] Loyalty to the Bolshevik cause was particularly questionable in Kazakhstan. The party was split along ethnic lines, and competing clans used the new Soviet institutions to air their own grievances.[16] A number of resilient, interconnected, authoritative, and administrative systems were composed of tens of thousands of Kazakhs and it is difficult to say to whom they felt loyal—to the Soviet government or to their own communities. Thus, it is as naive to think that Communist Kazakhs stood for the interests of the state as it is to think that they were covert agents for their own clans and personal networks.[17] Different levels of loyalty were often difficult to distinguish.

Most Soviet depictions of collectivization and sedentarization gave a positive twist by praising modernization, progress, and the establishment of socialism. They focused on increasing productivity, growing numbers of kolkhozes, and higher rates of alphabetization. It was, in principle, the standard paradigm for progress used in all works on Soviet agricultural policy until the late 1980s.[18] Today this interpretation is no longer considered convincing—it often mistakes ideals for reality. The extreme opposite, and a no less distorted version, is the radical nationalistic narrative that characterizes the Kazakhs as innocent victims of a Russian or Bolshevik plan to eradicate them. In the version that became popular after 1991, Stalin and his Kazakh party boss Filipp Goloshchekin, operated as willful annihilators of the Kazakh people.[19]

Some ethnologists studying the relationship between nomads and modern statehood offer a different interpretation: the case of the Kazakhs can be seen as one variation of the global theme on the difficulty that states have in disciplining highly mobile pastoralists and bringing them under control.[20] But some of this work loses sight of the historical context. The ethnologist Fred Scholz, for example, finds that "despite all its critical detachment," literature on the sedentarization of Eurasian steppe nomads "paints a remarkably pleasant picture."[21] Such studies focus on what is considered successful modernization, while opposite studies examine the fate of nomads, who, when seen from a global perspective, have come under considerable pressure. Here we find talk of cultural losses and complex processes of adaptation and transformation that always see mobile pastoralists as losers. The dichotomous picture has become more differentiated now that the practices of mutual encounter and the influence of indigenous populations on the societies of their conquerors and colonists have gained attention.[22]

Other studies explicitly explore famine and sedentarization in Kazakhstan.[23] Most authors agree on the following points: from the standpoint of the Communists, the nomads' backwardness and clearly negligible effort to integrate themselves into Soviet economic plans, as described by the Bolsheviks, made it absolutely necessary to put an end to nomadic mobility. It was about destroying the traditional social order, gaining power and control, and economic efficiency. Famine finally put an end to nomadism. The Bolsheviks pursued their interests regardless of the consequences. In the face of gigantic sacrifice, independent and free nomads were forced to settle and lost both their culture and their way of life in the process.[24]

Nonetheless, interpretations differ on a number of significant points. The extent to which the drive for sedentarization shaped the trajectory of events is controversial.[25] There are also differences of opinion regarding the significance of certain figures. The precise role of Kazakhstan's party secretary Filipp Goloshchekin and that of his successor, Levon Mirzoian, have been widely discussed.[26] It is also not entirely clear just what the Bolsheviks intended to achieve by their policy on the Kazakhs. Does *modernization* really capture what happened?[27] Was it a colonization project of the Soviet state?[28] Or might one say that in light of the vast replacement of the steppe population by outsiders, it was a case of ridding the area of nomads to make room for inmates from work camps and certain other settlements?[29]

The more or less received view has been that by 1935 sedentarization had been accomplished practically throughout Kazakhstan.[30] In fact, nomadism never recovered from the damage caused by Stalin's top-down revolution. Nonetheless, in some regions it did experience a remarkable renaissance.

Sedentism lost significance and as of the mid-1930s Soviet policymakers no longer pursued it as thoroughly as before. Nomadic practices, they discovered, allowed large-scale livestock rearing in the steppe. The Bolsheviks began to rely on what they had formerly rejected.

The Soviet state tried to supervise and to control its multiethnic population with the help of ethnologists and other scientists. With their knowledge, Soviet leaders emancipated ethnic minorities, founded national territories and republics, and translated their agenda into the languages spoken by the wide range of Soviet nationalities. They also let members of formerly "oppressed" nations join the apparatus of the party and state, in order to then form indigenous cadres that represented those national republics within the Soviet Nation. This policy of indigenization, or putting down roots (korenizatsiia), was at the heart of Soviet policy on nationalities. It anchored the Soviet system within the non-Russian population and let it radiate beyond Soviet borders.[31]

This "affirmative action empire" (as the historian Terry Martin has termed it) based on asserting Soviet ideology and dominance has been a focal point of research for about fifteen years. Other work on issues concerning the Soviet periphery, especially the Central Asian region, has explored the conceptions behind the Soviet policy on nationalities and described just how difficult it was to implement them.[32] In many instances ethnologists, anthropologists, agronomists, and statisticians had considerable say in wording the Soviet policy on nationalities. Tapping into their knowledge of the diverse regions and populations constituting the Soviet imperium was crucial for party leaders who themselves often came from the periphery but had little knowledge of the demographics and ethnic composition of the entire empire.[33] Stalin was one of the few Bolsheviks who had engaged himself deeply with the "national question" prior to 1917. In 1913 he published his thoughts on it, including his famous definition of a nation as "a historically constituted, stable community of people, formed on the basis of a common language, territory, economic life, and psychological make-up manifested in a common culture."[34]

Relevant work from the West on Central Asia in the early Soviet Union has emphasized the importance of Bolshevik nationality policy. This perspective led to exoticization of the region, making it a special case of Soviet activity.[35] But Soviet politics at the periphery was national in name only. In terms of content, it was socialist, or better: Stalinist. In other words, the

Bolsheviks' claim to power and their practices were the same across the entire Soviet Union. In all Soviet republics their indigenous party members, who may have sought limited rights to autonomy and self-determination, were particularly aware of it. An end was put to the support and promotion of formerly oppressed nationalities whenever they appeared to threaten the overall interests of the empire.[36]

VIOLENCE

Physical violence was omnipresent in the Soviet Union under Stalin. But it was more than just terror by the state or resistance by the people. Violence was also a resource that was available to every individual and that was used to create order.[37] Conflicts ignited by campaigns for collectivization cannot be described as purely two-sided affairs involving only the state and the population. Nor can we say unconditionally that it was a war of the state against the people, because outside of a few larger towns, there often existed no state worth mentioning that would have been in a position to wage a war.[38] In Kazakhstan's steppe regions, the Bolsheviks lacked power structures and institutions that are distinctive for modern statehood. This structural weakness was crucial for the escalation of violence wherever the Bolsheviks tried to assert authority.[39]

It was Stalin himself who stepped up the use of force and demanded ever more drastic action from his subordinates. Communist functionaries of every level endorsed coercion to achieve their ends. They believed in the power of crisis. Without pause, they generated and produced contention and struggle between classes, nations, clans, and party members.

The Bolsheviks were not devout advocates of clarity.[40] The system was built on confusion and terror.[41] By holding most of society in constant turmoil the Bolsheviks secured their authority and forced people to take sides. Crises sifted friends from foes, truths from lies. The Soviet project to rebuild society rested on the generation of perceived differences. Central control of the economy followed the same principle. The notion that high-flying plans for the economy were inconsistent with reality inadequately describes the evolution of failure.[42] The unbridgeable discrepancy between goal and reality was in fact an essential component of Soviet policy. Stalin pitted various institutions against each other to keep them under control.[43]

The Communists knew that the resolute implementation of terror and physical violence would break the seemingly insurmountable resistance and achieve their long-term objectives. They knew that millions would lose their lives. They were aware of the immeasurable cost and the destruction of resources. But that was irrelevant to them.[44] They would destroy the foundation of Kazakhstan's rural nomadic society. It was not enough to requisition grain and livestock, not enough to persecute kulaks and tribal elders and force people into kolkhozes. They would make the steppe's predominantly nomadic population settle permanently. The sedentarization of Kazakh pastoralists was not the emancipation of a suppressed nation. It was not about creating the "New Soviet Man." It was about gaining power and exploiting the economic resources of the steppe.

FAMINE

Students of the Soviet famine of 1932–33 have often focused on the social, political, and economic causes of famine and its demographic consequences.[45] Much of this research has suggested that under the circumstances of food shortage, frustrated people had no influence on the events dictated to them.[46] People affected by famine were mostly depicted as vague, passive, helpless victims with almost no agency.[47] What happens to people who starve, how they behave when threatened with death, and what it means to survive a food shortage have seldom been described.[48] Rarely do we read that people confronted with starvation become self-centered and asocial.[49] Post-Soviet historiography in particular has cultivated the myth that peasants and nomads formed mutually supportive groups to master the crisis collectively, but that, unfortunately, they failed.[50]

Unlike earthquakes and volcanic eruptions that cause radical change with great momentum, hunger crises creep up slowly.[51] It takes time for food shortages to wreak devastation. People see the worst coming and ward it off for a number of days (as when brigades carry off the last ounce of grain) or even for weeks and months (as when bad weather ruins a harvest). Food shortage is also a very personal condition: one's own body suffers. Undernourishment alters one's body and one's behavior. For an individual, a food crisis is a dramatic reality, while outside observers often do not see it until signs of malnourishment are visible or the first individuals die.[52] Privileged groups always manage to find esculents and other resources; few famines can be traced to an absolute lack of food.[53] Amartya Sen has shown that hunger crises occur when certain parts of the population are denied access to food—in other words, when, for whatever reason, the distribution of available resources breaks down. Sen calls this mechanism "food entitlement decline."[54]

Studies on the vulnerability of social systems have shown that concentrating on the economic conditions of famine in the way that supporters of Sen's approach have done disregards other factors like climate influence and social shifts. Behind starvation, however, often lies a complex interplay of political, economic, climatic, and social factors that make societies vulnerable.[55] Vulnerability research frequently ignores the strategies people might have had for mastering a crisis.[56] Concepts like "catastrophe" and "fatalism" obstruct the recognition of rational human behavior under such extreme circumstances. People are not solely and exclusively victims: they develop coping strategies that may be inadequate or fail dramatically, but that is a different matter.[57] It is particularly true when, as Gerd Spittler has shown, a crisis becomes so great that it can no longer be met with the instruments normally employed in such situations.[58] The social and economic costs of extreme events such as famine are directly related to the community's capacity to adjust, or to fend off threats.[59]

That was one of the problems with which the Kazakhs struggled. When the drive to collectivization began, the nomads no longer had the same mechanisms in place for mastering a crisis that they had shared some decades earlier. Their migration corridors had become narrower and they had become more dependent on the settled population. Many were impoverished. Severe weather had made the Kazakhs overall even more susceptible and vulnerable.[60] They had lost much of their capacity to resist external threats. And yet the outbreak of famine cannot be traced back to poor harvests and adverse weather conditions.[61]

The hunger crisis of the early 1930s took on dramatic proportions when Bolsheviks refused to end requisitions even after the disastrous outcome of the policy had become obvious.[62] Without heeding the consequences, officials squeezed livestock and grain from regions already suffering from shortage. As long as they could continue to do so, they could ignore the increasingly urgent pleas for aid and food from the provinces. The confiscation of agrarian commodities and the resulting massive shortage of grain in the markets was responsible for the outbreak of full-scale famine.

Relentless requisition drives quickly and irreversibly ruined the very foundation of nomadic existence. Without their flocks of animals, nomads could not survive in the steppe. In many areas hunger, violence, and exodus made the social structure collapse, which, in turn, left a crisis of authority. The dictates of shortage proved stronger than the dictatorship of the proletariat: starvation diminished the threat of terror and coercion. Hunger and flight had left large stretches of land depopulated, constant dearth generated a new kind of order. The hungry society was marked by ubiquitous violence, relentless competition, and eroded adhesion.[63]

The history of Kazakh starvation is also a history of mass flight.[64] Large parts of the Kazakh population tried to escape the impositions of collectivization and sedentarization. The Bolsheviks fought, pushed back, and isolated the so-called *otkochevniki*, the Kazakh refugees.[65] Hundreds of thousands nonetheless made it to neighboring Soviet Republics or crossed the borders to China and Afghanistan. These people posed an enormous problem wherever they went and the local people and functionaries tried to keep them at bay.

Although the hunger crisis was not premeditated, for the Bolsheviks, it was a welcome outcome of events. They accepted it across the entire Soviet Union, and in Kazakhstan, *as if* it had been planned intentionally. It became the crucial handle on power in the Soviets' pastorally dominated society. It was hunger that broke the resistance of the nomads who had fought bitterly to withstand collectivization and sedentarization.[66]

The Soviet famine of the early 1930s has sparked a controversial debate (not only) among historians. In the center of this dispute stands not the hunger in Kazakhstan, but the question of whether or not famine in Ukraine was an act of genocide.[67] This controversy has lasted for decades and has seriously damaged the relationship between Russia and Ukraine. Moreover, in the course of struggling with the legal concept of genocide, historians have entrapped themselves in a debate that brings little to understanding the dynamics of famine.[68] In addition, the discussion of the Ukrainian *Holodomor* has largely eclipsed events in Kazakhstan.[69] More recent contributions to the history of the famine have focused on the dynamics of the unfolding crisis and its contribution to decision making in the Kremlin.[70]

Was the hunger crisis in Ukraine (and in Kazakhstan) genocide? Continued, emphatic repetition of the hypothesis does not make it right.[71] The famine was not a genocidal program of mass murder. Three factors refute the notion that it was.

First, the hypothesis of genocide is narrowly restricted to Ukraine and, at most, the northern Caucasus and ignores hunger crises throughout other regions of the Soviet Union (including Kazakhstan).[72] But if the hunger crises were just as dramatic in other areas of the Soviet Union as they were in Ukraine, it seems less convincing that it was solely the result of decidedly anti-Ukrainian policy.

Second, to date no sound evidence has emerged to prove that Stalin pursued the destruction of the Ukrainian people. The signs that have been interpreted as such, namely, the string of secret police posts (OGPU) meant to stop starving peasants from fleeing, Stalin's "fear" of losing the Ukraine, and finally, the harrowing distress that burdened the population are not helpful arguments,[73] in light of the fact that the Bolsheviks tried to prevent other groups from migrating as well, including the Kazakhs.

Third, loose reference to genocidal intent prevents us from exploring how the nations themselves were responsible for catastrophes. Those presiding over the fates of real people, those responsible for the lives and deaths of the starving were not abstract Communists, they were themselves real, often locally rooted party members, peasants, and workers. And yet neither Ukrainian historians nor their Kazakh colleagues write much about the wrongdoers or the motivation of lower- and intermediate-level administrators.[74]

SOURCES

The history of nomads and settled societies is usually told from the perspective of the latter. My work is no exception. Nomadic culture is highly oral and leaves comparatively few written sources. The ethnologist Rudi Lindner noted that "historians dislike nomads," because the oral traditions of nomadic cultures conflict with the needs of a science focused on texts. In addition, written sources often portray nomads disparagingly.[75] This observation is true for large parts of the materials used in this study. My sources have something more in common that has shaped the perspective taken.

With only a few exceptions all documents stem in one way or another from the Soviet state and party apparatus itself. They range from Stalin's own notes and those of other members of the politburo to reports submitted by isolated party committees in the steppe. The documents may have been written by staunch Communists or opportunistic career politicians, either to promote the cause or for personal gain. But most important, whatever these authors put on paper served the purpose of communication within the apparatus. They wrote reports, letters, and telegrams in (often poor) Russian so that native and European officials could understand each other. Only very few documents from the 1920s and 1930s found in central Kazakh archives were not translated into Russian or written in Russian in the first place. Thus these documents present a certain view of society in the steppe that can be considered an outsider standpoint in two respects: it is Soviet and it is Russian. The documents are stored in four central Russian and Kazakh archives consulted extensively for the purpose of this study.[76]

One repository towers above the others in its significance for this book. Fond 719 at the Archive of the President of the Republic of Kazakhstan contains documents from the Kazakh party control commission. Its files have become accessible in the course of the past few years and were evaluated systematically for this work. They offer insight into both the state and party apparatus in provincial Kazakhstan throughout the crisis-laden early 1930s.

In archived documents the views of Kazakhstan's nomads, if articulated at all, are often mediated. Nomadic opinions come down to us as expressed by *others*. The reasons for this are easily detected: the purpose of archives is to preserve official communications. They rarely store papers from "common" individuals. And few ego documents at all exist for the subject of this book: hardly a diary, travel log, autobiography, or memoir tells of collectivization and famine in Kazakhstan.[77] Nomads lived an oral culture; very few were literate.[78] Letters and diaries are rare for this period. And until the Soviet Union imploded, the victims of collectivization and famine went unmentioned. By the time these topics emerged for discussion, most contemporary witnesses had died. Thus the testimony of the aggressors is often the only information we have. Whether events actually transpired in the manner that these witnesses relate is uncertain. Particular care is called for when accusations, conspiracies, suspicious networks, and the allegedly guilty are documented.

The spellings for Russian concepts and names used here follow the Library of Congress transliteration system. Some exceptions are proper names, geographic terms, and concepts for which the English language or press has its own forms.

1

KAZAKH NOMADS AND RUSSIAN COLONIAL POWER

"THE HOSTILITY OF centralized states towards the roaming pastoralists," wrote geographer Leslie Dienes, "is well known."[1] Nomads were militarily unpredictable as well as being at a partial advantage, and notoriously elusive to the state's attempt to contain them. The opposite of settled society, they were seen as an undesirable and sometimes frightening lot. State and communal leaders had strategies for dealing with the challenges of nomadism: battling it, seeking peaceful coexistence, or perforce paying tributes when it looked impossible to fight or keep the wanderers at bay.[2] Yet nomads and settlers often coexisted to their joint advantage. They knew reciprocal dependencies and negotiated mutual trade contacts.[3]

The demands of livestock husbandry outlined nomadic life and culture in Kazakhstan.[4] Traditional herds included sheep, goats, and horses, but the nomads also bred camels, which were indispensable for work and transportation in the steppe.[5] In the wake of late nineteenth-century Russian colonization, the steppe economy also saw a rise in the importance of cattle.[6]

Most Kazakhs lived in their yurts (felt tents), organized in auls (migratory units) consisting of up to five families, and trekked through the steppe with their herds.[7] Only the newcomers, the European peasant settlers, saw pastoral nomadic journeying as more or less meandering around the steppe. For nomads it was purposeful migration. Within a distinct geographic corridor, they moved from their winter to their summer pasturelands across longer or shorter distances. The Adai, who lived in the west, traveled up to one thousand kilometers a year, while the summer and winter pastures of some tribes in the east were just a few kilometers apart.

The Kazakhs trace their general lineage back to their (mythical) ancestor Alash.[8] Among themselves they distinguish various lines of descent. Kazakhs were taught to know at least seven generations of their ancestors. By reciting and imparting their lineage, they knew and disclosed their own place within the intricate society of the steppe.[9]

Steppe society was organized in three major groups called hordes. Members of the Seniar Horde lived in what is now the south and southeast of Kazakhstan. By the beginning of the twentieth century they numbered approximately 700,000. The Middle Horde included the nomads in Central Kazakhstan, to the east and north, and counted about 1.3 million. The Junior Horde, which around 1900 numbered about 1.2 to 1.3 million people, lived in what is today the west of Kazakhstan.

Besides belonging to one of the three hordes, Kazakhs were defined as members of a clan, which in turn was part of a migratory unit known as an aul.[10] Belonging to a clan was essential. It determined one's social status, whether one was related to other clan members or not.[11]

Contrary to the impression given to many observers, Kazakh society was neither egalitarian nor classless. Its groups were highly stratified and thoroughly hierarchical.[12] But when confronted with strangers or challenges, the auls often presented themselves as one entity. An aul elder was called an "aksakal" (white beard), leaders of smaller tribes were called "biis." The Bolsheviks used the latter term indiscriminately to refer to clan elders, wealthy Kazakhs, judges, and other members of upper ranks. Just as the designation "kulak" (wealthy peasant) was widely misused in the European regions of the Soviet Union, bii was used incorrectly in the republics of Central Asia and therefore—just like the term "kulak"—when it is found in the sources, usually gives us no true indication of the social and material status of the individual in question. It is certain, however, that Soviet functionaries saw biis as adversaries.[13]

Not all Kazakhs were nomads. Large parts of the population were seminomads or settled. During the second half of the nineteenth century, Russian colonization forced an increasing number of Kazakhs to stop wandering.[14] By the early twentieth century many families had permanent winter

FIGURE 1. A Kazakh aul in the region of Pavlodar, 1920s, TsGAKFDZ, 5–3489

quarters for themselves and their animals. The first Soviet census, compiled in 1926, shows that at that time a fourth of all Kazakhs were sedentary and more than 65 percent lived seminomadic lives, trekking in summer months only. A small minority of about 6 percent of the population was nomadic year-round.[15]

Land possession was of lesser importance to nomadic families: wealth was measured by the size of one's herds. External conditions were thus a constant threat to one's prosperity. Natural catastrophes, particularly winter storms that left the grass covered with impenetrable ice, could be fatal for both man and beast.[16]

Historically, the peoples of Russia knew considerable interaction with the steppe's nomads.[17] But it was particularly the struggles between nomadic tribes and the princes in Moscow that left deep traces in the collective memories of Russians and nomads alike.[18] The Tatar Yoke—the rule of Mongolian khans from the thirteenth to the fifteenth century—was an especially traumatic episode in Russian history.[19] It took centuries before the military threat posed by the nomadic tribes was contained and individual tribes, one by one, submitted themselves (at least nominally) to protection under the White Czars.[20]

The relationship between the Russian state and its nomadic subjects was in need of clarification. One solution was to settle the nomads. In the late eighteenth century, Czarina Catherine II unsuccessfully encouraged such sedentarization.[21] In the second half of the nineteenth century, after militarily conquering Central Asia, the empire increased its efforts to force "alien" nomadic tribes (*inorodtsy*) to settle.[22] The czar's officials chose one of the allegedly most effective ways of subjugating colonial realms at the periphery: they promoted the settlement of European peasants there. They saw the wide empty spaces of the steppe as a void for Europeans to fill and transform.[23] The Bolsheviks later harbored the same conviction in their attempts to open up the steppe.

The czar traditionally first sent Cossacks into newly conquered territory, followed by peasants from central Russian and Ukrainian regions who lacked land at home.[24] But European peasant settlement was subject to cycles: periods of immigration bans were interrupted by phases of new colony promotion.[25] Nonetheless, the number of those willing to seek their fortune in Central Asia increased continually. And once the fruitful region of Semirech'e in the east of what would later be called Kazakhstan was opened for settlement by the Stolypin Reform of 1906, people came in droves.[26]

When it came to distributing land, colonial officials gave preferential treatment to the incoming European settlers over the indigenous population, endangering the future of nomadism.[27] Land that was "leftover" after property had been distributed was put into the colonial public land fund and redistributed among newly arriving settlers. Within a short time, the best land had been taken from the Kazakhs and transferred to European peasants. A series of ordinances and administrative regulations further exacerbated conditions. The Steppe Statute of 1891 had determined that no one Kazakh household could claim more than approximately 16.4 hectares of land, which made wandering impossible.[28] Within a few years, Kazakh herd sizes were decimated, Kazakh migration radiuses minimized, and overall, the nomads became poor.[29] Many saw no option other than to settle and try their hand at farming.[30] This varied, naturally, from region to region. In areas with many large farms, adaptation was faster than in the endless steppes of central Kazakhstan, where Russian influence was less noticeable.

But for many Kazakhs, settling for purely material reasons was only temporary. Although Russian rulers saw no future for nomadism, they gave the nomads few incentives to take up agriculture permanently. In an exposé on colonializing Siberia, Russian prime minister Peter Stolypin and his minister of agriculture Alexander Krivoshein wrote that "the Kirghiz [i.e., the Kazakhs] cannot remain nomads forever, if they are capable of culture at all. Experience from recent years has shown that they are capable of moving on toward a life as farmers and that the Russian settlement in the steppe, which is inevitably linked to reducing land for nomadism, is the most powerful and for the time being, the only motivation for it."[31]

The Russians found the Kazakhs backward und unrefined. Control in the steppe was explicitly bound up with a mission to civilize them.[32] A typical report, for example, by a traveler from the late nineteenth century, says of the inside of a yurt: "That phenomenal Kirghiz dirt that settles in thick layers on all of a nomad's furnishings, leaves nothing one could sit or write on. There is no table and there are no chairs."[33]

In addition, many colonial officials were convinced that the Kazakhs wandered simply because they did not care to "bear the heavy yoke of agricultural work."[34] They apparently had no strong role models to represent the advantages of a nonmigratory, "civilized" life. Now, for lack of any better, the European settler colonists in Central Asia would "teach" them.[35] Most officials ignored the fact that the peasant homesteaders were hardly models of Europe's supposedly superior culture.[36] Count Constantin von der Pahlen, who was critical of the Russian colonial administration's activities, described the problem: "The majority [of the immigrants] were neither peasants from the land nor genuine factory workers but belonged to an intermediary class impoverished by circumstances in Russia. Lured by rosy prospects of a 'promised land' they had immigrated to Turkestan and were only too ready to lead an idle life at the expense of the state . . . and looked down upon the hardworking and disciplined natives."[37] The Russians, who came, as Dostoevsky wrote in 1881 in his famous diary entry on Russia's civilizing mission, "to Asia as masters," often resorted to arbitrary measures when they came into contact with those who had been colonized.[38]

Some have said that it was the czar's colonial policy that put an end to nomadism without developing any economically meaningful alternative plan. And that this was the challenge that the Bolsheviks faced after the civil war.[39] But while in the early twentieth century the Kazakhs were in a much worse economic situation than they had been before the Russian takeovers, this interpretation equates the normative acts of the colonial administration with the real conditions of the steppe.

What nomads and European peasant homesteaders had in common was originally little more than deep mutual aversion. They competed for the region's most important resources: farm land, pastures, and access to water. The peasants settled in the most fertile river valleys and at the watering sites of oases, shutting out the nomads who had watered and grazed their herds there before. In conflicts, the colonial officials usually took sides with the farmers in an alliance that the Kazakhs could hardly withstand. And conflicts—some of them violent—arose again and again.[40]

European coexistence with Central Asians created not only friction and new dependencies, it also opened up new and attractive perspectives for certain groups within the Kazakh population. Colonization in Central Asia increased the pressure on nomads to bring themselves into the economic and administrative elements of colonial society. Colonial leaders, in turn, needed the support of local middlemen who had an influence on the nomadic communities and acted in its interest. Locals were made community elders or given other posts in colonial administration. While fast social change created poverty for some, it also created new opportunities for members of Central Asia's elite.[41]

When it came to taxation and requisition, the czar's administrators were unyielding. Imperial authorities, whose powers in the Russian provinces often did not extend much further than taxation and resource extraction, had demonstrated repeatedly that relentlessness was the chosen method of rule. Whenever serious problems or uprisings occurred, the government sent armed units to remind subjects of its authority.[42] On the other hand, Russian policy was broadly tolerant of the nomads' Islam and of Kazakh customary law (*adat*).[43] The officials thought that nomads were less "fanatic" than the Muslims of Turkestan's oasis societies and that they were open to some sort of compromise, not least because it had been the Russians themselves who in the eighteenth century had spread Islam among the nomads in the hope that it would settle and "civilize" them.[44]

Intense contact with the Russian rulers also altered discourse among the Kazakhs themselves. Toward the end of the nineteenth century, Kazakhs familiar with European debates on national self-determination and modernity began forming a commitment to the creation a "Kazakh nation."[45] A small group of Kazakh intellectuals who had been educated and socialized in Russian schools and universities no longer argued over whether nomads should settle, but instead over how best to achieve it.[46] They agreed that without settling the nomads, the goal of their efforts—the creation of a "Kazakh nation"—was hopeless.[47] At the same time, influential leaders of Kazakh clans defended nomadism, which they saw at the heart of their identity.[48] Nonetheless, the reformers, as few of them as there were, played an important role: they constituted the core of the anticolonial elite that stood up for national self-determination, modernization, and the reform of traditional practices. They founded newspapers, associations, and political parties. During the tumult of civil war they made up the short-lived government of the Kazakh party Alash Orda. In the 1920s many of them belonged to the Bolsheviks' first generation of prominent local party members.[49]

No one single occurrence radicalized steppe society more than the Kazakh uprising of 1916, to which peasant settlers responded by massacring the insurgents.[50] On the face of it, the revolt had been sparked by the drafting of the male Kazakh population for work duty on the Russian western front, but the underlying reasons went deeper: the relationship had been poisoned by endless conflicts between peasants and nomads over access to land and water and by the arbitrary and disrespectful treatment of the local population by colonial administrators.[51] Rebellion quickly spread through large parts of the region. The epicenter of the conflict lay in Semirech'e, where the contrast between colonists and the colonized was most conspicuous. At first the Kazakhs were able to spread fright and fear among the Russians. But the latter soon responded with a military attack and gruesome acts of revenge by the Slavic settlers. The counterattack took many times more lives than were lost in the uprising.[52] Hundreds of thousands of Kazakhs fled to China to escape the violence.[53]

The region found no peace, even after the upheaval had been squelched. Eruptions of violence continued when the 1917 revolutions in Central Asia led to a long and bloody civil war.[54] Most of the Kazakh elite saw the end of autocracy as a chance for national autonomy. They founded the Alash Orda party as a collective movement of young Kazakh intellectuals with the goal of wide autonomy for the steppe within the framework of Russia. The Bolshevik's October Revolution in Petrograd gave them an opportunity to seize power. In December 1917, leading members of Alash Orda set up a government that would try to keep the upper hand during the months and years of civil war turmoil.

In Central Asia and other areas at the empire's periphery the Bolshevik revolution was initially a European matter.[55] It took place, if at all, where the

Bolsheviks had a noteworthy number of followers. Muslims were basically not represented in the soviets that arose in larger cities everywhere in 1918. The chaos of civil war brought most agriculture to a halt. Rule was by the right of the strongest. Akhmet Baitursynov, a leading Kazakh writer and representative of Alash Orda, put it simple, when he wrote in 1919: "In short, the [revolutionary] movement in the borderlands often manifested itself not as a revolution (as it is usually understood), but as complete anarchy."[56] Cities exploited the countryside. Pockets of red followers ruthlessly took what they needed from agricultural surroundings and let the local population perish. In 1918 many thousands of Kazakhs starved in the red-dominated areas of what later became Kazakhstan.[57]

The civil war in the steppe released dynamics that ultimately led to the downfall of the Alash government. On one hand the government's armed units fought the Bolsheviks more or less side by side with white generals and atamans. On the other hand its political representatives negotiated several times unsuccessfully with Lenin and Stalin over conditions for Kazakh autonomy within the Soviet state. When it became clear that the Bolsheviks would win the civil war, an increasing number of Kazakhs switched sides. Eventually, even the luckless leaders of Alash Orda submitted themselves to the Bolsheviks.[58] March 1920 formally ended the existence of their state. Soviet representatives had become—at least in name—the masters of the steppe.[59]

In August of the same year, the Bolsheviks founded the Autonomous Kirghiz Socialist Soviet Republic, which basically covered the territory of the Alash Orda state. Orenburg was its first capital. In the course of dividing up Central Asia, in 1925 the Kazakh Autonomous Socialist Soviet Republic was created to include parts of the Turkestan Socialist Soviet Republic that had been called out in 1918. After long negotiations the region around Orenburg was handed over to the Russian Soviet Federative Socialist Republic (RSFSR). At first the more centrally situated Kzyl-Orda and finally, in 1929, Alma-Ata became the capital of the young republic.[60] Organizing the large territory administratively was the first move on the long road to asserting Soviet rule in the steppe. The process would take years and cost more than a million people their lives.

2

SOVIET RULE IN THE STEPPE

"**C**OMRADES, THERE IS no Soviet authority in the auls," said Filipp Goloshchekin, the first party secretary of Kazakhstan in December 1925 to an extended group of Bolshevik leaders.[1] His audience was not surprised. Everyone knew the reasons for continued frustration and failure in the steppe. Between the end of the civil war and the onset of the drive for collectivization, the Bolsheviks had been unable to get a grip on the situation. Despite repeated efforts, their top-down interventions remained exceptions in a world that got along without the Communists, their philosophy, and their institutions. In many parts of Kazakhstan the soviets, as organs of local administration, existed on paper only. And where they did manage to establish themselves, they often became arenas for interclan conflicts.

The total number of Communists remained low and even the most optimistic observers doubted whether the majority of the party's members were loyal to the Bolshevik cause. Bolshevik ideas of socialism and modernity simply left no lasting impression on Kazakhstan's multiethnic population. It looked nothing like a strong state capable of effectively taxing and leading its citizens. Perhaps no other detail symbolizes the desolate state of things more clearly than a remark made by one functionary that the militiamen in his area did not have a single horse and therefore had to pursue their tasks literally on foot—in a country populated by pastoralists.[2]

Nonetheless, the state's claim to power did not go unheard altogether. The relationship between Communists and Kazakhs was not merely a series of deficits, lack of influence on one side, and indifference on the other. Even in the vast steppe, it was impossible to entirely ignore the state and its demands. Though it played little role in daily matters and issues, its lack of presence did not mean absolute absence. For all its weak points and problems, the Soviet state was a power that the inhabitants of even the most remote aul could not wholly escape.[3]

The Communists used various forms of intervention to assert their claim to power. Leaders and local representatives found their way to the auls when it came to collecting taxes, determining local powers, or deciding disputes over fertile land among various parts of the population. Such visits not only served revenue collection and other duties but also reminded the Kazakhs time and again of their Soviet citizenship, irrespective of how any particular individual might have interpreted it. When representatives of the state came, the people had to take some sort of stance toward it.[4]

The Bolsheviks believed that the Kazakhs would listen. But first they had to deprive traditional elites of their influence, an authority that had been successful in upholding all the practices and the Kazakh order that the Communists loathed. They sought at first figuratively, then later literally to decapitate Kazakh clans. In general, all the measures taken by the party either directly or indirectly targeted Kazakh society's elite with a twofold purpose: to deprive major figures of authority and to break up the social order. In a society where individuals identified themselves by their place in an intricate system of clans, destruction of the old social order could work only by replacing it with a new form of social collectivization and by providing the population with new figures of authority. The language of ideology called it "class struggle," but in fact it meant nothing other than the repression of influential Kazakhs.[5]

Although the Bolsheviks sought to revolutionize existing conditions, they were, of course, themselves products of their origins: they were members of the multiethnic society of the Russian Empire. Within the party in Kazakhstan and elsewhere, honor, patronage, and personal loyalty were paramount.[6] Among the Kazakhs, kinship and genealogy linked individuals, shaped clans, and generated trust. The party and the clans thus shared common principles: They were two separate networks of personal relationships that might intermingle and even absorb one another. The clans used Soviet institutions as they saw fit and sometimes even modified them.[7]

NATIONALIST IN FORM, SOCIALIST IN CONTENT

The Soviet state took on two different forms in the Kazakh Steppe. On the one hand it was an intervening and often punitive power, becoming active when taxes and contributions went unpaid, riots broke out, or a local potentate singlehandedly extended his tether. On the other hand, it also established formal relationships of rule between the center and the periphery by dividing the area into administrative units led by an apparatus of party and state officials. Yet the bare existence of such structures discloses nothing of how they worked. How did the Soviet state seek allegiance and loyalty at the local level? Who was involved in the Bolshevik project and why? What role remained for the clans?

"MEMBERS OF AN ALIEN NATION"

The Bolsheviks found themselves in a difficult situation: they were few in number, isolated from one another, and the nomads dismissed them. Most Kazakhs thought socialism was something for the Europeans. And because very few European Communists spoke Kazakh and only a tiny number of Kazakhs spoke Russian, the lingua franca of the multiethnic Soviet state, change was sluggish, if it happened at all.[8] In regions dominated by the Kazaks, the power of the Soviets and the Communist Party reached only as far as the local elites permitted.

The native population thought little of the comrades. Heavy taxation motivated many to leave the party and vigorous requisition further weakened it. Locals began to hate Communists. One report states that "persons who call themselves Communists terrorize the peaceful people with criminal connections and acts and thus contribute to the disorganization of Soviet work. No wonder the inhabitants of the steppe refuse to become party members and, on the contrary, are literally frightened by those who call themselves Communists."[9]

Thus it is hardly surprising that control commissions and the secret police (OGPU) constantly reported a lack of principles among the comrades: whole segments of the party seemed to be controlled by local *bais* (rich herd owners). Prominent party members openly lived their religion, and in polygamy. Some party members were alcoholics, brutal thugs, and rapists.[10]

FIGURE 2.   An aul classroom, TsGAKFDZ, 2–223

Anyone approaching a functionary with a request knew he would get nowhere without bribing. And a peasant settler said straightforwardly why he found the Soviet apparatus worse than colonial administration under the czar: not only did the czar have fewer officials but the latter also accepted smaller bribes.[11]

Kazakh territory was too large and the number of loyal party members too small for Moscow to successfully maintain functioning soviets. The Soviet state had little continuous, institutional influence on matters in the steppe.[12] In the mid-1920s some Kazakhs in the district of Karkaralinsk still took the Communists for "members of an alien nation."[13]

The party produced endless directives, appeals, and other papers, but many documents reached the borderlands only with considerable delay, or never at all. With few exceptions, infrastructure and communications in the steppe were in miserable condition. During the winter, some districts were isolated for months and left to their own devices.[14] Until well into the 1930s, post offices and telegraph stations neither accepted nor forwarded messages written and addressed in the Kazakh language.[15] Whatever information and directives reached the remote outposts of Soviet power in the steppe often remained indecipherable. Many party members were technically and politically illiterate: they could neither read nor write. When documents could not be translated into Kazakh, the most rational solution for aul leaders was simply to gather, acknowledge, and then ignore them.[16]

Some party members had only vague ideas of the fundamental principles of Bolshevik ideology. They had never heard of Lenin or Bukharin's *ABC of Communism*. Lower-rank functionaries could not explain what the party actually was.[17] European Communists, unable to speak the Kazakh language, were often met with suspicion and exclusion when they traveled to the auls.[18] The pastoralists could not understand agitators talking of class struggle, revolution, and the proletariat. The Europeans' abstract political discourse meant nothing to them at all.[19] These were not teething troubles, they repeated themselves year after year for decades. Yet no indignant report to the upper ranks, no decree, and no initiative could break the triangle of catastrophic communication (and the lack of authority it created), political and literal analphabetism, and ethnic conflicts within and surrounding the party.[20]

If Communists wished to be heard, they had to adapt. In nomad territory the difference between party and native hierarchy was blurred beyond recognition.[21] Most Communists could work only on the conditions dictated by the community to which they belonged. Many lower-ranking officials put their authority and knowledge in the service of their tribes and clans.[22] Even recognizably responsible party members, for example, saw nothing wrong with using party funds for Muslim holiday celebrations.[23] Higher-ranking cadres interpreted such cases not as misconduct, but instead, and rightly so, as symptoms of cultural imprint.

Except for a small troop of so-called professional officials, the party in the steppe thus consisted almost exclusively of men who were deeply involved in traditional society and upheld its culture, even in Communist garb. Some did do everything imaginable for their political comrades, even risking their lives during the years of civil war.[24] But they did not necessarily share all aspects of Communist ideology or live up to the ideals of a Bolshevik functionary.

The most prominent example of a national leader who joined forces with the Communists, was Tobaniiaz Al'niiazov, the so-called khan of the *adaevtsy* and chairman of the Revolutionary Committee for the Adaevsk region. Born in 1875, he was considered a descendant of legendary Kazakh warriors. He was arrested during the revolt of 1916, but released after the February Revolution. After neglecting the region in Western Kazakhstan for three years, in 1920 the Bolsheviks set up a Revolutionary Committee there and installed

Al'niiazov as its chairman.[25] The new man for the Adaevsk region thought little of radical social experimentation and much of comity among local tribal elites. Like a traditional Kazakh ruler, he was lawmaker and judge in one, guided by a combination of the Sharia and Kazakh customary law.[26] To his own delight, the people called him a khan. That title, he later said, was easier for the people to understand than the complicated designation "chairman of the Revolutionary Committee."[27] Multiple flare-ups of resistance by younger Communists against Al'niiazov's regime left him unscathed: the young men rarely ventured beyond Fort Aleksandrovskoe, the only fortified settlement in the region, while Al'niiazov moved primarily around the steppe. The public was on his side, seeing in him, as a report from the OGPU states, "the only Soviet official who supported the old patriarchal customs and traditions."[28]

But most important, Al'niiazov fulfilled his role as a patron and warded off continuous attacks on nomad territory by groups under the command of legendary Dzhunaid-khan from the Xorazm (Khorezm) region in the south.[29] To end the aggression, in 1921, Al'niiazov and a cavalry of three thousand men attacked the neighboring republic and progressed to the city of Qo'ng'irot (Kungrad).[30] The unprecedented assault helped establish peace between the inhabitants of the two hostile regions, but in the late 1920s that peace vanished again under the pressure of the drive for collectivization.[31] Al'niiazov's coup de main had, however, taken things too far. He was arrested and the guards at the southern border of the region disbanded (albeit without turning in their weapons). Al'niiazov was released in 1923, but tried in court again in 1925.[32]

None of this changed his standing with the public. He was seen as the top authority on all issues of relevance. Even Zhalau Mynbaev, chairman of the region's Revolutionary Committee, had to admit that Al'niiazov alone pulled all the strings.[33] In 1925 he got off lightly, but in November 1928 he was arrested again, this time together with a number of officials, and for the last time. They were accused of being responsible for the death of Sh. Eraliev, a member of the Kazakh Central Executive Committee (KazTsIK). In late 1930 Al'niiazov and the other conspirators were put on trial and sentenced. He broke out of prison in 1931 and went into hiding in the commotion of the next civil war, at which point he, a former member of the Kazakh TsIK, had irreparably become an enemy of the Soviet State.[34] His story shows how fragile alliances were between indigenous leaders and the Communists.

FACE TO THE AUL

The Soviet State formally saw its influence on the steppe grow continually. New members joined the party, an increasing number of people participated in elections to the soviets, and a number of other things seemed to indicate that progress was being made.[35] Yet everyone knew that behind the facade of Soviet institutions the old native power relations were still in place. When the Bolsheviks turned their "face to the aul", they found little that looked promising.[36]

Even the most ardent advocates of evolutionary change in Kazakhstan's auls had to acknowledge that all the talk and patience had been to no avail. Statistician Sokolovskii told his readers that it was an optimistic illusion to think that the influence of the clans would abate within the foreseeable future.[37] Revolution was not made by symbolic acts such as depriving *former people* of the right to vote or confiscating the possessions of the elite. Radical change demanded rigorous action. It was about sovietizing the aul. The term "sovietize" meant two things: it implied acknowledging that little had been accomplished in the past years and it meant taking a series of measures to change the unsatisfactory nature of things.[38] The party's leaders thought the aul Communists should take action, so that the auls could revolutionize themselves from within. Kazakhstan's party leader Goloshchekin, who had no firsthand familiarity with Kazakh life, also hoped that local Communists would provide authorities with information about events in the auls of which they were unaware.[39] Countless reports on the alarming state of the party show how unrealistic his expectation was.

In order to assess the situation on site, between June and November 1926 the Kazakh Party Control Commission spot-checked 85 party cells with 1,622 members and candidates across the entire republic. The controllers compiled a long list of deficiencies and painted a bleak picture of the party's basic organizations: they lacked guidelines and supervision, no one communicated with the Kazakh Communists in their native tongue, the party cells had no authority among the population, comrades distinguished themselves in no way from their non-Communist neighbors, all were influenced by the local notables and lacked discipline. Even when the party cells under scrutiny turned out not to be the worst in the country, the results of the survey were sobering. A total of 440 Communists (more than a quarter of all comrades) were fined. Over 100 were kicked out of the party permanently. Almost 200 party members were ordered to take political training.[40] The members of the commission had no other concrete measures to suggest. Their feeble advice was to strengthen communication with the cells and send strong comrades to the steppe, clamp down on discipline, and end technical and political analphabetism among the Communists of the auls.[41]

Party cells on the local level were mostly organized on tribal principles and subject to the authority of local bais. That meant a *total loss of party and class lines*, as one report from the westernmost part of Kazakhstan remarked. Party ethics had been undermined when comrades from one clan expressed sincere sympathy with a local notable whose horse had been stolen. Their loyalty made it impossible to battle such notables properly. They were miles from executing any political campaign adequately.[42]

Party and clan structures were amalgamated not only in the auls. Comrades at intermediate levels of leadership, and their respective followers, too, were organized along tribal, clan, and national lines. In September 1926 an instructor from Moscow's Central Committee reported that in the region of Zhetysu the entire party organization was entangled in tribal and clan disputes. Three out of four district party secretaries were involved in tribal conflicts. "In light of these facts," he reported, "the organization exhibits not even the slightest sign of closed ranks; on the contrary, it breaks down into all kinds of tribes, kinship categories, and so on."[43] Conflicts of this nature kept not only the participating comrades but also the general public holding their breath because normally they sympathized with one or the other of the antagonistic groups.[44]

Overlap was particularly apparent when it came to justice. Soviet law often served as a guise for decisions actually based on adat, the customary law.[45] People ignored abstract Soviet law, which they found incomprehensible, and settled their disputes before traditional Kazakh courts, which were more efficient and worked faster than the sluggish Soviet apparatus. And even then, as one observer wrote: "It is not seldom that our Communists and colleagues from Soviet institutions visit the *bais* in the company of poor or average farmers and request advice. . . . Communists often even participate in the courts of the elders. . . . *Bais* take a party worker who does so for the best Soviet worker in the entire aul. They respect him and see him as an authority among them."[46]

Without material support from the local notables, the Soviet state was hamstrung in the steppe. Many officials owned no horses, but only on horse-back could they fulfill their duties throughout the huge district. So they borrowed horses from the bais and were indebted to them, owed favors, and were particularly careful to spare the notables repressions.[47]

The Communists tried to recruit loyal followers from among the young men who lived at the margins of their communities in both the peasant villages of European settlers and in the auls. Taking sides with the Soviet state offered many among them opportunities for upward social mobility.[48] These young men (and few women) often belonged to minority clans in their respective auls and regions. Joining the Communists buttressed them against their rivals. Yet one often could not say just what it was that had led them to decline tradition. Had Lenin's arguments convinced them of the cause, or were they simply seeking personal advantage? The rural lumpen proletariat basked in its newly discovered strength. Many of them imitated the Bolsheviks' violent macho style. They publicly drank, smoked, swore, and ridiculed their victims.[49]

Anyone entering such an alliance with the Bolsheviks may have gained personal advantage, but could also be certain of clan scorn. Party membership did not exempt one from the necessity of getting along with one's neighbors and relatives. Wherever Communists appeared not to serve the interests of the aul elite, they were at best simply ignored and sometimes expelled from the community. In rare instances the bais sought outside support and appealed to higher Soviet officials to get a comrade or soviet chairman removed from the aul on charges of alleged offenses. In pursuing their own interests, local communities did call upon Soviet institutions when necessary.[50]

Being explicitly unpopular and braving derogatory nicknames were some of the lesser consequences with which Soviet activists had to deal. In some places they feared for their lives. In his book on the state of Kazakh auls, G. Togzhanov told of a man who came to him with tears in his eyes and described his hopeless situation. As part of a tax collection drive he had led a group of activists whose task it was to find livestock that the local bais had hidden from tax inspectors. Now he had to pay for this grave breach of the rules of aul life. Not only did the aul elite reprimand him, but the soviet leaders did, too, and tried to oust him as a *bozgysh*—a traitor to the interests of the aul—threatening him with imprisonment, exile, and as a last resort, death. The chairman of the Soiuz Koshchi, an association of poor Kazakhs without property, stated the view of the aul members in a nutshell: "How can anyone turn against the aul, against common opinion? Who is greater in number and strength—the aul, or that person?"[51]

SOVIET ELECTIONS IN THE STEPPE

Local soviets were the basic organs of Soviet power in the countryside. Elections to these bodies often meant a struggle between competing clans on the one hand and between the state and society on the other. At the local level, elections were about winning the majority of votes and filling two important posts: that of the chairman and that of the secretary of the respective aul or district soviet. These periodically repeated votes caused permanent problems for the Bolsheviks because clan elders often turned the councils into vehicles for the articulation of their own interests.

Clan elites either ran for office themselves or launched straw men who ran for office at their request. Once they had become members of the soviets, those candidates then pursued the interests of their backers, communities, and clans.[52] Most candidates had little similarity with soviet deputy ideals. Many of the elected made no secret of for whom they exercised their mandate. Sometimes competing clans produced artificial disputes between the wealthy and the poor simply to deliver a semblance of the class struggle that external observers so eagerly sought. In reality, as one report states, it was always about one clan aiming to suppress the others.[53] Sometimes candidates were uneasy with probable outcomes and took from the start to classical methods of voter corruption. In the fall of 1926 an instructor of the Central Committee reported from Zhetysu that if one invested between five hundred and one thousand rubles one could become the chairman of the district's executive committee. The sum bought a sufficient number of votes. A post in the aul's soviet cost less.[54]

Often local elites would reach some sort of consensus on vote outcomes long before elections took place. It reduced conflict to a minimum and promised control of the result. According to an article in December 1925 in the newspaper *Sovetskaia Step'* (Soviet Steppe), normally when the election committee's delegate arrived in the aul, the local soviet chairman gathered the most important dignitaries to decide on how to fill the most important positions. Once everything had been settled to the satisfaction of all present and every claim of all the clans had been met, the aul soviet chairman then convinced the outside delegate that it was impossible to hold an election meeting because people lived scattered across the plains, and so on. The same procedure helped fill positions in district offices.

Major conflict arose only when one group tried to gain complete control.[55] Elections to both the district soviet and the aul councils for the district of Mendeshevsk (Semipalatinsk) for the year 1925 exemplify how such conflicts were carried out. Two men who had been bitter enemies for years, Musatai Moldybaev and Adilev Ike, were cousins who throughout the final years of czarist rule and during the revolt of 1916 had taken turns holding the office of community elder. During the civil war, Moldybaev changed sides several times, eventually coming forth as a lifelong Communist Party supporter and partisan after the Alash Orda government had failed. In 1925 they each mobilized their supporters.

When Election Day came, the inhabitants of the district's aul gathered to vote. In Aul no. 2,[56] more than half the population appeared at a predetermined place and split immediately into two camps: the poorer people made up the group of Moldybaev supporters, while Adilev Ike's supporters represented the bais. Each side accused the other of tolerating people among themselves who had no right to vote in their aul. In protest, Ike and his supporters left the assembly place. In the belief that they were now dealing with impoverished Kazakhs alone, the people authorized to hold the election proceeded with voting. The result was that the candidates of those present won most of the seats in the new soviet. In the end, voting was a single group affair because the animosity between those supporting each of the leaders, who themselves had long ago lost the right to vote, was so great that they could not convene peacefully in one place.

In Aul no. 4 the atmosphere was not quite as heated. The person authorized to execute the election there reported that Musatai's group had won the support of the entire party cell. The comrades explained that Musatai's group was composed of impoverished voters and that although Musatai himself was a bai, he worked ceaselessly for the cause: "We call this group the 'Group of Village Poverty' and the other group the 'Group of Alash Orda and the Rich' and we believe that Musatai is an advocate of the poor and deserves our support because that group is disinclined to cooperate with the Communists."[57] Mock elections guided by fantasy class conflicts were standard procedure for local elections to the soviets. It was a Kazakh variation on the theme of *speaking Bolshevik*, that is, adopting Soviet ways of describing things in order to find an open ear for local issues.[58] But it also facilitated communication with the Communists in general.

In the auls, soviets, and party cells, simple party members, lower-rank Kazakh officials, members of the soviets, and the nomads had to cooperate with one another. Repeatedly alliances formed that left the Bolsheviks confused about where lines of loyalty and conflict ran within Kazakh society. Instead of working in the interest of the poor, comrades often stood up in support of a bai. And instead of battling exploitation, many people in the soviets fought for the hegemony of their own clan.[59] Time and again it became obvious that the auls knew no Marxist class struggle. The clans dominated economics and politics.[60] Edward Schatz has called these kinds of interrelations between traditional and modern elements "institutional syncretism."[61] Institutions took on a Soviet form, but content was determined by clan networks.

In Aul no. 1 in the district of Kasteksk the representatives of individual groups had consulted prior to the soviet election for 1927 and come to an agreement that only poor and average income peasants (*bedniaki* and *seredniaki*) should run for office, men who were wholly loyal to their bais and *atkamnery* (helpers of the bais) and would not violate the rules of the *yntymak*, that is, the rules of reconciliation and peace. Clan elites excluded Communists from the election preparations by insisting on observance of the yntymak and submission to its authority. Later, Communists had to admit that they had, in fact, remained bystanders.[62] One comrade added candidly that he had felt forced to appear quiet and reserved because "otherwise the representatives of the large clans would attack me and become my enemies and that would be of no advantage to myself or the party cell. I cannot do anything without the consent of the large clans, I must coordinate everything with them."[63]

The secretary of the party cell, described just how helpless local Communists felt: "I have to confess that on paper it looks like we are doing everything, but in reality nothing happens at all."[64] Yet he did not want to submit a complaint because past experience had shown that the district delegate had a mutual understanding with the three most important people in the aul. Understandably, local Bolsheviks sought trade-offs with them.

But who were these men commanding such great authority? Aul no. 1 was ruled by a triumvirate, which illustrates how clan hierarchy was combined with soviet positions.

One man was Bakir Ispataev, a dealer who knew every trick in the book, and who not only could read and write but also had profound knowledge of the law. People came to him for advice and mediation.

The second triumvir was Shaltabai Kudaibergenov, a wealthy man who owned more than eight hundred gelded male sheep and one hundred horses and who could afford five wives at once. Although he was a bai, he presented himself as being a truly Soviet person, a Communist since the days of Czar Nikolas II, who had always aided the poor. He was proud that all the members of his clan obeyed him without question and would defend him with their lives.

The third person was Musaev, the secretary of the aul soviet. Materially less well-off than the other two, he came from the same clan and was wax in their hands. His job was to represent Ispataev and Kudaibergenov's interests and give them an appearance of Soviet legitimacy. Whenever resistance arose, it was Masaev who reminded the people, and not always gently, of the principle of yntymak.

And then, finally, there was also the fairly insignificant chairman of the aul soviet, Nasypaev. As a member of one of the lesser clans, he could not articulate independent thought. Musaev often publicly disavowed him.

Under these circumstances it is not surprising that in Kasteksk's Aul no. 1, plenary sessions were nonexistent and the official representatives of Soviet power, Musaev and Nasypaev, did what was expected of them.[65]

For the leading cadre constellations such as in Kasteksk were proof that all plans for transforming the steppe were useless unless clan influence could be capped and clan leaders disempowered. And what was worse: under the circumstances, it was even impossible to control the Communists. In the 1920s across most of Kazakhstan the Bolshevik state was merely a local affair, where tangible rules were negotiated by local parties.[66]

THE SOCIALIST FUTURE OF KAZAKHSTAN'S NOMADS

Just where the Kazakh nomads fit into Soviet modernity was not clear from the start. Complete sedentarization had not from the very beginning been the Bolshevik's primary goal for Central Asia. The Communist plan was, rather, to change the pastoralists' nomadic behavior such that they would no longer question the state's fragile monopoly on power.

Thus the 1920s were preoccupied with struggles and debate over how to best integrate the steppe population into New Society in terms of culture and social order, and not least, in terms of economics.[67] Sedentarization meant nothing other than concentrating the population at clearly defined places or at least within clear boundaries. Could that be achieved by settling "backward" nomads, or should one let them remain nomadic? Could a state claim to exercise control over its population while tolerating that people of entire regions eluded its grasp? What could be done to raise the cultural level of the Kazakhs? And finally, was sedentarization an ideological or an economic necessity?[68]

BACKWARDNESS AND NEW CULTURE

For the Bolsheviks, who saw themselves as advocates of progress and modernization, nomadic culture was simply backward. Nomadic life was one of feudal exploitation, dirt, disease, ignorance, illiteracy, and religious practices that made women subordinate to men.[69] The Bolshevik view differed

FIGURE 3. Life in an aul, region of Pavlodar, TsGAKFDZ, 5–3617

little from that of colonial officials and ethnologists who had diagnosed the nomadic way of life as an inferior civilization and culture.[70]

The pastoralist life was one of mobility, and simultaneously one of inclusion, based on clan life that embraced all individuals sharing a common genealogy. But it also alienated Kazakhs from society as envisioned by the Bolsheviks.[71] For those who considered themselves guided by European standards, the ways of nomadic life were scandalous. The cramped, musty winter accommodations found the disapproval of physicians and advocates of modernization.[72] The ethnologist F. Slastukhin reported that in such quarters people vegetated "like bears in a cave," holding out through snowstorms in total isolation from the outside world, their neighbors, and their relatives; and that everything they owned and used was "filthy."[73] Life in the yurt, he said, and constant roving around, was responsible for it. The Kazakhs came to be seen as the epitome of what was not pristinely Soviet. The logical solution for all this nuisance, then, was sedentarization. Other authors, however, argued that making nomads settle posed a serious threat to the Kazakh way of life and its people: it was the summer migrations that kept them healthy. One could not recommend that they move into permanent housing.[74]

The Bolshevik's notion of the ideal socialist aul was clean, light, and practical. With limited resources, the party tried to acquaint nomads with basic principles of hygiene. Their cause was not philanthropic, it was to induce a cultural revolution in the steppe. The results were mixed: successful demonstrations of the medical art of healing got more attention than propaganda brochures written in Russian.[75] But to achieve a sustained effect, the Bolsheviks needed medical personnel who spoke the Kazakh language and stayed in the area.[76] Lacking those, many people relied on traditional healers and shaman cures instead of trusting distant doctors and unfamiliar medicine.[77] Moscow then sent Red Yurts to the steppe, staffed with physicians and paramedics.[78]

Like their comrades in other Muslim areas of the Soviet Union,[79] Kazakhstan's Communists tried to disseminate their agenda for progress, particularly among women. Woman's place in society was seen as an indicator of modernity or backwardness. One glance at the Kazakh aul convinced the Bolsheviks that clan women were oppressed, without rights, and disadvantaged. Promoting these women would break up and revolutionize rigid social structures.[80] Efforts to remedy the plight of women were, however, impeded by countless setbacks like a lack of women in the small cadre itself, language deficiencies, insufficient transportation, and so on. In the end, most Communist women's departments (*zhenotdely*) were staffed with urban Russian women and considered it a huge success whenever they were able to venture out to Kazakh women in the country.[81] All of this, however, did little to advance the cause of a "surrogate proletariat" in Kazakhstan.[82]

In contrast to conditions in Uzbekistan, Communists in Kazakhstan could not exploit the traditional veil as a symbol of female suppression.[83] Most pastoralist women wore a headscarf. Covering their faces, as was done elsewhere throughout Central Asia, was impractical for nomadic life.[84] Political activists thus had to fight other issues, particularly the payment of bride prices (*kalym*) and the practice of polygamy.[85] Paying a bride price, argued promoters of the "emancipation of the unveiled," degraded women to purchasable objects, unworthily exchanged for money or livestock. It also disadvantaged poor men who could not afford to buy brides and thus found households.[86] And widespread polygamy, the activists maintained, was a clear expression of female oppression in Central Asia.[87]

In the battle against bride prices and other aspects of Kazakh culture, activists rarely addressed the women involved, aiming instead at the men, who, as the Communists thought, did whatever they saw fit.[88] OGPU dossiers brimmed with reports of men married to three women at once.[89] Some fathers took money not only for their daughters, but for each grandchild born as well.[90] Party members apparently had no problem with such practices. Comrade Mukshchev from Akmolinsk, for example, paid kalym for a fifteen-year-old girl who became his second wife. The regional party secretary was informed, but did not intervene.[91] Only a fraction of all such cases turned up in the files and few of those that did were ever followed up. Large parts of the party were clearly embedded in precisely the cultural contexts that the party sought to eradicate.[92] On the other hand, Soviet emancipation programs did open the door to promotion and career opportunities for thousands of women who embraced the offer despite obstacles and in defiance of resistance from their environment.[93]

Another way to permeate society was to create a proletariat where none had existed before. If it had seemed difficult to create a labor force in Central Asia's oasis societies, the ambition seem hopeless for the steppe. Nevertheless, Communists began to forge proletarians to their liking. The first opportunity came in the late 1920s with the laying of the Turkestan-Siberian Railway (Turksib), the largest infrastructure project in the steppe up to that time. The line was to connect the Central Asian periphery to the European metropolis and tap into the region's resources more effectively. But the ambition was even larger than that. The railroad was seen as a means to Sovietize the remote steppe.[94]

Most of the over 50,000 workers engaged to work on the construction of more than 1,400 kilometers of rails were recruited from the native population. They were meant to become the avant-garde of a Kazakh proletariat. Several comrades expressed the hope that these men, once their work on the railway was done, would return to their respective auls as propagandists for the Soviet cause. But making proletarians out of the Kazakhs did not go smoothly. Violent clashes occurred between European workers and Kazakhs because the former were given preferred positions. Kazakhs abandoned the construction sites in droves when they felt poorly treated by superiors and coworkers.[95] The high expectations for change in collective attitude brought about by work remained unfulfilled. Nonetheless, work on the railroad attracted many from the margins of society, because it meant an opportunity for social advancement. For the first time it offered poor social strata an alternative to the traditional nomadic way of life.[96] And some of the new workers did adopt the Soviet project's ideals and became Communists. But those success stories were exceptions rather than the rule.[97]

DEBATE ON SEDENTARIZATION

The modern state was at odds with nomadism.[98] The Communist historical-material worldview foresaw a transition from a migratory, livestock-breeding society to one of permanent methods of production, but in Kazakhstan the process was slow. In the course of the 1920s the number of nomadic and seminomadic households there did gradually decline, but not necessarily due to any conscious shift toward modernity. Impoverished Kazakhs, who could no longer afford to roam, were more likely to settle than others. Wealthy Kazakhs remained pastoralists. In order to migrate with a yurt, a household, and an entire family, one had to possess a certain number of animals. The transition from life in the yurt to permanent living quarters almost always meant a loss in status. Therefore, as Anatolii Khazanov has shown, Owen Lattimore's claim that "the poor nomad . . . is the pure nomad" is incorrect.[99]

In order to survive, an increasing number of Kazakhs hired themselves out as farmhands to European settlers or tried to set up their own farms.[100] But many of them did so in an attempt to earn enough money to be in a position to take up nomadic life again—a behavior observed in many societies of a pastoralist nature.[101] Prominent Bolshevik Janis Rudzutak learned that during the famine of 1921. On a trip through Semirech'e he saw that many Kazakhs had settled out of necessity, not out of desire. "Some of these Kirghiz will . . . return to nomadic life, but clearly others will remain and work in agriculture."[102] And that is what happened. Even in the ethnically heterogeneous government of Semipalatinsk with it high percentage of Russian peasant settlers, over 80 percent of the 140,000 Kazakh households registered in the census of 1926 were nomads.[103] Under these conditions the comrades at first had no other choice than to allow nomads to continue their custom and practice of pastoral life.

But the Bolsheviks were neither politically nor economically inclined to leave society up to itself and wait and see what might transpire. They would control the historical process themselves and doing so required a coherent strategy. But what might be the role of nomads in socialist Kazakhstan? The

FIGURE 4   Nomads traversing the steppe, region of Pavlodar,
TsGAKFDZ, 5–3613

issue was pressing, as illustrated by the situation in Kazakhstan's north-west region of Adaevsk.[104] According to the Bolsheviks, the people who lived there—the adaevtsy—were the most backward people in the entire Soviet Union.[105] In contrast to the pastoralists of most other regions, the auls of Adaevsk wandered the steppe the entire year, without seeking any permanent winter quarters. They traveled distances of over a thousand kilometers along the eastern shores of the Caspian Sea, a practice that one report on the area deems a "primitive, barbarous kind of economy."[106] During the 1920s, conditions became increasingly difficult. In the north, European peasants had begun to settle where the adaevtsy usually had their summer pastures. And in the south the Adaevtsy were threatened by their enemies, the Turkmenian Iomuds.[107] Neither group dared to approach the grazing grounds north and south of the Turkmenian-Kazakh border for fear of attacks and raids.[108] Under these circumstances, the adaevtsy were forced to reduce the size of their herds and many suffered hardship.[109] When ten thousands of animals died of the frost and cold (*dzhut*) in the late 1920s, scores of nomads lost their means of existence.[110]

Some sort of universal solution was needed, but what? In short: Soviet macro-planners and economists voted for sedentarization while the majority of experts on the steppe economy and agronomists familiar with local conditions were against it. The former were heard, in part because leading Bolsheviks often preferred fundamental political deliberations to detailed expertise.

At first, however, the advocates of pastoralist-friendly policy appeared to have the upper hand. In 1926, a veteran of the Revolution, Sergei Shvetsov, wrote an essay on the issues of just how nomadism and the steppe stand in relation to one another and what would happen if the Kazakhs were to give up their nomadic way of life. His answers were clear. Under the conditions of the steppe, nomadic economy presented by far the most productive use of resources. Pastoralists, he wrote, did not migrate because they were primitive or because they had not yet reached the cultural state that their neighbors had attained, they did so because circumstances demanded it. As livestock drovers they were dependent on the environment. Nomadism was the only form of productivity in the steppe. And in the future, he said, pastoralism would become even more significant. "Destroying nomadism in Kazakhstan would not only mean the end of livestock breeding in the steppe and Kazakh economy, it would also turn the arid steppe into uninhabited lands."[111] As time eventually proved, the reality of it was much worse than Shvetsov had thought.

His concern, however, was indeed heard. One author even thought that Shvetsov's opinion was actually the most widespread one.[112] And others saw no alternative to nomadism for a long time to come: "Under present conditions no other use [of this region] is imaginable."[113] Kazakhstan's livestock was forecast to triple within two decades to number more than seventy million animals.[114] Nomadism would thus remain "the most important occupation of the native population for a long time,"[115] especially because settling all the nomads was out of the question. There simply was not enough land for so many potential new farmers. Preserving nomadism was thus, at least for the moment, economically both desirable and meaningful. Or, as one of the most prominent economic planners for Kazakhstan, Evgenii Polochanskii wrote: "The principal duty of the Republic of Kazakhstan is not to eradicate pasture livestock farming, but to end underdevelopment."[116] Expanding winter quarters had greater priority because it would make the nomads less dependent on climate. Traditional winter quarters provided the pastoralists with only rudimentary protection against the harsh steppe winter. Solutions that went further than ad hoc measures and emergency relief needed to be found for dealing with the regularly occurring frost storms.[117] Polochanskii designed generously dimensioned stalls and residential buildings for the cold season and campaigned to unite all members of the aul in cooperatives.[118]

Kazakhstan was to become an important provider of meat and animal products for the Soviet Union. Planners saw the steppe as crucial for supplying Kazakhstan's own market and those of the other Central Asian Republics, as well as for export.[119] This, the economists all agreed, could not be achieved with unsophisticated nomads who needed comparatively large domains because they drove their herds from one pastureland to the next without recultivating grazed areas and rarely laid up hay supplies for the cold winter months.[120] The nomads' animals were also seen as unprofitable because in comparison to herds kept in stalls, they built up no extra fat reserves.[121]

Since it therefore seemed impossible to make Kazakhstan's livestock breeding more European, the key word became "rationalization," a concept that combined several different ideas and measures that could be taken. Sedentarization was not necessarily a part of it. In January 1927, the members of the Council of People's Commissars of the RSFSR received a report estimating that in Kazakhstan as a whole, only about sixteen million desiatins of land (6 percent of the Kazakh Republic's entire territory) were suitable for field crops, either because they got more than three hundred millimeters of precipitation there per year, or because irrigation appeared to be technically feasible there.[122] It therefore looked more efficient to increase livestock breeding and use available resources to support pastoralism in any way possible. The desire was to double the size of herds within ten years' time and thereby increase the availability of animal products. It would take the work of various specialists, a string of fodder stations, more infrastructure in the steppe, affordable loan approvals, and other measures to reach that goal.[123]

Opponents did not hold back their critique of the policy.[124] It would be a mistake to improve conditions for nomadism. Instead, families owning few animals should be forced to settle as farmers. A. N. Chelintsev, a profiled advocate of this view, thought that over 60 percent of all Kazakh households should abandon their nomadic ways. Several political circles demanded the unconditional abolition of nomadism.[125] M. B. Murzin said that there was no solution for the disputes with European peasant settlers in the steppe other than to settle the nomads permanently.[126] Little attention was given to the fact that vast ranges and low density meant more than simply grazing land to the pastoralist population.[127] The nomads saw the steppe as a place, whereas for the Communists it was simply space, as the historian Matthew Payne put it.[128] And in the end the Kazakhs paid dearly for the Communists' colonial dream of limitlessly shapable space.

How could the nomadic way of life be reconciled with governmental notions of order? The question touched the very principles of the Soviet understanding of power. No one could say precisely where Kazakhs actually lived. In the early 1920s the Bolsheviks had tried to traverse the steppe in what they called Red Caravans, undertakings that served propaganda purposes and the gathering of information on the territories they desired to rule. Some in the expedition teams took the latter for the primary task.[129] Yet, even late in the decade, populations were discovered in the steppe of which no one had been aware. In a 1928 paper on redividing Kazakh territory for administrative purposes, we read: "Pastoralist life is incompatible with the exacting demands of administrative geography and forces us to draw future district borders arbitrarily."[130]

Statistician V. Sokolovskii illustrated the scope of the problem with a map of the Kzyl-Orda oblast: "If it were not for the railroad line, the city of Kzyl-Orda, and a few Russian villages . . . this would look like a desert absolutely devoid of humans that for some unknown reason has been divided by three bold lines into four parts as districts."[131] Simultaneously, he continued, regional administrative statistics show that 15,000 to 20,000 Kazakh households are scattered across 158 "peopled spots" throughout the area. These were not places with names, they were administrative auls. In contrast to traditional Kazakh auls, which in the summer consisted of 2 to 15 migrating households, administrative auls were composed of several combined auls. Just where such administrative auls were located could only be determined during the cold season, when Kazakhs stayed in their winter quarters.[132] Without native guides, Soviet administrators had no way of pinpointing the population at all. When Sokolovskii asked the Executive Committee of the Kzyl-Orda oblast to show him precisely where Kazakhs lived, the functionaries "waved their hands across the entire map saying, 'Basically, everywhere.'"[133]

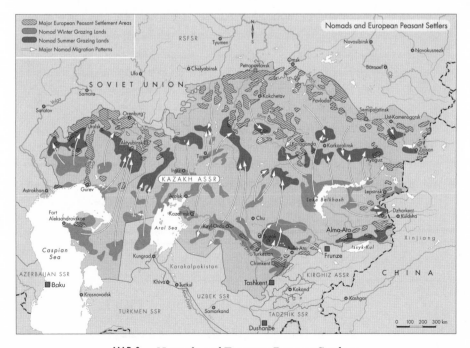

MAP 2. Nomads and Euopean Peasant Settlers

Such were precisely the ambiguities and chaotic circumstances that Soviet modernity was out to abolish.[134] A state that had no reliable information on the whereabouts, constitution, or even the number of its subjects could hardly substantiate any convincing claim to power. Its order was precarious and its legitimacy limited. Conditions in Kazakhstan questioned the fundamental necessities for any kind of administration at all.[135] Significant parts of the population could take down their tents at anytime and simply move elsewhere. The Bolsheviks wanted the Kazakhs to stay within a given district, or at least not to leave it permanently. Whether people lived in yurts or European-like villages was not irrelevant, but it was not paramount. Intrinsic to sedentarization was locating the Kazakhs in the first place. Were the Communists to exert any power at all, they first had to figure out just where the nomads lived.[136]

EUROPEAN PEASANTS AS OUTCASTS AND COLONIZERS

In the 1920s, the test for Soviet policy on nationalities was nowhere tougher than in the eastern part of Kazakhstan.[137] In hardly any other region of the Soviet Union were disputes among European and native populations heavier than in the regions of Zhetysu (formerly Semirech'e) and Semipalatinsk.[138] Peasant settlers and pastoralists harbored a deep mutual dislike of one another. Their lives and cultures differed fundamentally. They competed for the same resources and mistrusted one another. Neither the Kazakhs nor the European farmers had forgotten the violence of 1916 and the civil war.[139] The pastoralists remembered the immense and one-sided burdens of the post-1918 years of famine.[140] The Bolsheviks were unable to fence in the multifarious conflicts raging between the two groups, above all because they themselves lacked a coherent strategy for the future of the steppe. Should they always give preference to the needs of the former oppressed Kazakh nation, to the disadvantage of colonizers? Or should economic interests be weighed against the premises of policy on nationalities?

REFORM, HUNGER, AND NEW ECONOMIC POLICY

After the civil war the Communists had at first appeared as advocates of the former "oppressed" Nation of the Kirghiz. At that time many Bolsheviks thought that the revolution would spread from Central Asia throughout the remainder of what they called the *oppressed peoples of Asia*. The agenda was nothing less than to put an end to the European colonial rule. In 1919 Stanislav Pestkovskii revealed the vision—with Turkestan's Muslims on their side, Afghanistan and Persia would fall into their hands and pave the way to India and Mongolia.[141] Hostility toward "former colonizers" lent credibility to Bolshevik emancipation rhetoric. The Kazakhs, however, were not interested in a world revolution. They wanted revenge. They understood "equality for all" as driving out the Europeans.[142] Peter Holquist has noted that the Bolsheviks went on with the czarist regime's design, but switched the roles of expungers and victims. It was now the Kazakh nomads who were casting out the Russian peasants.[143]

The formal grounds for this policy constituted a politburo edict of June 1920 that stipulated the dispossession of all Russian peasants who had unlawfully appropriated land in Zhetysu.[144] Dispossessed kulaks and nonregistered immigrants stood to be deported. The focus was on settlers who after the revolt of 1916 had occupied property formerly owned by Kazakhs or who had illegally immigrated into the region. Kazakhs who had fled to China and now returned to their places of origin were to repossess their property. In addition, European immigrants were no longer to be privileged when it came to questions of land and water rights. Instead, attention was to focus on the question of appropriate cattle tracts through the steppe. The time had come, the edict continued, for all working people, whether they be Kazakhs or Russians, to have the same rights.[145] But what the resolution targeted as a measure against individual kulaks grew to become an attack on the entire Russian population. Disguised as a land reform, it was a demonstration of how the Communists envisioned the end of European colonization.[146]

For Russian farmers this reform marked the beginning of a long period of distress inseparably bound up with the name of a member of the Central Committee's Turkestan office, Georgii Safarov.[147] His arrival in the region in the spring of 1921 soon unleashed a regime of terror.[148] Tens of thousands of people were forced to leave their villages and embark on an uncertain future. Official statements say that over 8,000 families were relocated, over 621,000 acres of property seized, and more than 400 villages and settlements abandoned. The true numbers were much higher. In the Semirech'e alone, more families were displaced than the report indicates for the entire region.[149]

Even farmers from Vysokogo, a small place in the district of Chimkent that had been settled in the nineteenth century, were not spared. Despite having lived there for decades, under the dictate of land reform they were subject to relocation. Militiamen and soldiers from the Red Army drove them from their village to the nearest railroad station, herded them into freight cars, and threw them out again a few stations later. They persevered without a roof over their heads for over a month.[150] Villagers from Gorno-Slobodsk were forced to leave their homes within forty-eight hours. The Red Army threatened to execute them, if they did not comply.[151]

Wherever farmers resisted arbitrary treatment, the Bolsheviks took drastic action. In the area around Naryn, considerable unrest over land reform broke out in November 1920. Once the situation had been brought under control, a tribunal imposed harsh sanctions: many insurgents were shot dead, others sentenced to long imprisonments, and their families were deported. Janis Rudzutak, who was involved in the matter and in similar cases, had already demonstrated little sympathy with the practice of deportation, noting: "These evacuees are almost exclusively women and children. There are no men among them; the men have almost all been executed."[152]

The Kazakhs made land reform a form of revenge for the massacre of 1916. Attacks on peasants were frequent.[153] Adolf Ioffe, who often traveled the region as chairman of the Central Executive Committee's Turkestan Commission, said that Kazakh treatment of Russian peasants was terror run wild.[154] Neither did the horrible consequences of the reforms escape the few foreign travelers who happened to be in the area. A German visiting Semirech'e in 1922, Rudolf Asmis, wrote: "Along the roads one sees almost only house ruins, the sad signs of revolutionary struggles and especially signs of the peculiar revolutionary action that took homesteads away from wealthy farmers and gave them to the poor Kirghiz who ransacked them, but had no idea of what else to do with them. They returned to their yurts, even setting them up in the middle of the farm courtyards, and let the beautiful estates deteriorate."[155]

The longer Safarov operated in Turkestan, the more complaints were brought against him. Leading comrades came to the conclusion that he must be relieved of his duties as quickly as possible. An alarmed Cheka reported that if things continued as before, Russian farmers were going to revolt. Stalin soon joined Rudzutak and Ioffe in openly criticizing the merciless attack on colonizers. Lenin, however, stood firmly behind his protégé Safarov. His interest was not in local intrigues, but in the global political dimension of the events. It was damned important, he said, to prove that they were not imperialists by gaining the confidence of the natives and permitting no deviations from that course. Safarov, too, vehemently defended the course and tested Lenin's support by asking for his dismissal on the grounds that it was "impossible to work under these conditions."[156]

By the fall of 1921 Safarov was seriously under pressure. His hysteria caused confusion and his fight against the colonizers had long become the persecution of all Russians, wrote Turkestan's top Chekist (Soviet secret police agent) Iakov Peters to Lenin. Russian comrades had become increasingly apathetic and passive, while local Communists had become demoralized "monarchs."[157] Following lengthy debate, in January 1922 Safarov was finally excused from his duties.[158] But forced relocation continued. Not until the fall of 1922 did the Executive Committee of the RSFSR (VTsIK) put an end to land reform. Punitive measures were halted and kulaks were to be deported from Turkestan only in exceptional cases.[159] The excesses under Safarov's aegis had, however, lastingly poisoned the atmosphere between Europeans and Kazakhs. But even worse, the decisions made during the drive would not be taken back; all dispossessions and relocations were permanent.[160]

While only some peasants were affected by land reforms, Bolshevik procurement policy during so-called War Communism from 1918 to 1921 involved everyone. Unyielding disputes over grain had flared up between Communists and farmers.[161] In Central Asia the Communists stuck to exploitive practices that in other areas of the Soviet Union had been replaced in the spring of 1921 by more liberal regulations directed by the New Economic Policy (NEP).[162] Farmers were sanctioned when the authorities thought that they had delivered insufficient quantities. Comrades like Rudzutak, who was in a position to evaluate overall developments, pointed out how counterproductive this harsh policy was. Once all farmers were imprisoned or deported, who would sow and harvest? "This kind of food policy achieves nothing. It is not food policy, it is foolishness lacking the least justification.... If this food policy continues, we shall see a complete collapse and create a counterrevolution where previously there had been no reason for one."[163]

Rudzutak was not furious without reason. The effects of the Soviet famine of 1921–22 were felt in Semirech'e, too.[164] In the Kirghiz SSR alone, five of seven governments lacked food. It was said that more than 1.5 million people of the steppe went hungry. In the district of Atbasarsk over 100,000 peasants and pastoralists had little food. And still the local authorities did not refrain from requisition until the summer of 1922.[165] Conservative estimates suggested that more than 400,000 people died of hunger.[166] Between 1920 and 1923 the total number of households fell by a third, the number of peasant farmer households in the area was reduced by about 500,000.[167] Whether they were deported, emigrated or starved is unknown.[168]

In March 1922, the chairman of the Kazakh Executive Committee, Seitkali Mendeshev, described the catastrophic situation to Stalin: "In some villages, hundreds of people die of starvation every day. We are now not talking about eating cats, dogs, rotting carcasses and everything else, we are talking about cannibalism. The state of the nomadic Kirghiz population is particularly alarming. . . . In remote auls, entire families are dying."[169] No help could be expected from elsewhere, their own resources were depleted, Moscow provided nothing, and neighboring Turkestan offered only promises and well-meant resolutions. American relief, which had so significantly helped ease the hunger crisis in Russia, rarely found its way to Central Asia.[170] Officials did not have enough food to distribute. "Under these conditions," wrote Mendeshev, "we will only be able to save a very small fraction of those who are starving."[171]

In any case, the Communists disagreed on who should receive the scarce resources that were available. One said straightforwardly: "From the standpoint of Marxism the economically weak Kirghiz must die out; in times of famine they need no relief."[172] Turar Ryskulov, one of the most prominent Central Asian Communists, said cynically of those dying of starvation: "One can say that the dead have saved the Soviet Union, because if all these millions of starving people had come to us and demanded their share, they would have overturned and overthrown everything. We have to acknowledge that they saved the big picture, although we did not feed them."[173]

In the fall of 1922 the comrades brought themselves to abandon the principles of War Communism at the periphery of Central Asia and introduce the New Economic Policy there, too. The delay, said the chairman of the military revolutionary committee in Zhetysu, was due to the fact that the region "had not yet passed through the stages of revolution that Central Russia had gone through two years previously."[174] At the same time, the new policy also created a series of new problems. Some of the so-called kulaks evacuated in 1921 had begun returning to the area and now drove off the new villagers and settlers. Simultaneously the economic inequality between Europeans and Kazakh nomads increased because now the peasants could take their surplus to market themselves.

To the advocates of colonial revolution, it looked as if the pages of history were being turned back and an epoch they believed had been overcome was now rising again. Communists throughout the Soviet Union felt similarly. For years they had put all their effort into the cause and enforced the most radical measures. Now the very same leaders who had advocated the obliteration of all exploitation were lauding markets and private trade.[175] The Central Asian periphery saw the possible renaissance of dominance by European colonial settlers.[176] Functionaries like Turar Ryskulov, who wanted the greatest possible autonomy for Turkestan, warned of the danger of Russian hegemony returning to the region.[177]

But others saw these events differently: Abdrakhman Aitiev, the people's commissar for internal affairs, said that attacks on the kulaks should cease. They had, after all, brought elements of civilization to the steppe.[178] The Kazakhs should learn from them. Aitiev's deputy, Petr Struppe even went so far as to claim that it was not about nationhood. It was a waste of time to discuss nationhood when much more important problems begged for solutions.[179] To Ryskulov's dismay, few of the Kazakh leaders in Orenburg disagreed with Struppe.[180]

Comrades in Zhetysu, on the other hand, rejected deviation from the hard line against the Europeans. They had not fought them, only to row back now. They agreed to wrongdoing in 1921 by intimidating the kulak relocation villages with massive Chekist terror and not carefully distinguishing between so-called real kulaks and poor farmers. But the fault lay, they said, with the Russian and Cossack villagers, who had not sufficiently set themselves apart from the kulaks. The comrades regretted that some people now took up anti-Soviet positions and some families had yet to find a place to live, but the measures taken in land reform were right in and of themselves. The implementation of the NEP did not, they insisted, imply the end or even the revision of land reform. On the contrary, in order to underscore the previous year's success, property distribution must continue as planned.[181]

Despite statements such as these, the following years saw a fair amount of consolidation and détente. The NEP slowly took effect and conditions became stable at a rudimentary level. Famine was over, agriculture and animal husbandry were recovering, and attacks by anti-Soviet gangs declined noticeably. Farmers and pastoralists were no longer exclusively hostile toward one another. In general, a nervous peace and quiet set in where property distribution was permanent and the relationships between all groups living in one area were settled. Native inhabitants and newcomers had to get along under the conditions of the steppe. But they rarely trusted one another.

Whether voluntarily or not, an increasing number of Kazakhs abandoned their nomadic way of life and settled down. Most of them had neither the material resources it took, nor a sufficient knowledge of agriculture to do so. They could expect little support from the government. The committees for land distribution simply allotted them generous amounts of arable land and continued redistributing property in favor of the native population, while the wave of emigration by European farmers found no end.[182] And then new immigrants came to Zhetysu, seeking a safe future there.

CONFLICTS AND COMMISSIONS

The limit had been reached. In 1925, Kazakh party leaders declared that they would no longer tolerate people relocating in the republic. Before ascertaining exactly how much land their own native people required, they would not grant immigrants any property or allow them to occupy it. The chaotic influx into the Kazakh Republic over the past five to six years, they said, violated fundamental principles of Soviet land policy. It had previously been uncommon to initiate migration (and then only in an orderly manner), before the local population had been allotted land. This was particularly true when cultivable crop acreage was scarce, as it was in Kazakhstan. Most of the country could not be made arable without immense investments. Immigrants competed with the native people for land and the Kazakhs often felt they were at a disadvantage.[183]

This strict policy was a reaction to earlier attempts in Moscow to regulate the immigration question. In April 1924 the Council of People's Commissars of the RSFSR had already issued an edict on land grants to the nomadic and seminomadic population of Kazakhstan. In theory it put European peasant settlers and Kazakhs on equal footing, but in fact (as was the Kazakh comrades' custom) land and water grants followed a rank order (*ocherednost'*): Kazakhs were first in line, followed by immigrants who had worked in agriculture prior to 1918. These were in turn followed by those who had immigrated up to August 31, 1922. The last group consisted of

farmers who had arrived after August 31, 1922, but before August 7, 1924.[184]
Farmers of the bottom two ranks had no future in Kazakhstan.[185] Nomads
could count on generous loans and comprehensive tax cuts. Europeans
were expected to exit areas officially deemed nomadic or seminomadic and
settle elsewhere.

The peasants felt disadvantaged particularly in places where Kazakhs
held key administrative positions. In these so-called mixed regions unrest
grew among the European population. After all, complained the peasants,
they had left their homes and risked uncertainty, and worked hard and
frugally for years under inhospitable conditions and sacrifice to make the
steppe fertile and demonstrate European culture to the Kazakhs. And the
reward? As one pamphlet put it, the civilized Russian-Ukrainian population was forced into barbarism and nomadism. Their fields ran to seed, their
homes deteriorated or were used as cowsheds because the Kazakhs were not
inclined to live indoors. The goal of reforms had not been reached because
"the Kirghiz refuse to surrender simple shepherding and the free life of the
nomad in exchange for the hard work of a peasant."[186] Every line expresses
a deep aversion to the Kazakhs, the unruly nomads to whom the Europeans
felt superior.[187] Many farmers saw it as their duty not only to cultivate the
land, but to civilize the people, too.[188] In the early twentieth century thoughtful observers had already pointed out the dangers emanating from the Rus-
sian-European stance of superiority.[189]

Many peasants left Central Asia in resignation, returning to the European parts of the Soviet Union from which they or their ancestors had come.
Those that remained began to put up a fight. In their need, numerous farmers—especially from Zhetysu, where the worst conflicts raged—sought out
various levels of the central power, complaining of unlawful confiscation,
unfavorable land reform, and daily harassment by Soviet functionaries.[190]
They saw themselves as the victims of Bolshevist nationality policy, and the
equality of Kazakhs and Europeans as an affront. They submitted reports,
assailed regional officials, and sent delegations to Moscow, testifying to their
grievances. With variations, they all told the same story of brutal relocation
in 1921 and 1922, of never-ending disputes over property, and of discrimination at the hands of the Kazakhs.

In 1921, for example, a committee led by Uraz Dzhandosov had taken
land from the Cossacks in Stanitsa Kaskelensk and redistributed it among
local Kazakhs. Within a few years more and more Kazakh auls had installed

themselves around villages. The Cossacks now saw themselves "surrounded by a steel ring" that left each household only about twelve acres of land, "which by far does not suffice for farming, our most important and fundamental occupation."[191] They were particularly upset that large parts of their former property went uncultivated and was ruined. The nomads' cattle destroyed everything they had built up in decades of arduous work. But no one wanted to hear their grievances and when they brought the Soviet land laws to the attention of local authorities, the latter replied that those laws were "unjust and void." The Cossacks nevertheless insisted that they were loyal subjects of the Soviet Union who wanted nothing more than to follow the law. It was not their fault that no one trusted them and they were excluded from party membership.[192] Farmers from other villages reported similar circumstances.[193]

The situation worsened. As of the mid-1920s, Chekists in Zhetysu were constantly aware that violence might break out.[194] Goloshchekin saw the rising threat of violence and gravely warned his comrades of possible consequences: "If we do not come to a decision and provide them with land, the Russian population will take the matter into their own hands."[195] The farmers' patience was dwindling. In one complaint the inhabitants of the village of Obelinsk wrote: "We cannot accept that for some the Soviet Power is a natural mother and for others a harsh stepmother. If you come to our aid in a timely fashion, it will spare us the unwanted results that all of these misunderstandings are capable of producing."[196] In other places, exasperated farmers openly threatened "to cut the throats of all the Kirghiz 'when a better day arrives.' . . . Just wait" they said, "there will come a time when it will all be over for [the] Kirghiz."[197] They may have sensed that proclamations such as these did not go unheard.[198]

In Moscow several influential comrades listened carefully to the farmers' complaints. Petr Smidovich was chairman of a "Committee for Regulating Relationships between Native and Immigrant Peoples in Autonomous Republics and Territories." Knowing that it was not an exception to the rule, but indeed, a mass phenomenon, in April 1926, he wrote to Isaak Zelenskii, the chairman of the powerful Central Asian Bureau: "It is difficult to see these outcasts of Soviet Power . . . *virtually living outside of the law*. . . . How can you condone all of this, sit back and watch it, and even support it? In my opinion you are morally obligated to respond."[199]

The VTsIK set up several committees to examine the situation and solve the most pressing conflicts. The most important of them was led by Mikhail Serafimov and permitted to distribute land as it saw fit. Only extremely controversial cases were to be brought before the VTsIK. Serafimov was known to lobby forcefully for the interests of the peasant settlers and they sent him countless letters, petitions, and complaints.[200]

Serafimov made an effort not to disappoint the European farmers seeking his support. Within months he reported that several tens of thousands of households had been allotted millions of acres of land.[201] But in his own opinion, the only way to end contention permanently would be to create autonomous Russian territories. Most of the Russian settlers favored that very same solution. They did not want to be governed by Kazakhs. Like national minorities in other parts of the Soviet Union, they wanted to live in autonomous districts.[202]

Serafimov's plan was to take four districts inhabited mostly by Russians and Ukrainians and create an independent, autonomous region that would report directly to the VTsIK and not be controlled by Kazakh leaders. By switching territories, the percentage of native Kazakhs in the new region was to be kept to a minimum. As experienced farmers, more than 48,000 Russian and Ukrainian families could then produce grains for the cotton-growing regions of Uzbekistan and Turkmenistan. This, argued Serafimov, would end the hostility between the Europeans and the Kazakhs. He wanted the new territory named after the formal Soviet head of state, Mikhail Kalinin. He saw no obstacle in the fact that the four districts he had in mind lay partly in Kazakhstan and partly in Kirghizia, nor that they shared no borders and were not even connected by railway.[203]

If one ignored the many technicalities, at first the idea looked viable. It appeared to meet Soviet standards for solving ethnic conflict: Give far-reaching autonomy rights to certain communities in clearly defined districts. The theory held that if one could create ethnically homogeneous territories, different nationalities would leave each other in peace.[204] But while this worked for Uzbeks in Kirghizia, it did not apply to Russian peasant settlers in Kazakhstan.[205] Former colonizers had no claim to national autonomy at the Soviet periphery. To put things straight, in a telegram to the VTsIK executive committee, the chairman of the Kazakh TsIK, Munbaev, insisted that "there are and will be no independent Russian-Cossack districts or regions."[206]

Autonomous regions had been created for the purpose of encouraging a sense in ethnic minorities of becoming one nation. The fathers of Soviet nationalities policy felt not only that the Russians had already completed that step but also that their nationalism, in contrast to that of other minorities, was becoming harmful and needed some restraint. History, they thought, shows what happens when you give Russians free rein. Lenin distinguished the nationalism of oppressed nations from that of oppressive nations, and the nationalism of small nations from that of large nations. Large nations were guilty of oppressing small ones when they achieved their ends by sheer force.[207] As a nation, the Russians now had to bear the consequences. While it was a rather hypothetical imperative for those living in Central Russia, those living in other Soviet Republics knew what it meant to be labeled Russian chauvinists. In many places across Central Asia they had for the most part become the disenfranchised outcasts whom Smidovich truly pitied.

Although Serafimov's plan was never implemented, it sent a clear sign from central leadership to the Kazakhs not to take things too far, but the reprimand was not well received. Munbaev was furious:

> Who does all the work involved in land distribution? The special committee sent from the heart of the federation does it, while the hands and feet of local agricultural committee members are tied. . . . The fault lies with those sent by Serafimov's special commission, who have ignored all our plans for land distribution. . . . Serafimov dismisses orders from Kazakhstan, he finds it unnecessary to utilize the instructions, directives, and experience of the Kazakh People's Commissariat for Agriculture. He does what he wants. It gets us nowhere and I have been to Moscow and said that."[208]

Munbaev was apparently not the only one who had intervened in Moscow. Other comrades familiar with circumstances in Central Asia attacked Serafimov's work, too. Sanzhar Asfendiiarov, a member of the VTsIK, took Serafimov for an "aid . . . to the former White Guard" who had taken "many mindless steps in his struggle with local comrades."[209] Zelenskii claimed that Serafimov had "drowned his sanity" in alcohol.[210] Serafimov was accustomed to loathing, and dismissed the judgments. As he explained to his opponents: "The commission was formed to represent exclusively the interests of the state, not the interests of all parties."[211] But as pressured mounted, he was compelled to justify his decisions. He did not admit to having made mistakes.

Instead, he insisted that dissolving the commission would cause great damage.[212] But in 1927 he lost the last support from Moscow. In the presence of prominent Central Asian comrades Aleksei Kiselev, secretary of the VTsIK, asserted that Serafimov was "a morally corrupt person" and responsible for the whole mess.[213]

Naturally, things were more complicated than that. But the bitter quarrels over Serafimov were an indication of the increasing anxiety with which leading comrades in Moscow watched developments unfold in Kazakhstan. They wanted to support titular nations and no doubt the Russians, being former colonizers, would have to make sacrifices. But what price were they willing to pay for radically anti-Russian policy? If they allowed productive European farmers to be driven from the steppe, who would cultivate the fields and bring in the harvest? Every grievance brought forth by Russian farmers and every assault by nationally minded Kazakhs widened the gap between them.

Party leaders tried to balance the disparate interests. In January 1926, Stalin's confidant Viacheslav Molotov told party leaders of the Muslim republics: "I do not think that the Russian issue has changed over the past three or four years. We will proceed to decide as we have before, except that without a doubt more attention must be given to the question of the Russian farmers."[214] It was time, he continued, to stop negotiating pressing issues solely in national terms and to start bringing economic aspects into the picture. Careful observers knew what he was saying: The national republics should not needlessly put excessive pressure on comparatively productive Russian farmers. And in 1927 Andrei Andreev, who as candidate for the politburo could indeed be seen as one relaying directives from the highest instance, warned delegates at a party conference in Kzyl-Orda that their principle of *ocherednost'* was not a position in line with class policy.[215] That same year, party leaders sent a highly profiled commission to Central Asia. Chairman Aleksei Kiselev missed no opportunity to point out that he had come at Stalin's request: the general secretary wanted a solution and an end to the inundation of grievances addressed to him, Molotov, and the secretary of the Central Committee, Stanislav Kosior.[216]

Events went beyond warnings and setting up committees. In February 1926 the VTsIK turned down a Kazakh resolution regarding immigration on the grounds that it did not follow the Russian constitution. The comrades in Kzyl-Orda were advised to adhere to previously issued directives before proclaiming new measures of their own. After a few debates the Kazakhs decided, at least theoretically, to treat native and immigrant groups equally when allotting land.[217] Their solution met with Goloshchekin's approval. As he had told the delegates at a Kazkraikom conference in 1926, the time had come to allot land based on class, not on nationality. The decision was upheld, even though influential Kazakh cadre snarled that it was "colonizing by nature."[218]

Despite protest from Kazakh Communists, in April 1928 the ban on peasant settler immigration was canceled for good. Ambitious plans for relocating over five million people within the Soviet Union could not be executed without taking huge amounts of land from the Kazakh Republic.[219] Economists also argued that a generous amount of immigration to Kazakhstan was mandatory to ensure efficient exploitation of the area's resources.[220] This official reopening of Kazakhstan to another wave of immigration was a hard blow to the National Communists. Their plan to rescue the republic from further Russification had failed. As Terry Martin has noted, the decision marked a break with tacit policy on titular nations in general. For the first time Soviet leadership officially stated that titular nations were not entitled to constitute the majority of the population in their own republics.[221] Had these relocation plans, however, been brought to completion, the Kazakhs would have become a minority in their own country.[222]

Debate over immigration to Kazakhstan proved how difficult it was for advocates of indigenization to find an audience for their arguments favoring decolonization and national self-determination. The urgency of emancipation for formerly oppressed nations paled in light of a growing pressure for centralization that did not stop at the borders of national republics, and when faced with leaders who increasingly stressed solutions to economic problems.[223] The only way to protect national interests was to argue that they were economically promising. The implication for Kazakhstan was that nomads, who were just learning the principles of soil cultivation could not expect special protection. It was obvious that under these conditions Kazakhstan's nomads would fall further behind economically and that many a prejudice with respect to backwardness in the steppe would find confirmation. It had already been apparent in the early 1920s that when it came to drawing borders on either economic or ethnological criteria, the advocates of the latter would never entirely succeed.[224] And it was of little help that leaders in Moscow actually had little interest in Kazakhstan's struggles at all. Some leaders could not even find it on a map.[225] This was another reason that toward the end of the decade many leading Bolsheviks thought that nation policy should not be an end in itself. Even the policy's most ardent advocates had to accept that the Soviet Union's considerations of national ways and sensitivities were limited. Opening Kazakhstan for more colonization and marginalizing Kazakh-friendly positions were logical steps. It was perfectly clear: Moscow alone presided over the future of the Steppe.

CLAN LOGIC—PARTY LEADER NETWORKS

Kazakhstan's Bolsheviks were involved in constant quarrels, because the relationship between European and native Communists was uneasy.[226] "Former colonizers" and the "members of backward nations" misunderstood and mistrusted one another.[227] In March 1927, Leon Trotsky, who himself was soon to become an involuntary resident of Kazakhstan, noted that the two groups were so unamicable toward one another that they did not even play chess together.[228] While Kazakhs often accused the Europeans of being "chauvinists of Greater Russia," the Russians accused the Kazakhs of being nationalists. One of the 1920s' most influential Communists, Smagul Sadvokasov, firmly dismissed the accusation: "No party, and especially no Communist party, forces its members to hate their nation. Nowhere does Marxist literature say that the laboring class of civilized peoples will enter the kingdom of Communism over the dead bodies of oppressed nations."[229]

To complicate matters further, diverse networks of native party members competed for power and influence within the party. Competing factions formed when their spokesmen or leaders belonged to different Kazakh clans, or because they had existed before or during the short-lived rule of Alash Orda, or for other pragmatic, power-political reasons.[230]

To leaders in Moscow, the circumstances appeared to present as many opportunities as risks. If they could contain nationalist tendencies and pit separate networks against one another,[231] they might crowd disagreeable comrades out of high positions and break up competing groups within the Kazakh party organization. Central Asian Bolshevik politics saw a fine line between tolerating regional interests and reining them in. It was successful because Stalin and his party men at the periphery established themselves in local conflicts as respected appellation instances or arbitrators, as it were.[232]

Stalin's staff politics in the national republics took care of the rest. Residents of each titular nation were made heads of the Soviet institutions, but the position of the party's first secretary was, with very few exceptions, filled by someone of a different nationality. It was his duty to make certain that the native Communists' demands with respect to indigenization did not go too far. And he was to act as guarantor of central state interests.[233]

When the Kazakh ASSR was created in 1925 and Filipp Goloshchekin installed as its first party secretary, a phase of intentionally sparked and fueled inner party conflicts began. Exclusions from the party, purges, and repressive rituals became a common part of the increasingly bitter conflicts.[234] There was no doubt in the minds of comrades that the organization had to be purged of unreliable elements. To save their own skins many began to accuse others of deflecting, making agreements with the enemy, or, worst of all for Bolsheviks, creating factions (which was true to a certain extent).[235] In the best case, the losers of these struggles were shunted down to subaltern posts, but many were expelled from the party or repressed.

More than ever before, political survival was tied to a knack for clever networking and the skill of masking individual interests to make them look like Soviet interests. Lines of conflict ran not only between rival camps among the Kazakhs but also between Europeans and Kazakhs. What made these intrigues so confusing and even dangerous for those involved, was the fact that adversaries constantly switched alliances and forged tactical pacts with opponents of yesterday.

THE LANGUAGE OF THE MASSES

Native and alien comrades differed not only in culture and origin. They had also come to the party by very different paths and their ideas of the future of the steppe differed considerably. Kazakh Communists of both narrower and wider circles of leadership were repeatedly ignored by their allegedly more experienced and qualified European counterparts, or, at best, condescendingly smiled upon.[236] Newly arrived cadres, especially when they counted as long-time Bolsheviks, often presented themselves with an air of veteran revolutionaries who had come to teach Central Asians. Some candidly expressed their desire to leave the uncomfortable steppe as quickly as possible and admitted their disinterest in local problems. These functionaries often made important decisions without consulting or even informing their

FIGURE 5.   Filipp Goloshchekin, secretary of the Kraikom,
TsGAKFDZ, 2–91444

Kazakh colleagues. Native Kazakh Communists who dreaded becoming mere figureheads protested more or less vigorously, unwilling to accept the subordination forced on them.[237] But they also had to admit that little would change as long as some Kazakhs in the party apparatus went out of their way to comply with Europeans and their expectations.[238]

Next to the language barrier, many European comrades found the low level of education among many Kazakhs a severe challenge, especially when the latter turned down offers of help. On the other hand, many Kazakhs understood indigenization policy as a call to emancipate themselves from Russian claims to leadership. Sooner or later they found themselves at odds with both their European comrades in Central Asia and with party leaders in Moscow. Even indigenization's most convinced advocates did not see indigenization of the party and state apparatus as an end in itself. New comrades were expected to mature and learn to govern. To achieve that end, some functionaries even accepted temporary failure of the workings of regional Soviet institutions.[239]

But obviously, Soviet power would never fully assert itself in Central Asia if indigenization were pursued rigorously and without taking Kazakh interests into account. Functional *korenizatsiia* appeared to be the answer, in other words, not to automatically fill positions with Kazakhs based on the sole criteria of being Kazahk, but instead, to let individual qualification overrule position assignment by quota.[240] Molotov left no doubt about what that meant: "Now, as for the question of what can be done to colonize . . . the apparatus and educate national cadre who do not speak the national language: The first thing that we could do, and did do, and must pursue in the future is to Europeanize them. We need better qualified Europeans; without them we will get nowhere."[241] These insights uttered privately were the opposite of the official propaganda touting closed ranks between formerly oppressed nations and former colonizers. The advocates of integration sometimes dropped their disguise. Kazakh delegates at a party convention in Zhetysu must have taken for sheer mockery the words that Goloshchekin found to begin his speech: "Comrades, I would gladly give my speech in Kazakh, but as you see, I cannot, for I have no command of the language. But I believe that if one speaks communistically and in a way that touches the masses, that manner of speaking will reach the masses, whether or not the masses have a command of that language."[242]

And yet revolutionizing the Central Asian periphery and creating nations was not hollow rhetoric and none of it could be achieved without the participation of large parts of the Central Asian population.[243] Especially in Kazakhstan, where European peasant settlers and Kazakh pastoralists were continually feuding with one another over land rights and water access, Communists had to do all they could to keep things calm. Clever comrades knew how to use the sensitivity of party leaders to that cause. When in 1924 the first secretary of the Akmolinsk Government Committee was called back to Moscow, the ten plenum members staged a dispute. Instead of following the suggestion from Kzyl-Orda to ask the Central Committee to send an appropriate new candidate, they simply nominated a candidate of their own, Comrade Chirkov, and took a vote. Five voted for him, four against him, and one abstained. The Kazakhs had voted for him, the Russian comrades against him. Kazakh party leaders refused to confirm the vote on the grounds that it was not unanimous and that it revealed a deep chasm between Kazakhs and Russians. It was later discovered that the comrades in Akmolinsk had played with marked cards, manipulating the vote in hopes of getting an extra new colleague from Moscow. After realizing that their maneuver had failed, they unanimously voted Chirkov into office.[244]

KAZAKHSTAN'S CLANS

Kazakh networks vied for influence at all levels of the Kazakh party. In the mid-1920s most Kazakh Communists saw themselves as belonging to one of three competing mainstreams.[245] At first the most influential group was that surrounding Seitkali Mendeshev, chairman of the Kazakh Executive Committee. Its members controlled almost all important positions in the Kirghiz ASSR before it was replaced by the Kazakh ASSR in 1925. The *mendeshevtsy*, as they were called, sought cooperation with European comrades and recruited new members, for the most part from what a report on the individual groups called the "healthiest party element." The *mendeshevtsy* were present throughout Kazakhstan.[246]

Khodzhanov's group consisted mainly of former followers and members of Alash Orda and the Kazakh intelligentsiia, who during the civil war had at first been undecided as to whether or not to side with the Communists. Khodzhanov did not choose the Red option until late 1919. Men who had bet on the Bolsheviks from the start never forgave him the delay in making that decision. He joined the Communist Party in 1920 and quickly made a career. He became a member of the Central Committee of the Communist Party of Turkestan, led several People's Commissariats, and was editor of the newspaper *Ak zhol*.[247] In September 1924 Khodzhanov was made the second secretary of the Kazakh Party Organization and a member of the board of the KazTsIK.[248] It was crucial for his career that the network he had created became enormously important for Kazakhstan within a very short time.

While Khodzhanov built up a power base in Southern Kazakhstan, the leader of the country's third main group, Sadvokasov, focused on northern regions. He was Khodzhanov's most important opponent in the struggle for dominance in the newly created republic.[249]

The leaders of these three networks saw no reason, at least until 1925, to conceal the existence of these groups or to keep their own status therein secret. In a letter to Khodzhanov, Uraz Dzhandosov described a conversation he had had with Sadvokasov: "He said: 'The KSSR knows three groups (his, yours, and Mendeshev's); everyone belongs to one of them, it would be unworthy of a Communist not to.'"[250] The three leaders acted accordingly. When the Kazakh ASSR was created in 1925 the three men fought bitterly. Khodzhanov looked like the victor, but a few months later he had to admit the defeat. Sadvokasov's joy at his victory was also short-lived. By 1927 his star, too, was descending.

Khodzhanov had sought Stalin's favor. When in 1923 Tatar national Communist Mirsaid Sultan-Galiev came under pressure for alleged contact with Central Asian anti-Bolshevik insurgents,[251] Khodzhanov attacked the falling functionary. Stalin seemed to approve, saying:

> Khodzhanov spoke well in my opinion, and Ikramov did not speak badly, either. But I must mention a passage in the speeches of these comrades which gives food for thought. Both said that there was no difference between present-day Turkestan and czarist Turkestan, that only the signboard has been changed, that Turkestan had remained what it was under the czar. Comrades, if that was not a slip of the tongue, if it was a considered and deliberate statement, then it must be said that in that case the Basmachi are right and we are wrong. . . . Evidently, Khodzhanov and Ikramov uttered that passage in their speeches without thinking, for they cannot help knowing that present-day Soviet Turkestan is radically different from czarist Turkestan.[252]

Both men needed to correct their error, continued Stalin. But in general, Stalin appeared to like Khodzhanov. After the latter regretted the mistake, Stalin passed him a note that read: "You spoke well today. If you do that well at your job (of which I am not yet fully convinced), then I am prepared to be your friend and comrade."[253]

Stalin's favor was fleeting. In 1923 and 1924 in the course of political debate on dividing Central Asia up into republics, Khodzhanov made the mistake of strongly opposing the founding of new republics. Dividing the region up into separate republics, he said, was "like cutting up a living organism and asking that its head, limbs, and rump each live on by themselves."[254] In spite of his view, Khodzhanov made it to the position of second secretary at the Kazkraikom. He had made himself indispensable to the short-term first party secretary Viktor Naneishvili and to ambitious Nikolai Ezhov.[255] His climb came to a halt in 1925 when Filipp Goloshchekin arrived in Kazakhstan. Within a short time Khodzhanov lost his place as one of the prominent participants in the group struggle and was replaced by Ezhov.[256] This must have been particularly painful for him because a few months earlier he had approached Stalin on Ezhov's behalf and suggested that Ezhov be made first secretary.[257] But neither his presumed propinquity to the general secretary nor the ritualized admissions of guilt by Kazakhstan's party leaders could help him now.[258] Khodzhanov's career in the party was over.

Struggles within the party were not limited to the highest ranks. They sifted down to local levels, and local disagreements brachiated their way to the top. In the district of Chelkar, for instance, two irreconcilable groups were led not by local prominence, but by two well-known Kazakh functionaries: Uzakbai Kulumbetov and Baimen Almanov.[259] Kulumbetov was deputy chairman of the Kazakh Council of the People's Commissars and Almanov had been a leading figure in Alma-Ata Regional Committee since 1927.[260] Their feud went back to the time of the civil war and the choice of allies in the summer of 1919: whether the Red Division should side with the advancing White Guard and Alash Orda fighters or with the Red Army's retreating units. Kulumbetov and most combatants wanted to ally with the White Guard; Almanov and his followers hid in the steppe, awaiting the victorious return of the Reds. Once Alash Orda was defeated, Almanov and his followers got key positions in the region for their loyalty. But priorities shifted in 1920 when the Bolsheviks needed people from Kazakhstan's *intelligentsiia* with past experience with the opponents.[261] Striving for power and influence, Kulumbetov and his men penetrated the party.

It sowed the seed for years of disputes to come. Stylized as gangs defending their turf, both Kulumbetov's people and Almanov's people elicited loyalty in and outside of the party, threatened opponents, waived fees for friends, and used administrative resources and even arms to intimidate them. Tension loomed regularly just prior to Soviet elections.[262]

Network leaders gained followers and power as their careers progressed. By the mid-1920s individuals from both groups held administrative positions at all levels.[263] Chelkar's affairs were now relevant for all of Kazakhstan and changes in power in Alma-Ata changed conditions in other regions as well. Kulumbetov and Almanov went to great lengths to instruct and lead their followers, traveling to Chelkar often and summoning subordinates in order to give orders personally. Their activity did not have a lasting effect on grand politics: despite their dynamic growth, they were too small and insignificant in the long run. But by weaving themselves into larger political constellations, they did win repute in Kazakhstan's politics. Almanov and his people counted among the supporters on the Left surrounding Mende-shev and Ryskulov, while Kulumbetov's group tended toward the Right, especially the contentious groups surrounding Sultanbek Khodzhanov and Smagul Sadvokasov.[264] Kulumbetov managed to make himself appear indis-pensable when Goloshchekin rose to power and many other patrons faced their downfall.[265]

"WE DON'T HAVE A POLICY OF OUR OWN."

Filipp Goloshchekin lost no time. Soon after taking over the Kazakh party organization he began putting pressure on the so-called *gruppirovchiki*, the members of clan networks. New brooms sweep well, as Sadvokasov was soon to learn. After just a few months in office it was clear that Goloshchekin was deliberately stoking conflicts among Kazakh Communists. In a letter to Stalin, Sadvokasov complained that Goloshchekin was intentionally forc-ing the formation of separate groups and that he himself was powerless to halt it because by openly rebuking Goloshchekin he risked being labeled a gruppirovchik himself, which, as comrade Stalin knew, would be fatal. Sad-vokasov asked to be recalled from Kazakhstan, or at least that Moscow curb Goloshchekin's reins.[266]

Sadvokasov's complaint probably came as no surprise to Stalin. His new first secretary was performing as desired. Goloshchekin expertly created new tensions and let old conflicts escalate. Within a few months he not only had comrades reiterating old disputes that had once been settled,[267] he also began confronting Kazakh society with the new program of "Sovietizing the Aul."[268] Kazakhstan's new leader was executing orders from Moscow. Ezhov played an important part in it, as long as he remained in Kazakhstan. The man of small stature marching toward a huge and violent career agitated against all Kazakh Communists and networks. Not one of them was reliable, he said. The best strategy, he reported to Stalin, was to keep them all away from power by artificially fueling conflicts among them. And it would be clever not to send too many Kazakh delegates to Moscow where they could organize "Kazakhstan No. 2" and block measures taken by the party.[269]

Communists loyal to Moscow deliberately counteracted the various factions made up of their Kazakh comrades. But not all networks were easy to disclose. Some relationships remained in the dark and some groups would not be pitted against others. Besides openly attacking the *gruppirovchiki*, the men around Goloshchekin also tapped into OGPU resources. There they found what they needed to discredit Kazakh Communists. One group of European Chekists surrounding Anatolii Al'shanskii went about arranging all the means necessary to do so.[270] In the erroneous belief that Goloshchekin was unaware of events, one of the men involved wrote an anonymous letter describing the methods in use: OGPU members manipulated the testimony of imprisoned criminals as material against Kazakh comrades. They "murdered dozens of poor Kazakhs every year in order to isolate the poor and middle classes from Kazakh functionaries," and when they could not do it themselves, they acted through "Russian hooligans."[271] The OGPU accused Kazakhs in important positions of stealing horses from the Russian population and claimed that a large number of Russian kulaks and Kazakh clan leaders were agents who provided compromising material on native functionaries. The author of the letter may have exaggerated, but a number of comrades did have a real interest in fostering a lack of trust among Kazakhstan's Communists.[272]

As prominent victims of group struggles, in the mid-1920s Khodzhanov and Sadvokasov had made relatively soft landings. Party reactions soon became harsh toward those who had lost its favor. Comrades attacked in 1928 and 1929 for former attachment to Alash Orda while in the party or government were hit hard; many were expelled from the party or arrested. The bloodletting throughout the early phase of the collectivization campaign radically changed the constitution of Kazakhstan's Bolsheviks. With the exception of a small group of survivors, the entire first generation of Kazakh party members suffered the loss of influence and power. And with very few exceptions, those who managed to survive that wave of violence died in the wave of Great Terror.[273]

Goloshchekin and his praetorian guard among wider circles of leadership knew that Kazakhstan's autonomy was not as great as many of the Kazakh comrades had long thought or at least wanted to believe. Stalin's formula of affairs being national in form but socialist in content had always been taken as emphasizing socialist content. And under the conditions of Central Asia, to be socialist meant standardizing and centralizing the practices of governing. Stalin gave Goloshchekin free rein to do so, vindicating his policies in Kazakhstan as being "in principle, the only right thing to do."[274]

And yet it would be too simple to make Goloshchekin alone responsible for all of what was to come in the following years, as some Kazakh historians have done.[275] No doubt, the Kazakh party leader was not an uncompromising combatant for the Kazakh cause. He was less concerned with the interests of the people than with enforcing Bolshevik power in the steppe. Contrary to many a public statement, when implementing their policy at the Central Asia periphery the Bolsheviks made no particular effort to assimilate theory to local conditions. "Policy here is Central Committee policy," said Goloshchekin during a Kazkraikom debate, "We don't have a policy of our own."[276] What a difference that was compared to a few years previously when in April 1925 his predecessor Naneishvili had said at a conference, "Our Kirghiz [i.e., Kazakh] Republic is one great national republic . . . . Our Kraikom has the right to debate and decide on all issues," and no one had contradicted him.[277]

Goloshchekin's attitude differed little from those of functionaries in other regions. All Communists ordered to pursue the Cultural Revolution and enforce collectivization in the many different areas of the Soviet Union held their positions by the grace of Stalin. They all knew that they had not been chosen primarily to articulate regional concerns, but to establish centralist policy.[278] They had to be ruthless, resolved, and loyal. Goloshchekin, nicknamed the Czar's Murderer, certainly was.[279] Nevertheless, no one person alone could manage the huge task of taming Kazakhstan.

Team-Goloshchekin consisted of a small circle of comrades that wanted to put an end to the major division between the various groups and to the conflicts among them.[280] The circle included more Europeans than Kazakhs. Any native Kazakh who wanted to belong could leave no room for doubt about his loyalty to Stalin's squad of leaders. Uraz Isaev (chairman of the Kazakh Council of People's Commissars and the most prominent Kazakh leader) and Izmukhan Kuramysov (second secretary of the Kazkraikom) advocated Stalin's escalation strategy just as radically as Goloshchekin did himself.[281]

The deeds and demeanor of these pivotal agents can, indeed, be interpreted as acts of colonial rule. But that is only part of the picture. The events were not particular to Kazakhstan, they took place in the same or a similar manner all across the Soviet Union: those representing local interests had to struggle with those seeking to strengthen vertical power. And wherever members of regional networks appeared to lack loyalty to the central power, they were subjected to intense pressure. The practice of transferring responsibility to functionaries from other regions was also not restricted to Muslim parts of the Soviet Union, it was a genuinely Soviet affair. The fact that Kazakhs grappled with Europeans and that they were nomads competing with farmers for command of the resources does not alter the fact that it was all basically a struggle for power. The fact that native Communists used every means possible to defend their interests, including acting as a marginalized nation, shows that they understood the rules of the game. If playing the role of victims of "national oppression" and "colonial exploitation" seemed conducive to their interests, they did just that.[282]

But a party marked by political infighting cannot win. Or, as Stalin said, "The Party becomes strong by purging itself of opportunist elements."[283] Stalinists found it necessary to escalate conflicts in order to identify potential and real opponents and render them harmless. It was the only way to achieve the minimum of control and centralization necessary for seriously beginning to radically rebuild society. In 1928 the Bolsheviks felt strong enough to do it.

3
COLLECTIVIZATION AND SEDENTARIZATION

THE VISION PURSUED by Bolsheviks saw a radical restructuring and subjugation of the Soviet Union's entire rural population. Peasants, and in Kazakhstan's case pastoralists, too, were to become dependent agricultural workers who handed the fruit of their labor over to the state.[1] The plan was given top priority and enormous economic loss was taken in stride to accomplish it. While elsewhere in the Soviet Union dekulakization, material demands, and collectivization furthered the greatest possible confiscation of resources, in Kazakhstan collectivization, sedentarization, and the disempowerment of clan elites were instruments of control not only over the population and grain resources, but also especially of the livestock for a very large area.[2]

Collectivization and sedentarization worked in combination, followed the same logic of escalation, and served similar purposes. The Bolshevik slogan for Kazakhstan was "sedentarization by complete collectivization"[3] The attacks it unleashed were so devastating that it took the republic decades to recover.

Many historians have noted that the most important aim of collectivization was to increase the quantity of state-produced grain and to eliminate opportunities for peasants to interact in a free market.[4] To that end, in 1929, the "Year of the Great Turn," the Communists set the course for the largest possible collectivization of all agricultural production and did everything in their power to permanently silence the private sector.[5]

They had reason to act quickly: peasants were reluctant to hand over produce for the low prices offered them by government buyers. Soviet industry was unable to manufacture enough consumer goods of tolerable quality that peasants might want to buy, and the intended effect of artificially high prices for industrial goods evaporated. And finally, the leaders could not risk another massive drop in the overall amount of grain produced, as had happened in 1927 and 1928. Supply to the cities was threatened, which in turn weakened the Bolshevik's already precarious legitimization among workers. It was not possible to finance the ambitious program for industrialization without extracting resources from the villages. The Soviet Union risked its reputation as a nation of grain export as well as the loss of the foreign currency it so direly needed.[6] Stalin insisted that the peasants were called to solve the problem. In July 1928 he told the plenum of the Central Committee that peasants must pay an extra tribute to finance the plan:

> The way matters stand with the peasantry in this respect is as follows: it not only pays the state usual taxes, direct and indirect; it also *overpays* in the relatively high prices for manufactured goods—that is in the first place, and it is more or less *underpaid* in the prices for agricultural produce—that is in the second place. . . . It is something in the nature of a "tribute," of a supertax, which we are compelled to levy for the time being in order to preserve and accelerate our present rate of industrial development. . . . It is an unpalatable business, there is no denying. But we should not be Bolsheviks if we slurred over it and closed our eyes to the fact that, unfortunately, our industry and our country cannot *at present* dispense with this additional tax on the peasantry.[7]

If nothing else, for a long time the distribution conflicts that affected society as a whole were a source of the widespread notion in historical research that collectivization was a dichotomous struggle between the state and the peasantry. But once we look at the dynamics unleashed by the drives for collectivization in villages and auls, things look different. Individual villagers had different interests, and collectivization posed a crucial test for communities made up of both peasants and pastoralists.[8]

Bolshevik dominion over the population of the steppe was very fragile.

Across large areas of Kazakhstan they were unable to install people and institutions that reliably followed Bolshevik dictates.[9] They were unable to disturb nomadic society's networks built on loyalty and kin. Intervention in the world of nomads took extraordinary measures and the introduction of special authorities, troikas (secret police), and other (armed) representatives that could make the will of the central organ happen.[10] In other words, it took the threat or the employment of greater violence for Communists to enforce their will in the steppe, and even then success was often only sporadic.

LEARNING REPRESSION

The techniques for subjugating peasants and nomads to which the Bolsheviks resorted in the late 1920s had been learned during the Russian Civil War.[11] Stalin taught expropriation to his comrades in the provinces and officials followed suit. Bolshevik leaders knew that village and aul members and some of their own cadre would resist confiscation. The drive of 1928 gave them an opportunity to demonstrate their resolve, discipline the party, and give everyone a taste of the struggles to come.[12]

They first targeted the bais, Kazakhstan's equivalent of kulaks. The Communists had always seen the traditional elites of Kazakh clans as their major enemy in the steppe and left no doubt that sooner or later they would turn against them. If the bais represented the real power in the steppe, the Bolsheviks knew they had to undertake everything in their power to alter this power. They saw only one promising means for doing so: total expropriation to destroy the influence of rich men.

Lenin had known it in 1919. At the Eighth Congress of the Russian Communist Party, when asked about the future of the bais, he had told delegates from Kazakhstan, "Obviously, sooner or later we must address the issue of redistributing livestock."[13] The following years saw repeated attempts to undermine the economic role of the bais. In 1927 0.9 percent of all Kazakh households controlled more than 10 percent of the republic's total livestock. The number of households owning more than fifty farm animals rose quickly and the livestock of those families in turn increased at a disproportionate rate.[14] The Communists considered that trend, which was more likely a sign of agricultural recovery from the devastation of civil war and hunger, as an indication of increasing dependence and exploitation of the lower class.

Kazakhstan's government offered to introduce a voluntary tribute to be paid by wealthy households, which would then be used within the same aul. But the People's Commissariat of the Interior turned it down. The measure, said the officials, would achieve the opposite of what was intended. The rich would try to pass the entire burden of the voluntary tribute on to the average peasant, further aggravating the existing extremes. The People's Commissariat thought that the only way to effectively weaken the bais would be to tax them directly and much more heavily than before.[15] Their opinion gained the upper hand and the norms were set for higher taxes.[16] But it was not the only method the comrades pursued.

THE SEMIPALATINSK AFFAIR

It began with a telegram. On January 20, 1928, Stalin let Comrade Isaak Bekker know that he would no longer tolerate the difference in grain prices between the governments of Semipalatinsk and Petropavlovsk and the neighboring regions in Siberia.[17] Higher prices in Semipalatinsk and Petropavlovsk threatened Western Siberia's supply when it was more profitable for Siberian peasants and speculators to sell their harvest in Semipalatinsk. Bekker, at the time first party secretary of the Government of Semipalatinsk, and his colleague in Petropavlovsk, Raiter, had apparently ignored directives from the Central Committee and the Council of the People's Commissars. The general secretary said he would travel to the regions in question immediately and settle the matter.[18] Two days later Stalin ordered the party secretary to go to Rubtsovsk in Western Siberia, about 140 kilometers away.[19]

The details of their meeting are not known.[20] But we do know that in early 1928 Stalin traveled to the Ural and Siberia to teach cadres the Bolshevist way of collecting grain from peasants. The point was to build up "beastly pressure" and "seize" the "fortress that is grain procurement," he said just before leaving for the East, "no matter what the cost." Stalin's "Ural-Siberian method," as he later called it, set the style for requisition drives for years to come.[21] His lesson on dealing with peasants showed the cadres what he expected of them.[22]

Stalin apparently gave Bekker free rein to follow his example in driving in grain throughout Semipalatinsk. And Bekker proved himself to be an assiduous subordinate, dispossessing peasants throughout the land and confiscating grain that had allegedly been held back.[23] Although almost no other region of Kazakhstan was inhabited by more Ukrainian and Russian peasants, the measures were applied mostly to the Kazakhs. Initially, European kulaks, the most significant grain producers of the region, had little to fear. Officials in Semipalatinsk thought that the Kazakhs had been spared long enough. They were no better than the Russians, said Bekker, and it was now their turn to undergo confiscation.[24] Indeed, requisition fulfilled two purposes at once: grain supply and the disempowerment of clans and peasant communities. No one doubted the rationale of demanding grain from nomads. The Kazakhs had no choice but to buy grain and deliver it on demand. But because they had little or no actual money, they had to sell livestock to purchase grain. As a result, the price for livestock dropped and the price of grain rose. The grain supply quotas demanded of the nomads were thus a twofold burden for the auls.[25] Deadlines were also so short that it was practically impossible for Kazakhs to meet them, and delayed payments resulted in draconic penalties.[26] This practice of collecting grain from pastoralists was significantly responsible for the pauperization of large parts of the Kazakh population.[27] The method was devised and tested in Semipalatinsk.

The Bolsheviks certainly knew that they were inevitably depriving the nomads of their very means of subsistence. But functionaries surrounding Bekker had internalized the central axiom of Stalin's requisition policy: to judge outcomes not in terms of long-term economic development, but by their short-term success. It was paramount to make the plan become reality here and now. Pressure to present immediate results was generated top-down, as were the consequences of failing to achieve goals. Precisely how goals were achieved was less important. Everyone understood the conditions and acted accordingly. Such was the logic of administrative command-economy, where long-term goals were planned on paper, but in reality constantly overruled by acute needs.[28]

The taxation drives that Bekker triggered gathered huge momentum. Originally the intent had been to burden the bais, but soon higher taxes were expected from average, poor, and even urban Kazakhs.[29] Troikas took over in many places and interrupted regular administrative activity. Some households were approached by several different authorities, each demanding something more. Unlawful penalties were issued.[30] Afterward, no one was able to say just how many people in total had been affected by repressive acts. One court of inquiry later assumed that at least forty thousand people had been victims. But the actual number was probably larger.[31]

In Kzyl-Orda, Kazakhstan's capital at the time, signs of both the rewards and the dangers of the drive became clear very early on. This sent an ambivalent message to Semipalatinsk. The leaders' efforts to temper cadres in the northeastern region of the republic were half-hearted.[32] Bekker apparently believed that his activities found approval: his superior Goloshchekin had been to Semipalatinsk in February 1928 and attended a meeting of party leaders there dealing explicitly with expropriation.[33] And in answer to an inquiry from Semipalatinsk, the Kazkraikom had passed legislation on the use of property confiscated from the bais.[34] But one thing the officials in Kazakhstan's capital did not do was to issue written orders explicitly commanding Bekker to take action. Later the investigative committee concluded that the events were the government's fault alone.[35]

The entire population was affected. A group of people in charge who had little knowledge of local circumstances began to decide who was to pay which tax. They sometimes estimated herd sizes without ever seeing a single animal.

> An official visits the aul, calls the soviet to convene, and decides that one person has this much livestock and another that much. He is guided by visual appearances only. And then as if he were working in a laboratory, he writes up a report and determines taxes. But the people do not want to pay. We have heard complaints that in this manner livestock quantities were estimated for people who live over 200 kilometers away. The people live over 200 kilometers off, and yet the officials write up a report and register who owns exactly how many animals.[36]

Officials proceeded similarly in Russian villages. They used the presence of farm equipment, the number of working animals, and the number of family members to determine the cultivable acreage available to each family and define their tax load accordingly. The conjecture that they could theoretically cultivate a certain amount of land was fully sufficient for calculating a family's tax burden.[37]

Often the activists recruited in the auls were members of clans at odds with one another. Determined to damage an opponent, from the standpoint of one clan it made sense to burden the other with the tax load for an entire district. Livestock prices tumbled. Officials and comrades seized the opportunity to accumulate wealth at the cost of the miserable, often using their positions in the administration to do so.[38] Some officials admitted openly that they could not let such a unique opportunity slip by: "One member of the soviet says that today he is a member, but tomorrow he may not be reelected. He is a poor peasant and will buy cattle now. Another said that he needed a horse for travel. But the others . . . simply say that no one else takes the animals so they have decided to buy them for low prices to help the government."[39] Although Bekker and his cadres later tried to spread a different version of events, they held their comrades in the steppe on long reins and encouraged aggressive procedures. The activists achieved compliance by force and the employment of so-called administrative methods to affix authority to their demands. And yet their actions appear almost harmless when compared with later eruptions of violence during the drive for collectivization. Nevertheless, some people lost their lives during these months and others were thrown into workhouses and prison for dubious reasons.

The attacks on the auls soon caused turmoil throughout the government. Many people sought to protect themselves and their flocks by hiding in remote areas. Many bais tried to look impoverished by dividing their herds up among their followers and relatives. Others used the proximity to China's border and fled to Xinjiang, as they had often done before.[40] Memories of 1916 returned.[41] More than four hundred families crossed the mountain range, some of them poor, some from average households, and even some wealthy bais. It particularly aggravated the Communists that even leaders of the soviets, members of the Komsomol, and party members were seen fleeing.[42] Soviet border patrols stopped and arrested some, but they were unable to shut down the entire border.[43]

PRESSURE ON BEKKER

The obvious disregard for fundamental elements of the Soviet policy on nationalities eventually made the affair a scandal. The one-sided burden on Kazakhs contradicted all Bolshevik commitments to the Soviet Union's nations and the fact that it affected all social strata, and not just the rich, was inconsistent with rhetoric of class struggle. Tension grew so intense that Moscow had to react. In the spring of 1928 the Central Committee and the VTsIK sent a commission led by Aleksei Kiselev to the region to investigate the situation.[44] Kiselev's report stated clearly that Bekker had gone too far and that Kazakhstan's leaders were not guilty of causing the events: "The

Kraikom had issued no directives in this respect."[45] In late July the politburo removed Bekker from office and halted the drive.[46] In late September 1928 Bekker was called to Moscow where the Executive Committee of the VTsIK held him personally accountable.[47]

But Bekker defended himself, explaining that he had in principle pursued no other policy than what had simultaneously been followed in other regions of the Soviet Union and that he had received numerous, partly inconsistent directives that he tried to fulfill. Everyone wanted to reach the goals of the plan and had put pressure on him.

He understood that it was important not to stand alone as the sole individual responsible for the scandal, but to delegate part of the responsibility upward within the ranks. Naturally, he conceded, a series of grave mistakes had been made, but it was he who had always tried to temper the local comrades.[48] In some places, he continued, "we were forced to take exceptional measures in the auls," but that had always been done in close coordination with the Kraikom. Party leaders in Semipalatinsk supported him; they had always agreed on all important issues; one could not say that Bekker had ruled dictatorially.

Surprisingly, said one member of the commission, the so-called central directives mentioned by Bekker so often were not executed in any other part of Kazakhstan. In his role as chairman of the Executive Committee, Mikhail Kalinin went on to reprimand the commission for revealing serious misconduct, but not seriously sanctioning those responsible for it. Losing his office in Semipalatinsk was hardly a punishment for Bekker. Kalinin constantly received requests from comrades in that region begging to be pulled out.[49] The least they should do was to expel Bekker from the party and put him on trial.[50] Petr Smidovich saw all the success of recent years threatened: "Comrades, if White Guards had come and decided to destroy our work and the economy, would they have come up with a better strategy for achieving a counterrevolution in the region?"[51]

Bekker was an "honest Communist" who had made a name for himself in the civil war, added trade union leader Aleksandr Dogadov: "It is easy to talk in the office. . . . But the strength of our Bolshevist Party lies in the fact that once we embrace an issue, we do what needs to be done." No one would have acted differently in Bekker's place and putting him on trial would have serious consequences: "That would be perilous and we would end up putting 90 percent of our secretaries on government Executive Committees and government Party Committees on trial. The only one left would be Petr Germogenovich [Smidovich]."[52] Dogadov was right to a certain extent. A comrade was being reprimanded for deeds that were common Bolshevik practices in the country. All he had wanted was to see results. He did not care about how those results were achieved. Bekker, said Kalinin, obviously sought political renown. That indirectly confirmed what Dogadov had said: Success in seizing grain justified the means, but it did not necessary keep one in office. When the wind changes, today's triumphs can be tomorrow's crimes.

A decade later, people in Bekker's situation faced fatal consequences. But his landing was relatively gentle. For the duration of one year he was excluded from any responsible position within the party apparatus. And the Semipalatinsk affair hardly damaged his further career.[53] A few years later he became first secretary of Karaganda oblast and navigated the region through difficult years of famine. Bekker then became an authorized representative of the Party Control Commission in Uzbekistan.[54]

The matter was partly subjected to so much debate because in many respects it was an unprecedented case. It was in Semipalatinsk that for the first time anyone had come up with the idea of obtaining large quantities of grain from people who had nothing to do with crop farming. It was also one of the earliest drives for dekulakization and supply procurement where the criteria of ethnicity and nationality played a role just as important as social and economic factors.[55] The Kazakhs bore the main load, but other options might have been equally conceivable. In addition, these events took place in a remote border region. Bolsheviks gave such regions special attention because they had a propaganda effect for everyday Soviet reality ("windows of the revolution"), but also because they feared the "ruinous influence" that foreign countries might have on these neuralgic regions along the borders.[56]

By the fall of 1928, however, things had not gone so far as to warrant calling it the annihilation of an entire social class. In part this had to do with consideration taken of Nikolai Bukharin and his cadre who refused to comply with Stalin's aggressive course on collectivization.[57] Leadership in Moscow publicly demonstrated clemency and unity. Those whose possessions had been unlawfully confiscated during the course of the Semipalatinsk Affair were to be compensated for their losses. Sentences were to be annulled. Messengers were sent to the refugees in China to announce the end of exorbitant repression.[58] Resolutions were also passed in Kzyl-Orda admitting to the injustice done to the Kazakhs and promising reparation. The official wording was that Bekker and his subordinates had not properly understood the resolutions of the Fifteenth Party Congress. At the same time, Kazakhstan's party leaders declared that the exceptional measures taken had, in principle, been right for procuring grain, although they had been unduly applied to middle-income and poor peasants. It would not happen in the future.[59] At that time effort were still made to clearly define and limit terror in the country. The comrades were not interested in unleashing arbitrary spirals of repression, they wanted to get hold of their "enemies".

It was not entirely illogical to make Kazakhstan's Kraikom bear the costs of reparation. After all, Goloshchekin and his group were in part responsible for the Semipalatinsk Affair. But it put the comrades in Kzyl-Orda on the spot. Nigmet Nurmakov, chairman of Kazakhstan's Council of People's Commissars, conceded that while Kazakhstan was responsible for compensating losses, he did not know whether it would be able to.[60] Instead, he tried to tap into the RSFSR's budget. Kulumbetov was more specific: "Naturally, we will punish those who are responsible for destroying livestock, but that does not imply finding means to compensate those who suffered damage. . . . The government cannot be made responsible for all of the bungling."[61] It is not clear how much money actually went into reimbursing damaged households and how many animals were actually returned to their original owners.[62]

Semipalatinsk's devout Bolshevik party members were reluctant to accept these attempts to fence in the affair. Russians, especially, had welcomed the harsh approach to Kazakhs and were now critical. They supported Bekker and saw no need for the party to admit mistakes. One could, after all, simply "neglect the offended *seredniaks*."[63] The Russians could not understand why the party now complied with individual kulaks. This group of critics probably included the "former Red partisans" of whom leading Russian Communists in December 1928 had said—in a mixture of dread and admiration—that they still embodied the spirit of the partisans and were ready at all times to take the dekulakization of their villages into their own hands.[64]

But the events in Semipalatinsk shocked party members who took the policy on nationalities for more than power-tactical lip service. They demanded sanctions. It was out of the question, they said, to sacrifice the modest success they had painstakingly accomplished on issues of nationality in return for mere grain procurement. They wanted to see heads roll and reparation rendered. But in the end, they lost their case. Bekker's political opponents soon watched methods tested in the government of Semipalatinsk find routine application wherever grain was seized and kulaks were repressed—in other words, across the entire Soviet Union.

Disagreement over arbitrary acts under Bekker's aegis were merely part of a wider learning process. New cadres learned how to execute grain procurement and dekulakization, knowing that Stalin now saw no alternative. Despotism was widespread within the administration, and officials as well as activists saw physical violence as an option to be employed at will.[65] Stalin condoned the harsh strategy toward peasants. Like Bekker's advocates he knew perhaps from personal experience not to respect individual fate.[66] The trip to Siberia had cemented his conviction. He propagated radical measures, knowing how effective they were for defeating renitent peasants.[67]

LITTLE OCTOBER

In August 1928 the well-planned operation to expropriate "the wealthiest bais" began.[68] The drive, known as *debaiizatsiia* (debaiization), a Kazakh form of dekulakization, initially looked like a sequel to Bekker's solo efforts because at first it targeted the traditional elites of the auls. But this time,

FIGURE 6. Distributing the confiscated property of the bai Zaliev from the region of Akmolinsk, TsGAKFDZ, 2–27606

things were well-ordered and based on formal resolutions and clear direc-tives from the head of the party.[69] The plan was to dispossess "rich bais" and "semifeudalists" and chase them and their entire families out of their home-lands, and then to redistribute their possessions among the "poor popula-tion" in an effort to counter the unequal distribution of wealth and alleged widespread exploitation.[70] Officially, the drive was to hit the richest livestock holders only. Middle-income households and even those living in comfort-able circumstances had nothing to fear, said Communist activists. According to the resolution, only 696 bais in all of Kazakhstan were to be targeted. The definition of "rich" was the ownership of more than 400 animals in nomadic regions, more than 300 animals in seminomadic regions, and over 150 farm or productive animals in agricultural districts.[71] The Kazakh aul that had not yet felt the "breath of October" was now to become acquainted with the Bolsheviks.[72] The plan meant nothing less than the radical redistribution of livestock and possessions within Kazakh auls and the simultaneous dispos-session and banishment of the most influential clan leaders.

This so-called Little October heralded the commencement of collectiv-ization in Kazakhstan.[73] In May 1928, Goloshchekin explained the need for debaiization: While the drive focused on the most important men of the steppe economy, it was also directed against the most influential enemies and other "vermin." He hoped to propel the Sovietization of the aul forward and gave local officials free rein to accomplish it as they may, claiming that it was impossible to provide general guidelines on how to carry out con-fiscation. Without a doubt, the first party secretary conceded, individual regions would have to use very different methods.[74] Goloshchekin did not need to be more precise. When in August the final resolution on confiscation was passed, it sent through the entire republic a hitherto unknown wave of repression.

Although in principle they condoned confiscation, some Communists felt uneasy about it. At a meeting of the Central Asian Bureau, for example, Jusup Abdrakhmanov, for instance, chairman of the Kirghiz Sovnarkom, spoke up against Little October, not out of pity for the bais, but because he did not believe that the drive would have any positive effect on the poorer part of the population in nomadic regions. A diary note shows that for the time being, he intended to pursue no similar strategy in Kirghizia.[75] And Uraz Dzhandosov, who had been authorized to supervise the drive in Zhetysu, suggested involv-ing leading district officials as much as possible in the decision making. That would, he hoped, help to prevent exaggerated actions and simultaneously accustom local leaders to the true goals and dimensions of debaiization. But his proposal was ignored. *Etogo ne nado delat'* (that is not acceptable) noted someone (presumably Goloshchekin) in the margin of Dzhandosov's letter containing the suggestion.[76]

Kazakhstan's leaders were not going to take a different path, but to emulate what was happening all over the Soviet Union: they raised taxes and devised new tributes to be paid by wealthy peasants and kulaks. But most important, they took administrative measures to seize grain from the peasants. In 1928 confiscation once again became a normal part of governmental policy. War Communism had been revived.[77]

A brochure on the socialist reorganization of Kazakhstan stated unapologetically: "Current socioeconomic conditions in the aul cannot be altered by peaceful, normal ways of changing labor following the example of Russian villages. It will take revolutionary methods."[78] Little October quickly became violent in nature. In some auls the troikas merely threatened to use physical force. In others, they applied it, terrorizing victims whom they believed were hiding animals and possessions. The case of Aktau Adenov is typical: He had let his animals graze together with animals owned by a local bai. When the latter's livestock were confiscated, Adenov went to separate his animals from the bai's herd. But the commission from Alma-Ata in charge of the confiscation thought they could get more information out of him: "On that day the commission drove Adenov out into the steppe and staged an execution with him. They stripped him naked, bound him, put a gun to him, and tried to force thin rods into his sexual organ."[79] The men also tortured the bai, the actual subject of interrogation.

After that, the commission had little trouble with requisition. "People willingly handed over all their possessions to avoid becoming victims of harassment and abuse. Everyone understood the lesson taught."[80] Events were similar in other oblasts. The comrades' resolve also made a lasting impression on the Russian and Ukrainian peasants, who initially had not been targeted by the drive. But from what they observed they concluded that they, too, might soon be threatened: "At first the Communists were merciful to the Kirghiz while descending on us, the Russians, and pressing what they could out of us. But now they take the Kirghiz's livestock without remuneration and when they do that, they will soon begin taking ours."[81]

Debaiization was also used to settle old scores: loyal Bolsheviks attacked political opponents and "enemies of Soviet rule." Members of different clans and networks harmed foes of their own. The code to legitimize all kinds of damage was the passage of the resolution that extended the radius of potential victims far beyond the richest bais to include anyone whose possessions and social influence "impeded the Sovietization of the aul."[82] The passage opened the floodgates for administrative despotism. In the end, it was not the publicly touted economic rationale that made the drive successful, it was the pivotal desire to interfere with power relations in the aul. The attacks on the Kazakh elite aimed to destroy their authority at both the local and regional levels. The emissaries of the revolution prepared their offense across the steppe.[83] Repression soon affected not only the Kazakh auls, but former members of Alash Orda, Kazakh intellectuals, and unwanted native party and soviet officials as well.[84]

The state was clearly responsible for the escalation. But soon dynamics came into play that left the officials as bystanders, even when they made every effort to depict events as class struggle. At the Central Asian periphery, nothing was farther from the truth. Villages and auls knew no classes and no class struggle. People lived in clans and as members of tribes. Their communities were free of neither internal stratification nor strife. And many people did use the window of opportunity to escape, at least for a moment, life at the margin.[85] Having common origins in the same social and cultural milieu enabled them to pressure and, if necessary, be violent toward their neighbors. They knew where herds grazed and hid them from procurement commandos. They knew the dark spots in the biographies of their fellow men and mobilized hidden resentment and lingering conflict for their own purposes.[86]

The usurpation of Soviet organization and political campaigns by groups at local and regional levels was not new. What was new was the kind of consequence that now followed winning or losing: the total existence of the defeated, be they kulaks or bais, was at stake. And yet radical change in the social organization of the villages did not at first seem to be equally threatening for all peasants and nomads. Poorer members of local communities suddenly saw opportunities: by actively supporting requisition they got direct material gratification and chances at influential positions and social ascent.[87] And dekulakization offered many a welcome chance to rid oneself of old enemies and competitors. Collectivization was not only a war of the state against the people, it was also a war of the folk against itself.

The Bolsheviks had no illusions about the reliability of their organization in the steppe. If the authorities announced visits, it gave the bais time to prepare for confrontation. Utmost secrecy, the cadres found time and again, was paramount. In general, the bais had very close ties to other members of their aul. Thus demagogues like Dzhel'baev from the district of Kurdai claimed that it was not enough to simply relocate them: after deportation the bais maintained their influence through middlemen. They had to be "brought farther away and torn out at the roots and destroyed along with all of their relatives and close friends."[88]

When in November 1928 Communists from Alma-Ata drew their first conclusions with respect to the drive for collectivization, a local delegate had to admit that all attempts to keep confiscations secret before they happened had been in vain. The people directly involved knew what was coming before anyone else did. Other delegates reported similar circumstances. But the real reason the attacked were able to defend themselves was that they were very well networked with local authorities and even had their undivided support. Bisengali Abdrakhmanov,[89] chairman of the Regional Executive Committee told the delegates at the party convention: "The aul Communists ... nodded and when a bai walked toward any official from the district or the aul, the others moved over respectfully to give him a seat."[90] Many comrades were susceptible to bribes and some had relationships with bai daughters. The latter point aroused laughter, the proceedings tell us, for which Abdrakhmanov—playing the prude Communist—rebuked his audience: This was no laughing matter, indeed, it showed the difficult nature of the conditions one met when working in the aul.[91]

Abdrakhmanov's report was like many others. One heard from the district of Dzhetgarinsk, for example, that the district attorney had warned a local bai of an impending confiscation and taken ten male sheep in thanks.[92] Everywhere comrades seized opportunities to feather their own nests.[93]

Many of the people targeted used the weapons of the weak in their attempts to ward off intrusion by the troikas.[94] Without openly opposing the authorities, they simply did not hand over everything that defined their wealth and status. From many documented cases we know that rich bais divided their herds up among their relatives and dependents in order to appear less wealthy.[95] Others sold off their animals at regional markets and bazaars, which eventually led to dramatically falling prices, as had been the case in Semipalatinsk earlier in the year. And others, once again, fled across the nearby border to China to bring themselves and their herds in safety. The Bolsheviks had counted on open and armed resistance to debaiization. The Party Committee of Aktyubinsk, for example, had ordered the formation of an armed division to be called upon when needed.[96] But for the moment the Kazakhs remained, for the most part, quiet.

They were also reluctant to participate. Courting resentment from the Bolsheviks, many Kazakhs adopted a wait-and-see attitude. Large numbers of Kazakhs refused to engage in confiscation directed toward the indisputable leaders of their own nomadic communities, where each individual depended on the leader's benevolence. Native activists lived dangerously. One *bedniak*, for example, in the district of Chelkar was murdered for abetting confiscators. At the bazaar in Merke "the bai and former administrator Ulmar and his sons . . . publicly beat Utabai Peremkulov for disclosing the whereabouts of hidden property to officials."[97] In light of such events it was judicious to practice restraint. And often after sheep and goats taken from affluent bais had publicly been handed over to the poor, one saw them grazing in the pasturelands of their former owners soon after the troika had departed.[98]

Complementing solidarity within clans was a lack of it among clans. Clan acolytes in local administration offices did everything in their power to protect their own groups from repression as much as possible. Whenever unable to do so, they at least worked toward privilege for their own people when it came to redistribution. Thus in many places, debaiization exacerbated conflicts that already existed. That seems to have been the case in Chelkar, where in December 1928 the inhabitants of Aul No. 12 complained of unfair treatment. After property confiscated from their bai, Makhatarov, was redistributed, they found that about two hundred animals had been given to other auls. But the much larger part of Makhatarov's herds now strayed ownerless around the steppe. Their grievance was ignored. "We bedniaks, batraks, and komsomols," they wrote, "have been treated unfairly by the commission."[99] The commission had found them all already too affluent to warrant giving them more livestock, and this, in their opinion, was a mistake. They found the suggestion particularly appalling to award livestock to auls that had not been subject to confiscation.

Seasoned officials in the VTsIK saw through the Kazakhs' attempt to resemble impoverished innocents. They assumed (and rightly so) that this was primarily a matter of tribal conflict and wanted to investigate it. It was more than nine months a reply and in September 1929, Kazakh authorities responded that the inhabitants of Aul No. 12 were kin to Makhatarov and had supported him in his attempts to hide livestock. Several of them had been tried and sentenced, but no irregularities had been detected. Some of the applicants from the aul had actually not been given any animals but only because the commission "was uncertain whether the applicant would use the animals economically."[100] It seemed probable that the claimants were primarily interested in asserting their demands to the disadvantage of other auls and in securing the property of their own kin.

Many cases show that livestock was not distributed in accordance with the rules in other places, either. Nonetheless, already in April 1929, the party concluded that this had "no great political significance" for the overall outcome of the campaign.[101]

Zeineb Mametova would have disagreed with this conclusion. All the property of her husband Bazarbai Mametov had been confiscated following the resolution of August 1928, and he had been deported from his native region. Mametov was no common bai: he belonged to a small circle of educated Kazakhs who, as young men, had made Alash Orda careers for themselves and then joined the Bolsheviks. In 1917 at the age of eighteen, Mametov had become a member of the short-lived Alash regime. Then he switched sides. Following an intermezzo with the Cheka he had held various positions in the Soviet judicial apparatus. In 1925 he lost all his offices and withdrew to the steppe to devote himself to his livestock.[102]

Mametov's biography made him an ideal object of Little October repression. He was now imprisoned in Uralsk. On January 31, 1929, Zeineb Mametova sent a complaint to the district attorney in Kzyl-Orda. As the mother of two small children, she demanded that all sanctions placed on her husband be lifted and the case against him closed.[103] When nothing happened in her favor, she brought attention to her case in February and then again in April, both times unsuccessfully.[104] Her point was that the campaign was being used to settle old scores. A mixture of clan disputes, injured vanities, and malice among competing networks had resulted in her husband being accused of absurd offenses. She could not deny that he had been a member of the Alash Orda, but she made an attempt to belittle the role he had played in the former regime by saying, "Everyone knows that he has no talent at organization and takes no initiative."[105] The plea was unconvincing. And shortly after her first letter the district attorney determined that the procedure in Bazarbai Mametov's trial had been correct and the complaint was therefore void.[106]

The past shaped Iblia Kaimulin's destiny, too. Although he was by no means affluent, he lost all his belongings and was deported with his entire family from his native region of Petropavlovsk. In the mid-1920s he had taken the father of Abdrakhman Baidil'din to court and won his case.[107] Kaimulin, a Kazakh who owned barely more than thirty animals, knew that Baidil'din had been a leading member of the Alash movement and had forged new political ties with the Communists after the White Army's defeat. Baidil'din held a protective hand over his own father who prior to 1917 had been an important figure under the czarist colonial regime. He was also the head of a clan composed of more than two thousand families. Kaimulin complained that he had been treated unjustly. He did not have the means, he said, to defend himself against such "strong people."[108] Nothing helped. As could be expected, in March 1929 the Kazakh Control Commission exonerated Baidil'din of the allegedly defamatory charges and denied that he had played any role in repression against Kaimulin. The latter's expropriation and deportation were in conformity with a decision by "an assembly of the Poor Villagers, material from the OGPU, and a decision of local party and soviet organs."[109] Baidil'din had, it was mentioned, candidly and comprehensively informed the pertinent officials of his past.

Baidil'din's behavior was certainly not atypical. Districts and regions had been given clear instructions as to how many bais they had to track down. People in local networks did their best to protect their own contacts and shift the burden of confiscation to undesirable people. We do not know whether Kaimulin would have been more successful had he waited a few months before submitting his complaint, or had the gears of Soviet bureaucracy turned slower. For within a year, in December 1929, Baidil'din was expelled from the party on the grounds of "working for the secret service of Kolchak,"[110] put on trial, and convicted of engaging in a national-bourgeois conspiracy. He was executed in April 1930.

Even great merit for the cause of the revolution now no longer protected anyone from persecution.[111] Many aggrieved parties submitted information and complaints to various institutions, lamenting the injustice they had suffered. Complaints often involved unlawful confiscation, but more often the aggrieved tried to achieve a reversal of deportation orders.[112]

Debaiization was only the overture to the much broader collectivization campaign that followed without delay. It gave officials at all levels of the regime a prime opportunity to rid themselves of enemies and opponents. In contrast to a common Kazakh version of the events, it was not simply a case of Europeans positioning themselves against Kazakhs. Native cadres and activists were themselves deeply involved in identifying and persecuting affluent bais. Regional party committees dispatched almost exclusively Kazakhs to handle confiscation in the steppe.[113] And the behavior of confiscators was more often motivated by personal interest than by ideology. Old accounts and conflicts were settled. One report notes that not a single member of the administration could approach his task without prejudice.[114] That surprised no one except the few Communists who had come from elsewhere with orders to investigate exaggerations and excesses.

Leading Communists were not of one opinion in evaluating the campaign. Grand propaganda could not conceal the fact that the economic success of the drive had at most been small. They had even failed to reach the original goal of confiscating and redistributing 226,000 animals.[115] Goloshchekin tried to make defeat look like victory: a significant portion of those subject to governmental repression, namely, 136 of a total of 696, had not been pursued by the Bolsheviks because of their wealth, but because of their pasts as public office holders under the czar and counterrevolutionary activists.[116] And it was known, of course, that there were no true Soviets or party cells in the auls. Nevertheless, two-thirds of the target figures had been reached.[117] The Soviet apparatus's highly praised new authority in the aul was wishful thinking. Local Soviet organizations had proved to be the weakest link in the whole chain. It had become necessary to organize confiscations without informing the local apparatus at all. That is not what they had envisioned as strengthening local cadres. But in the end, that had not been the intention anyway.

On a small and manageable group, Little October tested practices that were later to be applied to the entire population. At first only specific individuals and their families were affected and they had been selected using more or less objective criteria. Despotism and violence had not yet grown to the dimensions they were later to reach, and for the time being, most nomads and peasants remained calm. Resistance was passive. The prospect of getting some of the goods confiscated from the bais gained the acquiescence of many people who otherwise would have been critical of Communist attacks.

As long as those suffering repression were few, others could counter their doubts with hope of personal gain.

While economic criteria were important, they were by no means the only grounds used to determine who might fall prey to debaiization. The foremost purpose was not to destroy the bais as a class in themselves, but to disempower the people seen by the Bolsheviks as potential insurgents: former officials of the czar's colonial administration, members of Kazakhstan's upper class, and most important, members of Alash Orda. The drive's political effect manifested itself in the process of selection and the far-reaching uncertainty sparked by repression.[118] Amnesties and promises from the time immediately following the Bolsheviks' rise to power lost their validity. Prominent ex-competitors of the Communists who had ascended to high positions in the state and party apparatus now found themselves just as targeted as the middle and lower officials of the short-lived national regime.[119] While Soviet propaganda vehemently announced release from the shackles of oppression, in reality a campaign of revenge had begun pursuing opponents who had long been anathematized by the Bolsheviks.

COLLECTIVIZATION AND DEKULAKIZATION

Peasants and nomads had to pay. The success of the first Five-Year Plan, an effort begun in 1929 to force industrialization on the entire country, depended crucially on complete control over the agrarian sector.[120] In the winter of 1929–30 hell broke loose in Soviet villages.[121] Kulaks were liquidated, resources seized, and peasants and nomads forced into kolkhozes. At a plenum of the Central Committee in April 1929 Stalin had said unequivocally: "The significance of the Ural-Siberian method of grain procurement, which is based on the principle of self-imposed obligations, lies precisely in the fact that it makes it possible to mobilize the laboring strata of the rural population against the kulaks for the purpose of increasing grain procurement."[122] In December 1929 the general secretary pondered the destruction of all kulaks as a class; one month later the politburo passed the corresponding resolution. It was now clear that grain procurement and collectivization meant waging war against the peasants and—in Kazakhstan—against the nomads as well. Sedentarization was now part of the program. Resistance meant facing the worst of Bolshevik resolve.

Local cadres seemed untroubled by the fact that they were exposing peasants and nomads to doom when, accused of resistance, they expropriated them of their last supplies.[123] On the contrary, leading Bolsheviks repeatedly encouraged and pressed their cadres to take such action. Molotov, for example, told party secretaries from the national republics in February 1930 that it was of the greatest importance that local officials demonstrate a "maximum of initiative" in confiscating animals.[124] Neither the population, the rural institutions of the Soviet regime, nor pastoralist economy would withstand the excesses of collectivization.[125] Stalin's top-down revolution overburdened peasants, nomads, officials, and comrades. And while it destroyed tradition, it made no realistic plans for the future.

DEKULAKIZATION RAIDS

The drive for dekulakization can be seen as an attempt by the Soviet state to split the rural population into two groups: the greater majority of all those who would later live and work in kolkhozes, and the minority of the

FIGURE 7. Grain procurement officials for the district of Irtyshk, May 15, 1929, TsGAKFDZ, 2–50517

kulaks and the bais, whom the Bolsheviks saw as their enemies. Expropriation, arrest, the deportation of entire families, and execution were the measures condoned by Stalin's party leaders for the purpose of "liquidating the kulaks as a class." About 3–5 percent of all peasant households were scourged by it.[126]

The decision about whom to repress was often highly arbitrary. Criteria were ambiguous and remained so in order to accommodate the diverse situations of Soviet peasants in different regions.[127] As early as 1928, Kazakh Communists' attempts to detail objective criteria had floundered. But now, as then, target numbers had to be met and victims were sought.[128]

There were two ways to do it: First, external commissaries had lists for determining whether individual peasants belonged to one class or another; these lists contained the names of all those who in previous years had been denied the right to vote because they owned too much property.[129] Second, those responsible for collectivization let villagers and local Communists inform them of what each individual peasant possessed. They must have known, however, that the inside information they were given served the interests of the informants more than it reflected true circumstances in the village or aul.

Nonetheless, there was reason to believe that nomads were hiding grain and livestock. Communists had experienced time and again that the rural population convincingly portrayed itself as being utterly impoverished, while hiding grain below their stalls.[130] The Communists had learned from events in 1928 how nomads made themselves look less affluent by parking their animals with other clan members. And Communists from rural backgrounds knew all too well that peasant complaints of poverty had always been a part of their communication with representatives of the state in the perpetual attempt to get a reduction of their tax load. Peasants and pastoralists had always tried to conceal their property from the covetous eyes of the state. Minimizing their tax load was essential to them.[131] Until the late 1920s it was taken as more or less acceptable folklore. But now it had fatal consequences. Now no one believed peasants who said they had already relinquished everything. And no one cared what it meant to their families to lose their last sack of grain or their last animal.

Comrades in the oblasts took one element of the resolutions and directives particularly to heart: the order to use any means necessary. Backed by that command, the troika responsible for Akbulak found it legitimate to define a dekulakization quota of 25 percent of all households for their district.[132] It could not be achieved without the threat and use of physical force and the responsible officials could imagine no other way to go about it. In the winter of 1931, for instance, the first secretary of the district of Kazalinsk, suggested entrusting authoritarian colleagues with the agitation of local pastoralists. The men, he explained to the party leaders, should be assigned to Chekists in order to "influence the psychology of Kazakhs on whom the presence of uniforms and Nagants has a positive effect."[133] One Chekist was blunt: "It seems to me that we shall not establish Soviet power in Sarysu without a good deal of bloodshed. The more bais we kill in the district, the better."[134] Officials like these had nothing to fear from their superiors. Goloshchekin had always pleaded for an increase in the exertion of pressure on peasants and nomads.[135]

Dekulakization turned into one huge raid organized by the authorities and secret police and executed and supported by villagers whose own material interests and personal animosities suppressed any scruples that they might have had. In several Kazakh oblasts every household was obligated to turn in grain. Nomads had to sell large parts of their herds to buy grain and fulfill their obligation. Then they were prosecuted for squandering livestock. When they were unable to fulfill the demands, the authorities abandoned all restraint. In the district of Zaural'nii officials beat men and women, drenched women with cold water, raped them, and then gathered for uninhibited carousing. They took men out into the steppe and tortured them with mock executions. They showed the men's families the empty rooms where their husbands and fathers had been arrested.[136]

Procurement officers often made exorbitant demands. One Kazakh peasant from the district of Kazalinsk was ordered to turn in over 1.6 tons of grain, although all he owned was two horses, one cow, and a camel. The demand rested on the claim that he was a Sufi. He fled to a different oblast and the rest of the village paid what he owed.[137] In the district of Enbekshil'dersk some comrades redeclared their seed as harvest and relinquished it in order to meet the target.[138] The decision was made with little regard for the implications it might have for the people.

To fulfill the quota, officials began taking preventive measures. In the district of Karmakchi, 283 households had to be dekulakized although that number had nothing in common with real conditions. Officials thus decided to proceed with families that one day *might become* kulaks: "In the resolution on their dekulakization we read that while they are not kulaks, their households are expanding and because it is clear that they will therefore one day exploit the poor, it was decided to deport them and confiscate their property."[139]

Those responsible for dekulakization threatened all who were unwilling to join a kolkhoz with confiscation of their property, arrest, and deportation.[140] In the village of Chemoldan, not far from Alma-Ata, Communists staged a so-called black boycott against resistant peasants. They nailed shut the windows of twenty-two homes and allowed the inhabitants to go out only at night and only to get water. In the district of Akkermerinsk, local comrades had another idea: "They formed a brigade with black flags and a bucket of oil and took to the streets. They went to a kulak's home, snatching up two bedniaks along the way, then smeared oil all over the walls, icons, and so on."[141]

The state's attack on auls and villages found by no means the disapproval of the entire rural population.[142] For example, in the village of Konovalovka in the district of Rykovsk, dekulakization began with a meeting of the local party cell. The village's five Communists gathered around Comrade Chernorod, a leading functionary from the district center, and compiled a list of thirty villagers who were to be exiled for being kulaks. The families concerned had to leave the village within a very short time and activists emptied their homes. Armed appointees relieved them of the belongings they tried to take with them. Records say that dekulakization was finished within a matter of hours. Two days after Chernorod had left the village, the dispossessed were allowed to return. They had held out in the steppe and many of them had suffered from frostbite. Meanwhile other villagers had rummaged through their possessions and taken what they wanted. Even days later the victims were stopped on the streets and their clothing was taken away from them.[143] Activists and plenipotentiaries from outside fueled conflicts such as these intentionally in the name of collecting information about presumed kulaks and expediting the subordination of village communities.

The campaigns developed an almost inescapable pull. Judges and district attorneys lost all credibility and left their offices to abet collectivization in the villages. The entire system of dispensing justice in the oblasts had become a will-less tool of authorized people and the OGPU, sanctioning even the farthest-reaching decision. It may have been what lawyers took for revolutionary justice. It also spared them all suspicion of being mild or yielding ("right deviation").[144]

The same held for leaders of the soviets. Their interest in removing kulaks permanently from the villages was even greater. When the campaign was over, representatives from the branch of justice would leave, while local officials would then be confronted with the victims, witnesses, and profiteers who remained.

Relocation meant being labeled a declassed element or special settler and deported to barren and remote territories to live at the margin of society where there were neither sufficient accommodations nor adequate food. More than two million so-called declassed elements vegetated and labored under catastrophic conditions across the entire Soviet Union.[145] During Kazakhstan's first phase of collectivization twenty thousand kulak families were exiled from the oblasts of Petropavlovsk and Kustanai and deported within the republic "in compact masses to regions of wasteland, far from Kazakhstan's centers of economic development and railroads."[146] It was followed by repression of the kulaks and bais in other oblasts. Kazakhstan's leaders were then obligated to accommodate thirty thousand kulak households from those other parts of the Soviet Union.

Seen from Moscow, Kazakhstan was considered an ideal destination for deportation. It lay at the periphery and had ostensibly unlimited and economically underused space.[147] Agronomists and hydrologists expressed confidently that if one had a sufficient workforce and could relocate the small groups of nomads who already lived there, one could cultivate and harness the steppe.[148] Expanding the Gulag to include Kazakhstan in the early 1930s was done based on those criteria.[149] The further these projects evolved, the more Kazakhstan's officials found themselves incapable of continuing what they had achieved by early 1930: until that time they had successfully deterred the absorption of kulaks from other regions in the Soviet Union.[150]

And yet, as resolved as the Soviet state was about removing specific segments of the population from certain regions, the officials in target regions were equally passive and unable to cope with the numbers. Sometimes a mere telegram amid their own collectivization commotion warned them of the upcoming arrival of thousands of uprooted people. Kazakh leaders simply told local officials, who often enough had no idea what to do, that they were responsible for creating adequate conditions for the new arrivals. Newcomers were expected to fend for themselves and do heavy physical work. Although the evacuation of kulaks from other oblasts was already well under way, Bolsheviks were still debating whether investments and food supplies were necessary.[151]

A report from the far western oblast Gur'ev described how the families of repressed kulaks and bais lived cut off from the world in a special colony on the shores of the Caspian Sea. They had no living quarters, were not paid for their work in the fields, and, for lack of equipment, harvested hay with their bare hands. The village soviet in charge forced the men to fish out on the sea for days without providing them and the women and even small children on the boats with food. Many died. The telegram closes by reporting that "it came to frequent flights and suicides among kulaks and bais."[152]

BOLSHEVIK SPEED

Stalin's "revolution from above" needed immediate, direct results. In November 1929 Molotov said, "We have . . . just four and a half months left . . . for a decisive breakthrough in the economy and at collectivization."[153] Competition was fierce among top party leaders in the republics and oblasts; all of them wanted to reach the highest rate of collectivization within the shortest period of time. The numbers coming from Kazakhstan were unconvincing and officials there came under pressure.[154] In November 1929 Kazakhstan's people's commissar for justice, Dzhanaidar Sadvakasov,[155] ordered district attorneys to intensify repressive measures. "Your reports show that punishment and confiscation has been administered to a very limited degree," thereby reducing government pressure to "null."[156] Such reprimands brought results. Local officials set about their tasks knowing that they would be held accountable for failure.[157]

Within just a few weeks, numbers rose rapidly. According to official statistics, 50 percent of all households had been subject to collectivization by the end of March 1930. In some oblasts such as Pavlodar, with its higher-than-average number of European peasant settlers, officials reported on May 1, 1930, that more than 96 percent of all households had been successfully organized in kolkhozes.[158] It was efficient to let oblasts compete for the highest rates in collectivization, a practice that became particularly absurd in Kazakhstan's pastoralist territories. Even the districts considered the most backward fought to be recognized as now fully collectivized. It was not just about loyalty: collectivized areas were permitted to deport kulaks and bais without themselves taking in people deported from elsewhere.[159]

No one bothered to inspect conditions in the kolkhozes, which were said to be sprouting like mushrooms throughout the land. And no one looked all too closely at the dekulakization rushing through the country at breakneck speed.[160]

Many historians have interpreted the Bolshevik's enormous hurry for collectivization and other projects (e.g., the absurd attempt to accomplish the Five-Year Plan within four years) as proof of the Communists' particular affinity for modernity and acceleration.[161] Faced with the possibility of war on one or more fronts, Soviet leadership is also said to have sought rapid industrial recovery.[162] The more or less conspicuous irrationality of the plan has been said to have exacerbated the strain and necessitated revised plans time after time.[163]

Nonetheless, that view ignores the mentality of the men surrounding Stalin who insisted on "Bolshevik speed" for collectivization and industrialization for the very reason that it provoked and escalated conflict. They saw themselves at war and acted accordingly.[164] Crises were instrumental: the more the population was pressured, and the more relentlessly, the easier it was to discern friend from foe and to destroy the latter.[165]

During the civil war the Bolsheviks had used a similar strategy of sowing discord to successfully parry the crushing advantage of the enemy, despite ostensibly hopeless circumstances.[166] Thus when peasants and nomads across the entire Soviet Union rebelled against collectivization, they were doing exactly what the regime wanted.[167] Turmoil in rural areas came as no surprise. Stalin himself had said that victory in collectivization would follow bitter battles with the kulaks.[168] He continued to pursue that policy even after devastating consequences and extreme hunger crises had become obvious.[169] In November 1932 he wired comrades in Alma-Ata that in light of the sabotage by kulaks, Kazakhstan's leaders had no other choice for grain procurement than to use "the rails of repression."[170] A few weeks later Goloshchekin told delegates at the Fifth Plenum of the Kazkraikom: "Not only can we not abandon the methods of force, violence, and harsh repression toward the class enemy, we must step up the efforts."[171]

HELPLESS IN THE STEPPE

During the drive for collectivization the Kazakh Communists in charge of the operation there detected weakness in the Soviet claim to power. Oblast collectivizers were not up to the task. In the district of Chelkar the comrades from the oblast's center had no detailed instructions: "Those authorized to work in the auls have been insufficiently instructed. They know that they must collectivize everything, and that they should round up the livestock, but no one knows what to do next."[172] Things were not much better in other oblasts. No one knew of a plan. One report mentions that districts sent to the steppe people who had no idea of how to organize a kolkhoz. New commissions were constantly coming to the auls with contradicting directions and discarding what those before them had said was right. They confused the inhabitants who had no conception of collectivization at all.[173] The ignorance of those in charge was not a question of education, they were being kept in the dark for strategic reasons. Higher-ranking officials often left local cadres in a state of helplessness that led them, in turn, to reconcile their disassociation through a particularly harsh treatment of peasants and nomads.[174] When even the representatives of the state did not know exactly what was expected of them, the people lived with uncertainty and fear. From their viewpoint, collectivization, requisition, and dekulakization created a tightly organized and comprehensive attack on their entire existence.

When the campaign for collectivization reached its zenith in early spring 1930 in the district of Chubartavsk, local party leaders recruited as activists young and motivated students from a technical school in far-off Karkaralinsk. The party deliberately chose men from hundreds of kilometers away to make certain that they had no personal or family ties to the population that might undermine the success of dekulakization. One of the students was Shafik Chokin, who later wrote down his experience.

After he arrived in Chubartavsk, local party leaders sent Chokin to a remote aul that had until then successfully eluded dekulakization. Inexperienced as he was, Chokin was on his own. The aul expected him; the locals demonstrated reluctance and animosity. It took considerable effort to find a man who would halfway reliably assist him by providing information on other aul members.

When a rumor spread that Great Britain had declared war on the Soviet Union and defeated the Bolsheviks, Chokin's position became untenable. The nomads wanted to kill him. Simultaneously they prepared to attack the administrative center of the district, the town of Barshatas. For days Chokin and a local activist named Aitbek Tolendin hid themselves at a Muslim cemetery, assuming correctly that no one there would suspect them. When they finally came out of hiding and made their way to a neighboring aul in search of food and information, they discovered that the rioters were seeking them, but now to beg for pardon. The rumors of the end of the Bolshevik regime had proved untrue and the attack on the district center had been staved off with bloodshed. Fearing sanctions, the nomads now took pains to gain the favor of the young man they had persecuted just days before. They organized a generous feast for Chokin and Tolendin and apologized. Then they asked Chokin to swear that he would not leave the aul without their permission. Chokin swore as requested, but fled a night later to Barshatas, ten kilometers away.

His flight almost cost him his life. He approached the town under fire not only from the men at his heels but from members of the Red Guard at Bolshevist outposts in the steppe. As soon as he was in safety, Chokin denounced the insurgents' spokesmen and ringleaders. They were later arrested and sentenced.[175]

Executors of the dekulakization campaign lived dangerously, as Chokin's example shows, especially when they were on their own and unable to assert any authority in local communities. Emissaries from the Soviet regime were threatened, beaten, tortured, and murdered when they collected tributes or tried to force people to join the kolkhozes.[176] In those auls marked by strong social cohesion, little was gained by pointing out abstract provisions and instructions, little was gained through arbitrary measures and pressure, and the Soviet claim to power reached its limits. The Kazakhs were flexible and clever. To subvert Soviet policies they sometimes took up arms, but they also sometimes pretended to be loyal subjects and followers of the Bolsheviks who made mistakes, admitted their failures, and asked for forgiveness.

On March 2, 1930, Stalin reduced the pace. In his famous article published in *Pravda*, "Dizzy with Success," he explained that the previous practice of collectivization had led to excesses because its "voluntary character" had gone unheeded. That had to end.[177] But Stalin's piece ultimately only elicited a short interruption in the race for the highest rates of collectivization. Soon the chase for the best numbers began anew. Gerhard Simon has called Stalin's maneuver the "dizzy with success trick"—an attempt to use the results of self-inflamed radicalization against subaltern officials. The point was to identify scapegoats to blame for the many failures of forced collectivization, which was typical of Stalin's method of governing.[178]

The peasants thought that they understood the message and hundreds of thousands of them left the kolkhozes. In Pavlodar alone almost 60 percent of all peasants living in the oblast left the kolkhozes within three weeks.[179] The abrupt stop signal had a dramatic effect on the apparatus and the progress of the entire drive for collectivization. Weak administrative structures were unable to cope with a rapid change of course. Officials were left to deal with the new situation by themselves.[180]

Matters in Pakhta-Aral illustrate what this meant for comrades on the scene. In April 1930, a local trade union official, Kisliakov, who was responsible for promoting collectivization in the area, wrote to a leading member of the OGPU in Central Asia.[181] Caught unawares by the unexpected turn of events, the heads of kolkhozes, he wrote, responded with complete helplessness and refused to even mention Stalin's call in *Pravda*. At the general assembly of the Sacco and Vanzetti kolkhoz, the chairman of the district executive committee said not a single word about Stalin's address. It was not discussed at all until the Kazakhs inquired about it repeatedly.

The people interpreted Stalin's message as meaning: "The Central Committee and Comrade Stalin oppose kolkhozes." Within a very short time, not much was left of the collectives, Kisliakov wrote: "On March 25, they began to deteriorate. In a state of anarchy, the Kazakhs took their horses, cows, small animals, and property and on March 26, all Kazakh kolkhozes were practically ruined. According to tentative estimates, less than 10 percent of the population has remained in kolkhozes." It was not only devastating news to the Communists. The exodus had serious tangible consequences, too: it was time for spring sowing and no one knew what to do. Should they support individual peasants and provide them with seed, or distribute the seed among the remaining kolkhozes?

District leaders were no help; they insisted that the district remained one of complete collectivization with everything that followed from it. The uncertain circumstances caused Kazakhs to abandon the area in droves, although the schedule for sowing was not even half met. Kisliakov and his men had not received any directions in a long time about how to proceed with collectivization. All their inquiries were answered with promises of instructions to come the next day. Everyone was irritable; well-known advocates of collectivization were threatened and beaten. When the OGPU had several rebels arrested, more than one thousand people gathered to demand their release. Similar scenes played out in what remained of the Progress kolkhoz, where it was said that more than two hundred armed men lay hidden in the steppe, ready to attack the village at anytime. Faced with the dangerous situation, district leaders chose to disappear and even avoided meeting with the members of the brigade who were supposed to discuss the next steps with the people in charge. Kisliakov said straightforwardly that Soviet rule no longer existed in this territory.

The highly explosive mixture of incompetent officials, constant changes in plans for the worse, growing uncertainty among the people, and the arrival of countless plenipotentiaries from elsewhere sparked outbreaks of violence again and again all across Kazakhstan. In the seminomadic district of Chubartavsk, which had not one single permanently settled village, local leaders were entirely overwhelmed by the situation, the burdens, and the demands made of them and, for the most part, simply quit work. When the first party secretary returned from a conference in Alma-Ata with a new, even more demanding plan for tributes, people refused to believe that it was genuine. One comrade lost the document and as they had already been given so many different versions of the plan, they confused them and no longer knew which one was valid. Shortly thereafter the district's nomads rebelled, depriving the Bolsheviks of all livestock from the whole area.[182]

In light of the pressure exerted on the comrades it is not surprising that very few of them openly expressed unease or admitted to having scruples. One Communist handed in his membership book saying he would rather be shot than return to the countryside to procure grain.[183] But such incidents were rare. Many believed the propaganda about the advantages of kolkhozes, having had it hammered into them time and again.[184]

On the other hand, numerous reports of the men's enormous consumption of alcohol and their excessive carousing perhaps indicate that many suffered emotionally from the strain of their duties. Not all those involved in forcing collectivization and carrying out dekulakization were crusaders for the cause. Many were unconvinced, but they were far too few, especially in Kazakhstan, where thousands of officials and employees of Soviet organs were posted involuntarily.

Among the executors of collectivization were the "best sons of the fatherland," mostly young workers recruited to help collectivization attain a major breakthrough.[185] Often they had only a vague idea of rural life and they knew little about the nomadic aul. Finding themselves fairly isolated in unfamiliar surroundings and pressured to deliver results, many panicked. When escape was not an option, many saw no other way to protect themselves other than exhibiting undue and blatant harshness.[186]

David Tsirkovich, a Ukrainian worker, was one such young man thrown into the steppe. He was a party member from Kharkov (Kharkiv) and was sent to the village of Znamenki in Semipalatinsk where he tried to prove himself as chairman of the Morning of Freedom kolkhoz. From the start, he complained, he had never gotten support of any kind except commands and instructions. While no fewer than six district plenipotentiaries had come to the kolkhoz during the sowing season, each had different ideas and gave different orders and interfered with his work. Tsirkovich felt bound to official directives and powerless vis-à-vis the autocratic functionaries: "For example, Zukovich, the commissioner for grain procurement, ordered me to send off our grain reserves at a time when the kolkhoz had absolutely no surplus. When I pointed out that we should never haul off reserves I was removed from my post and accused of opportunism and pursuing a kulak policy."[187] The same had happened to one of his colleagues, he said. They were held accountable for numerous problems and mistakes. It was no wonder, Tsirkovich reported, that many had abandoned the region. One young man could not cope with the pressure and attempted suicide.

APPROACHING ECONOMIC CATASTROPHE

Grain procurement and heavy livestock requisition ruined the Kazakhs within a very short time. Functionaries all over Kazakhstan took recourse to methods they had tested in Semipalatinsk in 1928—they demanded grain and seed from nomad livestock drovers. As had been the case in Semipalatinsk, the nomads could only comply with the immense demands by selling off their animals. Prices for grain shot up at the markets, while livestock lost value. Those unable to pay their tributes in grain became victims of repression.

In the spring of 1930 Mausumbai Kuderin, for example, was charged to pay an additional tribute of 40 poods (about 1,500 pounds) of grain. Being a cattle drover, the Kazakh could pay the tribute only by first purchasing grain on the market. Then one new and higher tribute demand followed the next. Kuderin bought and bought grain and paid his debt. When he finally realized that the authorities would never give him peace, he put an end to the farce. In the fall of 1930 he was arrested for having sabotaged the delivery plan. The

Chekists charged him and his male relatives with having formed an anti-Soviet gang. Within six months his family had been destroyed financially, its male members were in jail or had fled, and their wives and children faced an uncertain fate.[188]

In Balkhash, representatives from the district center forced nomads to pay tributes in grain although they had sowed nothing. People sold their animals at bazaars, where they got very little money for them. When there was nothing left to buy, money lost value and grain became the most important means of payment. Within a short time people stood on the brink of famine.[189]

This method of collectivization destroyed Kazakhstan's herds. Even those in charge of the collectivization campaign understood the consequences. One official from Chelkar reported: "At first they decided on how to collectivize the herds and ... decided that [each family] would be left one cow or goat. But in the summer months the Kazakhs live almost exclusively on milk and *ayran* [a yogurt drink]; those are their staple foods. The present method of collectivization, then, means that because of the gigantic amount of territory assigned to the kolkhozes, the Kazakhs are not merely doomed to hunger rations, they are left to starve."[190] The dramatic loss of livestock influenced events between 1930 and 1934 more than any other single factor. The exchange that nomads and settlers had practiced with one another in the past ground to a halt and the economy collapsed. The pastoralists' source of existence dried up: they lost their mobility and with it the foundation of their entire identity.[191] This distinguished them from European peasant settlers, who were often hit just as hard by procurement drives, but the peasants remained peasants, even when they had lost everything. For nomads it was different.

The Kazakhs were not alone in their concern about the decimation of livestock. In both state and party organs awareness mounted concerning the crisis that lie ahead. In the winter of 1930–31 all oblasts reported substantially smaller herd sizes than they had a year previously. But requisition continued as before and by the summer of 1931 the amount of livestock in Kazakhstan had been reduced by over 70 percent. According to official statistics, in 1929 almost 36 million productive animals lived in Kazakhstan. Two years later they numbered not quite 9 million. By the winter of 1932–33, Kazakhstan's auls had practically no more animals. In 1929, an average household had owned about 41 animals; in 1933 they had only 2.2. Across

TABLE 1: LIVESTOCK IN KAZAKHSTAN FROM 1926 TO 1934
(IN MILLIONS OF ANIMALS)

YEAR	HORSES	CATTLE	SHEEP/ GOATS	PIGS	CAMELS	OTHER	TOTAL
1926	3.04	6.75	23.1	0.43	—	—	—
1927	3.57	7.72	26.1	0.52	—	—	—
1928	3.84	7.68	26.6	0.37	—	—	—
1929	3.79	6.74	23.83	0.27	1.13	0.04	35.82
1930	2.61	4.12	12.77	0.02	0.79	0.04	20.36
1931	1.77	2.58	3.97	0.04	0.47	0.02	8.85
1932	0.69	1.59	2.72	0.09	0.16	0.01	5.26
1933	0.45	1.61	2.70	0.13	0.09	0.01	5.00
1934	0.43	1.58	2.15	0.12	0.08	0.02	4.39

Source: Data are taken from *Pianciola, Stalinismo di frontiera*, 392.

Notes: Sums are not precise because numbers have been rounded. For the years 1926 to 1928 (statistics ending January 1), see GARF 6985-1-4, 38. For the years 1929 to 1934 (statistics ending June 1) see GARF, 6985-1-19, 105.

Kazakhstan more than 90 percent of all livestock had been lost. Predominantly nomadic oblasts were hit even harder.[192]

By 1934 about 4.4 million animals were left in Kazakhstan. Statistics show that the largest loss, from over 26 million down to about 2 million animals, involved sheep and goats, the nomads' most important productive herds. But cattle, horses, and camels were also lost by the millions.[193] The economy in the steppe now lacked desperately needed pack animals for transporting food and other goods to the auls and kolkhozes.

The bleak figures represent nothing less than the collapse of Kazakhstan's economy. The hubris of extracting as many animals as possible from the private sector in the shortest possible time without preparing to provide for that sector in any other form led to economic catastrophe. It is hard to imagine a more devastating scenario for a society whose entire economy thrives on breeding livestock.

Even then the regime hiked its demands for livestock, meat, and other animal products. New plans were issued for exploiting more resources, and certain quarters of the year were identified as being crucial. When plan fulfillment faltered, as it did in January 1931 when just more than 20 percent of the quantity demanded was registered as having been delivered, Moscow sent emissaries to get defaulters moving. The drive permeated everything. As Stalin told representatives from the national republics who were in charge of livestock breeding: "I know that many of you try to say one thing but do another. . . . Many sovkhoz [state farm] directors and chairmen of livestock combines have double plans, one that they publicly applaud and another that they carry out. . . . But no tricks are allowed when we are talking about an army and workers that must be fed!"[194] In contrast, whether any real plans existed for the proper use of the resources garnered by those constantly enhanced plans appeared to be negligible. Procurement offices showed only marginal interest in the plight of the confiscated animals. Sovkhozes and kolkhozes were left alone with the livestock driven to their gates. In early 1930 there existed few plans for what to do with collectivized animals.[195]

In a scathing report of January 1931, Danilovskii, the authorized representative of the OGPU in Kazakhstan, laid out what the Kazakh branch of the Soiuzmiaso, the agency for livestock procurement, had achieved over the course of the winter. When devising their plans for individual oblasts, he wrote, the agency's employees had obviously taken no consideration of local circumstances or the financial potentials of certain areas. The outcome was widely disparate success rates. While the plan for Belovodsk was fulfilled to 627 percent, Iany-Kurgan only reached 5 percent. Almost half of the livestock purchased consisted of costly young animals that had not yet attained slaughter weight and were useless for immediate meat production.[196] Animals were also driven across great distances through the steppe for collection and slaughtering without sufficient fodder reserves along the way and they lost weight or died. In an attempt to prevent total losses, the animals were driven through villages and auls to eat any hay they found along the way.[197] Without veterinarian expertise, no one isolated sick animals from the others and more animals caught diseases and died. A sudden snowstorm on an open field could kill huge numbers of animals; there was little hope of rescuing them.

The Bolsheviks responded with their standard methods. The OGPU arrested some of those responsible, they issued directives with concrete instructions, and Stalin intervened. The way they had treated the animals that winter in Kazakhstan, he wired to Kazakhstan's leadership, had "cheated the working class and the state," and the guilty would be held accountable.[198]

A few months later, nothing had changed. In November 1931 Danilovskii's successor Mironov reported his concern: Winter was coming soon, no fodder reserves had been deposited along the corridors used for driving livestock, and at the collection spots no one knew when or how many animals would arrive. No one knew exactly where the herds were on any given day. Workers in charge were incompetent and irresponsible. The same held, in his opinion, for the entire Soiuzmiaso, from top to bottom. For example, about sixty thousand animals assigned to the Taldy-Kurgan meat combine stood near the Karatal train station. Without fodder and shelter they were in danger of freezing to death. But the procurement organs continued driving ever more animals to the overloaded combine. There were not enough butchers and the combine's few workers soon left when they were given no food for themselves.[199]

FIGURE 8.   Transporting agricultural equipment, region of Pavlodar, 1931, TsGAKFDZ, 2–38907

Slaughtering did not solve the problem. Transport, cooling, and preservation capacities were limited. During the winter, when temperatures dropped, meat could be stored outdoors and transported in a frozen state. But that changed with the thaw. In January 1931 authorities from Gur'ev in the west of Kazakhstan reported that 250,000 kilograms of fish and more than 100 tons of meat needed to be dispatched urgently, before warm weather set in.[200] At Nurinsk, a train station along the Akmolinsk–Karaganda line, workers soon learned what that meant. In the spring of 1931 about 160 freight cars of meat were hauled into the station. The contents of 70 cars showed "clear signs of decay. The meat was bad, black, rotten, and smelled putrid."[201] Unloading the cargo became a "veritable bacchanal" with workers carelessly tossing the meat onto the platform and into corners. Workers from various organizations split the freight cars among themselves and bartered off the contents. Living animals became emaciated without fodder, while at the same time several thousand tons of grain stored in the open at the same station went to waste. More than a thousand plows rusted in the snow and tanks full of kerosene stood around unlocked.[202]

It all took place before the eyes of the very people whose means of subsistence it destroyed. More and more peasants and nomads arrived from the steppe to Nurinsk to deliver wagonloads of meat that they had carted across hundreds of kilometers in early spring temperatures. In Nurinsk they were turned away or sent home with their spoiled products without compensation for their work, or food for their horses and camels. The exorbitant waste and lack of respect for animals, supplies, and wares of all kinds must have filled the people with bitterness, especially when they themselves owned very little and constantly had to comply with new demands. "We need not say another word about the mood among the peasants," says one telling report on these events.[203]

Procurement officials were not interested in livestock and grain alone. They also wanted hides, bones, and leather, and they collected these resources en masse. In Gur'ev they demanded one pood of wool per mutton, in Iliisk two poods of bones and one dog hide per household, and from nomads in Kzyl-Orda and other regions they took the felt mats right out of the yurts. An order from Alma-Ata directed that all horse manes and tails be cut off and collected. It was supposed to be a voluntary contribution but as one report tells us, "The instruction that this work was urgent, combined with the strict observance of its execution, inhibited all sense of voluntariness . . . and the shearing of horsetails began everywhere."[204] The economically most absurd action of the campaign took place in Akkemirsk where, under the threat of arrest for failure to comply, nomads were forced to "slaughter dogs, mules, and camels and deliver their bones."[205] In Karkaralinsk cadres demanded the shearing of twenty thousand sheep just when winter was imminent. About one-third of the sheep froze to death in the following months.[206]

Although the comrades claimed the opposite, the guilt for the unprecedented loss of livestock lay not with the nomads who slaughtered their own animals or drove them across borders to save them from confiscation. And the order to deliver meat only partially explains the massive loss of animals. Between 1929 and 1931 it would have taken only about 9.5 million animals to fulfill the state's plan to 100 percent. "Thus," said one reporter in November 1931, "the huge number of missing livestock, namely, about 17.5 million animals, was wasted by predacious destruction and squander."[207] The large sums of money budgeted for this sector of the economy were pointlessly lost and none of the Kazakh comrades seriously investigated the causes for it.

By custom the pastoralists owned only as many animals as their region could nourish. They split their herds and trekked through more or less defined corridors in the steppe, allowing the grasslands time for regeneration. Forced livestock concentration abandoned these customs. Herds could not thrive when too many animals shared too little space. Without fodder, many animals perished, especially in the winter.[208] Disease and contagion spread faster among crowded flocks than when nomadic herds lived scattered and separately.[209]

The economic damage resulting from the drive for collectivization was not caused by confiscation in and of itself. The damage emerged afterward, when all the valuables and resources collected went without preservation or further processing. The weaknesses intrinsic to the system of the Soviet planned economy were conspicuous: each actor was keen on producing and exhibiting the greatest possible numbers with little heed to the consequences of his own actions. The functional logic of Stalin's regime wanted results, not farsighted vision. Comrades continued to confiscate livestock even when buyers were lacking. It was rational to concentrate exclusively on fulfilling orders.

Foreign agronomists were aware of the consequences of this kind of policy. Among them was Andrew Cairns, who in the 1930s studied the state of Soviet agriculture for a Canadian research institute. In one report he mentions a conversation with a German agricultural scientist, Otto Schiller, who had traveled Kazakhstan in mid-1932. Schiller, one of the leading experts on Soviet agriculture, had told Cairns that he never would have imagined developments such as those taking place in Western Siberia and Kazakhstan. While he had seen livestock everywhere during his previous trip in 1925, he had now not seen a single animal while traveling to a farm near Semipalatinsk. In his opinion, because they were all nomads and could not survive without their animals, one million Kazakhs would die of starvation.[210] Schiller was right.

THE SEDENTARIZATION CAMPAIGN

While the drive to collectivize Kazakhstan's auls had been dramatic for the nomads, the attempt to settle these people was tragic. The campaign was poorly planned, carried out by amateurs, and refused by the those it targeted. In the end, "sedentarization based on collectivization" cost hundreds of thousands of people their lives.[211] Why did that occur? What plan did it pursue and what happened at the "settlement spots?" What were the consequences of the drive's failure?

CALCULATION

Izmukhan Kuramysov, second secretary of the Kazakh party leadership, spoke clearly. At the Kraikom plenum in December 1929 he outlined the grand feat awaiting the comrades: nothing less than the sedentarization of the nomads and a socialist reorganization of agriculture. Kazakhstan had an enormous amount of land, he said, that was utilized improperly or not at all because nomadic communities could not build a socialist economy. His plans were bold: within the first five years, 65 percent of all nomads were to be settled. If one added all the Kazakhs who were already no longer migrating, one would have almost 90 percent of the population of Kazakhstan settled.[212]

Kuramysov's lecture revealed the thoughts of Kazakhstan's party leaders.[213] It was impossible to install socialism with nomads. Their way of life was an "impediment to a more profitable exploitation of the territory," as the plan for sedentarization written up by the Sovnarkom unmistakably phrased it. The measure was necessary, furthermore, to destroy the influence of the bais once and for all because "the existing nomadic and seminomadic structure is the source of continued exploitation of the bedniaks by the bais." The case was even more serious because subjugation there took on "half-patriarchic and half-feudalistic forms." And it would be "meaningless to end this exploitation," said Kuramysov, "without reorganizing those backward forms of economy."[214]

How did the Bolsheviks plan to reach the ambitious goals? In November 1929, as part of the first Five-Year Plan, the Kazkraikom proposed an overall procedure for developing Kazakhstan's agriculture that included measures for executing sedentarization. A few weeks later the procedure was approved by the plenum of the party commission.[215] Although the original concept was subject to change over the following years, the first numbers and deadlines it set remained the most important point of reference for all future deliberation.

The first step was the transition from an "extensive" nomadic economy with its characteristic customs to an "intensive" and "rational" use of land. Livestock breeding was to remain the most important branch of the economy of the steppe, but the area under grain crops was to be extended to include all the currently unproductive territory of Kazakhstan. It would be necessary to establish gigantic kolkhozes consisting of up to three hundred households each. The plan went far beyond simply settling the Kazakhs. It designed an economy that included sovkhozes, factories, and mines that worked in close coordination with kolkhozes. Sedentarization would create a proletariat class in Kazakhstan, freeing up more than 300,000 laborers to work in industry and agriculture, planners believed.[216] They wanted to settle more than 540,000 nomadic households. Based on an average family size of 4 people, they were talking about settling more than 2 million people. Within the first 4 years, in other words, by the end of 1933, the entire nomadic and seminomadic population of northern and southern Kazakhstan, or 430,000 households, were to have become permanently settled. A longer preparation phase was calculated for the central steppe regions; the goal was to be reached there by completion of the second Five-Year Plan. If all the measures take hold as projected, the planners claimed, by 1933 the area of cultivated land will have increased from 470,000 hectares to more than 2.7 million hectares. Household incomes would triple during that period from an average of 238 rubles to over 740. Rational management and a focus on labor-intense produce would increase yields by more than 1,000 percent.[217]

It was almost impossible to seriously estimate the price of the utopian project. Like so many other Soviet statistics, the apparently exact lists nonetheless suggested thorough planning and preparation.[218] They calculated costs totaling 364,036,400 rubles of which 96 million would be covered by the state budget.[219] The rest would be borne directly and indirectly by those involved. Approximately 130 million rubles was to be financed by money that the (yet to be established) kolkhozes and sovkhozes would have to borrow. About 130 million rubles would have to come directly from the population to be settled.[220] No one questioned how the kolkhozes would cope with such tremendous debts from the start, or how the vastly impoverished Kazakhs were to raise such astronomic funds.

The People's Commissariat for Agriculture (Narkomzem) in Moscow was skeptical of the plans. They were not troubled by the desire to settle nomads for the purpose of making land available for resettled peasants. What troubled them was the speed expected of the comrades in Kazakhstan in fulfilling the plan despite the fact that they had neither the resources, nor the technical expertise, nor the administrative capacity for doing so: "The pace is inacceptable. It is not only unrealistic, it may lead to extremely disadvantageous results. Beyond collectivization, even in its simplest form, planned sedentarization cannot be done. We have very little practical experience with collectivization in these regions and at the present moment we have no reason to expect that nomads will come together on a large scale and join kolkhozes. Any attempt to force the nomads to join kolkhozes would lead to the irrevocable disorganization of all livestock rearing in Kazakhstan."[221] Grigorii Grin'ko, a planning expert also expressed concern.[222] Although he did greet the plan of resettling nomads elsewhere to make land available for immigrants from other regions who "had lost their livestock and under current material-historical conditions had no prospects of rebuilding their farms," he found several points of the plan questionable. The numbers for the Kazakh development of livestock levels, he said, were much too optimistic, and in light of continued losses it would be impossible to reach the levels of 1929 by 1933. Instead of the projected 443,000 households, at most, 380,000 households could be settled in the coming years.[223]

But despite the objections, Narkomzem officials did not fundamentally oppose the plan. They urged that the overly optimistic targets be carefully revised and made some suggestions for reducing the burden on the state's budget.[224] The closing statement worded by the People's Commissariat said that the plan for Kazakhstan was, in principle, reasonable and realistic.[225]

Meanwhile, all the deliberations and plans for sedentarization assumed that even after settling and becoming members of kolkhozes, most Kazakhs would continue to migrate as livestock breeders. The expansion of crop fields did not question the foundation of the Kazakh economy. The deputy chairman of the Kazakh Sovnarkom, Uzakbai Kulumbetov, underlined once again in November 1930: "Whoever says that sedentarization is linked to a reduction of livestock in the livestock-breeding areas affected by sedentarization is absolutely wrong and does not understand that we will combine sedentarization with seasonal migration, albeit with a limited radius of nomadic trekking."[226] An anonymous writer added: "It is entirely clear that where it is more profitable to bring the herds to the 'mountains of grass' we will not bring 'mountains of grass' to the herds."[227] And an article in the journal *Narodnoe khoziaistvo Kazakhstana* noted that the success of sedentarization would be measured by the growth of the herds.[228] Local officials thought the same. A party secretary from the district of Dzhambeitinsk outlined a solution that he found tenable: "The number of households in kolkhozes must be based on the number of dairy cows: one cow per household. Everyone else must emigrate to the republics of Central Asia."[229]

But by the spring of 1931 the rapid loss of livestock caused by procurement campaigns meant that in many parts of Kazakhstan the prerequisites for a planned settlement policy were no longer given. But this obstacle did not halt those in charge of sedentarization.

PRACTICES AND CONFLICTS

No one in the oblasts really understood what sedentarization was about. On the long way from the detached plans elaborated by the people's commissars to the actual measures that were necessary for implementing them, motivation dwindled and knowledge of the long-term ends dissipated. Most regional and district administrators were occupied with other work—collectivization and procurement demanded all their attention. Many comrades turned to sedentarization "in moments of leisure only."[230] No one thought the idea was important and little pressure was put on local officials to deliver tangible results. In many places the whole program was almost forgotten. Little happened until June 1930. In Semipalatinsk those in charge simply lost the plans for settlement. In Karkaralinsk the plans were stamped, filed, and archived. In Pavlodar they built one dwelling for settlers by July— to ease their consciences, as one official put it.[231]

Sedentarization was accompanied by administrative chaos. It involved numerous institutions, people's commissariats, and economic structures in one way or another. Each actor was interested only in the part assigned to him and did not ask what contribution he made to the total picture. The campaign remained piecemeal in many places.[232] Party leaders in the district of Enbekshi-Kazakhsk, for instance, watched how their plans for irrigating projected settlements were torpedoed by various other organizations. Once they had convinced the office of water management of the usefulness of their project, and the construction work on an urgently needed canal had progressed considerably, the kolkhoz bank refused to lend any more money because the funds for irrigation were meant exclusively for projects in cotton-planting regions. It made no difference that all settlement in that district depended on the canal.[233] And then another problem arose: the workers involved in building the canal were not given enough food and diverse people's commissariats blamed each other for it, without finding a solution.[234]

Surveying and distributing land was one of the essential prerequisites for successful sedentarization.[235] In most of Kazakhstan's oblasts this work had gone undone for years. No one knew exactly what territory belonged to whom and who had rights to it. Often the land administration could not settle land conflicts between kolkhozes.[236] Opaque circumstances encouraged greed. Newly founded kolkhozes tried to secure "inheritances" of expropriated kulaks. Sovkhoz directors and kolkhoz directors competed with various state organizations and the leaders of (proposed) large-scale operations for the best land. Finally, the OGPU and the People's Commissariat of the Interior intervened on behalf of their special settlements and labor camps that needed gigantic pieces of property. Often the fragile kolkhozes that had neither permanent buildings nor qualified personnel could not compete with the financial and political supremacy of government operations.[237] Faced with powerful competitors and interests of that kind, the pastoralists had little to say. They were often left with what no one else wanted. Individual families did not stand a chance when surveyors simply ignored their claims and left them with nothing but shabby winter quarters or drove them away from previously designated settlement spots.[238]

Land distribution was often based on ethnicity. Whether Europeans or Kazakhs received priority hinged to a considerable extent on the local decision maker's nationality. In Petropavlovsk in northern Kazakhstan the comrades in charge handed over the largest and best property to Russian kolkhozes because, in the year before, the Kazakhs had been less productive than their European neighbors. The Kazakhs had simply made too many mistakes, the responsible comrade later said to excuse the injustice.[239] Kazakh officials, on the other hand, argued that they had to take care of the nomads during the transition period by providing special support in the form of land and other privileges.[240] Turar Ryskulov, who in December 1930 had publicly warned of demanding too much of the people living in nomadic and seminomadic areas, spoke up again and, pointing out the custom in countries like Argentina and Australia, pleaded the case for rationalizing livestock breeding in the steppe instead of settling the nomads.[241]

But the success of intervention was limited. To a large extent the drive was understood as an attempt to Russify the Kazakhs and rob them of their identity. Large parts of the Kazakh population that could not make any other sense of being forced to settle were not the only ones who thought so.[242] Many native officials shared the same sentiment. They conjured up (and not entirely unjustifiably) an image of a vulnerable Kazakh society susceptible to contagion, whose national characteristics were in danger of being lost: "We will not benefit from settling. The Soviet regime wants to drive us into a pen and feed us from one big kettle, but we Kazakhs are not used to that and will contract numerous diseases."[243]

Often sedentarization meant nothing more than bringing nomads to barren, arid property in the steppe and abandoning them to their fate.[244] When in June 1931 a commission in the district of Enbekshi-Kazakhsk went to examine conditions at the settlement spots, they found that at least two kolkhozes had been located in bad places. The soil was salty, the groundwater was brackish, and the entire area was infested with malaria.[245] Kulumbetov reported a case from the district of Irgiz where the comrades in charge had had no better idea than to settle the nomads in the middle of the desert without access to groundwater. The houses had been erected on old graves, which was a monstrous sacrilege in the eyes of the Kazakhs.[246]

When in the district of Balkhash the Kuvashi kolkhoz was to be settled, at least a technician came to the location. After hurriedly inspecting the territory he chose a place for the village that the members of the kolkhoz unanimously rejected. Later the VTsIK sent a commission that also found the place "fully inappropriate for cultivated life" because there was not enough water "to secure the continued existence of an entire village."[247] Some kolkhozes underwent an odyssey before being assigned a permanent settlement spot.[248] But when Kazakhs complained about the "nomadic method of sedentarization," the officials in charge threatened consequences.[249] In the district of Kazalinsk they were told: "If you don't want to be settled you can sit around hungry because we will take away all your animals and grain."[250]

The most radical—and for the Kazakhs most dramatic—form of sedentarization was raid. When the procurement officials confiscated all the animals of a whole aul, they sentenced the nomads to immediate immobility. Without sheep, goats, and cows it was senseless to migrate; without beasts of burden it was impossible. The nomads could no longer transport their yurts and belongings. It meant the end of the journey for the aul. The inhabitants often had no hope of getting the slightest support of the kind that was offered to Kazakhs who officially agreed to settle. They were on their own. And the consequences were disastrous. Sedentarization through expropriation turned nomads into refugees and beggars. Many Kazakhs understood what was happening. The inhabitants of Aul No. 11 in the district of Balkhash, for example, declared that the government was taking measures to settle them in order to control them and their property, and to tax them more heavily. And, they added, nomads could more easily conceal their livestock and property from the inquisitive eyes of tax collectors than settlers.[251]

The efforts at settlement exacerbated Kazakhstan's already precarious economic situation. Poorly planned and hastily executed settlings caused an immense loss of resources. And more resources were needlessly tied up in futile projects. Yet, as grave as the immediate losses were, another aspect proved even more consequential. Disregarding whether people actually settled permanently, as soon as an aul was officially involved in sedentarization, the statisticians counted its inhabitants as settled. This meant that officially they now (at least on paper) had arable land at their disposal, cultivated crops, and harvested yields, which, in turn, were taxable. Based on the aggregated data concerning all the allegedly successfully settled households, the planners in Moscow and Alma-Ata determined delivery quotas that had nothing to do with real conditions.[252] This fueled a fatal trend—the outcomes of plans that had been structurally impossible to implement in the first place were now exacerbated by imaginary numbers.

The sedentarization campaign was also exploited by clever officials and their networks seeking to protect their own interests, gain control over livestock, and simultaneously secure funds designated for the settlement of nomads. For example, in the district of Karkaralinsk about nine thousand people were to be settled in 1932. But due to migration and flight, the population had sunken by a third or more. District leaders did not deny the numbers. But when the plenipotentiary for sedentarization pointed them out, they told him to obey orders. The actual size of the population was irrelevant, they said, they had to garner as much budget for sedentarization as possible. The chairman of the executive committee was just as careless about real conditions in settlement locations. When it was brought to his attention that not one of the fifty proposed settlement sites had been examined for suitability and that the majority of them had no water, he replied: "The details don't interest us, just tell us the total number of settlements and make your budget suggestions."[253] And still more functionaries seem to have welcomed sedentarization as an opportunity to damage their competitors and opponents by assigning them unsuitable settlement spots.[254]

In some regions no suitable places existed for settling households permanently, at least not without first carefully exploring them geologically and digging new wells and irrigation canals. But it made practically no difference and settlement places were determined almost haphazardly on crude maps.

The disillusioning beginnings of the campaign were followed by ever more new decisions of an increasingly greater scope. Sedentarization, it was decided in 1931, should be completed within a short time, preferably before the close of the period covered by the first Five-Year Plan.[255] The goal was indeed unrealistic, due not least to the slow and sedate apparatus itself. Many officials did their best to ignore sedentarization, while others—generally Europeans—rejected it on the grounds of unprofitability: Why waste so much money on such incompetent people?[256]

They were not alone in finding sedentarization unreasonable.[257] By 1932 skepticism had grown at Kazakhstan's People's Commissariat for Agriculture and among members of the Committee for Sedentarization (Kraiosedkom). One member expressed the opinion of many, namely, that "the settling of the Kazakhs is exclusively a matter of the Kazakhs themselves and not an issue for oblast administration." Another added: "I have always said that we should not settle Adai on soil of Russian Cossacks, they are all bandits and loafers."[258]

By the end of 1932 leading comrades had had enough of the endless debates and idle discussion. They suspended the old structures and established a new Department for Agriculture in the people's commissariat. The work of the latter would be guided and controlled by Kazakhstan's party leaders.[259] This newly founded "sector" was given powers that the old Committee for Sedentarization had never had.

NATURALLY, YOU WILL BUILD EARTHEN HUTS, NOT PALACES

The greatest challenge for the settlement campaign was to immediately erect houses and facilities for hundreds of thousands of people. The construction program stumbled from the start: no one knew exactly where to build and there was a lack of building material and experts.[260] One official reported that construction had stalled in his region because the drawing showed mason foundations for residential buildings, but no one knew where the stones were to come from. No one dared to ignore the plan, so they simply quit building.[261]

Using local building materials like clay bricks appeared to be a solution. One calculation from November 1930, however, figured that the poor building material provided for Kazakhstan would allow the construction of only 15 percent of the 41,250 homes planned for construction in 1930 and 1931 (which incidentally would have provided for only a quarter of the households to be settled in the same period). And even that was purely theoretical because it was based on unrealistic completion targets.[262]

Meanwhile, the production of local building materials made no progress. Although Kazakhstan had plenty of clay in its soil, it was impossible to produce a sufficient quantity of bricks. The clay had to be dug out, molded, and dried: "One molder produces an average of 50 bricks a day. The work is done essentially by adolescents for whom not the least provisions have been made. They get no bread, tea, or sugar. They work without pay.... There is no technical supervision."[263] Goloshchekin was not interested in the practical side of sedentarization. Worried regional officials bored him with their endless complaints of a lack of stones, wood, and bricks. His priority was sedentarization for the purpose of changing the social structure of the aul in order to put an end to exploitation. It made no difference whether they lived in yurts or houses. And in any case, production facilities were more important than housing for the population, he said. Crucial for the success of settlement, claimed the party secretary, were stalls for the animals, sheds for equipment, and barns for the harvest. Incidentally, he preferred a focus on the sedentarization and concentration of large populations in sovkhozes and industry.[264]

In 1932, two years after the drive had begun, Iakov Belikov, the Kazakh people's commissar for light industry, robbed local comrades of their last illusions about building supplies.[265] Successful sedentarization, he said, would have to depend on local means and ways. The previous year, he reported, the republic had only received 9 percent of the actual quantity of round timber that it needed and even that was sent to the large construction sites in Karaganda and Kazmed on Lake Balkhash. Everyone understood that scarce resources went first to large industrial projects. Settling nomads was secondary.

In the same vein, Nikolai Zalogin, the former deputy people's commissar for agriculture, said there was no hope of getting experts. Successful settlement in areas that had ethnically mixed populations would have to rely on support from Europeans building earthen huts. His audience was speechless. Earthen huts? "Naturally," he replied to his stunned listeners, "do you think you're going to erect buildings of armored concrete? Naturally, you will build earthen huts, not palaces."[266]

Many of the irritated delegates seemed now, in January 1932, to finally grasp for the first time what sedentarization actually meant—the impoverished and homeless population of Kazakhstan would have to build up a new existence under inhospitable conditions and without outside help. It was no relief to be told they should use the remains of existing buildings and local construction material.[267]

A report of 1934 summarized the campaign's modest success. It was a story of decline: in 1931 the plan to build more than sixteen thousand houses had been surpassed. One year later, less than even half of the proposed eleven thousand buildings were completed. In 1933 construction had begun for two thousand homes and the same number of previously begun homes was completed. Without mentioning the substantially greater number of simple dwellings that people had set up for themselves,[268] these statistics reveal the chasm between intentions and reality. The data on completed production facilities of all kinds looked even worse. While the plans had been fulfilled to some degree, one glance at the absolute numbers revealed how little had actually been achieved in settlement places.[269]

And the statistics said nothing about the quality of the houses built without technical expertise. One typical example comes from the Akkul kolkhoz in the district of Novo-Talassk. After three years all homes completed in 1931 were in urgent need of repair. To have been built meant nothing other than that houses stood around half-finished in the steppe. They had neither windows nor doors, the walls were crooked. The roofs were not insulated, and water ran down walls that threatened to collapse. Most houses had no window openings on the sunny side. Inside it was dark and damp. No one had thought to arrange the houses in any manner and they stood disordered in the steppe.[270] The buildings themselves looked haphazard, without a touch of symmetry: "One window was directly below the roof, another down near the ground, and a third one someplace else, as if the builder were completely oblivious to the inner design of the edifice that they here call European-style homes."[271] Many Kazakhs preferred to continue living in their yurts, which were most suitable for the extreme climatic conditions of the steppe. They used the houses, at the most, as winter quarters.[272] Farsighted comrades wanted to change the course of the construction program and pushed for the erection of cattle sheds to enable the Kazakhs to live under a roof separate from their animals in the winter, and for the construction of homes that better met the needs of the people.[273]

But the "settled" Kazakhs had other reasons for not abandoning their yurts. In light of the fact that until 1932 it had been the practice in Kazakhstan to combine many small auls to become one very large unit (a practice later condemned as "gigantomania"), sedentarization often meant merely lining up the nomads' yurts in rows at the designated settlement locations. Sometimes hundreds of yurts were arranged in file along "village roads" named after revolutionaries and Soviet leaders.[274]

Concentrating the nomadic population artificially in such settlements in Central Kazakhstan's inhospitable regions was to have dire consequences. It was impossible to feed hundreds, even thousands of people using the meager soil of the steppe.[275] The "Gigantic Settlements" soon died out. Hundreds of abandoned yurts stood in the steppe in absurdly precise rows as haunting witnesses to Bolshevik hubris during the famine.[276]

THE TOP-DOWN PERSPECTIVE

The problems of sedentarization created a burning issue for officials at the periphery. But the mighty macro planners in Moscow governing the distribution of resources and scarce materials were more interested in grand industrial projects.[277] They cared little about the hardship of Kazakhstan's kolkhoz peasants trying to survive the winter in the steppe in roofless houses without doors. While in 1933 sedentarization was put on the agenda of the Sovnarkom several times, the topic was postponed repeatedly in favor of other, more important issues.[278]

TABLE 2: SEDENTARIZATION IN KAZAKHSTAN

SOURCE/CONFIRMATION	KAZAKH HOUSEHOLDS
1. For the year 1928	828,000
2. Number indicated by the Gosplan for the year 1931	706,000
3. Most recent figures (minus 5% bai households)	670,000
4. Of 3 above, the number of those already settled and living in villages	
4a. Figure resulting from measures taken in the past two years	50,000
4b. Settled by 1930	70,000
4c. Settled auls that coincide with village centers	30,000
Total for 4a to 4c	150,000
5. Number now working in industry or in sovkhozes, according to the census of 1931	20,000
6. Number that will enter in industry in 1932	30,000
7. Number to join sovkhozes in 1932	30,000
8. Number to work in fish processing	5,000
9. Number to work in the transportation sector	2,000
Total for 5 to 9	77,000 [*sic*]
Total subject to sedentarization	443,700
Rounded off	400,000

Source: GARF, 5446-13a-2451, 22.

The lack of attention given the campaign by Moscow's top leaders matched their disinterest in and disdain for the fate of the nomads. Almost no one focused on the precarious situation. When, in February 1932, the chairman of the Kazakh Council of the People's Commissars, Uraz Isaev, reported to Molotov on accomplishments and future projects, he added a little list to his letter (see table 2). It revealed how carelessly the Communists juggled the lives of several thousands of Kazakhs.

Without a trace of shame, Isaev let several thousand families simply vanish from the list and out of sight for the officials. His table shows that the bais apparently had as little right to be settled as the more than 40,000 families that were simply dropped at the end of the list. An attached comment mentions that another 191,000 households should be subtracted from the 400,000. By 1932, it says, 114,000 of them had been assigned land as planned and another 77,000 had been absorbed by other segments of the economy. One need only take measures, then, to settle 209,000 households.[279]

The document illustrates not only radical Bolshevist thought but also its grasp of reality. By early 1932 famine had already eliminated countless victims and tens of thousands of Kazakhs had fled from the republic. Officials like Isaev were not concerned that the rounded off numbers reflected people who might later return to Kazakhstan. Communists were not interested in individuals, they were interested in labor. They paid no heed to the needs of real people, they produced the groundwork for collectives. All of it necessitated control. The nomads had to be settled. The (human) cost was negligible. When it came to materializing the one gigantic project, the alleged "backwardness" of the nomads had, in terms of argumentation, disappeared into the footnotes.[280]

Much more important was the circumstance that sedentarization was an essential prerequisite for the large-scale relocation of special settlers, Gulag prisoners, and later also "enemy nations" in Kazakhstan's steppe.[281] Whenever the planners spoke of opening up gigantic areas of land for development following sedentarization, they thought of the development as a task for the people they would deport from elsewhere. Nomads were in the way and had to leave to make room for the victims of Stalin's repression; it was they who were to live and work in the steppe.[282] This was especially true of territories selected for Gulag camps. According to a resolution of May 1930 the OGPU wanted more than 110,000 hectares put at its disposal to accommodate "the enormous politico-economic and cultural significance of the camp to be erected" (that was later to become Karlag).[283]

Sedentarization often camouflaged interests that had nothing to do with the conditions of nomadic life. The drive was used to excuse the failure to meet delivery quotas or to undermine them; opportunities for corruption and nepotism emerged wherever scarce building materials and funding could be garnered; and settlements turned out to be fighting grounds for competing groups. Indeed, whenever entire communities were relocated, the point was to free up territory. While throughout all these events the people concerned were relevant only inasmuch as they presented a problem that called for a solution, they were also exploited as the solution to other problems.

The attempt to settle Kazakhstan's nomads failed miserably. Almost none of the ambitious goals were accomplished. Bookkeeping tricks could not make the targeted numbers look halfway achieved. And instead of the projected yield increases, the results were catastrophic losses in all sectors. What at first looked so promising turned out to be fatal in the long run. Settlement happened on paper or manifested itself as crumbling ruins in inhospitable places. Sooner or later the misplaced Kazakhs would return to the scene as beggars, refugees, and warriors.

4
CIVIL WAR AND FLIGHT

THE "ROAD TO socialism" led to mass flight, civil war, and famine. Millions fled from imposition and repression. Hundreds of thousands resisted. To evade the blessing of collectivization meant to disrupt the socialist project. Whether they fled or took up arms, nomads were sought out, attacked, and killed. Within a few months large parts of Kazakhstan were caught up in a long, smoldering civil war with the Red Army, OGPU troops, and militia.[1] Violence spread and soon one could no longer tell combatants from noncombatants. The Kazakhs as a whole were eyed with suspicion.

State aggression meant violence and terror. But it did not fall on a tranquil society. The steppe had never been a place of peace and harmony. When pastoralists and their flocks fled to other regions, they often began struggles with other nomads already living there. In 1929–30, the steppe was not a tinderbox ready to explode at the tiniest spark, but once aflame, it showed the Bolsheviks the limit to their power. In the end the regime won by the superior means of terror at its disposal and because it made no distinction between warriors and refugees. And finally, it profited from the famine that caused the nomads to fight primarily for survival.

FRAGMENTED CIVIL WAR

In April 1930 Kliment Voroshilov received a report on West Kazakhstan: "Soviet rule and party organizations have prevailed in larger towns only. For several hundreds of kilometers across large stretches of territory, for instance, from Turgai to Aral'sk, there exist no Soviet rule and no party organization."[2] A year later the situation had grown worse after individual Kazakh tribes allied with the Turkmen Iomud tribe, toward whom they had been hostile for years.[3] In Turkmenistan and Kazakhstan former enemies now closed ranks against the Bolsheviks.[4] These trends greatly alarmed the comrades: "The entire zone along the east shore of the Caspian Sea is marked by banditry, which reaches 350 to 500 kilometers into the heartland, including Turkmenistan."[5] An internal report by the OGPU in August 1931 said that conditions had "worsened incredibly."[6] The Bolsheviks had lost control over vast parts of the western Kazakh steppe and some functionaries were frightened. Aleksandr Popkov, the first secretary of the district of Gur'ev in the far west of Kazakhstan, wrote in August 1931 to his political mentor, Central Committee member Emel'ian Iaroslavskii: "This is how banditry looks now in the district of Mangistavsk . . . the so-called *adaevtsy* have united three clans. One clan, the fourth, remains neutral. The nomadic population of the district encompasses about fifty thousand people. Between seventeen and twenty thousand of them are hostile toward us. We used to search for the bandits and now they're after us."[7] Inspecting the region at about the same time, Kulumbetov, the deputy chairman of the Kazakh Council of People's Commissars, shared Popkov's judgment of the situation. Up to 60 percent of the population harbored anti-Soviet sentiments, he thought.[8] Rebels attacked and destroyed kolkhozes, factories, and cooperatives. They attacked Fort Shevchenko, the most important town on the Mangyshlak Peninsula, several times; Red Army and militia units narrowly managed to protect the fortification. The steppe had become a deathtrap for prominent Communists.

The events in the western region of Kazakhstan were part of the civil war that—triggered by forced collectivization—broke out between 1929 and 1931 in almost every rural area of the Soviet Union.[9] In most places it was peasant resistance to local developments and posed no serious threat to Soviet

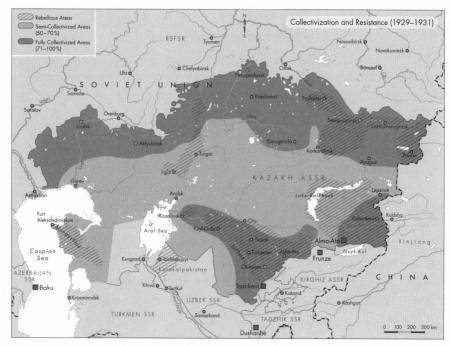

MAP 3. Collectivization and Resistance

dominance. But in other places, such as the Caucasus, Ukraine, and Central Asia, things were different. Struggles there became so fierce that in some places maintaining Soviet rule was at stake.[10]

Until recently these armed conflicts have been interpreted as struggles between the Soviet state and its own people, struggles that the Communists won, albeit barely and not without exhausting every possible means. The notion of the state versus the people has taken on various forms, but dominated research in general. Differences have been explained by the disparate roles played by insurgents: Were they "bandits" spurred on by "anti-Soviet elements," as Soviet authors say? Or were the eruptions of violence anticolonial uprisings or even "national liberation movements," as some Central Asian historians have argued since 1991? Or were peasant and nomadic communities battling the imposition of collectivization and fighting for the preservation of their tradition?[11]

The desire to reduce the reasons for violence to one single motive is more misleading than helpful. The same holds for the assumption that all forms of (rudimentarily) organized violence always targeted activities and representatives of the Soviet state, in other words, that they were occurrences of planned "resistance." Resistance alone can explain neither the motives of individual aggressors nor the dynamics of spiraling violence. The state, indeed, could only be the target of violence when its representatives were present and in a position to assert the state's claim to the exclusive use of force.[12] That was only partly true in nomad country. It is thus advisable to distinguish different levels of struggle and view them as a fragmented civil war, not as a dichotomous conflict where two indistinct groups fight one another. It was, rather, an ever-smoldering domestic war in which various groups and actors pursued certain aims with varying degrees of violence.[13]

Most of the so-called insurgents were not keen on ending Bolshevik rule; they had local interests in mind and thought little of abstract political concepts. Nomads and peasants alike had conservative goals: they fought mainly to save their immediate environment where they dealt with the real problems of land ownership, pastureland rights, herds of animals, how to minimize their tax load, and their refusal to join kolkhozes. The inhabitants of the steppe sought to retain the traditional social order that they saw threatened by incessant Communist attack.[14]

Indeed, not all Kazakhs pursued restorative ends. Many welcomed the expropriation of the bais, profiting as they did from the redistribution of confiscated livestock. Many understood how to use the Soviet system's thirst for new cadres for their own purposes. And now the profiteers suddenly found themselves closing ranks with those who are frequently the most important advocates of resistance: young men with thwarted opportunities for social ascent.[15] They stood at the forefront of a broad generation-straddling alliance within Kazakh society that overcame social differences and was held together by the external threats of collectivization and requisition.

When the people stood up to them, the Soviet state's rickety institutions collapsed. When the crucial moment came—that is, when the plan to enforce collectivization and organize the confiscation of livestock and grain came into effect—local soviets and party cells proved to be weak. The Kazakhs locked up, murdered, or drove off Communist officials and when they were gone, the traditional pattern of social order returned. Fear of Stalin's top-down revolution strengthened the standing and authority of local elites more than it undermined them. In times of crises people gathered round an elite that had resources, connections, and status, in the hope that these men might rescue them from the impending catastrophe.[16]

EXPECTATIONS

Bolsheviks saw the resolve with which peasants and nomads resisted their policy as the doings of diligent class enemies. Because similar forms of resistance cropped up in all regions of the Soviet Union at about the same time, they had no doubt that they were dealing with well-organized opponents. Their goal was to discover and destroy these enemies. Solomon Bak,[17] the OGPU's representative for the region of Orenburg, had written in May 1929 to his boss, OGPU deputy chairman Genrikh Iagoda: "To our disgrace, in many districts the authority of the popes and mullahs is now greater than the authority of the local party cell and the village soviet."[18] Observations such as these reinforced the comrades in the belief that they were surrounded by enemies that must be fought with any means necessary. The sense that the number of opponents grew, instead of shrinking, followed from the logic of a system based on the continued instigation and escalation of social crises.[19] Growing resistance in the villages and auls confirmed the theoretical premises and the experience of earlier crises.[20] When struggles began, resistance was just what the Communists wanted. It helped them to count, identify, isolate, and remove "anti-Soviet elements."[21]

Because the comrades clearly assumed that the socialist rebuilding of villages would lead to class struggle, they were initially not troubled by resistance from the rural population. In fact, they were irritated by any lack of it. In February 1930 some of the most important Central Asian party officials appeared before the Central Committee in Moscow in an attempt to justify their modest success in creating kolkhozes. When Zelenskii, the chairman of the Central Asian Bureau spoke on the situation in Uzbekistan, a conversation arose between him, Stalin, and Molotov that clarified the results Moscow's leaders expected from the campaign for collectivization:

STALIN: Was there no confrontation with peasants due to enforced collectivization?

ZELENSKII: No. What kind of confrontation? They occasionally fight with one another, that does happen, but there has been no confrontation of a political nature.

STALIN: Well, maybe something like this: They gather together and some say they won't [join the kolkhoz] and the others say they will, and then they have a little shooting. Anything like that?

MOLOTOV: You don't have a single gang because of collectivization and dekulakization?

ZELENSKII: Not yet.

MOLOTOV: Perhaps you don't have the most recent information?

ZELENSKII: Naturally, I don't have the latest information, but nevertheless, we don't have any gangs due to collectivization.

OTHER VOICE: Not yet, but it will happen.

ZELENSKII: Naturally, it will happen a bit.[22]

A short time later Molotov would no longer have had to ask. Central Asia was shaken by a wave of violence. Bitter peasants and nomads rose up in every region. Now it was the turn of officials seeking Stalin's continued favor to report on their success in battling the bandits. Some Communists reported that they had tens of thousands of opponents. They proved their vigilance and determination by destroying the so-called enemies. To a certain extent it was practice for the use of power that regional potentates would display during the years of mass repression in 1937 and 1938: the more enemies they could identify, the more they could demonstrate loyalty and devotion. Goloshchekin, too, knew what Moscow expected of him and never tired of reporting of the Kazakh OGPU's success in fighting the bandits.[23]

Most uprisings began when the people of an aul or district were confronted directly with representatives of the regime and realized what enacting the orders implied for them. Nomads and peasants felt immediately threatened. Single, situational acts of violence quickly developed into mass movements led by influential elders. When in early September 1930 the people of the district of Kazalinsk realized that they could not reach the grain procurement target for their district because it asked for ninety thousand poods more than their actual harvest, bai Kulembetov organized four hundred men to hunt down the Bolshevist officials in the auls. They had few weapons: about fifty hunting rifles and two revolvers. The rest of the men used makeshift cold weapons. Nonetheless, they soon numbered over one thousand men.

In Kazalinsk the alarmed Communists created a staff that began negotiating capitulation with the rebels in order to gain time. But the nomads refused as inacceptable the Bolshevik's demand that they turn in all weapons and hand over their leaders.[24] Within a few days the Red Army had defeated the revolt and reported the silenced uprising: "The dzhigits that . . . had flown returned to their auls. Life in this raion has returned to normal."[25] Among the rebels taken as prisoners was one Russian (apparently a peasant) who had participated in the Kazakh's revolt. He told interrogators that "it was not the people who started the tumult: it was begun by those enforcing grain procurement."[26]

Things were similar in the district of Akkul' where in April 1930 an uprising broke out just as the person in charge of grain procurement for that aul was beaten by an angry crowd. The news spread quickly and soon more than one thousand people (three hundred of whom were equipped with all kinds of primitive weapons) invaded Akkul' and destroyed the site completely. Local party leaders had already run off. No one stood up to the mob. The nomad leaders distributed the confiscated grain and declared the uprising over. To secure order they elected five members to a board. News of the victory quickly made the rounds in the auls. But it did not last. A report by the OGPU summarized the events: "The arrival of our unit restored our power."[27]

Apparently the nomads of Akkul' were content to destroy the district's main town in an act of wild violence, chase off the Communists, and regain possession of their property. Spontaneous eruptions of violence such as this, limited in scope and aim, constituted a large part of the resistance to collectivization measures taken in Kazakhstan. As soon as these "rebels" were confronted by superior forces overpowering commanders, they retreated to their auls. However—and this aspect was particularly threatening to the Bolsheviks—there was no guarantee that they would not take up arms again for similar reasons or cooperate with other insurgents. The members of the OGPU thus found themselves constantly searching for the minds and organizations behind the uprisings. And because they were always afraid of having overlooked someone, the Chekists struck hard more often than necessary.[28]

To a certain extent both nomads and Communists worried constantly about what the other side might do. Worry and fear can discourage patience and fuel violence. Uncertain of the other side's plans, some try to create certainty by taking things in their own hands. The ethnologist Jürg Helbling has shown that groups often embrace violence when the risk of waiting things out seems too great.[29] Peace, Peter Waldmann once said, "thrives on the conscious and intended consent of the parties involved," while violence often reproduces itself.[30] This may explain why the Kazakhs in Kazalinsk revolted. Faced with absurd demands for grain and ruthlessness they perhaps had nothing more to gain from patience and negotiation.

In rising up, the Kazakhs demonstrated that they were not mere passive objects of expropriation. Or, as the sociologist Dirk Baecker says, "Violence keeps people in the game and ensures that the next moves will have something to do with them."[31] Here the players also articulated rural morals that often break out in "dosed" quantities.[32] Such violence is not necessarily directed toward the state or other authorities. But in contrast to nineteenth-century Russian villages, for instance, where peasants and representatives of the state (normally) kept violence under control and knew how far they could go, the Bolsheviks reacted with great severity to the slightest sign of insubordination.

While the more or less spontaneous outbreaks of "the people's wrath" were annoying, albeit controllable events, several well-organized uprisings presented a greater challenge for the Chekists. Throughout Kazakhstan Muslim clerics, influential clan elders, and followers of emigrated veterans of the anti-Soviet resistance called for a "holy war" against the Bolsheviks. Their demands were similar: Drive the Communists off and erect khanates, accept Sharia law, disband the kolkhozes, and return confiscated property and animals to their rightful owners. Their promises were similar, too: support from abroad was on its way, Bolshevik power was coming to an end, and uprising had begun across the entire Soviet Union.

The standard repertoire of resistance agitators always included rallying cries that perhaps sounded credible to the downtrodden, but were otherwise unverifiable.[33] But the ringleaders of rebellion were not the only party speculating about the future: almost everyone joined in. A myriad of rumors and other news confirmed and contradicted one another, mirroring the people's insecurity throughout collectivization.[34] Rumors thrive in frightened societies where people are uncertain of their own situation and futures.[35] And in Kazakhstan unverified news was often the only information available for both the nomads and the Communists because during times of unrest the Soviet regime's already desolate communication systems broke down entirely.[36]

In the north of Karakalpakstan, organizers of resistance visited the auls in the late summer of 1929 and informed influential clan elders of their plans.[37] They claimed that they had sufficient weapons and that their group of followers was constantly growing in size. But most important, they explained, they were in contact with Dzhunaid-khan who was hiding in Afghanistan and had promised them his support.[38] Dzhunaid-khan was a prominent and influential opponent of the Bolsheviks who had made a name for himself as leader of the Basmachi in Central Asia.[39] The insurgents' alleged affiliation with him perhaps convinced the local elite in Karakalpakstan that their cause was not lost from the beginning and deserved their support.[40]

Once the initiators of the uprising had secured the advocacy of decision makers, they attacked. On September 27, 1929, a group of over thirty armed men rode to Takhtakupir, the administrative center of a district in the northwest of the autonomous region. At the bazaar they called the people to join them in destroying the city and annihilating the Russians. More than a hundred people took up rods and complied. They invaded the buildings of several Soviet organizations and laid them to waste, tearing leaders' portraits from the walls, shooting at them and mocking them, and threw pictures of Karl Marx and Lenin out onto the street to be trampled by horses.[41] The attack on objects and symbols was followed by attacks on Europeans and anyone else suspected of having cooperated with the Communists. They beat and killed several officials and employees of the local authorities, Russians and native Kazakhs alike.

The rebels had gotten their information from locals. They proceeded particularly brutally with an aul correspondent from the local newspaper, first chopping off his right hand, then tearing out his tongue, and finally executing him.[42] One Tatar named Lanshakov just barely escaped being murdered. Although he had shown an angry crowd that his penis was circumcised, in other words, that he was Muslim, he was chased and beaten until he lost consciousness because "somebody . . . yelled . . . 'that's a Russian!'" The rebels abused and raped Russian women and girls.[43]

The OGPU had discovered the insurgent plans ahead of time and brought squads to Takhtakupir. But these men had been lured out of the city, diverted by false information that the rebels had gathered outside of town.[44] Ninety minutes after violence broke out the squads arrived, struck down the insurgents, and arrested those responsible for it.[45]

The incident in Takhtakupir was investigated by both the Kazakh party office and the OGPU. Several officials lost their positions and were put on trial. Moscow's Central Committee sent an investigative committee, too, led by Aleksei Grichmanov.[46] At a meeting of the Kraikom Bureau in January 1930 Grichmanov divulged his findings, which were as scathing as they were predictable. The "enemy of the people" had taken advantage of the many excesses that had happened and the mistakes that had been made during requisition and dekulakization. The apparatus was "contaminated" and in urgent need of purging. The OGPU had taken inadequate measures to prevent the revolt, although information had suggested that it might occur. The Kraikom had issued instructions unsuitable for conditions in Karakalpakstan, and finally, the region's Communists had followed orders from the central organs merely "mechanically."[47]

Kazakhstan's party and OGPU leaders denied the accusations. Chekist Al'shanskii strongly objected to the accusation of being careless. Not only had his organization had early knowledge of insurgent plans, it had also arrested several agitators. The incident on September 27 had been "an attempt of the remainder of the counterrevolutionary group to go through with the plan that the ringleaders had devised before we arrested them."[48] Takhtakupir, he argued, had not seen a revolt, but only a slight uprising. The rebels there were part of anti-Soviet networks spread throughout Central Asia and commanded from abroad, especially from Afghanistan.

In reply to the claim that Kazakh leaders had ignored problems in Karakalpakstan, Goloshchekin pointed out that the region had been getting increasing attention. He admitted having made mistakes but he did not surrender. There was no truth to the complaint of excesses happening during grain procurement: "On the contrary, when it came to grain procurement, [the Communists in Karakalpakstan] understated it. . . . They should have given the wealthy bais the toughest, intensified grain procuring treatment. . . . But they did not. . . . They should have, and now they must defeat the semi-feudal bais in the severest way possible."[49] It would be ridiculous, he said, to curb repression now.

Goloshchekin's relentlessness told the comrades in both Kazakhstan and Moscow that he would not deviate from the course of massive repression. In January 1930 he thought that unyielding severity solved all problems.[50] He also believed that he had the staff and material resources necessary for it. At this meeting Al'shanskii and Goloshchekin made it clear once more how they would handle resistance. They would eliminate not the cause of opposition, but its initiators.

WAGING WAR

Uprisings continued. In early 1930 a man named Asadulla Ibrahim declared the outbreak of "holy war" and called people from everywhere to rise up against the Bolsheviks.[51] They were not alone in their fight, he told his audiences: they were part of a larger movement. "Soviet rule is finished everywhere. Uprisings are happening across the land. Units from Afghanistan will come to our aid. The Soviet regime has not only toppled in Central Asia, it has also collapsed very close to us, in [the cities of] Turkestan and Chimkent."[52] Words like his were welcomed in the auls surrounding Suzak.[53] The region's insurgents came together under the leadership of Sultanbek Sholakov.[54] As the OGPU later discovered, Sholakov and his men had planned the action meticulously. They exploited the fact that in that district Soviet institutions existed on paper only and that most of the few Communists around were sympathetic to the preparations for revolt. All the militia in the region were among the coconspirators.[55] For that reason, the Chekists had to admit, there was no one left among local comrades to actively counter the uprising or at least even inform the officials of the imminent threat. And what was worse, when the insurgency broke out, the party organization was "fully demoralized." Kazakh Communists who until then had stood on the sidelines now chose to join the rebels who guaranteed them exemption from punishment.[56]

Early in the morning on February 7, 1930, more than four hundred insurgents rode into Suzak where they joined the members of their group who had infiltrated the city for days and recruited allies there. "The entire male population," it was later said, armed themselves with "primitive weapons" and joined the gang.[57] First the mob freed prisoners, then gang leaders invaded and ravaged state and party buildings and burned files and documents. At least twenty-four people—mostly Communists—were "brutally tortured to death."[58]

In contrast to other places, where the fighters sought to leave the conquered town quickly, insurgents in Suzak tried to establish themselves there. Sholakov was declared "khan" and gathered a council of twenty to manage the affairs of the community. The most important task was to recruit new troops and produce weapons and ammunition in order to be prepared for an expected attack by Red units. Not only did the insurgents already have detailed mobilization plans, they also set up a factory for manufacturing rifles and bullets. They sent envoys to nearby auls to organize weapons and appeal to the people for assistance.

Sultanbek Sholakov began his short-lived rule by staging a number of public events designed to demonstrate that Communist and European rule were over. Fifteen comrades and employees of Soviet institutions were condemned at a propaganda trial. People were publicly whipped for not conforming to Sharia precepts or for dressing in "European style."[59] Well-known Communists were forced to carry white flags through the town and repeat prayers publicly. Similar scenes played out in several auls surrounding Suzak.[60]

The color white was particularly significant because it distinguished the insurgents from the "Reds." In addition, for Central Asian cultures, especially for the nomads, white represented authorities and elites.[61] Thus, forcing Communists to bear white flags in front of the locals not only visualized their defeat but also demonstrated symbolic capitulation to the power of the khan.

The new leader of Suzak was a devout Muslim who took the Sharia as the guideline for his deeds and dressed his appeals to the people in religious phrases. "The time has come to defend religion," he said in one appeal that has survived. "Each of you must engage in the works of destruction, be it through agitation, or by using your own animals, or your own strength . . . this is the guarantee for our well-being in this and the other world, and God will help us."[62] The Chekists noted that obviously the people of Suzak objected little to Sholakov and his group. On the contrary, the fighters had been welcomed and cared for. Apparently (at least that is how the Communists later explained things), nationalistic and religious slogans and "provocative rumors" of the alleged establishment of khanates in other regions had a part in it.[63] In the surrounding auls that were also controlled by insurgents, the distribution of confiscated animals and grain among the population may have increased the rebels' popularity.

After nine days, on February 14, 1930, Sholakov's rule ended in a bloodbath. Cadets had arrived from Tashkent and conquered the city in just hours. More than three hundred insurgents lost their lives, including the "Khan" and his closest advisers. Another three hundred were taken as prisoners.[64] The attackers recorded only three injured. The Political Department of the Central Asian Military Commando (SAVO) concluded in its final report that the "speed and resolve with which the unit proceeded made a great impression on the people. . . . They hid in their tents and did not come out. Every tent was decorated with red flags. After things had calmed down a little the entire population, even the oldest of them, walked around wearing red armbands and shouting, "There is no God, I belong to the Komsomol'. . . . It is typical that one group of bandits that could not hold out against the officer cadets shouted the same things."[65]

To regain control of the situation, a Revolutionary Committee was set up immediately after Sholakov's defeat, consisting of what was left of the party cell, a few combatants from the voluntary militia, and comrades from the district executive committee for the purpose of temporarily managing the district's affairs. The uprisings in Suzak and elsewhere, especially in West Kazakhstan, troubled the comrades. The Sovietization of the aul seemed to have failed completely. But other than appealing to the vigilance of local activists, the Bolsheviks had little to offer, especially nothing that might persuade the people in nomadic regions to switch sides.[66]

Insurgents who had occupied larger towns and cities posed no great threat to the better-equipped units of the Red Army. But the steppe was a different matter, where very mobile nomads with thorough knowledge of the terrain were extremely dangerous opponents. They could always split up into small and even tiny groups that were difficult to find. The more Kazakhs joined such loose gangs, the more nervous it made the Communists. In the spring of 1930 the extent of uprisings was troubling. Faced with endless attacks by armed "bandits" and ever new blazing conflicts, leading Communists in Alma-Ata began to seek help. They appealed repeatedly to the SAVO, and even to Stalin personally, to put larger contingents of soldiers, automatic weapons, and especially airplanes at their disposal to fight the nomads.[67] If they were to gain control over the rising number of uprisings, they needed well-trained troops and superior weaponry.[68]

Goloshchekin thought it necessary to appear personally in Moscow in order to mobilize additional units.[69] The practice of deploying militia against insurgents had failed because they were insufficiently trained in battle and often defeated by the enemy. In addition, the voluntary units consisting of Communists (komotriady) often capitulated to the "bandits" at the first opportunity, taking their weapons with them when they changed sides. That was how the rebels in the region of Kzyl-Orda had come to possess machine guns. In connection with this, the Kazakh party leader told Stalin that these circumstances were unlikely to change in the future because "the battle against banditry is hampered by the fact that . . . no regular units of the Red Army are stationed in Kazakhstan. OGPU divisions promised to the regions of Syr'-Darinsk, Aktyubinsk, and Kustanai have not come. We request the acceleration of organizing units on Kazakhstan's territory."[70] The requests were reasonable. The above-mentioned Popkov said clearly that in the summer of 1931 the situation was dramatic: "There have been cases of individual departments being entirely destroyed (Turkmenistan, Zhilaia Kosa). . . . The solution is to get more units to strengthen our impact, including units of the Red Army and Party forces, and it must happen as fast as possible, or it will be too late."[71]

Supplying weapons and lining up units, however, was heavily impeded by competence struggles and a lack of infrastructure.[72] And the Red units were often poorly equipped. Soldiers often took mounts and food from the local population, leaving the locals "unhappy," as one party secretary from the district of Karmkchi euphemistically wrote to Goloshchekin. The correspondent did not fail to mention that the battle against the "bandits" would be complicated if they did not get more financial and material support.[73]

The lack of reliable communication paths also hindered an effective war. Battles often spanned a territory "the size of any medium-size European country," making it absolutely necessary that units stay in contact with one another and exchange information regarding their own and the opponent's positions.[74]

Relatively small contingents of troops were sent into the field to fight insurgents. For instance, in the summer of 1931 Belonogov, an OGPU-official, commanded barely four hundred men (members of the OGPU and voluntaries) for the purpose of defeating resistance in West Kazakhstan.[75] Confronted with thousands of Kazakhs, Belonogov requested support from the Kazakh National Cavalry Division. Besides the fact that the cavalry unit was one of the few Red Army formations stationed in Kazakhstan at all, Belonogov had another reason for wanting their deployment: most of its members were Kazakhs. He feared that an overly large presence of "Slavs" in the battle against insurgents would evoke a negative reaction among native Kazakhs and provoke greater willingness to join the resistance.[76] Nonetheless, from time to time, units from other Soviet republics were sent to Kazakhstan. Among others, the OGPU dispatched troops to Kazakhstan from Azerbaidzhan and the Middle Volga region that attacked the Kazakhs with shifting success.[77] The officer cadets from Tashkent were deployed all over Central Asia, for example, in Suzak.[78]

The only groups that could survive conflicts under the conditions of the steppe were those that had uninterrupted access to water. Water was essential for the insurgents because as large groups of nomads, they often fled with their entire families and herds. Without water, these slow-moving groups were doomed to perish. Wells and other water sources were thus often the sites of the worst struggles. Insurgents barricaded themselves there and tried to defend the vital resource.[79] Red Army units and the OGPU exploited that circumstance and operated systematically near wells and oases in order to ensnarl the insurgents in encounters and force them to capitulate.[80]

The nomads had few firearms. They had taken most of the three-barrel rifles and revolvers in their possession from militiamen or captured them during the course of smaller skirmishes. They also used a number of different hunting guns and old models from the First World War and the Russian Civil War.[81] To use valuable rifles the most effectively, the best weapons were assigned to the best marksmen. Most combatants had to make do with pikes, spears, axes, and swords.[82] Before a campaign the men organized themselves in groups of a hundred, and then split into smaller groups led by experienced combatants. When one was injured, even slightly, the others relieved him of his weapons and ammunition to prevent their falling into the hands of the opponent.

The nomads tried to avoid direct encounters and restricted themselves to assaults and ambushing. If they could not avoid confrontation they relied on numbers and encircled the opponent: "The gangs began forming huge masses, knowing of the psychological affect that a large group would have on small units of the Red Army; they also used the crowd's herd instinct to follow one leader and be inspired by one personal example."[83] The Communists were not only intimidated by the sheer size of the nomad groups, they were also at a disadvantage because of the opponents' better horses and their precise knowledge of local conditions that enabled them to perform even complex military maneuvers. "These groups of bandits call themselves the White Army. They are well-armed, have commanders, and know the art of warfare. They dig trenches and lie in ambush in the mountains. In comparison, our units are smaller in number and not familiar with local conditions."[84] Caught up in dynamics that they had once sparked off themselves, the Communists overlooked the fact that they were pushing the spiral of escalation too far. The violence became so extreme that in some places Bolshevik rule began to falter. Years of continued tension, actively involving tens of thousands, if not hundreds of thousands of people, and violent conflicts that turned entire regions into war zones forced the Communists at least temporarily onto the defensive.[85]

LOSS OF RESTRAINT

"On both sides, bitterness has reached its limit" reads a report on the steppe from spring 1930. Insurgents fought with the courage of the desperate and rumors spread of Kazakh cruelty: "They take no injured men as prisoners. They kill every prisoner of war, especially the natives, the Kazakhs. They disfigure the corpses of their countrymen, cutting off their noses and sexual organs and slitting their bellies. After recent struggles they left the dead naked. Two heavily injured people were burned in a fire."[86] The insurgents fought with determination, often continuing to fight even after defeat. Next to having inferior weapons, their doggedness was another reason for disproportionately high numbers of casualties. On June 24, 1931, near the town of Ust'-Urt, the Red Army came upon five hundred people, killed seventy-five of them, and took another thirty people as prisoners. The Red Army itself lost only two soldiers along with Fetisov, the chairman of the OGPU in Gur'ev.[87]

The loss of restraint on all sides was fed by events such as those that occurred in Shetsk. Chekists there publicly executed insurgents in a brutal demonstration meant to discourage revolts. In April 1931 some members of the OGPU went to various auls and executed prisoners who had fled from the Karlag as well as leading figures of the revolt who had shaken the district in March.[88] The brutality of these men exceeded even the generous standards of the OGPU. The men responsible were arrested and punished in the presence of their colleagues.[89]

In other places secret service agents tried to kill prominent insurgents. One such undertaking succeeded for the OGPU in Karakalpakstan where they were able to smuggle two agents into a group surrounding a man named Klichbai. In November 1929 two Chekists received orders to gain Klichbai's trust, join his group, and eventually kill him. The plan seemed doomed from the start. When the agents tried to join the group, Klichbai grew suspicious and decided to hand them over to two rebels of influence in the region.[90] In an effort to make the agents' camouflage seem credible, the OGPU arrested some of their relatives, called for a boycott of their families, and confiscated some of their property. That convinced Klichbai that he was dealing with like minds and he let the men join the group. It was months before a favorable moment came to carry out their plan. One night in early March 1930, the agents killed six of the leading "bandits," including Klichbai. As proof of their successful mission they presented the severed heads of their victims to their superiors.[91]

Considering conditions in the steppe, it made sense for the OGPU agents to present their commanders with the heads of the men he had been after. Most of the enemies that the Bolsheviks thought surrounded them seemed invisible, showing themselves only—if at all—through their deeds. They were livestock drovers, peasants, or even party members that had first become "enemies," in the Bolshevik interpretation of the word, through the act of collectivization. The Bolsheviks only had clear ideas of the men behind the insurgents such as legendary Ibrahim Bek, the influential Dzhunaid-khan, or Klichbai.[92] It was important to them to see and present the heads of those leaders. Displaying the enemy's corpse satisfies a need to confirm one's power, and in this case, perhaps also to reassure oneself of the ability to keep up with an unseen opponent.[93] The historian Michael Riekenberg has pointed out that opponents often use the same forms of violence, such as mutilating the dead, to demonstrate their equality—not in goal or position, but in the capacity to use force.[94]

As unrest and conflict dragged on, the distinction between insurgents and peaceful nomads became blurred. Resistance and flight often went hand in hand. A report on the exodus of the nomad population written by Sergei Mironov, an authorized representative of the OGPU in Kazakhstan, says: "In a number of districts in this region resistance turned into armed struggles, the development of gangs, and acts of terror . . . but it especially meant exodus for the nomadic and settled Kazakh population."[95] An unknown author of a resolution presented to the Kraikom came to a similar conclusion: "Exodus is the enemy of the people's form of resistance to the socialist offensive that is unfolding."[96] Thousands of Kazakhs tried to flee from collectivization and sedentarization to presumably safer regions while insurgents simultaneously trekked through the step with their entire families, herds, and all their belongings. Normally they only left their families unprotected behind when they were off somewhere on a military mission. From a distance it was difficult to tell who was traversing the steppe for what purpose.

The Bolsheviks decided how to handle the confusing situation—if it were impossible to distinguish combatants from the peaceful population then all nomads migrating to regions "contaminated by bandits" were suspected of resisting Soviet power. In case of doubt the commanders were therefore more likely to order an attack than to try to find out with whom they were dealing—especially because many of the Red units were from European areas of the Soviet Union and not familiar with the steppe and its inhabitants. They reacted with violence to every group they encountered.[97] Confrontation with representatives of the Soviet state did not automatically end in combat. But such encounters did mark the end of flight because livestock and other possessions were confiscated, group leaders were interrogated, arrested, and sometimes killed.[98] It meant acute hardship for the nomads who could not move without their animals. Any new trek through the steppe meant a perilous venture. The situation revealed the Soviet state's attitude toward fleeing nomads: They were enemies for refusing to submit themselves to the Bolsheviks unconditionally.

This loss of restraint toward violence is typical of civil wars where permanent pressure and constant instability radically cut short planning horizons and time frames: "People are willing to do things that they might not do if they were under less pressure."[99] Sönke Neitzel and Harald Welzer have pointed out that soldiers combating irregulars or partisans often tend to see a potential opponent in everyone. They attack and kill anyone whose suspicious behavior *could* be interpreted as a hostile act.[100]

The Chekists in charge encouraged their troops with orders and instructions that left little to be desired by way of clarity. Solomon Bak, leader of the Semipalatinsk OGPU, explained to the Chekists entrusted with fighting the gangs: "The liquidation of these groups must occur exclusively with arms. Anyone negotiating capitulation will be held accountable. Notify everyone."[101]

Yet without negotiations the Red Army did not know with whom they were dealing. Bak's orders sanctioned massacres on nomads. Once regular combat operations were completed, the attacks on nomads were simply declared the "war on gangs." In addition, in one of his numerous commands to the district leaders of the OGPU, Bak ordered that repressive measures target not only active gang members, but also bais "who were not immediately involved in uprisings, but did spread provocative rumors."[102] "The affair with the gang movement," we read in another order by his pen, must be completed "within a week." And anyone choosing not to follow this order will personally be held accountable.[103]

Increasing pressure from Soviet troops began to erode the cohesion of nomadic alliances. By interrogating Kazakh prisoners the Chekists learned of internal tension and conflicts. Allied by necessity, disputes within nomadic communities were eventually inevitable. One Kazakh man named Mukan Kevilev, for example, who had been taken prisoner in June 1931, reported that his group was about to break up: more than fifty men wanted to surrender to the Soviet troops, while the remainder were willing to fight "to the death."[104] The Chekists must have found such statements encouraging, especially because their own agents reported growing discord between Kazakhs and Iomuds in the Turkmenian Karakum Desert. When water became scarce the differences between members of various clans came to the fore.[105] Some Kazakhs even asked Soviet commanders for free passage in order to bypass Iomud influence.[106]

Not all uprisings ended in devastating military defeat and not in every case did the majority of the Kazakhs involved lose their lives. Some uprisings led to negotiations. Prominent Kazakh Communists sometimes went to the insurgents to convince them that their efforts were futile.[107] But most promises were empty. Not only were leaders arrested, the repressions affected simple followers as well. It was not without reason that the Kazakhs who had been found guilty of resisting Soviet power were among the first prisoners to fill the newly established Karlag.[108]

Armed disputes ended when the nomads' capacity for resistance waned. Widespread famine, a serious loss of livestock, and the superior military capacity of Red Army units that fired even at refugees gradually led to resignation among the Kazakhs. When they tried to flee by emigrating, they ended up as beggars. In the long run, they could not compete with the OGPU, voluntary militias, and the Red Army. They never had a real chance. No additional significant armed uprisings were recorded following the last and largest uprising in West Kazakhstan, the uprising that had caused Comrade Popkov such concern and was crushed in September 1931.[109] Nonetheless, years later some smaller groups were still operating in a few regions, supporting themselves with robbery and theft.

WIDENING THE WAR ZONE—WAR IN THE SINO-SOVIET BORDERLAND

The fragmented civil war was fought particularly bitterly in the Sino-Soviet borderland.[110] From early 1930 until mid-1932 permanent combat took place on both sides of the demarcation line: between Soviet and Chinese border troops, Kazakh refugees, small groups of professional border crossers, and resolute opponents of the Bolsheviks. The confusing situation was complicated even further by the fact that within Xinjiang armed struggles over power in the province were also going on.[111] Hundreds of thousands of Kazakhs tried to reach safety on Chinese territory. The Red border troops took every instance of migration as an act of resistance, which they tried to stop with increasing brutality.[112] Groups of Kazakh refugees were more and more willing to fight their way to freedom. Both factors contributed to the escalation of violence.

DEMARCATIONS

The American sinologist Owen Lattimore once remarked that national borders meant nothing to the Kazakhs who had always moved back and forth from Russia to China as political circumstances dictated.[113] But nomads were, indeed, aware of borders and their implications. As wanderers between worlds, pastoralists were accustomed to overcoming demarcation lines.[114] Members of Kazakh and Kirghiz tribes lived and used pasturelands on both sides of the border. The nomads' excellent knowledge of the routes through the impassable mountain areas of Tian Shan also predestined them for the smuggling that flourished in the borderland.[115] Illegal transfers of goods and people were unthinkable without the well-networked Kazakhs who profited from far apart checkpoints. The Bolsheviks found that the tradition of smuggling "and the historical ties between a certain part of the population and those who live in China no doubt influence the uncritical, irresponsible stance that the population has toward violating borders."[116] The Communists found it highly problematic and dangerous that besides smugglers there were also bandits and others whom they saw as political opponents, operating from Chinese national territory. It meant not only that the nomads avoided the Bolshevik right to control them, but that they had established a stronger system in the borderland than that of the Soviets.[117]

The refugee march to Xinjiang followed the traditional pattern of Kazakhstan's nomadic communities—strategic escape to presumably safer regions in times of danger. Following the nomad uprising in 1916 hundreds of thousands had fled to the Chinese province for fear of revenge by Russian peasants and the czar's army.[118] When in 1928 the Communists unleashed the campaign to expropriate wealthy bais, part of the population from the east regions of Kazakhstan also sought protection beyond the border. The more radically the Bolsheviks attacked the pastoralists' social order, the greater the stream of refugees grew. It peaked in the early 1930s.[119]

The Bolsheviks were obsessed with national boundaries and border regions.[120] To have more control over these sensitive regions, along the demarcation lines they defined border zones extending twenty-two kilometers into Soviet territory where the OGPU's border troops had almost complete authority.[121] In the 1920s the plan had been to convert these regions with their trans-frontier settlements and numerous ethnicities and nationalities into models that would promote the Soviet idea abroad. They were therefore equipped with many privileges.[122] But propaganda was only effective where foreigners had access to the country and its residents. And those foreigners threatened to introduce anti-Soviet attitudes and spies. Thus control was continually tightened until the border regions became "institutions of isolation."[123]

In the early 1930s the Bolsheviks were highly alarmed by the muddled situation in Xinjiang. Tension in the region, its confusing power relations, and porous borders all created ideal conditions for spies and other foes. The comrades were convinced that English and Japanese agents were active just behind the border, waiting for an opportunity to infiltrate Soviet zones and perform acts of sabotage. Remainders of the White Army from the days of the Russian Civil War were also still in the region. And then there were reports of a "Great-Kazakh Khanate" to be founded with the support of the English. One letter to Zelenskii, the chairman of the Central Asian Bureau, says: "West China is the showplace of the Kazakh counterrevolution. Within West Chinese territory, and heavily influenced and aided by the English, diversion gangs have been organized that at the moment of intervention will come in large groups into the regions of Semirech'e and Ferghana for the purpose of severing these economically important regions from the USSR in a war between partisans and the Soviet power."[124] Individual conflicting parties, on the other hand, tried to gain the Soviets' favor. Ma Shaowu, who had acted as a warlord on his own since the end of the 1920s, tried to convince the Bolsheviks to support him with automatic weapons and soldiers so that he could gain power in the province. He offered them considerable influence in return, saying straightforwardly: "You shall get what the Japanese have in Manchuria."[125] That was sufficient legitimacy for engaging in his conflicts.

BORDER CROSSERS

Crossing the border to Xinjiang was a dangerous affair. Off the beaten track of official and severely controlled crossing points on mountain pass roads, the demarcation line ran through impassable mountain country that could not be traversed without a guide familiar with the area. When debaiization began in 1928 and increasing numbers of people decided to leave the "paradise of workers and peasants,"[126] the connections and systems of smugglers and border crossers became more important than ever. They brought refugees across the mountains and protected them from Soviet border patrols. The Chekists knew it: "The absolute majority of Kazakhs migrating to China are accompanied by armed gangs."[127] These men rarely acted for altruistic reasons. They either let the nomads pay them for their services or they used the opportunity to invade kolkhozes and villages on Soviet territory and steal livestock.[128]

By the spring of 1930, at the latest, the border troops considered the "internationally active" gangs a grave problem. Not only did they attack kolkhozes and snatch the fruits of their labor from the "peaceful population of the border region," they also enticed the residents to go abroad.[129] The commander of a border troop department stationed in the town of Zaisan explained in April of that year: "Recent months . . . have been marked by border violations and bandit attacks from the Chinese border regions that are unparalleled in illegality and arbitrariness. The criminal element from our regions near the border . . . finds like minds among the Kazakh population of the Chinese border region . . . and rages against our population in the border region."[130] Kolosov, the Soviet consul in Ghulja (Yining) on the Chinese side of the border, saw things similarly. The gangs had knowledge of the area and were very well-organized and networked with contacts reaching from bandits on Soviet territory to Chinese administrators. The refugees turned to these people because they were frightened by the Soviet border troops. Some bandits were "commissioned" to smuggle relatives, livestock, and other possessions into China. The leaders of these groups could easily recruit followers from among the impoverished refugees. What Kolosov found particularly threatening was the fact that besides smuggling people and stealing from the "peaceful population" the bandits also worked as spies collecting information on the stations and number of Soviet units.[131]

One group, for example, was led by Alimdzhanan Kutanov and Bazarbek Nurtazynov. Both men originated in the district of Malai-Sariisk and had long been professional border crossers. In 1927 Kutanov was sentenced to ten years in prison, apparently for criminal business transactions, but he had been able to escape to China first. In the years to come he would be seen many times on Soviet territory.

Nurtazynov had been a smuggler in the past and was known to Soviet authorities. In 1930 the two men organized an armed group in Xinjiang consisting mainly of refugees from their region of origin.[132] They wanted to help relatives and members of their clan flee to China. In mid-November 1930 they crossed the border with more than sixty people on horseback and went in small groups to auls in the district. The Chekists attributed several attacks on kolkhozes and sovkhozes near the border to Nurtazynov and Kutanov's followers. Some local functionaries were kidnapped and their fate remained unclear. Hundreds of Kazakh households moved toward the border and were not deterred by clashes with Communist voluntary units.[133]

The border troops mobilized a heavily armed department that found the nomads after a few days. The Kazakhs could not defend themselves against machine guns and grenades. The fall of darkness alone spared them from total annihilation. The assault continued the next day. But then violence escalated, as one soldier described it, because some Kazakhs threw themselves at the border soldiers in desperation. One of them, armed only with a knife, attacked a soldier. In a close fight he was injured by another soldier, but held on to his victim and bit off one of his fingers. Another Kazakh attacked a soldier and tried to pull him off his horse just when the soldier was reloading his rifle. The two fought until the soldier hit the Kazakh fatally with his gun barrel.[134] Later the Chekists were keen on calling these episodes characteristic of the entire operation. But their stories speak more of a massacre of the Kazakhs than of bitter war struggles. The soldiers appear to have killed every man they met. Only one soldier of the Red Army was wounded, two horses were either injured or killed. The opponents suffered 243 casualties; 50 women and 30 children were taken as prisoners. There is no mention of wounded or arrested men. The troops also rounded up 600 horses, 100 camels, and 200 loads.[135] To conceal the obvious massacre, the final report on "the liquidation of Kutanov and Nurtazynov's gangs" stated that the "bandits" had suffered such large losses because after smaller clashes with poorly trained voluntary units they had been "surprised" by the fighting capacity of regular army units.[136]

The radical brutality with which both the OGPU's border troops treated refugees had several sources. For one, the men's profession was to protect the border and pursue defectors. Many of them may have thought it a question of honor to achieve the best possible "results" and prove their expertise. Good soldiers were rewarded and lauded.[137] But most important, the men could expect serious consequences if they did not capture refugees.

Another source of this brutality was that leading comrades in Moscow and Alma-Ata put full power into the hands of the executors of Soviet policy at the borders. In February 1930 the politburo passed a resolution allowing the confiscation of all the belongings of families trying to cross borders with their animals and the taking of "especially harsh measures" against anyone driving livestock across the border. They also resolved to send "qualified" comrades to the border regions of Kazakhstan and other Central Asian republics with orders to stifle emigration at the first signs of it.[138] In April 1930 the Kazakh Council of the People's Commissars resolved to relocate all bais and kulaks at least one hundred kilometers deep into the country's interior if they had been caught organizing emigration. The same held for everyone who had already brought their families or their possessions across the border and for family members who had been left behind.[139]

The number of troops at the border in the region was hiked considerably.[140] They gave harsh treatment to every Kazakh they found near the border. The luckier Kazakhs were merely arrested, sometimes beaten, and had their possessions confiscated. The rest were shot. Women and children were not spared. In a perhaps incomplete list of illegal border crossings for the year 1930, the OGPU reported "enemy losses" of 734 dead and 38 injured. More than 3,600 people had been arrested during the period covered by the list. The border patrol itself suffered 24 casualties and 15 injured.[141] That was a much greater number than a year before, when only 250 households (about 1,000 people) had been prevented from crossing the border.[142] According to other sources, however, more than 1,000 people were killed in 1930 in the Ili Valley where a large part of the refugees tried to pass the border.[143] One report simply states: "Our border patrol has received instructions to halt emigration to China by any means possible; they made the greatest effort in this respect and in doing so it often came to serious excesses."[144]

Emigrants kept moving, despite the massacres. But they changed their strategy, as one report to Goloshchekin says: "They used to move in masses, but now that they have suffered heavy losses, they emigrate in small groups."[145] These groups had no similarity to the well-prepared and armed fleeing masses that the border troops had dealt with before. Their flights were the desperate acts of impoverished Kazakhs trying to escape starvation. As an old woman, Nazira Nurtazina remembers how in 1933 at the age of six she made it over the mountains to Xinjiang with her family. They started off together with two other families. The men "decided to cross the border by a roundabout route . . . because the direct road was too dangerous: the Soviet border patrol forced people to return or shot them." The trek across the icy mountains took more than fifteen days; they could only make progress at night. Although she was just a little girl, she traveled the entire way by foot. Just when their supplies were dwindling, they reached Chinese territory. Many others died trying to cross the border.[146]

Despite the dangers, most of the Kazakh flights across borders were successful. But many people found themselves worse off afterward: civil war had broken out in Xinjiang and supplies were scarce. Uprisings and political assassinations plagued the region for years. Warlords struggled for political influence.[147] Conditions were becoming increasingly precarious. Bandits marauded and famine gripped parts of the province. In 1932 and 1933 many Kazakhs died of starvation on Chinese ground, still holding Soviet currency in their hands. Food was so scarce in Xinjiang that their money was worthless. Kazakh refugees were a burden for an already struggling area.[148]

Nonetheless, few Kazakhs dared return to the Soviet Union. The majority, said one who did go back, feared revenge by the Soviet state. And indeed, in one report we read that such anxiety was not without reason: in some cases poor peasants returning from China were arrested. And local authorities refused to give any kind of assistance to completely impoverished repatriates.[149] When civil war broke out in Xinjiang in 1933, the Soviet Union intervened with massive military means. For some years the province was a puppet state dependent on Soviet influence. That left the nomads with no way to escape.[150]

The fate of Kabimolda Zheksembaev shows how difficult conditions were for Kazakh refugees in China. After fleeing, he had trouble gaining a foothold in his new surroundings. After a while he found employment in a small factory. In the spring of 1934 the factory owner was arrested and disappeared without a trace. Meanwhile Zheksembaev's parents and other relatives who had left the Soviet Union with him had all died of one or another illness. On his return to Kazakhstan he told border guards: "The faltering economy and famine in the region make life almost impossible for immigrants and because I do not feel particularly guilty toward the Soviet Union, I decided to come back."[151] But his return and the return of those with him became torturous. Due to famine they could survive only through thievery. They stole horses and other livestock, and they were themselves robbed. By the time they finally reached Soviet territory, they owned nothing.

ON BOTH SIDES OF THE BORDER

The OGPU border patrol was not satisfied with preventing "bandits" and refugees from crossing the border. In several cases Red units followed Kazakhs into Chinese territory and attacked them there. Consul Kolosov informed his superiors in Moscow of such cases, adding to his report a letter from the Chinese provincial administration that warned clearly of the consequences for such border violations.

What had happened? In October 1930 a Chinese border patrol observed a group of Red Army soldiers chasing two hundred to three hundred Kazakhs that were already up to fifteen kilometers deep within Chinese territory. When the Kazakhs realized the threat, they scattered in panic "in all directions." The soldiers captured some of their livestock and looted their possessions. After they were gone, Chinese officials inspected the scene of the crime and found "traces of the Red Army's brutal reckoning with the Kazakhs: more than ten of them had been murdered on Chinese territory."[152]

In early December Chinese soldiers found more than fifty dead Kazakhs, including women and children, and blamed the Red Army. Some had been killed by bullets, others by the sword.[153] Kolosov noted that the responsible officers of the border troops did not deny the events. The deputy commander for the unit in question had informed him that they had killed three hundred Kazakhs in the December campaign.

In his capacity as a diplomat Kolosov pointed out that the Chinese had already protested border violations by Soviet units several times, stating that such violations were "factual violations of the sovereign rights of a neighboring country."[154] But at the same time he tried to refute the widespread belief (shared particularly by border troops) that Xinjiang's administration welcomed Kazakh immigration. On the contrary: Chinese officials had informed him repeatedly that they were concerned about recent developments. In addition, the Chinese border patrol had received instructions to deport all refugees from their territory. In the spring of 1930 more than two thousand people had been forced to leave the country. Kolosov did not need to stress how ineffective these measures were for coping with the ever-growing wave of new refugees. With respect to the border patrol of his own country, he insisted, "None of the harsh measures that our border soldiers have taken against refugees trying to cross the border have achieved any real results . . . even when they use the worst methods."[155]

The overly motivated soldiers were not the only group to ignore the border in their determination to track down refugees. Leading comrades found armed action on Chinese territory an effective strategy. In early January 1931 young Iusup Abdrakhmanov, chairman of the Kirghiz Council of the People's Commissars, thought of sending soldiers across the border disguised as Basmachis, saying, "That's probably the only way to destroy the Basmachis on the other side of the border."[156] Postnikov, the Soviet general consul in Kashgar, went even further, writing that measures had to be taken for Soviet units to destroy Basmachi leaders on Chinese territory, where they operated more or less without obstacles.[157]

The Soviet border patrol repeatedly demanded that its Chinese colleagues arrest and hand over well-known "bandits." But for the most part these demands went unheard, as we know from a frustrated report of April 1930. The Chinese said they did not know the whereabouts of the wanted persons and that they had to deal with a number of otherwise not-specified difficulties, which made them unable to comply. Without the assistance of local warlords and clan leaders the Chinese authorities could not achieve much: "Kazakh Prince Alen' Zhipyskanov [who lived on Chinese territory] refuses categorically to execute instructions asking him to return Kazakhs, on the grounds that they are his brothers."[158]

Such obvious signs of weakness prompted the Soviet border patrol not to take their Chinese colleagues particularly seriously. What they observed from a distance confirmed their conviction that they must take things into their own hands. A report of January 1931 on some Chinese frontier posts states: "Although the Chinese government has issued orders to take strict measures regarding border violations, the border is poorly protected. The men at the posts spend all their time gambling and smoking narcotics like hashish and opium. Anyone caught violating the border can free himself by [offering] a bribe."[159] Other reports tell of poor provisions and modest lodgings for border soldiers, some of whom the Soviet secret service believed would have liked to desert to the Soviet Union.[160]

The Soviet soldiers assumed—and perhaps not incorrectly—that their Chinese counterparts not only tolerated border crossings, but actively supported them. It was unacceptable and against the rules of conduct among "neighborly states" said the angry commander. The consul must intervene energetically, he said.[161] But real relief could only come from soldiers. The failure to distinguish between armed bandits and desperate refugees contributed to the radicalization of violence, even on Chinese territory. And the conduct of Soviet troops in the region was enabled by the fact that government in Xinjiang was rudimentary and the Chinese government had only limited influence there.[162] While similar events would have been unthinkable at the Soviet Union's western border and would have had incalculable consequences, the weak representative of China's central regime had only feeble protest to offer. Soviet border patrollers took advantage of the power vacuum for their own ends. In line with their belief in the power of order they ruthlessly exploited their strong position when their surroundings lacked real government. From their viewpoint, they were not widening the battle zone by ignoring the border, they were exercising a legitimate form of self-defense.

FLIGHT

The *otkochevniki*, hungry Kazakh refugees, became the emblematic figures of the years of crisis. Between 1928 and 1932 larger and smaller groups from all over the republic packed their belongings and embarked on an uncertain future in an attempt to escape the immense pressure of the grain procurement campaign, dekulakization, sedentarization, and especially, the threat of starvation. After the summer of 1930, mass emigration could no longer be halted. Some nomads believed they would only find safety beyond Soviet borders, others tried to find safety for themselves and their herds in neighboring regions such as Western Siberia or the Central Asian Republics of Turkmenistan, Uzbekistan, and Kirghizia. But the majority of the refugees wandered aimlessly about within Kazakhstan's borders.

Migrating to presumably safer regions was one of the elementary and existential strategies of nomadic communities. They migrated, for instance, when drought or ice storms left their animals with nothing to eat, or when their own communities were beset by stronger hostile clans.[163] But while such forms of flight were normally regional and limited in duration, the escape that began in the 1930s was different. Collectivization and sedentarization threatened the very core of nomadic culture. One pastoralist justified his flight with the words: "A Kazakh can no longer live in Kazakhstan."[164] The entire society of the steppe began moving. The Kazakhs became a people on the run.

"IT CHANGES THE CULTURE, IT DESTROYS TRADITIONAL CHARACTER"

In the newspaper *Sovetskaia step'*, Filipp Goloshchekin, welcomed the September 1931 wave of refugees as a sign of socialist progress: "The Kazakh who never left his aul, who knew no life other than that of the nomad, now easily moves from district to district within Kazakhstan, he goes to Russian and Ukrainian kolkhozes, goes to work, goes to help build up the Volga region and Siberia. Naturally, this changes the economy, it changes the culture, it destroys traditional character, destroys the old economy."[165] Many a comrade found Goloshchekin's tenor inappropriate: "One can hardly agree to that sort and manner of rebuilding character and the economy" someone wrote in a letter to Moscow.[166] But in crucial respects, Goloshchekin was right: the nomads left for other regions of the Soviet Union and the "traditional character" and "old economy" were in ruins. Little was erected in their place, however. Instead, the flight of the Kazakhs left their society broken to pieces. And nothing was further from the truth than the claim that they now moved from one place to the next "with ease."

The steppe was full of refugees seeking food and shelter.[167] No one knew how many. In the summer of 1932 the authorities in Alma-Ata estimated that the number of households in "constant movement" must lie between 180,000 and 200,000. Comrades from the OGPU thought, and probably more realistically so, that the number must be much higher. They estimated that about 280,000 households were traversing the steppe, in other words, about 1.2 million people. A year later, when the administration in many places was on the verge of collapse, the numbers rose again.[168] During the years of famine about 1 million people left the Kazakh ASSR. About 400,000 later returned. And about 200,000 left the Soviet Union permanently.[169]

In February 1933 at a meeting in Moscow a representative of Kazakhstan had to admit that he had no exact numbers with which to quantify the exodus: "We had no special instrument for counting and watching the movements of fleeing Kazakhs and it is impossible to perform that kind of special observation."[170] Regions bordering Kazakhstan were flooded and overburdened by the masses of refugees. In Western Siberia authorities said that the wave was mounting, but they had no exact numbers. The most detailed estimates assume that about 100,000 Kazakhs fled to Western Siberia between 1931 and 1933, although that number rests on unreliable statistics.[171] In the Middle Volga officials calculated in March 1932 that during the past three years more than 50,000 people had come to that region from Kazakhstan.[172]

The large number of escapes that remained undiscovered early on and the fact that now and then local Soviet officials had themselves engaged in emigration proved to the Chekists that the "lower Soviet apparatus" was unreliable and instable. In resignation they complained that the party lacked influence on its own members: "When the clan flees, your everyday Communist will flee, too. Family ties are often stronger than affiliation with the party."[173] Many aul officials tried to give their clan's flight the look of legal migration by collecting approvals, certificates, and documents. They often led the escapes themselves.

Many regions openly welcomed Kazakhs who still had livestock. To the dismay of Kazakh officials, Turkmenian authorities in Krasnovodsk courted emigration-inclined Kazakhs. The secretary of the district of Mangistau's party committee submitted a complaint to Turkmenistan's party leaders that their officials had orders to let all Kazakhs pass through the border to Turkmenistan, while passage in the opposite direction was prohibited. The embargo did not apply to Turkmenian procurement officers doing their work on Kazakh soil who paid better rates for produce than the Kazakh authorities. His region, wrote the secretary, could not reach the quota that it was supposed to deliver because Turkmenian procurement officers ran off with the goods. The Turkmens replied, of course, that both Turkmenistan and

Kazakhstan were Soviet republics and therefore their procurement served the Soviet state as a whole. But they did not leave it at that. When a commission from Kazakhstan arrived in Krasnovodsk to investigate the whereabouts of Kazakh refugees and their livestock, the members of the commission were arrested and detained for weeks without explanation.[174] As bitter as the complaint from Mangistau was, it failed to mention that the Adai moved south because the markets in the north were bare of grain. Radical procurement had put an end to all trade. For the nomads that meant either butchering their animals or moving south.[175]

The Turkmens' plan was clear: Kazakh herds were delivered right to the doors of procurement officers who were then able to fulfill requirements that they otherwise could not have met. Specifically, the comrades in Krasnovodsk had already lost whatever control they may have previously had over vast areas of the Turkmenian steppe. And if many regions of Kazakhstan could not be considered successfully Sovietized, things were much worse in Turkmenistan. Across large stretches of land there was little evidence of Soviet power even in the early 1930s.[176] The Kzyl-Kum Desert that lay between Uzbekistan, Kazakhstan, and Turkmenistan was (in several respects) unknown territory, making it attractive for refugees from the north seeking shelter. Chekists estimated that by late 1931 more than three thousand households and about five hundred bais were hiding in the desert. Outside of all civilization, the nomads could only hold out at that blank spot on the map because relatives from Karakalpakstan supplied them with what they needed for survival.[177]

The Chekists realized how serious the situation had become and the Kazakh OGPU's second highest leader, Anatolii Al'shanskii, appealed to Goloshchekin to reprehend the Turkmens who were using every possible means to stimulate Kazakh emigration.[178] Their concern was great because in August 1930 very similar things were happening at the Uzbek border in the south of the republic. Smugglers had tried to drive a large flock of sheep across the border to the neighboring republic and were stopped by Kazakh border patrollers. It came to gunfire involving Uzbek militia engaged by the speculators. When a few days later the animals in question were offered for sale at a bazaar (where their brand marks unmistakably identified them as belonging to Kazakhs), the Uzbek militia remained silent, supposedly because they had received no orders.

Leaders from Alma-Ata sent angry telegrams to the Central Asian Bureau and to Uzbek leaders, but they got no tangible results, perhaps because it was well-known that the Kazakhs also had scouts out in the field ruthlessly confiscating livestock.[179] Their official mission was to stop smugglers from reaching Uzbekistan. But these "politically illiterate" and "poorly informed" fighters stole from kolkhoz members who had never intended to leave Kazakhstan and were operating on Uzbek ground. Uzbek authorities did not believe, and rightly so, the Kazakh authority's claim that these were simply groups of "common bandits."[180]

The Kazakhs sent both troops and agitators to the refugees in an effort to convince them to return to the regions of their origin. They were often received with gunfire, however, and chased off by both refugees and the local elite. The two groups cooperated together in the district of Tamdinsk, for example, where numerous immigrants from Kazakhstan lived in Aul No. 6. When members of the OGPU turned up in the aul to put an end to unlawful conditions there, they met with armed resistance organized by the party secretary and the chairman of the soviet. In neighboring Aul No. 8 it was the district's man authorized to execute the procurement campaign himself who led a group of twenty men to obstruct the Chekists and attack their replenishment lines.[181] These alliances between the militia and the livestock thieves show how closely the state and society collaborated at the local level. But the incidents also illustrate the limits of solidarity among the republics and regions and mirror the immense lack of trust and the uncertainty that ruled the steppe.

The situation became more precarious for Kazakh refugees, the longer they had to hold out in Central Asian republics. Tension increased between the refugees and the native population. In Uzbekistan's city of Kamir "ten to twenty Uzbeks used sticks to beat Kazakhs working in settlements. Many Kazakhs left for fear of similar treatment by the Uzbeks. They roam from place to place. Uzbeks threw out some Kazakhs working at a settlement and insulted them by saying that they eat human flesh."[182] Local networks and kolkhozes were wary of the nomads. The latter were also constant competitors for other groups energetically defending their traditional pasturelands and water sources. The refugees lost their herds: animals were taken from them, or the Kazakhs sold them at bazaars. The officials lost all interest in impoverished newcomers. They wanted the immigrants' property. The marginalized paupers got no relief from the soviets or from party organizations. A letter to Goloshchekin testifies that Uzbekistan's officials simply did not bother with what happened to refugees in their districts and cities.[183]

As beggars, the Kazakhs soon became a burden for the Central Asian republics. They had to be fed, they needed shelter, and they needed work. Solidarity was expensive and became an organizational challenge for the soviet authorities. Assisting destitute Kazakhs used up funds already allotted for other purposes. Officials at all levels of the administration, from the leaders of the Union's republics right down to local soviets, had good reason to shrug off the pauperized Kazakhs. Administrators basically had two strategies for dealing with these people: ignore them or chase them away. As long as the Kazakhs lived quietly far off in the desert, far away from "civilized areas," they could hope to evade attention from the officials. But as soon as the unwelcome guests caught their eye by invading villages and kolkhozes or by coming too close to settled areas, the administration's well-known mechanism kicked in: Chekists began searching for bais and other "enemies of the people" among the nomads.

SIBERIAN CONDITIONS

In Western Siberia Kazakh refugees lived in squalor. In that region, to which tens of thousands of people had fled from the northern and eastern regions of Kazakhstan, much of the population and many of the officials rejected the *otkochevniki*.[184] An OGPU report of January 1932 sums up the situation:

> Beginning in the fall of 1931 Kazakhs began fleeing from Kazakhstan to the bordering regions of West Siberia. More recently these treks have become massive in character. As many as 1,300 refugees from Kazakhstan are in the district of Baevsk. As many as 10,000 Kazakhs have been counted in the district of Slavgorod. . . . The Kazakhs on the run live crowded and in filth and epidemic diseases spread among them. Many have no lodging and sleep on the street. The refugees have no belongings, they work nowhere, and the great majority of them go hungry. They beg, they eat carrion, and they steal cattle and horses. Some of the Kazakhs have left their children to fend for themselves. There have been several cases of emaciation.[185]

Andrew Cairns, an agronomist who was traveling the region at the time, observed destitute Kazakhs in Slavgorod begging desperately for bread.[186]

In Siberian cities, children's homes were so full that they had to turn away orphans.[187] Many officials could not cope with the situation. A woman heading the department for women's issues in the district of Kliuchevsk described how more and more half-frozen women came to her, some with their dead children still in their arms. They begged for bread and to be allowed to place their surviving children in the custody of the state. Her report closed with the words: "Comrade Vostrotina, what should we do with all of these Kazakh orphans?"[188]

Villagers in Siberia eyed the aliens as competitors for resources that were already getting increasingly scarcer. The refugees cost money and endangered the survival of the peasants already heavily marked by the drive for collectivization.[189] Language and cultural barriers were also reasons for the Siberian peasants to reject the Kazakhs: very few Kazakhs spoke Russian and their behavior did not seem to banish ethnically connoted prejudice. Siberian peasants chased and beat the aliens from the south, treating them as second-class humans who could not be put to work and with whom one need not bother. The chairman of the Trudovik kolkhoz in the district of Uch-Pristansk understood those sentiments and issued an order "not to accept Kazakhs into the kolkhoz . . . because of the differences between the two nations."[190]

Peasants were particularly afraid of losing their animals and provisions. Nothing fueled the spreading hostility toward Kazakhs more than the livestock theft attributed to them. And the number of animal thefts did, indeed, rise as increasing numbers of famished refugees poured into Western Siberia. In some regions the rate of animal theft climbed by 1,200 percent.[191] Peasants and local Soviet institutions in solidarity with one another closed ranks to ward off the menacing aliens. With applause and support from the peasants, party officials in districts and villages declared war on the Kazakhs: "Terrorize the Kazakhs," was the district of Isilkul'sk's party secretary's command to the chief of the regional militia. "They have overrun us with their thievery. If we demonstrate lenience, we shall never recover from it," he said. And another added: "Those Kazakhs are such dogs, almost all of them are criminals and all they're good for is crime."[192]

The organs of justice registered petitions from peasants asking that all Kazakhs be prohibited from staying outdoors after sunset, or that they be deported from the district. The grounds for that were seen in the immense rise in crime rates in the villages. And there were countless rumors and stories of attacks, rape, and other crimes that the Kazakhs had committed against the Russians. Such accounts spread so heavily in the area surrounding the city of Barnaul that the local district attorney saw himself obliged to publicly state in the local newspaper that the rumors were totally unfounded.[193]

Observers from elsewhere were shocked to see how Kazakhs were treated. Many refugees worked under merciless conditions and for miserable pay in the mines of Leninsk in Western Siberia, as one M. A. Kalnin reported to Kalinin. Kazakhs went begging all over town, yet the local authorities seemed to ignore "this abnormal and shameful phenomenon."[194] The result brought about by Kalnin's letter exemplifies the Soviet apparatus's disdain for "extraneous" people in general. A lower-rank employee at the VTsIK in Western Siberia inquired about the "phenomenon" described by Kalnin. Months later Moscow received the reply that "the Executive Committee for the Region of Western Siberia informs [the VTsIK] that the district and regional organs have taken measures to improve the situation of the Kazakhs."[195] The satisfied clerk checked the matter off his list and filed it.

The officials were much more interested in the reactions of local residents. It was unfortunate, for instance, when an OGPU report on famine conditions in various Soviet regions had to mention that "the refugees have a negative effect on the political opinions of kolkhoz peasants in the region of Western Siberia."[196] But the comrades were truly alarmed when their own young cadres started asking questions. Pilot trainees in Orenburg, for example, could not understand why famished people were wandering the streets: "If they are bais, they should be relocated somewhere, but if they are our own people, poor and average-income peasants, then something must be done to remedy their tragic situation."[197] The young pilots' naive observation touched a sore spot. When it came to dealing with refugees, the Soviet state abandoned its own concepts and values. This was particularly true on-site, at the local level.

Representatives of the state and party did little for refugees and sometimes the militia simply overlooked obvious assaults. When in the West Siberian city of Kemerovo Kazakh workers were attacked and beaten and ran to the nearest militia station, they were told to go and get the guilty persons, because the officials did not know whom they were talking about.[198] And Moldagaliev, the commissioner of the Kazakh Council of People's

Commissars for the Middle Volga Region, noted: "Due to the entirely unsympathetic attitude of district cadres toward the needs of Kazakhs who are unable to work, many of the famine refugees are in a very difficult situation. They are in acute need of cereal and shelter. . . . In Orenburg those without relief are starving, many are bloated, many have died of hunger. The enemies of the people beat famished Kazakhs, there have been two executions, and still the chairman of the city soviet refused to give nomads work or even promise relief."[199] Local officials had to admit that their practice of driving away thousands of Kazakhs was a failure. "Presently about three thousand people are registered in Orenburg who were sent back to Kazakhstan but returned to us. . . . Our efforts are futile."[200]

The only nomads with any real chance at finding work and a livelihood were men capable of labor. They were assigned to the "large socialist construction sites," sent to the forests to fell wood, and put to work in the mines of Siberia. Often they had been lured to these places with the prospect of earning enough for themselves and their families. But frequently the promises were false, the weak men were not familiar with the work, and they could not complete the amount of work demanded of them. The language barrier further impeded communication between the brigadiers and the workmen. The directors of factories and sovkhozes, who were under considerable pressure themselves, saw the Kazakhs as a burden and got rid of them as soon as an opportunity arose. Common methods included simply not letting the Kazakh men begin working when they finally arrived after searching for the place for months, or hiring them as seasonal laborers only. When winter came the men had no work and were left to fend for themselves. They dug dwellings in the ground and tried to survive the harsh winter months on little food. Very few had any real chance of survival.[201]

Pay and food rations depended on individual work performance. Many of the men were so weak on arrival that they could not accomplish the tasks expected of them. They found themselves in a vicious circle with no escape. The weaker they became, the fewer prospects they had for ever fulfilling the work requirements, and the less food they were given.[202]

One such voluntary work migrant was Umurgali Aukeev. In a petition to the Central Committee he described the miserable situation in which he and his friends found themselves: "Many, many Kazakhs look for work in the Siberian cities of Barnaul, Viisk, and Rustavka. One man finds work, another doesn't. The cadre department at the Viisk sugar factory said frankly that they do not hire Kazakhs. They hire Russians, but chase Kazakhs away. Some factories hire single men only and will not accept families. Workers are relieved when their families die. Others abandon their families, leave them behind, and wish they didn't have them."[203] By the summer of 1932 the situation had become so desperate that leading comrades in the region of Western Siberia could no longer look the other way: ethnic tension had become a threat to safety in the region. Prominent authors wrote a series of newspaper articles on the dangerous potential of "Great-Russian chauvinism."[204] Robert Eikhe, at the time head of the party in Western Siberia, called on the Communists to end discrimination against Kazakhs and to more closely observe the principles of Soviet policy on nationalities from now on.[205] He had reason for the demand. Not only was disturbing news coming in from cities and villages, compelling him to take action, but Moscow, too, had been dispatching ever more impatient inquiries into the unrest. It was not without irony that of all people it was Kazakhstan's party leaders themselves who repeatedly brought the unfair treatment of "their citizens living temporarily in Western Siberia" to Eikhe's attention.[206]

As a result, those guilty of "Great-Russian chauvinism" were sentenced in public hearings and assemblies. Judges and speakers severely criticized the increasing number of attacks on members of the Kazakh minority, especially because entire villages and sovkhozes lost control when dozens of people began assaulting one another for inane reasons. One court in Kemerovo, for instance, sentenced two men and a woman to long prison terms for playing a leading role in riots at the Udarnik sovkhoz in August 1933.[207]

But court trials were exceptions and helped little to calm things down. Russians who attacked Kazakhs could expect superficial and slow investigations, especially if they were party members or functionaries who had attacked Kazakhs for no apparent reason. In Liubinskii District, leading comrades passed an incriminating file from one desk to another for months: Three sovkhoz managers were accused of having Kazakhs arrested and brutally tortured for no reason. Although outside commissioners pointed out the urgency of the matter several times and demanded that the guilty be punished, it took intervention by an envoy from the district attorney of the region of Western Siberia before a public trial was arranged and the men were sentenced to long prison terms.[208]

In November 1933 a party leader for the region of Western Siberia summarized the efforts undertaken up to that point. The results were not flattering: The soviets' work among Kazakhs was inadequate, immigrant accommodations were shabby, and the newcomers were treated badly. Their children were beaten at school, and the large number of written complaints about such conditions stood in no relation to the slow rate at which they were processed. But the worst flaw was that "chauvinism" was constantly on the rise among Siberian workers, peasants, and officials. And that could not be expected to change, wrote the party leader, because no one was interested in the problem, and posts in the responsible organs and institutions were held by incompetents. The region's department for national minorities did not have a single coworker who spoke the Kazakh language, the report said. [209]

The refugees in Western Siberia and elsewhere found themselves in a dilemma—they could not return to their homeland ravaged by famine and civil war, and most of them did not want to. But it was also difficult for them to stay in their new surroundings. No one in the villages and districts felt responsible and most of the people rejected them. Many of the hungry refugees got no relief from the institutions of Soviet society. They were forced to survive at the margin, as part of the "dark mass" that gave a poor and miserable look to Soviet cities in those years. [210]

5

FAMINE

BETWEEN 1930 AND 1934 at least a quarter of Kazakhstan's total population perished. Ethnic Kazakhs were hit hardest. More than 1.5 million died of starvation, illness, and disease. Enormous suffering began when grain was taken from the auls and animals were driven away. Misery was ubiquitous: one saw emaciated children at railway stations and corpses by the side of the road; bloody fights broke out over a bit of bread, family ties unraveled, and were inured to cannibalism.

People went hungry all over the Soviet Union. Worst hit were Ukraine, North Caucasus, the Volga Region, and Kazakhstan.[1] Leading comrades in Stalin's inner circle were well-aware of the facts and sought to gain control. Beginning in the fall of 1932, Bolsheviks reacted to lower procurement results by marginally limiting the demands of the drive, passing a number of politburo resolutions, devising relief programs, replacing personnel, relocating multitudes of people, and planning emergency measures. But the mid-range result was that a once serious famine soon became a major catastrophe that shattered Kazakh society.[2]

The crisis reached its peak *following* the introduction of measures contrived to remedy it. The Bolsheviks were not interested in saving the people per se, they wanted to rescue a faltering economy and restore control. For

them, it most important to reach the goals of procurement and collectivization. That was the sole criterion for judging the success or failure of people
in the government and administration.[3] Relief for the starving was secondary, especially when it meant rerouting reserves set aside for other purposes.

Some Bolsheviks were troubled by the millionfold misery but took the
loss as a matter of course. Undoing the fabric of society, they realized, presented an opportunity—it prepared the way for dependency and subordination. People had no escape from the institutions and framework of the Soviet
state. Cooperation had become a matter of life and death. Ultimately, famine
sovietized Kazakh society. It was both a prerequisite and an instrument of
Bolshevik power in the steppe.

SCOPE

Catastrophe was not sudden and did not befall all parts of Kazakhstan at
once.[4] In the winter of 1929–30 authorities recorded a significant increase
in malnourishment and consumption. And they saw the first people dying
of starvation. Initially two areas were affected most by famine: the predominantly agrarian districts in northern Kazakhstan where the collectivization
drive had first been introduced on a large scale and from which grain could
be hauled off easily, and the western part of the republic, where the population, including the Adai, depended on grain sold at markets. In 1929 those
markets were bare.[5]

In early 1930, alarming reports came from northern Kazakhstan. Conditions worsened considerably within weeks, especially in the Pavlodar oblast.
In February comrades warned: "We are not panicking . . . but the Oblast Committee Bureau sees itself compelled to inform party leaders immediately
that in the Pavlodar oblast there is a very real danger of the party's whole
policy failing."[6]

The comrades reported of villages consisting of women only because
men sought work and food elsewhere. Cultivated land had been reduced to
such an extent that they were forced to buy grain from Siberia. Other regions
reported similar conditions. In June 1930, authorities estimated that more
than 100,000 people were starving and in urgent need of food in the northern
regions of Kazakhstan. In the Aktiubinsk oblast more than 40,000 people

went hungry. Kazakhs were not alone in their plight; Russian and German peasants also suffered bitterly.

Time after time, delegations from the villages and auls went to administrators asking for grain. Distraught women assailed the officials with pleas for bread. In some places the needy formed mobs and stormed warehouses and barns, often only to find that their grain had already left the region.[7] Some officials closed their doors to hungry people "willing to do anything."[8] In the Kazakh capital Alma-Ata administrators felt "bombarded" by telegrams from local officials complaining of shortages. They replied irritably that the comrades must handle the problems themselves.[9] At first higher officials tried to depict shortages as isolated, unrelated occurrences. And they did make singular attempts to provide certain groups with a minimum of support.[10]

At that point, in the summer of 1930, a condition gradually became conspicuous that was to have dramatic relevance for the months and years to come—amid the confusion over competence and responsibility, not only the requests pouring in from the oblasts but also the assignments going forth from the administrative centers began to evaporate into thin air. Paperwork confirmed that relief was being sent to the starving. But when the responsible organizations lacked the resources or had other plans, decisions were not followed by action. In the summer of 1930, for instance, the Kazakh branch of Soiuzkhleb was commissioned to deliver 30,000 poods of grain to help the people of Petropavlovsk oblast. Time was short: local authorities had already begun excluding certain groups of people from receiving provisions. The center confirmed the order and requested that the regional branch release the grain, although everyone knew that the warehouse was empty. When urgent inquiries arrived from the oblast, the Soiuzkhleb center simply confirmed that yes, the grain supply had, indeed, been commissioned. The same authorities simultaneously put pressure on the branch in Petropavlovsk. "Instead of a real solution," says one report, "what we got was a game of telegram leapfrog."[11]

Leading Bolsheviks focused on reaching their targets for grain and livestock procurement, organizing collectivization and sedentarization (both more difficult than they had imagined) in the midst of armed struggles, and mass emigration. Caught up in the dynamics that they had themselves set in motion, they were blind to the imminent catastrophe. And at first things seemed satisfactory. Although all economic indicators looked disappointing, the harvest of 1930 enabled the survival of most of the steppe's inhabitants. But in 1931 the problems returned and were now more dismal than ever. Contrary to expectations, poor weather spoiled the harvest.[12] That was fatal for Kazakhs who had been forced to settle. Their freshly cultivated fields produced only modest yields, if any at all. They had no noteworthy reserves for emergencies and they had no experience in farming to know how to prepare for and survive crises. Later Uraz Isaev was to say that the attempt to turn arid steppe soil into cultivated land by a stroke of the pen was a major cause of the disaster.[13] And fodder for livestock was nowhere to be found. It had been carted off to meet procurement targets. Nomads began killing their animals and soon they had consumed a large part of their own source of subsistence. Procurement drives and kolkhozes did the rest: the Kraikom declared the "complete socialization" of livestock, rounded up droves of animals, and let them perish.[14] In summer and early fall throngs of recently settled pastoralists began abandoning the steppe.

The cadres grew nervous, even in agrarian areas inhabited predominantly by Europeans. "All of the seed has been taken from the district. What shall

FIGURE 9. Kazakh refugees in the winter of 1930–1931, TsGAKFDZ, 5–3621

we sow?" wrote one distressed agronomist from Ubagansk, saying in closing: "I have written this in the hope that the system of kolkhozes and the Soviet regime are not as feeble and inattentive as to . . . allow such mismanagement that one of the richest parts of the steppe becomes transformed into empty, unpopulated grassland."[15]

In 1932 everything collapsed. Agriculture broke down. Reserves were depleted, the harvest was even smaller than a year previously, and the Bolsheviks took even that and the remaining animals.[16] A state of emergency governed almost all of Kazakhstan's oblasts. People fled from famine everywhere. The steppe regions of Central Kazakhstan were practically depopulated. In December 1932 more than half of the population of the district of Zhana-Arinsk had fled. Only about five thousand families still lived in the region of Turgai. And no one knew where the inhabitants of Chubartavsk had gone. A 1933 report from that district states that "according to recent statistics, about 1,500 households, that is, a total of up to 7,000 people, have remained. But emigration counts rise as the food problem grows more acute. The district has no grain reserves and the measures taken by district organizations to halt emigration have produced no positive results. Despite the ban enacted by the Oblast Executive Committee, seed reserves were distributed for consumption in November and December."[17] In many places the already poor communication between administrative centers and the oblasts now broke down entirely. Particularly during the winter months beset by snow storms, entire districts were cut off completely from the outside world.[18] Comrades in administrative centers had only a vague idea of what was happening in remote areas.[19] Often they lacked even a rough estimate of how many had died. Statistics were piecemeal and selective.[20]

Official numbers did not reflect the jumbled situation but by purporting to be precise they made the catastrophe look manageable. One OGPU bulletin, for example, noted that for Kazakhstan as a whole, between December 1931 and October 1932 a total of 14,549 people had died of starvation and related illness.[21] The true number can hardly be determined: deaths were not recorded, no one knows how many refugees left never to return, and the most important demographic calculations rest on highly unreliable censuses taken in 1926 and in 1937. This calls into question the statistics that claim to show the proportion to which individual ethnic groups contributed to the total number of 1.5 million victims.

It is clear, however, that in absolute numbers the Kazakhs suffered by far

FIGURE 10.   Famine refugees in the region of Pavlodar, 1932,
TsGAKFDZ, 5–3569

the greatest losses when compared with other nationalities living in Kazakh-stan.[22] The true scope of the catastrophe could not be captured by statistics. It is found in the countless reports from the oblasts that expose the authori-ties as incapable of coping with the situation.

STARVATION AND SOCIAL BREAKDOWN

Famines are often characterized as times of disorder. We read that chaos erupts, social relations deteriorate, and people begin disregarding the authorities and taking matters into their own hands.[23] Famine can also be held responsible for the erosion of the ordering principles that had governed Kazakhstan. Under relentless pressure, solidarity and social cohesion dwin-dled until little was left. Paraphrasing a thought put forward by Jan Philipp Reemtsma, one can say that in Kazakhstan one of society's most fundamen-tal parameters had become meaningless: the trust and confidence that in our interactions with others we can normally expect others to have benign intentions.[24]

Famine ripped society apart both within and beyond the pale of its grip. No one could escape violence and its consequences. The hungry turned to barbarity and inevitably swept others along with them into the dynamics of famine. And yet the extraordinary circumstances did not fully atomize society, as has occasionally been suggested.[25] Out of the crisis there evolved new kinds of social structures that differed from the social order that had existed before.

SIGNS OF DETERIORATION

People began eating grass and plants. They consumed dogs, cats, birds, mice, and whatever else could be caught in the villages and auls. They boned and ate horses and cows as they wasted away. They excavated carcasses and made them edible.[26] But such substitutes could only tide them over a while. Then they had no choice but to leave. They dragged themselves to larger towns, railway stations, sovkhozes, and construction sites because whenever food was available, there was often no way to get it to the auls and villages.[27]

Gafu Kairbekov, a Kazakh author born in 1928, recalls scenes from his childhood in Turgai:

> It is a small town, a district capital, and it stands on a hill. Below there is a little river and all the streets slope steeply down to it. We children used to run to the river barefoot. In my memory there are people out in the streets—many grown-ups. They can't walk; they're crawling on all fours so feeble they can hardly move along; they have no strength left. When they can't go any further they start scratching at the earth with their nails; they lie on the earth like dogs. We step over them as we go. On our way down to the river we have to step over several of them. Down there, on the riverbank, an animal is being killed. It is towards that slaughter that the hungry people are crawling. Those who manage to get there will drink the blood of the animal.[28]

In his classic study *Crowds and Power*, Elias Canetti points out the consequences that persistent hunger and violence can have for multitudes of refugees. Fleeing crowds initially exhibit a high degree of solidarity forged by hope of rescue and fear of the external threat. Leaving danger behind them and striving to reach a common goal, they begin to cooperate. Even when the prospect of deliverance seems slight, refugees keep together.[29] Wolfgang Sofsky has described things similarly. Mass flight releases an "equalizing effect" because "a movement of many invokes a solidarity that goes beyond the instinct of individual survival."[30] But as circumstances grow more precarious, solidarity falters. And when obstacles loom large, solidarity breaks down. Panic and animosity grow. "In the end, each man flees alone."[31] And that is what happened to the Kazakhs. During their month-long treks through the steppe, their communities fell apart. Many aspects of their destiny indicate that the pace of disintegration quickened when social relations lost stability and resilience.[32] At first the burdens of flight and the threat of encountering Red troops caused many groups of Kazakhs to split up into smaller units. Later, when food reserves were depleted and no help was in sight, they began to leave their helpless, weak, and sick members behind. Yet even when faced with conditions threatening their very existence, not everyone was uncompromisingly willing to do only whatever it took to secure individual biological survival.[33] Patterns of disintegration often halted at the door to the core family. Even under the most difficult conditions, the core family tried to stay together and cope.[34] In a description of one such odyssey through the steppe, Mukhamet Shaiakhmetov, for example, says that it was the extreme solidarity between his mother and siblings that made survival possible for all.[35]

The longer the famine persisted, however, the greater the number of children orphaned. Thousands of children were picked up all over Kazakhstan. In October 1932 officials registered more than twelve thousand children deprived of parents in the seventeen districts of eastern Kazakhstan alone. More than ten thousand of them were "tended" by various organizations.[36] By mid-1934 the number of orphans across Kazakhstan was over sixty thousand.[37] Taking into account the mortality rate in children's institutions from the years of 1932 and 1933, where in some months more than 10 percent of the charges died,[38] and considering that many orphaned children were simply not registered, the real number was probably much higher. Many children lost their parents to illness and death. And others were abandoned.

The abandonment of children secured the survival of members of the group who could work and procreate. The number of eaters had to be kept at a minimum.[39] One Kazakh adage taught, "When a camel dies, you fall behind; when your own child dies, you catch up with the caravan."[40] But rarely was a child set adrift without any prospect of rescue.[41] Most parents who left their children behind tried to envision at least an abstract chance of their survival. They hoped for mercy from the better-off. They left infants at the doors of soviet buildings or placed toddlers in the arms of passersby.[42]

Others saw no option other than to sacrifice their children. In the early 1990s, the Kazakh literary scholar Mekemtas Myrzakhmetov told of the most traumatic moment of his life. In the summer of 1933 his mother, faced with certain death by starvation, took him and his sister to relatives in search of help. On the way they were surrounded by wolves. The steppe had little prey to offer the hungry animals. The situation was hopeless. Either all three would die, or his mother had to sacrifice one of her children. She left her daughter to the wolves. Later she told her son that he was more important for the family's survival.[43]

The authorities could not handle the situation. In March 1932, administrators for the city of Semipalatinsk saw themselves forced to open three new orphanages for four hundred children each. But they had no funds and the existing twelve orphanages were overcrowded and unable to feed the children already there.[44] Inspections and revisions revealed dramatic circumstances in Kazakh orphanages: countless children were undernourished, many had contagious diseases, the buildings were filthy and devoid of the most elementary furnishings and supplies. Some feeble children sat in their own excrement.[45] Orphanage staff embezzled food and supplies and left the children to their fate.[46]

In Ozersk functionaries used only four thousand of the sixty thousand rubles set aside for the orphanage. The rest of the money was never found.[47]

In Pavlodar officials took all the children they collected in town to an empty house. Conditions there were disastrous. "We will not report in detail of the dying and the dead that lie in the front yard, the corridors, and the house itself. We say only in general that the children in this 'asylum' are neglected ... they get only one bowl of *kasha* or soup a day ... they roll about in dirt on the floor and stove, they are left alone in pitch darkness, they cry, and those with no strength left to cry just moan and wheeze."[48] Relief that actually did arrive was often insufficient or even inappropriate for children. In some places the children were fed for days and weeks with nothing but unground rye, which led to intestinal illness and mortality rates of over 80 percent.[49]

Elsewhere authorities began deporting children and adolescents to

remote villages where so-called children's communes became deathtraps
for their young inhabitants. In July 1932, inspectors sent to the village of
Steklianskoe (about twenty kilometers from Semipalatinsk) were greeted
by horror. They found about five hundred children living in half-dilapidated
buildings whose former proprietors ("kulaks") had been exiled. A few weeks
earlier the headcount had been twelve hundred. Meanwhile seven hundred
children had either died or run away. The remainder were undernourished
and many were ill. The only doctor's assistant around said the majority had
no chance of survival. Their dwellings were filthy and food delivery was
random. The inspectors found the staff on the premises wholly unsuitable.
Other staff stayed in Semipalatinsk and left the children to their doom.[50]

The problem of neglected orphans exasperated the nation's leaders. They
called for a solution time and again and regularly reproved officials for ignoring it. At a congress in November 1933, for example, the party secretary of
the district of Ianikurgansk said that within his district lived about four
hundred homeless children for whom he was entitled to money from the
oblast; yet to that day he had not received a single kopeck for their care. For
that reason, and because their food rations were stolen, the mortality rate
among them remained high, he said.[51] The hungry orphans were on the bottommost rung in the hierarchic food rationing system, and because they
were not part of the workforce, they could not hope for access to scarce
resources.[52] Supplies for the children were easily misappropriated; detection was rare and minors could not file complaints. Adolescents and children
ran away from the cramped orphanages in droves. They formed gangs that
gave them a sense of safety and some protection from attack and robbery.[53]
And they hunted for food together using any method they could.

After all reserves were exhausted, some of the starving began to eat
human flesh. News of it spread rapidly and set everyone in a state of alarm.
Bazaar and market meat was suspicious. Children were endangered, too easily snatched, and supposedly more palatable.[54] Some such incidents were,
indeed, documented.[55] Most of the children concerned were not consumed
by strangers but by relatives and acquaintances. Some parents had eaten
their own dead children.[56]

There were also reports of hungry gangs attacking, killing, and devour-
ing others out of sheer desperation. As the famine peaked, the danger of that
happening was so great in some areas that even experienced officials were
reluctant to travel there.[57] Mansur Gataulin depicted his findings in July

1932 at a kolkhoz near Karaganda, where cowsheds were full of corpses. "I went outside again. There was shouting coming from the road. Desperate ragged women were attacking my driver with knives. I shot into the air and they ran off. I looked around and a short way off there was a cauldron over a fire. Something was cooking. I walked over and lifted the lid; in the bubbling water a little foot floated up, or a hand, or a child's heel."[58]

For the winter of 1932–33 the OGPU recorded multiple instances of people being lured, caught, killed, and eviscerated.

> On the eve of March fourth an unknown Kazakh woman with two children ages six and eight went around the aul of Karamunii in the district of Taldy-Kurgan, asking to stay at the house of an aul inhabitant, Toigembaev. The latter, together with six other people, then killed her and the children. Their hearts and lungs were cooked and eaten that night and the rest of their flesh was discarded....
>
> Eighteen kilometers away from the Guliaevki Station the body of a man was found whose entrails had been removed. Along the way one found ten adult corpses and the bodies of five children, some of which showed traces of murder; meat had been severed from the adult bodies.[59]

Cannibals threaten the cohesion of a community by violating one of the most fundamental principles of human socialization, namely, that people do not eat one another.[60] They could not expect compassion when caught. The community's hate and fear focused on them and they were hounded and killed.[61] When inhabitants of the village of Sartuma discovered people among them who ate body parts and killed children, they "locked them into a cold earthen hut, bolting all the doors to let them die of hunger."[62] By the time they were discovered a while later, one was dead and the others were dying.

Whenever the militia and the OGPU discovered such events they carefully noted the condition of the corpses. They listed scalped heads, ripped out kidneys, hearts, and livers, extremities scattered about, and body parts floating in cauldrons.[63] The reports filled with anthropophagic practices not only document deviant human behavior but also served to rationalize the horrific events by pathologizing those involved. People who did that must be sick. Rarely did the authorities write that "enemies of the people" or "kulaks" had incited people to eat human flesh.[64]

In February 1933, Uraz Isaev received a letter from the district of

Karamakchi on the eastern shore of the Aral Sea. A leading soviet official described conditions there:

> Death by starvation has become the fate of the masses. . . . On the fifteenth of February I personally ordered the police chief to search the town and he found thirty corpses. On the sixteenth he found eleven bodies. At the district center two hundred emaciated people beg for bread every day (and many more are in need). The chairman of the district executive committee just returned from the kolkhozes and reported that the roads to the district's capital are lined with corpses. . . . District employees report that not one single kolkhoz has no dead or people wasting away. . . . When authorities ride out to the kolkhozes they take their horses into the house with them at night and have them carefully watched by day because there have been cases of people stabbing horses in the neck in broad daylight in hope of getting a little horse-meat or blood.[65]

The steppe had become one gigantic zone of death.[66] In many places the authorities were in a position neither to help the living nor to bury the dead. No one dug graves for the bodies dumped into ditches and pits.[67] Often reminders from outside officials were necessary before the basic regulations of human remains disposal were once again enforced. Neither the local people nor their functionaries had the strength to handle it properly. Often the only solution left was to reward people with bread or grain for each body they collected and interred.[68]

The dead demonstrated to the living what they had yet to expect, while simultaneously inuring them to the sight. "When I reached Semipalatinsk," wrote a newly arrived official in the summer of 1932, "I saw at the station . . . two Kazakhs who had died of starvation, but no one was bewildered."[69] In larger towns corpses lying around had become a normal street scene. In the steppe it was much worse. Roads between settlements were lined with carcasses of those who had starved. "Gigantic settlements" presented the particularly haunting sight of rows and rows of hundreds of abandoned yurts, in which only dead lay.[70] Corpses were seen openly "all over" the district of Chubartavsk, wrote one official in September 1933. Within a one-kilometer radius of a kolkhoz his men had found more than twenty dead. There were no living inhabitants in the yurts of Aul No. 10, only dead bodies and human bones, "presumably meal scraps," he noted.

The people knew of many similar death sites. And it is telling not only that the body of the chairman of the District Control Commission lay unburied in the steppe but also that several dead bodies and even skulls lay scattered around in the immediate proximity of the OGPU building, without anyone taking particular notice of them.[71] When someone mentioned to a sovkhoz director that body parts and a skull had been found on sovkhoz grounds he replied frankly that he had too much to do and no time to take care of it.[72]

With the exception of a few towns, well-ordered life came to a halt. Agricultural production ceased where there were no people to work the fields. In some kolkhozes "not a single person could stand upright."[73] Whatever animals were left soon disappeared. The only people who could now survive in the steppe were small groups living off predation and pilferage.[74] And when people became scarce, wolves and other beasts of prey reconquered the steppe. Uninhibited gangs and wild animals became a lethal threat to anyone moving outside the bounds of villages or kolkhozes.[75]

THE COUNTENANCE OF STARVATION

Going hungry radically changes people. They do not suddenly become recognizable victims. Over a longer period of time their figures, facial features, and ultimately their natures begin to change. Death by starvation is not sudden and unexpected. It announces itself gradually over days, weeks, even months. From various contexts in which people have suffered from undernutrition for longer periods of time, we know how permanent deficiency changes the human organism. The hungry lose weight and look haggard and boney. Their skin loses suppleness and becomes pale. Muscles atrophy and warp posture. The starving often become apathetic and passive toward their environment.[76] Finally they lose interest in anything except food. Starvation blocks out all other emotions and induces a condition in which people tend to develop extreme forms of what, under other circumstances, they would consider their "normal" behavior.[77]

The faces of the starving frighten and horrify others. Their countenances speak of imminent death. Others may feel as if the radical change in facial expression comes from a loss of individuality and personality. Giorgio Agamben tried to explain why the faces of the dying in German concentration camps evoke such horror. He believes their faces are like mirrors: "Everyone

... recognizes himself in [a man's] disfigured face," the look of a starving person "marks the threshold between the human and the inhuman."[78]

The surviving descriptions of starving Kazakhs illustrate an intermediate state between life and death. Mukhamet Shaiakhmetov saw "not people, but walking skeletons ... their arms looked unnaturally long and their eyes sunken and terrifyingly lifeless, ... an appalling sight."[79] Gazing out the window of his father's club car onto the station in Kazalinsk, young Kamil Ikramov, son of the first party secretary of Uzbekistan, Akmal Ikramov, saw "skeletons, living adult skeletons with child skeletons in their arms."[80]

Other officials reported that when they encountered half-starved children their hands shook uncontrollably and they could not sleep for days.[81] All of these reports are about first encounters with malnourishment and the sight of starvation. Outside observers were particularly shocked to see beggars, hungry children, and dying people lying in the streets, scavenging food from rubbish pits, and fighting over a few pieces of bread.[82] The sometimes absurd coexistence of Soviet normality and human tragedy raised indignation. One controller could hardly contain himself while reporting to Stalin and Molotov that a small store in the district of Taldy-Kurgan had nothing to sell but "three pairs of rubber galoshes and portraits of Comrade Goloshchekin." "Is there any more hideous way to ridicule the starving population?" he added.[83]

But after experiencing the initial horror many people—at least outwardly—became complacent and callous. No one could handle constant confrontation with misery. It was true of the tough Chekists just as much as for those who were not involved. Agnessa Mironova-Korol', the wife of Sergei Mironov, the OGPU's authorized representative in Kazakhstan at the time, wrote of a trip to Karaganda in 1931, when she accompanied her husband. Mironov and his colleagues did their business in town and returned in the railroad club wagon in the evening in a depressed and thoughtful mood. In the luxurious club wagon with all its comfort and fine edibles they were able to relax, joke, and exchange anecdotes.[84] While the privileged men of the OGPU could at least momentarily block out what they had seen, most people had to find some other way to cope with the atrocity.

The majority gradually became accustomed to the starving around them and resigned to accepting it. The longer they were confronted with hungry people, the less it bothered them. While most people in the steppe, the auls, and the villages went hungry, things looked different where Soviet infrastructure still worked reasonably. In the cities, at railway stations, at Five-Year Plan construction sites, and in the sovkhozes there were always plenty of people—officials, employees, and even workers and their families— who did not go hungry or who were at least not subjected to continual shortage. The famous Swiss adventurer Ella Maillart who traveled in the Central Asian Soviet Republics in 1932 described begging children as part of the picturesque scene at a train station and less as an element of famine.[85] Her travelogue explicitly mentions the fate of the Kazakhs only a few times in passing, as in a description of a woman she observed in a "Kazakh wagon": "A woman rewinds her white turbaned head-dress, the only article of her clothing which is not in shreds. . . . Her baby, hanging to her gown, supports itself on thin sticks of legs, whose knee bones stick out prominently. There is no flesh on its little backside, which looks like a wrinkled bladder hanging in numerous folds. Whence do they come? Where are they going?"[86]

No one wanted to have anything to do with the starving. They were said to pose a threat and have contagious diseases. Established communities that often enough fought for their own survival saw the starving as a threat to stability and safety. In January 1933 the OGPU reported from Karaganda that the steady flow of famine refugees had worsened conditions in the city. The Chekists worried less about weak people vegetating in the streets at freezing temperatures and under open skies than they worried about crime. Crime got out of control when the refugees combined to become small groups and attacked bakery shops, robbed shoppers on the streets, and attacked people on horses to purloin the animals. Ten horses had been stolen on a single day, the report said, and two bakery shops robbed. An attack on a flour warehouse had been thwarted at the last minute.[87]

Anyone who raised his hand against the refugees had rarely to expect sanctions. When they marginalized, isolated, and deported hungry refugees, the comrades could generally count on tacit tolerance from the majority of the population that was not starving. No one intervened when the militia and the OGPU escorted the weak from public spaces.[88]

Rejection of the starving often enough turned into overt hostility. In April 1933 a letter to the editor of the local newspaper in Akmolinsk, the *Akmolinskii udarnik* said: "The Red Market is open and can only be called red because blood flows there every day. Individually or in groups, famine refugees grab food from the hands of dealers and shoppers who beat them until they draw blood, beat them unconscious, and sometimes beat them dead."[89] The longer the exceptional circumstances lasted, the more frequent outbreaks of violence and self-administered justice became. The starving formed society's lowest stratum. They were chased off, threatened, and often killed. They were strangers and beggars. Refugees were part of an undifferentiated gray mass with no future and a past that interested no one.[90]

It is no coincidence and it was not for a lack of camera equipment that there are few photographs of starving people in Kazakhstan. The catastrophe had no countenance and it was to be given none. The cloak of silence had to be opaque. Valentin Groebner has an explanation for why the powerful prevent or at least suppress the availability of horrific images:

> The more familiar elements are included in the "unimaginably" horrible images of the sufferings of others, the more effective they are. Collective memories are built from selection and invasion; we are supposed to remember and shudder, but it must be caused by the right, the relevant images. That is why atrocities that have not been photographed are somehow less grave in a vague and cynical way. And that is why ultimately images of the horrific tell us so much about the visual order of our own environment. The images that we find unacceptable are those that violate [our] political rules of what may be made visible.[91]

The Bolsheviks knew exactly what shocking and mobilizing effect might by triggered by pictures of starving people.[92] During the famine of the early 1920s they had intentionally—and successfully—used such photographs to encourage international solidarity with the downtrodden.[93] Under exchanged banners, ten years later they did everything in their power to prevent any attention to news and dire pictures from the suffering regions.[94] Like the experience of physical pain, experiences of starvation cannot easily be put into words.[95] But images of emaciated bodies do tell us something about starving people. We can see what we cannot communicate.[96] The less attention those in power gave to the starving, the easier it was to isolate them.

An example of this took place in July 1933 at the Kazakh party leader's sixth plenum. Among other matters, the agenda included a discussion of errors and excesses that had occurred in recent years. The speakers dissected the humanitarian catastrophe with abstract concepts and compartmentalized it as reflecting various problems. They lectured on the difficulties involved with supply, expressed concern over the reduction of livestock, and debated over how much land to reserve for new crops. They did not talk about starving people.[97] Only Khasen Nurmukhamedov, at the time deputy chairman of the Kazakh Planning Committee, spoke up: "We talk a lot about the loss of herds, which is no doubt an important factor for our economy, but often we forget the most important element of our productive forces, namely, the people. In some regions the population finds itself in a very difficult position. I have to say it: In Kazakhstan we have eighty thousand orphaned children. We can't bring this up just as a complaint, we have to talk about it to raise awareness within the party organization for our battle against the consequences of emigration, our battle against the neglect of the children."[98]

For this comment Nurmukhamedov was heavily criticized. Gdalii Pinkhasik, party secretary of the region of Uralsk, called out: "Livestock breeding, says Comrade Nurmukhamedov, is not the most important issue. In his opinion the most important point is that Kazakhstan has eighty thousand orphans and that people look awful and have faces that are dreadful to see. I don't think that the plenum can agree with that kind of medical standpoint. We are politicians and cannot endorse such a bourgeois-philanthropic view."[99] That was the point, and Pinkhasik knew it. Precisely because the sight of figures and faces was so shocking and imprinted itself indelibly in the memories of those who saw it, the Bolsheviks could have no interest in people talking about it. Nurmukhamedov admitted having made a mistake: "I provided too much detail when describing the calamitous situation of the decamped nomads. This led my comrades to conclude that I was taking a philanthropic view of the situation. In this respect I accept the negative comment that Comrade Pinkhasik made. I should like to point out, however, that I did it in order to draw the plenary session's attention to our fight against the consequences of the decampment."[100]

MARGINALIZATION AND ISOLATION

Food distribution points were set up everywhere in Kazakhstan in cities and at important railway stations. They were sites to which the starving were banished and left to die. The official rations to be distributed among the starving there were insufficient for survival: a family of four was given 25 kilograms (55 pounds) of grain for one month. It meant that children got 150 grams (5.2 ounces) of bread per day, nonworking adults got 250 (8.8 ounces) grams of bread per day, and workers got 350 grams (12.3 ounces) of bread per day.[101] And these skimpy rations were only theoretical and maximum portions. Reality looked different. In Karatal, says one report, "the midday meal (consisting of water and flour) fed only half of the people, then they poured water into the pot and gave that to the rest of them."[102]

In the city of Aulie-Ata the local distribution point had lost its function. Mortality rates were enormous: "Due to a lack of equipment . . . , entirely unhygienic conditions, and a lack of food, death from epidemics and emaciation continues. Between the tenth of February and the third of March this year [1933] we have registered the deaths of 1,023 people who came here. . . . Within two weeks 108 of the 252 new arrivals died. Of the 295 children brought to the children's home, 78 died within 38 days."[103] Wherever the militia picked up starving refugees they brought them to these provision points and reception centers that were always at the periphery, at the outskirts of town, next to train stations, or in remote villages. The sites were allegedly chosen to prevent contagious diseases from spreading and to facilitate the coordination of relief measures. In reality these camps marginalized starving refugees and isolated them from the rest of the population.[104] On a small scale it reflected what characterized the Soviet Union as a whole: The conviction that useless people must be cleared away and disposed of as waste.[105]

The authorities made regular attempts to clean up the cities and stations and drive away the starving.[106] A steady flow of new arrivals replenished the spaces left by deported refugees, however, leaving the officials with modest success at the most. The practice was nonetheless continued in an attempt to keep the situation under control. In the summer of 1932 so many famine refugees arrived in Alma-Ata that the city soviet closed down the local provision site. The militia complained that they could not control so many "elements."[107] Their terminology is telling: the militia, OGPU, and parts of the Party had begun to see the uprooted people as a safety issue. Individual groups had become "declassified elements" and were thus no longer within the reach of relief measures, said one OGPU report from the summer of 1933. These Kazakhs would steal, speculate, beg, and harvest fields illegally.[108] In many towns the authorities were content to simply remove starving people from public spaces and then leave them alone.[109]

In Semipalatinsk "all organizations sent whomever they wanted" to a building at the edge of town called Barracks No. 6. These included famine refugees, "Russian adventurers," "parasites," and other "problematic cases."

But no one felt responsible for supervising and supplying the barracks.[110] In the district of Chu authorities had erected barracks where more than six hundred people vegetated under abominable conditions. The ill and dying lay on the filthy floor amid their own excrement. No one supervised the distribution of food, and the weakest got none at all. The dead were not buried, they were simply covered with stones and snow. There was not one single latrine on the entire grounds. The buildings stood in a trough and were flooded by a nearby lake when the snow melted in the spring. Although various administrative authorities had pointed out the catastrophic conditions several times, nothing was done about it. It took intervention by superior authorities before at least the worst problems were temporarily corrected.[111]

High mortality rates at provision points and reception camps were not due solely to the problems of feeding the inmates and finding medicine for them. New arrivals were not simply isolated, they were also "filtered" in order to identify bais and other "enemies" among the refugees and eliminate them. This aspect was particularly important at every reception point that (at least theoretically) all Kazakhs returning from other Soviet Republics and elsewhere might pass through. If food was available at all, it was distributed in the most bureaucratic and clumsy procedure imaginable. In the district of Merke it went like this: "First, employees register new arrivals on a list of that day's returnees. The list is then presented to the Operative Troika for confirmation. Upon confirmation the list is handed over to the Authorized Representative to be rubber-stamped and then passed on to the department for handing out bread and other products. The list is then handed down to the provisions sector that commissions the baking of bread and its distribution the next day."[112] Under these conditions countless people starved to death at that reception camp.[113]

In many instances local authorities actively sought to rid themselves entirely of the starving people by simply deporting them to other places. The miserable people were chased from one place to another. In the city of Turkestan, where snatched up starving people vegetated under awful conditions in dilapidated houses at the outskirts of town, responsible authorities loaded more than eighty people into a wagon, gave each individual 800 grams (1 lb., 12 oz.) of bread and sent them off on a trip of several days to Aulie-Ata. When the train arrived there the deported people were in pitiful condition. Several had died on the way.[114]

In the spring of 1933 more and more famished refugees surrounded the canteen and workers' living quarters at a factory construction site in the district of Merke. The director, local party representatives, and worker representatives resorted to drastic measures. They parked a truck nearby and put two buckets of food scraps onto the loading space. When the hungry people rushed to the food, the rear door was latched and the truck drove to a far-off mountainous area where the people were abandoned. "We made several trips like this," says one report. "The OGPU organs do not know what happened to the people."[115] Wherever they could, the comrades fended off crowds of refugees as best they could.[116] From all regions of the republic officials submitted complaints to Alma-Ata about how passive and arrogant their colleagues were in handling the matter.[117]

From the perspective of many European officials at their important perches within the Communist organization, the famine was simply Kazakhstan's own problem.[118] And many European comrades were unable to muster empathy for the impoverished and ill refugees whose condition seemed to confirm all their prejudices about the Kazakhs as lazy and filthy people. Branding Kazakhs collectively with those terms permitted European comrades to pursue every kind of discrimination. Despite orders to the contrary, in sovkhozes and factories European directors excluded needy Kazakhs from provisions and left them to their fate. For many, the hungry were simply "locusts that ate up everything"[119] and endangered the already meager crop yields. Many comrades thus found it acceptable to distribute food and seeds not according to need, but among those who were thought to be more productive, namely, in general, the European peasants. Niccolò Pianciola has said that officials in ethnically mixed regions sought to control impositions such that they mostly affected the Kazakh part of the population.[120] In November 1933, for example, the party secretary of the district of Atbasarsk mentioned in a conversation with Kazakhstan's party boss Levon Mirzoian that there was no grain in the district. When asked by Mirzoian how many people would go without grain, the secretary replied simply, "The entire Kazakh part of the population." With winter approaching, that confession was a death sentence.[121]

At the local level many officials acted like little dictators and did what they wanted with the starving people. One such man was the sovkhoz director Druz from Karatal'sk. When Authorized Representative Bokhov inspected Druz's sovkhoz he said that "no English colonizer, not even a Spanish colonizer had with such nonchalance committed deeds of the nature committed against Kazakhs under the conditions of the dictatorship of the proletariat in the Kazakh Soviet Socialist Republic in a Soviet rice sovkhoz in the district of Karatal'sk."[122]

Several hundred famine refugees lived and worked at the sovkhoz. They were beaten, treated worse than the Russian workers in every way, were not permitted to move into vacant houses that had been erected for special European settlers, and received no pay for months, while the Russian workers got their wages. Druz ordered the bread rations to be cut by a third for all Kazakhs who were too weak to keep up with work expectations.[123] The director admitted that most of the brigadiers in his sovkhoz were former kulaks who vented their anti-Kazakh resentment there. Druz himself was known to hate nomads. In March 1932 he banned a group of Kazakhs to a remote salt lake on the sovkhoz's territory so that, as he put it, "the air here is not befouled by the horrible stench of these kolkhoz members." More than one hundred people died from drinking the brackish water, more than a thousand more fled. Among the 150 families that were settled on ground belonging to the sovkhoz in the following months, more than 180 people died.[124] Bokhov said: "Here we take these to be entirely normal phenomena."[125]

Druz and his men had no consequences to fear. As a member of the Alma-Ata oblast Party Committee he was almost sacrosanct.[126] It was clear to men like Druz that hungry refugees would not enable them to cultivate unused farmland and celebrate production acclaim. They wanted workers to perform. If that was not the case, they knew how to get rid of them. "Who told you to come here? You came of your own choice, so do what you want. I have no food for you," said one kolkhoz chairman from the district of Dzhambeitinsk to a group of enfeebled refugees asking him for help.[127]

It had become widespread practice to hire Kazakhs by the season only and fire them in the winter. Administrators of sovkhozes and construction sites did not feel responsible for the survival of workers. The consequences could be seen on the streets of Karaganda in the summer of 1933: during the months of July and August alone the militia counted more than eight hundred corpses on the roads, most of which were the remains of people who had worked at industrial construction sites in the area and had been fired for not fulfilling work expectations.[128] "He who does not work shall not eat" was the slogan of the early Soviet years and it applied to everyone, even refugees.

Ethnic tension in the steppe culminated during the years of famine. The bitter battle over scarce resources was fought for the most part between

European peasants and Kazakhs. Kolkhoz farmers who still managed to grow cereal crops in 1933 were constantly and existentially threatened by raids of their fields. Collective operations began organizing units for their own defense that would protect their harvests from hungry people. Violent struggles and shootings among scavengers and crop watchmen were the result. Often thirty or forty hungry people stormed crop acreage together.[129] The phenomenon took on such dimensions that in some regions the threat of significant harvest losses loomed. The authorities then not only permitted the implementation of kolkhoz militias, in the summer of 1933 they even organized mobile rapid deployment forces to keep hungry people off the fields.[130] Taking measures such as these did not put an end to the problem, but they do illustrate how the authorities and the nonstarving part of the population closed ranks to pursue their interests.

Some peasants took the law into their own hands and punished alleged "criminals."[131] In early August 1933, four horses were stolen from the pasture of peasants from the village of Kamishlovo. A while later Sannikov, deputy chairman of the village soviet, apprehended a Kazakh seen with one of the horses. The man said he had purchased the animal from a "well-known horse thief" who lived in a neighboring aul. Sannikov took four armed men and rode with them to the nearby aul. On the way they took every Kazakh they encountered into their custody, took their horses, and beat the individuals unconscious. Boikov, the chairman of the regional soviet, happened to come along and join them and he, too, took part in the violence. When they got to the aul where they expected to find the horse thief, the men found only a few of his relatives who could say nothing about the incident. The Russians yelled that Kazakhs were all dogs and thieves and one could not waste good words on them, and they beat two of the suspect's family members. They bonded one of them and took him back to their own village, torturing him along the way with feigned executions in an attempt to get answers from him.

A day later they let the battered man go. Rumors spread that the man had been clandestinely murdered.[132] The peasants had punished him as they saw fit. They had always believed that they had a right to self-administered justice; in their communities every effort to enforce the state's monopoly on violence had not changed that conviction. And the belief was reinforced when the representatives of that state themselves engaged in the violence. Although peasants did turn to state courts to settle other matters, when it came to animal theft they relied on their own methods and notions of justice.[133] Compared to complex court decisions, the criteria for arriving at judgments in rural self-administered justice were clear: Rustlers deserved death, especially if they were Kazakh.

In an urgent letter to Kazakhstan's party boss Levon Mizoian a few Kazakh Communists warned in the spring of 1933: "The current catastrophic condition of the Kazakh part of the population . . . confirms the [European] prejudice that the Kazakhs are by nature imperfect, wild, and crude. This fuels, evokes, and compounds chauvinism."[134] The comrades were not alone in making that observation. Even advocates of a more Russophile line, who had little sympathy with far-reaching plans to infiltrate the party and governmental apparatus with native Kazahks (indigenization), were appalled by conditions in Kazakhstan. Grigorii Aronshtam, the former first party secretary of Turkmenistan, for example, wrote in a letter to Stalin and Kaganovich, "One can say, without fear of exaggerating, that Great Power chauvinism rages in Kazakhstan. . . . There are a number of instances . . . of purely zoological hate for the Kazakhs."[135]

What Aronshtam, using correct party terminology, called "Great Power chauvinism," had fatal consequences for the Kazakhs affected by it. They were fired systematically, excluded from food rations, and driven away. Starving people who could not contribute to the already faltering economic development threatened to bring it to a halt. In many places Kazakh workers were seen simply as "waste." They were given minimal bread rations, if any at all.[136] "Declassed elements" were identified, chased off, and marginalized all over Kazakhstan. No orders had been given to do so and the process was not coordinated or controlled by one central office. And yet at all levels of the administration, from the local soviets to party committees for entire regions and Soviet republics, comrades followed the same pattern—they did everything imaginable to get rid of the famine refugees because they either could not or did not want to bear the cost of what it took to provide for them.

THE CADRE AND THE CRISIS

Officials at the lower and medium levels of the state and party apparatus played a key part in managing the famine crisis: they presided over the destiny of the people. The positions of comrades throughout the oblasts presented them with both opportunities and risks. If they did well, they could stabilize their own position of power and strengthen their own network. But making mistakes in dealing with the refugees was the risk. There were no practical rules for what to do with starving people and doing it poorly could mean one's own demise.[137]

The outline and rigid grid of Soviet population categories had no rubric, no class for famine refugees. They were often seen as mere surplus that burdened and depleted local budgets. As Kazakhs they were members of a "young nation" that had a right to be defended against European Great Power chauvinism. Based on their class membership, the majority of the poor and average-income peasants had a right to support. But as "declassified elements" straying in the cities they became the targets of "cleansing" operations. All these factors determined how comrades behaved toward the famine refugees: whether they helped them, tolerated them, or chased them away.

DYNAMICS OF FAMINE: DISTRIBUTION NETWORKS, VIOLENCE, EXCESS

No one in the state and party apparatus had illusions about whether his own position or that of his comrades was secure.[138] Targets and plans constantly contradicted one another such that meeting one meant disappointing the other. Paradoxically, the lack of clarity was a defining characteristic of a system that claimed to create clarity.[139] According to Stefan Merl, "From the first establishment of the command economy in the early 1930s, breaking with the norm had been a condition of satisfying the dictator's production commands at all."[140] That contradiction was the predetermined breaking point for every Soviet career. Illegal was whatever superior instances and people deemed illegal. Stalinism knew no permanent and authoritative criteria for what was right and what was wrong. The decisive factor was the opinion of whoever happened to be in charge at the time.[141]

Officials holding exposed posts could be swept one way or another by changes in personnel, the relocation of staff, or periodical house cleaning. Everyone filling lower positions was constantly breaking Soviet law and subject to sanctions at any time on purely formal grounds. At other times that very same behavior was seen as sign of Bolshevist resolve and brought praise and recognition. There was never any certainty. Bolshevist cadres acted and worked with this in mind and ultimately the uncertainty became a stabilizing factor of the system.[142]

The best way to escape the dilemma was to be tied into one of the networks described above whose mixture of personal loyalty, the granting of material advantages, and the reciprocal knowledge of incriminating details secured the workings of the Soviet system in the steppe and elsewhere.[143] Without such personal connections even the most rudimentary form of Soviet rule would not have worked.[144] Personal networks protected one from incessant inquiries and revisions issued by various Soviet control authorities. That could be important, for example, when causes were sought for failed campaigns. But they also guaranteed that what was structurally impossible, such as the fulfillment of contradictory plans, did not completely paralyze the organization.[145]

These alliances were necessarily fragile. The comrades involved thus tried to increase their security by bribing as many others as possible or making them confidants to illegal procedures. Violence, corruption, and organized theft were integrated components of practical Soviet power.[146] In kolkhozes and auls this Soviet way of "organizing authority" went hand in hand with the providence that local potentates exercised in the name of their clienteles, or, in other words, as a system of "socialist paternalism," as Lewis Siegelbaum has called it.[147]

Paternalistic networks of that kind organized the society of starvation. They were most often based on kin and membership in the same clan, but they could also be based on ethnic distinctions, local affiliations, or political loyalties. Wherever hunger began to threaten an oblast, networks established themselves for the provision and distribution of food and other resources.[148] To be included in one of those networks was almost an indispensable prerequisite for surviving the famine.[149] Those who starved were people who had either fallen out of survival networks or had never access to them in the first place. Networks were closed to outsiders and their members did everything in their power to deny outsiders access to the resources they controlled.[150]

Whether or not the locals could prevent strangers, that is, famine refugees, from invading their networks became a matter of life or death. The OGPU reported incidents from all over Kazakhstan where food had been held back, distributed among one's own people, or sold at the bazaar for exorbitant prices.[151] The result was always the same: by excluding the starving, the people who were part of the distribution networks were able to survive.

Comrades from a party cell in the Turgai oblast, for example, decided to give the inhabitants of their aul 600 grams (1 lb., 5 oz.) of food relief per day, while refugees from other auls were to get only 4 kilograms (8 lbs., 13 oz.) per month, in other words: 135 grams (4 oz.) of food per day.[152]

An emissary also from Turgai, an oblast that comrades in Alma-Ata already considered particularly backward, reported that there individual clans had monopolized the distribution of livestock and food. The mighty clans had placed their own activists and Communists in local administrations and thereby cut off weaker groups from the resources. Members of the latter were the first to die of malnutrition. As in so many other cases, once again it was Kazakhs who exploited the weaker position of other Kazakhs.[153]

The pattern repeated itself in other regions. In August 1932 seven kolkhoz peasants starved to death in an aul in the district of Urdinsk. They had begged their aul soviet for help several times but their requests were denied because they belonged to a minority clan within the aul. Two party members who controlled the distribution of supplies in the aul had decided to give the scarce resources only to members of their own clan.[154]

One OGPU report said that bais had been able to bring soviet institutions and kolkhozes under their control and thereby "gotten a strong economic weapon in their own hands . . . with which they could influence antagonistic and weaker clans." In addition, theft was a prevalent element of clan conflict and used as "an instrument to economically destroy competing clans."[155]

Leaders in Alma-Ata were eager to depict the collapse of the economy as having been caused by the damaging ways of locally operating groups that had allegedly acted against the interests of the state and its kolkhozes for years. One example was the May Day kolkhoz in the district of Akbulak. There a group of leading comrades had been acting as "counterrevolutionaries" and done everything they could to destroy livestock, let harvests go to ruin, and break equipment. But their worst offense was that they provided for themselves and their families. After their arrest the accused admitted openly that they had split up everything delivered from the district to the kolkhoz among themselves and not given anything to poor kolkhoz members who were dying of starvation. The group also admitted to having embezzled grain when it was weighed and manipulated documents. Their activity had not remained secret for long at the kolkhoz. They resorted to threatening other members of the kolkhoz to silence them. Nonetheless, in the end fourteen men were sentenced to death by the bullet in this affair. The rest were sentenced to long prison terms.[156]

Despite the prospect of draconic punishment, comrades continued to organize networks for the purpose of representing the interests of "the state" in a way that they deemed meaningful and useful. Officials who took matters into their own hands justified their actions with rhetoric of the class struggle and whatever terminology was currently popular with the party. Personal enemies were "counterrevolutionary elements" and "exploiters," vendettas were a fight against "gangs" and "rioters."

When the famine began, disputes between competing networks and clans grew worse because setbacks in heaving one's own clan members into crucial positions meant a loss of easy access to resources that were becoming scarce.[157] That could have grave consequences as a few officials in the Aralsk district learned in 1933 when their competitors inside the apparatus excluded them entirely from provision procedures and they were faced with death by starvation within a short time.[158]

The marginalization of whole groups was sometimes the result of conflicts that had already existed for a long time. In the district of Chubartavsk two large clans opposed one another: the Tulenget and the Kerei. The district's (nomadic) "center" was on territory roamed by the Tulenget clan and there they held all the essential administrative positions. In 1932 the Kerei were able to move the "center" to their own territory and then began filling more influential positions. Conditions got out of hand when some of the former leaders were arrested in connection with the murder of a local official. Intrigues flourished.[159] No one knows how the conflict ended and it is probably irrelevant for this study. The point is that local cadres were caught up in endless fights over power while the people around them were dying like flies. In Chubartavsk conditions were still catastrophic in September 1933, when famine in other regions was subsiding.[160]

If one wanted to win battles for power, one could not be squeamish in one's choice of means. In early 1933, Dzhangaziev, the newly appointed party secretary for the district of Mangistau, presented an impressive example of radical will to power. In the far west of Kazakhstan he had discovered perfect conditions to provide for his followers and patrons. Within just a few weeks he had installed one and a half dozen men from his clientage at crucial posts in the apparatus, although very few of them fulfilled even a minimum of the criteria generally required for becoming a Bolshevist functionary: His new chairman of the trade office had been banned from the party twice and his new inspector of finances had played an important part in the Alash Orda regime. Some had been penalized by the party for engaging in "group fights," others had rather dubious social backgrounds. In short, Dzhangaziev had gathered men around him who had little to lose and who saw the chaotic conditions of famine as a window to opportunity. They relieved former officials of their offices by accusing them of diverse misdeeds and ordering the organs of justice to sentence them accordingly.[161]

Dzhangaziev was a distrustful man who saw control as the best way to prevent conspiracy and betrayal. He forced all comrades in the district to participate in an incessant series of sessions of the district committee and its subcommittees. No one was permitted to miss a conference that could last up to ten days. Dzhangaziev kept the reins in his hands, but the oblast was left entirely to itself, said a report from the local OGPU branch investigating the affair.[162]

Another feature of the Stalinist exercise of power was the high degree of will to violence exhibited by Soviet officials.[163] Especially because representatives of the state—apparently in the name of and on orders from the state—were the perpetrators, we often find that incidents of violence during the crisis years were considered incidents of "state violence."[164] Trutz von Trotha has pointed out that "arbitrariness and violence in particular are by nature expansive. For governmental arbitrariness and violence that means that under conditions where no effective institutions and normative precautions exist to curb it, arbitrariness and violence pervade all of people's interactions with the governmental administration."[165] That sense of arbitrariness and violence left considerable leeway for Soviet officials, which leading comrades encouraged them to exploit. One could gain the esteem of Stalin and his followers by solving problems "the Bolshevist way."[166]

Thus, seen from the bottom up, it made sense for local networks to use threats and violence. In complex times, physical violence solved problems efficiently. Strikes and blows could destroy, readjust, reset, and cement social order and relations. It affected not only perpetrators and their victims, but third parties, too, for whom a message was intended.[167] Acts of violence bonded perpetrators. There was, however, a downside to using violence in local networks—in the long run, joint offenses, bribery, and other forms of personal gain did not promote trust among the culprits themselves.[168]

In the aul of Akir-Tiubinsk in the district of Aulie-Ata local soviet leaders set up a regiment of terror. "Brutal blows were the only thing the kolkhoz masses understood," says an OGPU report on the situation. Violence was directed not only toward prominent leaders of local society, but against the entire population of the aul, especially women. They cut off their hair, which was one of the worst humiliations for Kazakh women.[169] On a different occasion they forced women collecting wheat in the field to sit on thistles. "Soviet secretary Isakulov arranged the thistles such that they 'reached their destination.'"[170] The comrades employed such tactics to demonstrate their unquestioned superiority. Whenever victims had no way to defend themselves, a readiness for excessive cruelty grew. The women's frailty and helplessness incited the powerful to devise more perfidious methods.

Outgrowths of brutality such as occurred in Akir-Tiubinsk did not happen everywhere. In many places merely threatening the people was sufficient for securing their compliance. But that could only be done successfully when there was no doubt that deeds would follow words. That happened in the district of Iany-Kurgan where leading comrades cooperated with one another because it enabled them not only to control the grain supply for their oblast but also to divert resources for their own families and clientele. "Now we've got the chance, we must seize the moment. The district is in our hands," they said, as reported by the OGPU.[171]

True to that slogan, they installed their own followers at key posts in the auls and kolkhozes and instructed them to put pressure on kolkhoz members. When a representative from the oblast administration visited the district, the chairman of one kolkhoz was said to have openly threatened peasants: "Whoever imagines accusing us, no matter who you are, will not live long in the district of Iany-Kurgan. If you don't want to die, then watch your tongues." One peasant later testified that an influential kolkhoz director added: "District leaders are at our mercy, they get bread and meat from our kolkhoz and that's why it will be hard for them to accuse us."[172]

In the district of Karmakchi leaders of the Odraza kolkhoz secured support from officials in the district's capital by regularly supplying them with grain and meat while their own peasants ate "cats, dogs, and badgers" or went hungry. One desperate mother went so far as to wed her eleven-year-old daughter to the brother of a kolkhoz leader. After a few days of "using her as a woman" the much older groom threw the girl out of his house. It was also said that kolkhoz leaders took work animals and food from local stock for themselves.[173]

Reciprocally corrupt relations between district leaders and kolkhoz leaders that were advantageous for both sides and could only be dissolved by risking one's own demise ensured that the majority of the kolkhoz members were excluded from getting the bare necessities while friends and families of officials and kolkhoz leaders were supplied. Officials used threats, repression, and violence to buttress the local power relations that had emerged through such connections. Such patterns of internal group integration based on the exclusion of outsiders were not only important for the relationship between the leaders and the people suffering from shortages but also shaped relationships between the cadres struggling for power and influence in the steppe.

Others demonstrated publicly how little they cared for the tasks assigned to them while people consigned to their "care" starved. Aleksei Pogorepov, chairman of the district department of the OGPU in Talgar, was a heavy drinker and cultivated close relationships with anyone who could get him alcohol, especially doctors from the district hospital and the director of the local hard liquor factory. In June 1933 Pogorepov confirmed his reputation by skipping a meeting of the district executive committee and riding drunken in an open car through town together with the schnapps producer. They circled several times around the club building where the meeting was being held, which led to "unhealthy conversation among the participants at the plenum."[174]

Leaders from the district of Bostandyk took things even further. Abdulin, the party secretary, Babaev, chairman of the District Executive Committee, and Ileev, the state attorney spent the summer of 1933 in an endless series of drinking sprees with prostitutes and other "friends." The height of bacchanalia was reached one evening when the three men staggered around drunk. Ileev undressed and "scandalized" himself naked in the street, trying to rape the wife of another official. The incident was no secret. Neither were the frequent rides of the troika through the district guised as "checking up on the work," as they called it. In reality they exploited their power and let the kolkhozes pamper them.

And even those were not the only accusations brought against them. Babaev had been thrown out of the party in 1929 but then made a career for himself by using a fake party book issued for his brother. Illeev was said to undermine party policy by having kolkhoz peasants arrested at random and then letting them starve in prison without any formal charges or trials.[175] Such explicit demonstrations of arrogance and indifference were not rare. They were fueled by the awareness that many mid-level officials had of their power and their belief that they had secured their positions sufficiently. At the same time, they were dancing on a volcano. In many regions circumstances were so hopeless that comrades simply resigned and quit working and did whatever they could to divert their attention from dismal reality.

In the district of Zharminsk in eastern Kazakhstan some lower-level officials exploited their posts to embezzle hundredweights of food and to slaughter livestock for their own needs. The result was that at least eighteen people starved and a large part of the remaining population fled. Sometime later fourteen men were arrested, including the entire direction of the kolkhoz in the aul in question. The affair was turned over to the local militia inspector who was less interested in investigating the case than in seeking his own gain. After receiving fifty rubles each from two of the accused, he let them go and closed their cases. That did not end the affair, however. The "particular gravity" of the matter necessitated sending a commission to the aul to prepare a propaganda trial. On arrival, the four members of the commission set to work immediately: They drank with the accused men at an eight-day-long carousel that the accused had organized for them, which cost several hundred rubles. They slept with the wives of the accused several times, and raped at least two wives of kolkhoz peasants.[176] One of the women lost her child because of it. When the wife of the defendant Makenev refused to use her body to redeem her husband, all their property, which had already been confiscated, was sold on the spot. After several days all the accused were released and the commission moved on to the next auls where they "solved" similar cases in the same way.[177]

Excesses and assaults were on file because they happened in public and the protagonists were careless (or self-confident) enough to vex others, for example, by raping their wives. That crossed the line between tacitly tolerated debauchery and conduct worthy of sanctioning. Where the boundary lay between the two forms of behavior was a matter of interpretation in a society where practically everyone was forced to constantly violate rules and law and the only question of significance was who was judging and who was sentenced. The (alleged) core of the matter was almost irrelevant.[178] When officials were charged with corruption, personal gain, or uninhibited violent behavior, such accusations were often only an excuse to get rid of disagreeable comrades and competitors.

Famine hardship offered local despots an opportunity to play out their power fantasies. Under conditions of existential adversity, the population was at the mercy of the local officials. Refusing to follow the comrades' arbitrary commands meant risking one's freedom. This was true even for the representatives of the Soviet system in the steppe who were also constantly confronted with danger. They accused one another of belonging to anti-Soviet groups and of being corrupt. The accusations were not actually false, but everyone was guilty of it anyway. It was inconceivable to pursue a career in the party without constantly violating "socialist legality." It was therefore imperative for functionaries to develop highly branched networks that would protect them from detection and investigations.

Several consequences resulted from it. First, one had to avoid the slightest look of forming any kind of group. Second, it was absolutely necessary to secure networks vertically as well as one could. This was done by bribing influential officials or incorporating them. And finally, one promising strategy was to attack opponents and competitors by accusing them of forming objectionable groups themselves. One had to make it as difficult as possible for outsiders to identify or even gain access to one's networks. The specific conditions of Stalinism made that behavior logical. But it was just as logical to always expect one of the state or party's numerous instruments of control to intervene.

Networks in Kazakhstan came under serious pressure when in January 1933 Goloshchekin was removed from his post and Levon Mirzoian from Armenia was appointed the party boss for Kazakhstan. The change in office was accompanied by a mass cleanup campaign within the party organization because a common feature of such post replacements was that the new man in Alma-Ata brought a number of his own confidants along and placed them in key positions.[179] Mirzoian's inauguration introduced a massive exchange of cadres at the lower and intermediate levels. For him these purges were a fundamental prerequisite for exercising power efficiently; the former cadres were mostly Goloshchekin's men and thanked him for their careers. They served as scapegoats for the dramatic condition in which the oblast found itself.

The more pressure the Control Commission and the OGPU put on the officials in the region, the more important it became for them to prove in word and deed that they no longer followed the old league and were independent of its groups. An opportune moment for them to do so came at the plenum of the Kazakh Kraikom in June 1933, which became a session of reckoning with Goloshchekin and his followers.[180] Many were removed from office before and after that discussion.[181]

Throughout 1933 the OGPU apparatus in Kazakhstan and elsewhere devoted its attention to comrades that had abused their positions, wasted resources, or engaged in clientele networks.[182] Authorities became susceptible for stories of corruption and administrative violence. Chekists painted a devastating picture of the state and conduct of the Soviet apparatus in the oblasts. Party members indulged in alcohol and had lost self-confidence and perspective, wrote the newly appointed party secretary for the district of Kazalinsk in April 1933. There was not enough food to feed even the most important comrades, forcing party workers to commit "all kinds of crimes" to get food.[183] Following an inspection trip to the district of Karatal'sk one delegate from the Kraikom came to a pessimistic conclusion: "I am deeply convinced that we will never successfully solve a single problem in the aul on time if we uphold the current set of officials. . . . One must keep in mind that the current functionaries in the village have been ruined to the core by the former leaders and we have been unable to change that."[184]

ANSWERS AND NEW DEPENDENCIES

By the summer of 1932 vast parts of Kazakhstan's population were bound to lose their fight for survival. Agriculture was on the verge of collapse and livestock continued to decrease. Catastrophe looked inevitable. But no one wanted it to end that way. Even Stalin and his cohorts had no interest in completely wiping out the Kazakhs. Leaders believed that they could overcome the crisis as long as the production facilities were not entirely destroyed. The first step they took was therefore to regulate access to food even more carefully.[185] Their priority, however, was not to save lives but to preserve economic assets and enforce order and discipline. To that end they excluded some parts of the population from supplies while privileging others. They also wanted (more) control over the flow of refugees.

The Bolshevist elite interpreted the famine as manifesting the final struggle between peasants and/or nomads and the state, a struggle that would end as soon as the peasants and nomads surrendered and began to cooperate. The most prominent expression of that belief was Stalin's correspondence with the author Mikhail Sholokhov in the spring of 1933 in which Stalin claimed that the hungry peasants of the Northern Caucasus were fighting a war of attrition against the Soviet power, a "fight to the death."[186] Once the Bolsheviks had conquered the kulaks and bais, he believed, then sabotage, wastefulness, and the entire crisis would be a thing of the past.

Cynics in the politburo recognized the advantages created by the dramatic conditions: The famine gave them the opportunity to subordinate all Kazakhs once and for all. Chaos dealt them a good hand. If the impoverished Kazakhs were going to halt their own demise they had to give in to the Soviet State, its institutions, and above all, its various representatives in their land. The answer to the crisis was to agree to dependence. The end of the famine meant the Sovietization of the steppe.

RESOLUTIONS AND DECISIONS

If one wanted to date the end of the famine in Kazakhstan, one might say September 17, 1932.[187] On that day the politburo in Moscow passed its resolution, "On Kazakhstan's Agriculture and Livestock Breeding."[188] The resolution said that sedentarization had been successful and that meanwhile more than half of the entire arable land in Kazakhstan was under cultivation. The next step was to erect European-style villages but to use local materials in doing so. Further, when establishing new kolkhozes it was important not to mix clans in one and the same kolkhoz. It also mentioned that about forty thousand tons of food and seed had been set aside for the nomadic and semi-nomadic regions. In addition, the populace in those regions was now exempt from all grain and meat procurement demands and all taxes for a period of two years. The type of collective economy that had dominated the country up to that point, the *artel*, was to be abandoned in favor of the TOZ, or Cooperative for the Communal Cultivation of the Land.[189] Wherever regions could be considered "economically settled" each household was entitled to own two or three cows, ten to twenty sheep and their offspring, and the same number of pigs. Another passage of special significance regulated livestock breeding in nomadic regions. An exception was made for nomads: each Kazakh household was allowed to own one hundred sheep, eight to ten cows, three to five camels, and up to ten horses. The resolution thus marked the end of the old policy of collectivizing livestock entirely, whenever possible. Together with the new rule on the private ownership of livestock, the reduction in procurement demands and taxes enabled hundreds of thousands of people to avoid starvation. For a while the concessions contributed to livestock recovery.

But as meaningful as the politburo's resolution on Kazakhstan's agriculture and livestock breeding seemed, it was not an isolated document but part of a series of regulations elaborated in reaction to the kolkhozes' inability to provide the rest of the Union with sufficient food. The measures outlined by Stalin's leaders did not renounce the priority of providing for the cities, industry, and the army by exploiting the rural population. They did, however, take true circumstances in villages and kolkhozes more adequately into account. The focus lay on changing the dysfunctional procurement system. Instead of putting demands on the kolkhoz collectively, now each kolkhoz peasant had to turn in a specified share of certain goods such as meat, grain, and milk. Beginning in 1933, private arable land and herds became relevant economic factors. The intent was to increase "affluence" among kolkhoz peasants. The state promoted private food production and supported, to a certain degree, the purchase of livestock. Planners thought that if peasants could, for the most part, sustain themselves, then more of what the kolkhoz produced would end up on the market.[190] The land of the peasants and the animals of the nomads were meant to secure the survival of kolkhoz members for decades.[191]

In light of the indisputably alleviating nature of the changes that Stalinist leaders granted kolkhoz peasants at a time when famine still swept the land, historians have often debated whether or not the resolution implied a retraction of state policy based on an insight that the methods advocated in the past had led to a catastrophe.[192] Some authors saw only tactical concessions made by the Bolsheviks to the peasants, and no sign of their having learned any lesson. The latter interpretation is supported by the fact that the politburo simultaneously passed tough laws to protect "socialist property." The infamous so-called Law of Spikelets, issued in August 1932 and applied with unyielding severity, prescribed draconian prosecution for the theft of even minute amounts of grain (with sentences ranging from a minimum of ten years in prison to the death penalty).[193] All these measures put more pressure on individual households that were now made responsible for the survival of livestock, a responsibility that had once been transferred to the collective. The comrades thought, and they were to be proved right, that transferring this responsibility back to private households would lead to quicker livestock recovery. In early 1933 they also established so-called polit-departments at all machine and tractor stations (MTS) for the purpose of controlling the kolkhozes and sanctioning misconduct. These departments were independent of local networks and party structures in the region and answered directly to the Central Committee as an extension of it.[194]

New plans demanded new faces. Signs emerged quickly that Goloshchekin, who was associated like no other with the machinations and disastrous consequences of sedentarization, would have to go. Even his most loyal allies began carefully disengaging themselves from him. The first to distance himself was Isaev, who in 1932 dared to write a letter to Stalin criticizing the almighty Filipp as being essentially responsible for the fiasco: "Personally, I believe that Comrade Goloshchekin, who has done enormous work in Kazakhstan . . . will not have the strength necessary for a decisive change of course."[195] The "pharaoh of the steppe" was unmoved. In December 1932 he once again defended the hard line in a speech to delegates at a party meeting.[196] But soon thereafter he had to leave his post. In late January 1933, he was replaced by Levon Mirzoian from Armenia.[197] Goloshchekin's ejection from office was accompanied by a loud propaganda campaign against him and the "old leaders." Between January and June 1933, newspapers and magazines printed numerous accounts of the economic catastrophe, making more than passing mention of its dimensions and (in agreement with new party policy) accusing Comrade Goloshchekin of being responsible for it.[198] The party's first secretary, said Isaev, had no idea what was happening in the country because he had never once visited an aul to inform himself.[199] Goloshchekin complained about the disparagement and tried to justify himself.[200] After his arrest in 1939 he was still decried for the part he played in "building socialism" in Kazakhstan. But even then he failed to see that his successors needed a scapegoat to legitimize their new policies, and he continued to make "bais and bourgeois nationalists" responsible for the problems.[201]

When Mirzoian arrived in Kazakhstan he found a gigantic task awaiting him. The plummeting economy was in need of stability, the refugee problem in need of a solution, and food shortages in need of an end. Before embarking on the journey he had known, as he later wrote to Stalin's confidant Lazar Kaganovich after arriving in Alma-Ata in February 1933, "that conditions in Kazakhstan were complicated," but once he got there, he realized that conditions "surpassed his [worst] expectations."[202] As the newly appointed head of the party he immediately requested more investment in communications infrastructure to improve communication with the republic's most remote regions, and he called for better personnel.[203] Then he focused on four projects.

First, he took the budget scheduled for the sedentarization of nomads and used it to provide for famine refugees. The policy of ignoring the refugees was no longer tenable and uncontrolled deportations by provincial potentates had to be replaced by a general party policy on demographics. He also stopped settling "nomads in the former sense of the word," as he wrote to Stalin in the summer of 1933, because "today Kazakhstan has no nomads or seminomads who are not on the run. In reality, the entire nomadic and seminomadic populace consists of refugees" and the state "is responsible" for them all.[204]

Second, starving people were no longer to be provided for in the cities and at train stations—they were to be cared for in their kolkhozes, villages, and auls. Third, many famine refugees would be denied return to their original home regions and would instead be sent to areas in need of laborers. And fourth, the comrades began rigorously redistributing livestock from the kolkhozes.

After one year, Mirzoian reported that his plan had been implemented. In early 1934, at the so-called Party Congress of the Victorious, namely, the Seventeenth Party Congress of the Communist All-Union Party of the Bolsheviks, he told the plenum: "While we saw enormous rates of emigration from Kazakhstan until late 1932, we have not only halted that migration in 1933, we have also achieved the return of a large number of households."[205]

In fact the new head of the party in Kazakhstan could at that time take pride in having "halted" famine and mass flight and to this day the Kazakhs venerate him for it.[206] But Mirzoian was not the compassionate philanthropist that many of his admirers still see in him today; he was a scheming Stalinist official who knew that relief for the starving was not an end in itself.

Nothing had greater priority than getting livestock to the people. For that purpose the Bolsheviks began buying large quantities of animals from Xinjiang. The livestock were intended to enable the subsistence of kolkhozes and individual households as well.[207] In reality, deliveries were heavily reduced and entirely abandoned for a number of regions; livestock breeding was ended in kolkhozes, and what remained was distributed among the peasants and nomads as regulated by the resolution of September 1932. If possible, all households were to get their fair share of the animals and only bais and other "enemies" were to get nothing. But even these measures could not alter the fact that there were not enough animals for everyone.

At the end of 1933, authorities estimated that 125,000 Kazakh households still owned not one single animal. And matters were even worse concerning the lack of cows (*beskorovnost'*): Of the 670,000 households in Kazakhstan, 410,000 had no cow of their own. Statisticians warned that the number would rise with the number of Kazakhs returning from other Soviet Republics. The estimate for the end of 1934 stated that approximately 170,000 households would possess no livestock, even though more than 100,000 animals had been purchased in China, sovkhoz livestock had been noticeably attenuated, and animal-breeding cooperatives had been dismantled for nomadic and seminomadic regions.[208]

In light of the shortage of livestock, individual hardship was not the factor that determined who got animals. The pivotal question was whether a given household had fodder and could bring the animals through the winter. Where there was doubt, a family was passed over, which meant that famine refugees had little chance. Most of them had already lost everything and even those who had found work in a kolkhoz rarely had any reserves. Famine refugees went away empty-handed; once again they were at the greatest disadvantage.[209]

Personal connections were also important when it came to redistributing the livestock left over after kolkhoz farm shutdowns. The peasants to receive animals were those who had good relations with the comrades in charge and with influential kolkhoz directors. Some officials went by the rule that whoever had collectivized more, got more in return: they returned the livestock to the bais from whom it had once been confiscated.[210] In other places European cadres favored Russian peasants.[211]

Some people thought the reason they were given animals was because "bais, mullahs, their aids, and activists" were looking after their interests and because "food was [now] being handed out as compensation for [past] excesses," as one report states with indignation.[212] And as had been the case during debaiization in 1928, now many officials used the opportunity to get the best animals for themselves.[213] Many comrades claimed to have made mistakes in the past when kulaks, bais, and false activists had been given livestock "under the banner of otkocheveniki." Party leaders had no doubt as to what had been the true nature of the affairs. In November 1933 Mirzoian attacked Senshibaev, the party secretary for the district of Enbekshil'dersk, before an assembly of party leaders from nomadic and seminomadic regions:

MIRZOIAN: Did district activists get animals?

SENSHIBAEV: No, aul activists got some, but district activists did not.

MIRZOIAN: It looks as though in your district even employees from the land administration office were given ten sheep.

SENSHIBAEV: We are currently trying to put that livestock into more reliable hands. We gave the animals to people who have hay to feed them.[214]

The majority of the cadres from the oblasts apparently shared Senshibaev's standpoint. They all knew that under conditions in the aul it was unrealistic to give animals to families without means and to simultaneously neglect half-loyal foot troops of the Soviet apparatus. One comrade from the district of Aiaguz said: "Aul activists who are really honest comrades, irrespective of whether they are party cell secretaries or executive committee chairmen, have in any case the right to livestock for their own use. Why should they not?" Isaev interjected: "In other words, you are saying that we must give animals to the aul activists." "Yes," was the reply, "I think that honest activists should get livestock for their own purposes, and *it can be seen as a certain tactic.*"[215] This obviously reflected a struggle between local leaders and local comrades. Loyalty and allegiance, and reciprocal swap relationships among locals were more important than orders issued by some far-off regime. And because Soviet hierarchies worked according to that principle at all levels, with the exception of sporadic interventions, little changed.[216]

Herds continued to shrink. Undaunted by draconian penalties for killing animals, many Kazakhs slaughtered the sheep and goats just given to them. Sometimes the Kazakhs were even encouraged to slaughter livestock by officials who apprehended the advent of other circumstances: "You have been given the animals for the winter only, to feed them, for in the spring they will be taken away again."[217] In the Turgai region one official told kolkhoz peasants that the Central Committee had decided to completely dissolve kolkhozes in their region and the people could do whatever they wanted with the reprivatized livestock. The Kazakhs were skeptical and asked whether a kolkhoz peasant would be allowed to slaughter the animals he got. The answer was yes, "Since the livestock was handed over for personal use, it means that it can be slaughtered. You must not die of starvation."[218]

But it was not the misinterpretation of orders that was responsible for the continued loss of livestock. The greatest losses were caused by numerous epizootics and the grave shortage of fodder and hay during the winter months. People were eating anything they could find and little was left for animals. Thousands of animals starved and froze to death in the sovkhozes. Yet the Bolsheviks insisted that wastefulness and "unprincipled butchering" were responsible for the loss. The "two-legged wolves," they said, presented the greatest threat to the recovery of stock.[219]

As Isaev told Stalin in June 1934, party leaders gradually realized that "awareness among Kazakh cattle drovers" was a crucial factor in sustaining herds. The Kazakhs, he conceded, "had never quite understood the meaning of collectivization" anyway.[220]

After shutting down kolkhoz operations the redistribution of their livestock salvaged what was left of the once huge herds of Kazakhstan. And in the regions gripped tightest by famine, where food supply had been throttled for years, handing out animals secured the survival of countless people who then had some sort of, albeit modest, means of sustenance. But concessions came not without strings attached. Faced with considerable consequences and penalties if they failed to do so, it was the nomads and peasants' responsibility to keep the animals alive.

REPATRIATING FAMINE REFUGEES

The mass flight of the Kazakhs strained Kazakhstan's relations with neighboring Soviet republics. People everywhere struggled with the outcome of the collectivization campaign and suffered from grave deficiencies and hunger. Under already precarious conditions, the inflow of refugees to neighboring republics was an immense burden for them. Beginning in 1930 bitter disputes arose between the leaders of regions that shared borders with Kazakhstan—who wanted to be rid of the uninvited guests—and officials in Alma-Ata, who wanted to prevent or at least retard repatriation.[221]

Robert Eikhe, the party's first secretary for the region of Western Siberia, and the men around him saw the only solution to the problem in sending refugees back to where they came from. But unless the situation in Kazakhstan improved, few Kazakhs would return voluntarily. When the first refugees starting showing up in cities and at railway stations in Western Siberia in 1930, authorities tried to arrange convoys to take the people back to Kazakh territory in the company of armed units. Many people died during the procedure because, as Kazakh authorities lamented, no one had given the returning migrants provisions for their journey of several days. Thousands of people were stranded in the cities and stations near the border. The city of Pavlodar in northern Kazakhstan became one huge refugee camp.[222] But in light of the growing numbers of refugees fleeing to Soviet republics at Kazakhstan's borders, forced repatriation was negligible. The problem required overall fundamental regulation.[223]

Yet the worse things got in Kazakhstan and the more famine scourged the land, the more vehemently Goloshchekin and Isaev tried to prevent refugees from returning to their places of origin. In debates with Siberian and Central Asian comrades they first claimed that the people leaving Kazakhstan were labor migrants. If bais and other undesirable elements had mingled with the "enthusiasts," it was up to each republic to act accordingly, argued Goloshchekin, and give the rest of the migrants full support.[224]

Eikhe was furious at the effrontery. In a remarkable letter of March 1932 the head of the party in Western Siberia tore up Goloshchekin's arguments, accusing his Kazakh comrade of violating mutual agreements made "in Moscow" and of pursuing the wrong strategy in claiming that the *otkochevniki* were not famine refugees. Obviously, said Eikhe, Goloshchekin was ill-informed. It was not new, he continued, that

> bais and kulaks had mingled with Kazakhs and spread counterrevolutionary propaganda. The question was why bai-kulak counterrevolutionary agitation had been so successful that year that they were able to seize thousands of poor and middle-income households. [And furthermore,] organizing relief for those households is only possible in your own oblasts and on your side [of the border]. . . . You are entirely right that kulaks and bais must be detected, but that can only happen in Kazakhstan at the points to which we return the Kazakhs. After examining them it is up to you to send kulaks and bais to special settlements. . . . We cannot organize that kind of investigation.[225]

Faced with Eikhe's refusal to accommodate and filter the fleeing, Kazakhstan's officials searched for some other way to delay any organized flow back of the refugees. The solution was to request that colleagues in Western Siberia first announce how many Kazakhs they planned to return and from which regions those people originated. This, said the authorities, would improve the coordination of their reception. Now it was Leonid Zakovskii's turn to write an angry letter. The OGPU's representative for Western Siberia wrote: "You want to make our oblast a testing grounds for separating your people by district and status. You want us to write up statistics, gather and provide for your people, and then send them back, but only upon your request. I do not agree to it!"[226]

Faced with mounting pressure, Kazakh officials had no choice but to send squads to neighboring republics and enforce the return of emigrants. Kazakh refugees were frightened of these men who hunted them down and drove them out of Western Siberia.[227] When rumors of their approach spread, refugees took down their tents and left the area immediately. One report to Eikhe from the state attorney for the region of Western Siberia says: "When one thinks of the extreme distress in which Kazakhs live here with us, one can easily imagine that things in Kazakhstan are much worse."[228] In fact, many Kazakhs who did return, whether voluntarily or not, found things in Kazakhstan so disastrous that they saw no alternative but to flee anew.[229]

The winter of 1932–33 made things worse everywhere. All across the Soviet Union hungry peasants left their villages for a chance at survival elsewhere. The situation was particularly dramatic in Ukraine, in the Middle Volga, and in the Northern Caucasus.[230] The mass migration of sick and hungry people willing to do anything was a challenge not only to the safety of the interior, it also brought the catastrophe to towns, cities, and regions that had been spared the problem up to that point. Isolated initiatives could not solve the problem.

In early 1933 the Bolsheviks got down to business. On January 22 Stalin and Molotov signed orders designed to deter "Ukrainian and North Caucasian peasants from migrating en masse to the cities. . . . Counterrevolutionary elements are to be arrested and the remainder of the refugees returned to their former places of residence."[231] Although the paper referred to the situation in Ukraine and the Northern Caucasus, it was clear that the underlying plan to define famine regions and deport the starving to them had now become the rule. Closely connected to this resolution were operations for "cleansing" Soviet cities of "declassified elements" and "drifters," most of whom were deported to Siberia.[232] "Hooligans" at railway stations were to be handled by armed officers.[233] It would have been impossible to set up barriers around famine areas in Kazakhstan in the manner done in Ukraine: there were limits to what the Soviets could do in the steppe. But nonetheless, the OGPU troops stopped refugees wherever they could and sent them back to their original districts.[234]

With respect to the refugee issue, Mirzoian had to prove himself more conciliatory than his predecessor Goloshchekin and could no longer refuse to take back the *otkochevniki*.[235] But unlike the comrades in Ukraine, the new leaders in Alma-Ata could trust that their demands would be heard in Moscow for the entire economy of the Kazakh Republic was at stake and threatening to collapse.

Turar Ryskulov became a pivotal figure in these disputes. Due to his position as deputy minister president of the Russian Soviet Federative Socialist Republic (RSFSR) and his excellent network inside the Kazakh party apparatus, he was presumably the one man in Moscow most knowledgeable of Kazakhstan's predicament. Ryskulov had been the one time and again to put on the agenda the *otkochevniki* issue and the conditions in Kazakhstan's regions gripped by famine, and his opinion of the matter was heard. He had warned very early on that the refugee catastrophe might destabilize the entire region. Between September 1932 and March 1933 he wrote several detailed reports in repeated attempts to make Stalin and other top officials of the state and party more aware of the famine in Kazakhstan.[236] His texts count as among the most well-known sources on the catastrophe. Kazakh historiography has often seen them as evidence of Ryskulov's deep bond with the Kazahks.[237] Stalin read Ryskulov's reports with apparent interest.[238]

Ryskulov was assigned the task of finding a solution for the refugee problem. For Kazakh comrades this was a double-edged affair: they were in dire need of relief, but they were also frightened of being held accountable for the unprecedented destruction of Kazakhstan's material resources. Goloshchekin would not be the only one sacrificed as a result of the crisis.[239]

In February 1933, as the famine catastrophe reached its peak, Ryskulov chaired a newly formed commission. At first its members attacked those they believed had cause the malaise and listed their shortcomings: Kazakh comrades were uncooperative and responded to inquiries with vacuous telegrams, said a delegate from the Middle Volga region.[240] Delegates from Kirghizia had complaints, too: In the spring of 1932 Kirghiz authorities had generously provided sustenance for the refugees, while the Kazakhs merely roamed the land, registered the refugees, and robbed them of their last money by exchanging it for worthless "certificates."[241] The comrades also noted the Kazakh authorities' ignorance of valid agreements and their lack of interest in the chaos around them: "In one case we . . . collected five hundred children and took them to the district of Alma-Ata at the Kazakh government's request. For three days the party's district committee and executive committee refused to take these children in. Finally they decided to accommodate them but by then some of them had already died because they had been forced to stay at the railway station."[242]

The members of the Ryskulov Commission then proceeded to report in detail on the success of their previous undertakings. They confessed to having made some mistakes and asked for additional funds because their "local budgets" were exhausted. But they also insisted that Kazakhstan begin repatriating its refugees as soon as possible, preferably before it came time to sow crops again.[243] Kazakhstan's representative did his best to ward off the inevitable: He agreed that conditions were dreadful and that mistakes had been made. But, he said, if Kazakh officials had made mistakes in other republics, it was not the fault of leadership in Alma-Ata, it was the personal fault of the men who had overstepped their competences. Kazakhstan, he said, saw itself in no position to repatriate all the *otkochevniki* and provide for them adequately.[244]

The consultations closed with a compromise. Everyone understood that Kazakhstan could not possibly deal with the refugee problem alone, if for no other reason than that it was impossible to rope in the entire steppe and, while one could try to prevent nomads from emigrating, it would never be fully achieved. The "Ukrainian solution" would thus not work for Kazakhstan. The neighboring republics would have to pitch in and absorb at least part of the refugees. The final agreement was that those neighbor republics would keep the refugees who were already on their territory and Kazakhstan would try to prevent any additional migration.[245]

Time would soon tell that the plan was to fail. Neighboring republics neglected their part of the agreement and Kazakhstan was unable to shut its borders. But the resolution had been passed, which meant that each republic could take recourse to it for its own purposes. Ryskulov frequently reminded his counterparts about the obligations accepted at the meeting in Moscow.

While the Ryskulov Commission negotiated in Moscow, the comrades in Alma-Ata were not idle. They declared the end of the flow of refugees to neighboring Kirghizia, ordered all authorities to cease processing refugees, and prohibited sending refugees back to Kazakhstan on the Turksib (the Turkestan–Siberia Railway). The Kirghiz were outraged at this "irresponsible decision" made by the Kazakh Council of People's Commissars. It freed Kazakhstan of all responsibility for refugees who had managed to get beyond Kazakhstan's own borders.[246]

Kazakh comrades then began haggling with Uzbek leaders over which of the refugees in Uzbekistan would be allowed to return to Kazakhstan and which would not. Each side wanted control of the auls that owned livestock, especially work animals, and wanted the other republic to take care of the impoverished Kazakhs. In late February 1933 they finally agreed that Kazakh authorities would take no administrative measures to encourage people to return. All movements were to be voluntary and all conflicts—for example, regarding the households' unfulfilled duties in Uzbekistan—were to be decided consensually.[247]

Comrades in the Bashkir ASSR had made a mistake in early 1932 by unilaterally deporting all Kazakhs from the area. Firm intervention from Moscow reproved the Bolsheviks in Ufa for that decision and compelled them to repeal it.[248] The Bashkirs took that as grounds for demanding an enormous budget of five million rubles for the purpose of erecting about 2,700 homes for Kazakhs who stayed on their territory. Debate over it continued for almost a year until finally the Council of People's Commissars of the RSFSR approved 10 percent of the money requested.[249] That money went unused, however, and authorities continued to deport Kazakhs.

Ryskulov was angry: Bashkir comrades had neither ended deportation nor begun settlement, despite repeated calls to do so. If they did not soon take the necessary steps, he would have to report it to the Executive Committee's Central Control Commission.[250] Bashkir leaders then admitted to mistakes but blamed them on recalcitrant local authorities who had not recognized the "political significance" of working with famine refugees. And, complained Bashkir comrades, it was not easy to work strategically with people who wandered constantly "from one place to another."[251]

Having any way to regulate the flow of refugees put some regions at an advantage. Influential regional leaders like Eikhe in Western Siberia could dictate conditions to their Kazakh comrades and use *otkochevniki* as leverage for the pursuit of their own interests. Weak republics like Bashkiria were at a disadvantage. Refugees became a tool for deciding the outcome of struggles among provincial leaders over resources and influence in Moscow.[252] When shortages ruled everywhere, stressing the precarious situation of the refugees was one way to get procurement rates reduced or extra grain deliveries granted. And comrades tried to raise esteem for themselves by accusing others of neglecting the *otkochevniki*. Under Stalinism it was customary for officials not to wrangle directly, but to live out their rivalry in a roundabout manner through their connections, in other words, by involving Moscow.[253] No telegram and no resolution was too insignificant not to be sent in copy to Moscow. One of the steady behavioral patterns of officials in charge was to inform Moscow of one's own deeds and of the errors made by others.[254]

Leaders in Alma-Ata were in an unpropitious position. They needed cooperation from neighboring regions to minimize the number of returning refugees. But their stalling tactics and adamant refusal to repatriate greater numbers of refugees annoyed comrades in other republics. Dissatisfaction on all sides fueled a struggle over power and influence among the leaders of separate republics. And the struggle was contended at the expense of the very people for whose interests the leaders allegedly fought.

In mid-March 1933 the Sovnarkom of the RSFSR decided that a total of 1,005 tons of grain would be set aside as relief for refugees in Western Siberia, the Middle Volga region, and Kirghizia.[255] But leaders of a union republic could not authorize shipments of that order on their own and the resolution required the approval of the Council of People's Commissars of the USSR.[256] In addition, all Kazakhs still found in those three regions were to be settled permanently there. There was mention of more than 20,000 Kazakhs who would find work in factories and sovkhozes. But not a word was wasted on the discrepancy between that low figure and the conspicuously much higher real number of refugees.[257]

In terms of decisions and plans, the resolution of March 1933 at least marked a certain turn of events because it meant that Kazakh leaders had finally met one of their goals—for the time being, none of the other European regions in the Soviet Union would send refugees back to Kazakhstan. It did not hold, however, for the republics of Central Asia. Most of the Kazakhs stranded there were sent back.

But resolutions are one thing and implementation is another. Delays in grain supply postponed the employment of Kazakhs.[258] And many district and regional administrators of Western Siberia simply ignored the resolution and continued deportation.

In May 1933 Isaev made one last attempt to prevent or at least postpone a mass flow of returning migrants. With a dramatic telegram to Molotov he sought revision of the resolution. His arguments sounded familiar: Kazakhstan lacked resources for any accommodation of the ever-mounting stream of repatriates because thousands of other refugees were still wandering about within the country's own borders. Neighboring regions, especially in Central Asia, must therefore be persuaded to keep and settle those who had gone there.[259] In reply, three weeks later someone from Molotov's staff wired Isaev that Moscow would not again discuss the sedentarization of refugees outside of Kazakhstan's borders.[260]

Comrades in Alma-Ata now had no other choice but to accept returning refugees. They knew that the death rates would rise in the winter. There simply was not enough food for everyone. Party leaders discussed the matter openly and Mirzoian himself informed Stalin of the dilemma.[261] The Kazakhs surrendered to the inevitable. They sent a number of representatives to neighboring Central Asian republics and began organizing the return of refugees. Local administrators helped them track down refugees in Kirghizia, Uzbekistan, and Karakalpak. As representatives from the old home country they made big promises to the impoverished Kazakhs, telling them of the resolution of September 17, 1932 and promising livestock and seed as well as exemption from all taxes for the next three years. It was welcome news. Lured by the prospects, many people in the neighboring republics, and also people in Xinjiang, began planning their return.[262] Later Soviet literature would call this phase "the completion of the planned transition to sedentariness for nomads."[263]

In preparation for hauling them off, returnees were sent to railway stations near larger towns. In April 1933 about eight hundred Kazakhs gathered at the Pishpek station near the Kirghiz capital Frunze. They said a representative had instructed them to wait there for their journey home. But no one had made provisions for them and many died. Officials registered as many as eleven deaths a day. The Kirghiz government refused to take responsibility and denied the people any relief. Not until the OGPU had intervened several times and heard their many excuses were the Kirghiz authorities ready to give food to the hungry.[264]

The Kirghiz's reluctance to help may be explained by the fact that at the time Frunze was literally surrounded by Kazakh yurts. Even in the city, yurts filled "every vacant space"—over a thousand tents in all. Iusup

Abdrakhmanov, chairman of the Kirghiz Sovnarkom had noted in his diary as early as February 1932: "Near Frunze a second city mushroomed, a city of yurts belonging to Kazakh citizens who moved there out of hunger and their dependence on alms. It is the result of Filipp's [Goloshchekin's] work."[265]

Faced with the dire conditions, Abdrakhmanov stopped reacting to Rys-kulov's impatient telegrams inquiring into the state of things at Kirghiz distribution centers and how the return of the famine refugees was coming along.[266] The young top official came to his own conclusions. Supported by other leading comrades, Abdrakhmanov refused to fulfill grain delivery targets for 1932 for fear of overstraining his own people. He understood the risk: "I would rather have them oust us for not fulfilling the plan than for letting our Republic become what has become of Kazakhstan."[267] In May 1933 Abdrakhmanov was removed from his post.[268]

Organizations that did fulfill their obligation to send grain and other food to the collection points for refugees in other Soviet republics often sent inferior goods for which they had no other use. When the Kazakh Central Administration for Grain Procurement, for example, received orders to send several wagonloads of grain to Kirghizia to provide for refugees, the cereal was mixed with sand. The bread made with it was inedible, but nonetheless handed out to Kazakh refugees. One official reported: "When food distribution began at the station the locals laughed: 'Is that bread? Look how Kazakhstan feeds you! Today half of your food is sand. And when you return you'll only get stones!'"[269]

Kazakhs stranded in Karakalpakstan suffered miserably. In the spring and summer of 1933 more and more people gathered at the collection point on the southern shore of the Aral Sea. Most of them owned nothing but the rags on their bodies and many were weak from long foot marches through barren terrain. There in the isolated region that was considered very backward even by Central Asian standards, authorities were wholly unable to cope with the constant stream of hungry people. They had neither the provisions nor the logistic means to feed tens of thousands of people. There was no food, housing, or medical service. Diseases spread quickly and killed many. And scores died of starvation.[270] In September 1933 the desperate people waiting for return to Kazakhstan saw no other way to draw attention to their precarious situation than to lay the corpse of a starved man in front of the Waterways Administration Building.[271]

Some months later, in May 1934, conditions again worsened dramatically.

Authorities in Uzbekistan and Turkmenistan had stopped relief for refugees in an effort to force them to return to Kazakhstan. According to OGPU estimates, now more than ten thousand Kazakh households, that is, at least forty-five thousand people, were stranded in Karakalpakstan. And there were thousands of orphans. Local authorities could provide a minimum of food for—at most—only half of these people, in part because leading comrades had embezzled funds. The number of deaths rose and peasants from local kolkhozes feared for their harvests because the starving took everything that looked edible.[272]

Communists in Karakalpakstan said they could permanently settle a maximum of three thousand households; the other seven thousand would have to leave as soon as possible. Lengthy negotiations ensued in which the People's Commissariat of Inland Waterway Transportation calculated that it would take five months to ship the people from seven thousand households across the Aral Sea to Kazakhstan, on the condition that their passage be paid and provisions be made for the passengers.[273]

And once again Kazakhstan's officials tried to prevent the return of the refugees. Isaev thought that the Karakalpaks were taking this opportunity to rid themselves of Kazakhs who had resided there for years. And he demanded that funds be noticeably increased.[274] But his efforts failed.[275] It is unclear whether there was any substance to his claim that among those to be deported were families who had lived there for years. The complaint does not seem to have been entirely contrived because the deportation of refugees did enable the administrators of neighboring republics and regions to rid themselves of unwelcome groups. The desire to deport them was particularly strong wherever Kazakhs could not be grouped together to form "national kolkhozes" or autonomous administrative districts because they had been "settled into" existing villages.[276]

It was no coincidence that famine refugees were treated and deported in the same way and manner that hundreds of thousands of so-called special settlers had been treated and deported to Kazakhstan and Siberia in the early 1930s.[277] In both cases it was the purpose of local officials as well as leading comrades in the capitals to purge entire regions of "socially alien elements," "kulaks," impoverished vagabonds, and people belonging to other ethnic groups. What happened to these people when they reached their destination was of lesser importance. From the standpoint of those in charge of deportation, the problem was solved when the people were gone. From the perspective of the regions absorbing the refugees, and for the refugees themselves, arrival at their destination meant a whole new set of challenges.[278]

Mirzoian meant precisely those challenges when he spoke of migrants returning from Karakalpakstan at a meeting of the Central Committee in June 1934: "And now the *otkochevniki* are coming back and need to be fed and accommodated and even if we demand that they deliver their share [of what it takes to fulfill the procurement plan], we will not get meat."[279] The conversation that followed revealed how little leaders in Moscow understood what was happening in Central Asia and how little they cared. Kazakh refugees meant nothing to them. The people's commissar for defense, Kliment Voroshilov, replied to Mirzoian's remark on the problems involved with absorbing returning migrants: "Then take fewer of them back."

MIRZOIAN: But the resolution of the Sovnarkom of the RSFSR from some commission or another of the Council for Work and Defense instructs us to take back 7,000 from Karakalpakstan. Our neighbors welcomed the Kazakhs when they came with their livestock, now they're returning them to us in droves.

KALININ: They belong to you.

MIRZOIAN: They do, that is right, but we must take back fewer of them.

STALIN: You were the ones who wanted those orders.

MIRZOIAN: No, Comrade Stalin, on the contrary. We are the ones at odds with the Central Asians over this issue.

STALIN: Well, why did you not complain, if the decision was wrong?

MIRZOIAN: We received the resolution [just] before departing [for Moscow] and we intend to submit a complaint. It also mentions [taking back] 7,000 from Turkmenistan.

GRIADINSKII: You can get more back from Siberia, too.[280]

By the time Vladimir Shubrikov, the party secretary from the Middle Volga region, followed Mirzoian in addressing the party leaders, the latter were bored by the issue. When Shubrikov explained that due to food shortages last year part of the people had migrated to other regions of the Soviet Union and were now returning, Stalin interrupted him: "*Otkochevniki*? You really have *otkochevniki*?" The minutes recorded at this point: Laughter. All Shubrikov could do was to reply, "No, we don't," and then discuss other issues.[281]

As of the mid-1930s the wave of people returning to Kazakhstan included tens of thousands of people who had escaped the famine by fleeing to Xinjiang, but who now saw no future for themselves there because of the civil war.[282] The OGPU worried about that trend, fearing that spies and bais might mingle with the returning migrants. Border officials therefore were given clear instructions "not to stimulate" immigration and to exhaust all options that "would permit the refugees to return to China." But between October and December 1934 alone more than ten thousand people, mostly Dungans and Kazakhs, crossed the Sino-Kazakh border. Chekists claimed that the presence of returning migrants threatened to incite "excesses" in regions along the border and thus deported them to interior regions. Reluctance to comply meant a refusal to enter the Soviet Union. The re-immigrants were organized in villages modeled after the "special settlements" and subjected to the same restrictions as deported kulaks.[283]

People returning from other Soviet Republics were not free. They were distributed across Kazakhstan, assigned by the administration to certain places based on quotas. Mirzoian gave regional party leaders exact instructions and held them accountable for upholding the decision.[284] Returning migrants were preferably to be settled in kolkhozes that had an MTS at their disposal and were sufficiently established to absorb the newcomers. Newcomers were only to be organized in new kolkhozes when it was impossible to integrate them into existing ones. Officials tried to follow that rule. Their statistics say that in 1933 alone more than 60,000 households were "added" to existing kolkhozes, while only 7,700 families were organized in independent collectives.[285] The OGPU helped reduce numbers by tracking down "anti-Soviet elements" within those groups.[286]

Thousands of families were deported to regions with which they were unfamiliar and forced to do work for which they had learned no skills. When settling these people the officials no longer took their places of origin into consideration. They sent them to cotton-growing and sugar beet sovkhozes and kolkhozes in Kazakhstan's south where, due to an inclement climate, unbearable work conditions, and widespread malaria, they had difficulty finding laborers.[287]

And yet neither the measures taken nor the resources available were sufficient for handling the large numbers of returning refugees, especially while Kazakhstan still struggled to fulfill the high procurement quotas demanded from it. Although he probably knew that it was senseless, in June 1934

Mirzoian once again appealed to Moscow to rethink the precarious circumstances:

> We have been able to fulfill only 86 percent of our livestock obligations. We
> have problems distributing the remaining 14 percent. . . . If we were to ful-
> fill our obligations entirely, we would have to distribute the burden across
> 552,000 households. We have only 560,000 households in the entire republic,
> but based on the Central Committee's resolution [of September 17, 1932] we
> must exempt nomadic and seminomadic households [from turning in their
> share of livestock]. There are at least 150,000 such households. And that
> leaves us with 400,000. We simply do not have enough households to meet
> the targets."[288]

It is typical that in May 1934 only 78,000 of the 150,000 households registered as having returned to Kazakhstan after June 1933 were considered
"settled."[289] In other words, just half of the returning migrants were involved
in one form or another in governmental measures for sedentarization. The
rest was left up to itself.[290] Some Kazakhs complained about the situation
and demanded that promises be kept. If not, says a letter from returnees in
the district of Kzyl-Tussk, "the district will depopulate anew."[291]

By the end of 1934 most refugees had returned to Kazakhstan. Nonetheless, careful estimates say that more than thirty thousand Kazakh households
remained in Soviet republics outside of Kazakhstan, waiting to return in the
following years.[292] Some of the late returners came back when neighboring
republics and regions tried to "purge" their territories; others returned once
they were convinced that the famine was over. The Great Party Leaders saw
them as "isolated incidents."[293]

DELEGATING CATASTROPHE

Soviet population policy was defined solely in terms of agricultural productivity, and famine refugees were mere objects. Channeled migration helped
overcome shortages and steer uprooted people toward regions with labor
force deficits. Relocating people enabled social culling and the detection of
enemies and opponents. But above all, transforming and moving large parts
of Kazakh society gave the Soviets an opportunity to assert their claim to
power there once and for all.

For that reason, in the spring of 1933, when large groups of refugees were being brought back to Kazakhstan from neighboring republics, politics also cracked down on inland refugees. The militia and the OGPU began systematically "cleansing" cities and railway stations.[294] Most food distribution points were closed in favor of decentralized provisions for kolkhozes and sovkhozes, which also served to select workers.[295] "Emaciated people and children" had a right to food there, if they could work. This method forced the Kazakhs to join kolkhozes and sovkhozes where they would allegedly find food and work.

Kazakhstan was not alone in choosing that method for freeing cities and major junctions of hungry people.[296] It was in line with Stalin's plans for the entire Soviet Union. In February 1933 he had said that "lazy people" deserve death by starvation and two years later he justified the sacrifices of the famine years with the successes of industrialization.[297] In 1933 the bulk of governmental measures taken for famine regions consisted of "cleansing" the cities, relocating the hungry to the villages, auls, and kolkhozes, and providing food for workers only.

One important measure was the introduction of inland passports. The crisis of 1932–33 had triggered huge waves of migration all over the country and washed millions of uprooted and impoverished people into the cities. In order for the state not to lose all control over this Soviet "quicksand society" (Moshe Lewin's phrase), living in the city was restricted to those who had been registered and issued a passport. Peasants unable to get the document were thus bound to the kolkhoz; "cleansing" the cities now had normative grounds. The undisclosed details of the resolution specified a number of "elements" that would be denied residence permits or passports. The list included escaped kulaks, people without steady work, and criminals.[298] The passport system became a major component of Stalin's repression machinery.[299] Within just a few months hundreds of thousands of people were banished from the cities and exiled to Siberia and other far-off regions, some under atrocious circumstances.[300]

Displacing refugees from Kazakhstan's cities coincided with new regulations. A high-ranking commission from Aulie-Ata decided that it was time to "cleanse" the city of *otkochevniki* without hesitation.[301] In Aktiubinsk officials decided that all "rovers" were to be banished from the city as soon as possible.[302] But in April 1934 the City Party Committee was forced to acknowledge that despite several "cleansing" actions the town was once again full of *otkochevniki*, including numerous kulaks and bais disguised as refugees. Previous attempts to free the urban area from these people had brought no satisfactory results. On the contrary, some individuals had been picked up by the militia three or four times. A decision was made to give food only to those who were willing to work. The rest were chased out of town for being "lazy."[303]

Local administrators bore the brunt of this new course. They were deemed responsible not only for economic conditions, but for repatriating Kazakhs as well. They frequently requested more food supplies but the response was always the same: Every region was allotted a specific amount and there were no extras.[304] When functionaries from the district of Aksau complained that they could not feed the endless stream of refugees, more than 2,700 households, with the food rations assigned to them, the party secretary for the region of Alma-Ata, Il'ias Moldazhanov, told them to find a solution to the problem "that very night" or accept the consequences: "I am informing you that you will be arrested on the spot if you do not feed the *otkochevniki*. I am informing you that the chairman of the executive committee for Balkhash has been arrested. If you remain passive, we will do the same with you."[305] Under those circumstances, regional officials had no choice but to set priorities with respect to whom to feed. A later report by the Kazakh Narkomzem said that "measures taken to settle refugees must unconditionally focus on providing for households to be settled with minimal amounts of food and other supplies and concentrate on bringing them into the normal process of productivity."[306]

With a letter to the chairman of the political section of an MTS in the district of Aulie-Ata, Mirzoian explained just what that meant:

A special decision made by the Kraikom says that all kolkhoz peasants and immigrants who do not work and who do not want to work shall get no food. Nonworkers are to be excluded from food distribution at all costs. We must educate the people to understand that they will only get bread if they work and that lazy people and the idle get nothing. You must undertake this task jointly with the district committee and if there are any individual kolkhozes, districts, or cooperatives that get grain but are reluctant to work, you shall cancel their grain supply and allow kolkhozes inhabited by good-for-nothings to derail.[307]

Bureaucrats in the Kazakh Sovnarkom and in some oblasts worked out detailed plans for whom to give how much relief, and where.[308] In theory, strict guidelines regulated the distribution of foodstuffs and grain and not one gram was to be handed out before the district executive committees had confirmed the lists of names of the needy that had been compiled by the kolkhozes. Those in charge at the kolkhozes were to render monthly accounts of how means had been utilized and then order what they needed for the near future. The procedure was the same at the district and regional levels. In theory.

Immigrants were often seen as trifling beggars. In 1932 in the district of Karmakchinsk administrators received more than 24,000 rubles to provide for the starving. Between July 1932 and January 1933 they spent just a tad more than 1,400 rubles of it and most of that went to staffing costs and for wiring telegrams abroad. They spent 120 rubles on repairing living quarters and buying garments for refugees.[309] The figures illustrate how little attention local officials there paid to famine refugees.

A list compiled in December 1932 by the Kazakh Sovnarkom shows the extent of losses. Over the past year the state had provided 57,000 tons of grain either as direct relief or in the form of loans, but only 33,000 tons had actually been handed out.[310] The remaining 24,000 tons were composed of fictitious supplies that existed only in the statistics, grain still in storage, and the significant shrinkage of over 10,000 tons that were no longer in central storage but had never been distributed.[311] The discrepancy between the plan and (reported) reality meant the death of tens of thousands of people. Sometimes the grain that was delivered as relief was returned to fulfill procurement demands.[312]

Officials began imposing harsh punishment whenever waste was recorded. In 1933 Kazakhstan's public prosecutor began preliminary investigations into 800 cases, 600 of which came before the court. These were incidents of embezzling relief and committing fraud related to settling repatriates. Of the 1,800 people convicted, about one-third (566 people) had some function in the party or state apparatus, somewhat more than 20 percent were marked as being "bais, kulaks, or other alien elements." Ninety people were condemned to death, but most of the offenders were sentenced to ten years of detention camp (1,084 verdicts).[313] Although the list is incomplete, it does indicate that few cases involving functionaries and local elites who had profited personally from the supplies intended for the *otkochevniki* were investigated and brought to trial.

But even leaving waste and personal gain aside, there was a major lack of grain and a lack of transport capacity. Administrators complained constantly of having no camels or other beasts of burden.[314] At times distribution failed because the auls sent no lists of the number of needy to the grain storehouses and without the lists, those in charge refused to hand out grain. In some regions this was the reason that even the few supplies that did exist were not distributed at all.[315]

In fact, without party leaders first intervening, it was often impossible to get the institutions that had grain to distribute it as planned. No one dared to stop the tactical maneuvering and stalling among procurement organizations, whose directors knew very well that every grain of cereal that did not leave Kazakhstan to fulfill procurement demands had negative consequences. When regional supply processes collapsed, the blame was often placed on those immediately in charge, in other words, the local party boss instead of the director of a large regional grain warehouse who had refused to open his doors.[316]

Such inaction corresponded to the ever greater misuse of means designated for the integration of refugees. Officials and Communists everywhere filled their own pockets with those funds. A tried and proved method for doing so was to scale up the number of households in need of relief. The lists were full of "deceased persons."[317] In April 1934 the Party Control Commission found that it did not know where more than a half a million hundredweights of grain dispersed after October 1933 had gone. The controllers registered alarming conditions in districts where the control of food distribution was in the hands of "enemies of the people," who requested much more than they needed, while people continued to die of starvation because the relief never got to them. The situation was similar for fabrics and industrial products. A report by one control commission states that it was impossible to say where all the goods were, but "what is clear is that only the smallest amount ever reached the refugees."[318]

By mid-1934 signs emerged that Moscow's leaders were no longer willing to send thousands of tons of grain to impoverished Kazakhs, especially when the effort appeared to have no noteworthy economic effect. Famine refugees lost their status as victims in need. Policy turned to excluding as many as possible from relief and a trend began of viewing the starving as "declassed elements" and "idle persons." Many officials publicly endorsed the opinion that "the majority of the *otkochevniki* are criminal, stray elements and kulaks ... that one need not provide for."[319]

That perception certainly found support when controllers discovered cases of individual households that profited from taking relief intended for the *otkochevniki*. Communists from Semipalatinsk reported a particularly serious case in March 1934. Officials discovered that of 150 Kazakh households settled in kolkhozes organized especially for them, 114 were falsely registered as refugees and received relief to which they were not entitled. A "spirit of dependency" had grown among the Kazakhs, said the report, not without reproach. No one wanted to work, everyone wanted the state to provide for them.[320] Comrades were beginning to think that many people were only concerned with getting some material advantage out of their situation.[321]

In 1934, Vasilii Sharangovich from Kazakhstan's Party Control Commission and his subordinates strongly pushed for a thorough reform of the food system.[322] They saw misuse and waste everywhere. There was absolutely no control over to whom grain was given, how much grain was given, or even what criteria were used in decision making. No one knew how kolkhozes and districts came up with their lists. Even the most rudimentary forms of accounting and auditing were not practiced in kolkhozes, regional administrations, and at other administrative levels.[323] Since October 1932 more than 1.1 million hundredweights of grain (55,000 tons) had been delivered to Kazakhstan, without anyone knowing anything at all of its whereabouts.[324] Simultaneously the members of the commission believed that an attitude of reliance on the state for food was spreading among the Kazakhs. Of Kazakhstan's 121 districts, 116 received state support of some kind.[325] The controllers wanted to see an end put to that mentality: All regions were in a position to feed their own population by "mobilizing their own resources," said Sharangovich. The controllers demanded that, with a few exceptions, after the imminent harvest, the distribution of food must cease.[326] The Kazkraikom wasted no time turning these demands into a resolution that prescribed tough penalties for any officials passively continuing to condone such "waste."[327]

Now it was more or less up to the peasants and kolkhoz directors to cope with the growing numbers of newcomers as best they could. The newcomers' chances of gaining access to local distribution networks were slim. They were on the bottommost rung of a hierarchy shaped by personal links and mutual dependencies. In August 1933 the Central Committee in Moscow declared that all kolkhozes that had welcomed newcomers were to organize extra food supplies for them.[328] Officially this measure looked like support for impoverished families but, in a telegram to the party secretaries in oblasts, Mirzoian explained the details and said unmistakably that now the responsibility for the survival of repatriates lay with the kolkhozes: "The volume of these provisions will be decided by each kolkhoz at its kolkhoz assembly, and depend on the harvest and on the number of *otkochevniki* living there."[329] There would be no more external help to count on.

No one and nothing in the kolkhozes were prepared for the people returning from other Soviet republics or being driven out of the cities and away from railway junctions. They were given the dirtiest and most exhausting work and they lived in abject conditions.[330] Despite promises to the contrary, they were not given livestock.[331] Many local functionaries refused to give newcomers valuable animals. It made no sense, they said, to distribute animals among the Kazakhs who had arrived at the kolkhozes so late in the year that they had no time to put up fodder and hay for the winter.[332] The argument gained increasing importance because the survival of the few remaining herds now had top priority. Every goat, sheep, and cow was carefully guarded and kept alive at almost any cost. Slaughtering an animal without permission was reason for severe reproof and punishment. Some comrades openly declared that they would only welcome *otkochevniki* who brought their own animals with them.[333] Leaders in Alma-Ata increased the pressure on the repatriates and kolkhoz directors by reminding them that any food distributed at all was only a temporary measure and families that slaughtered the animals they were allowed to keep not only would not get any additional animals, they would be excluded from all further relief.[334]

When they arrived, most of the repatriates quickly realized that kolkhoz members saw in them a burden for their already fragile survival networks. Serious conflicts broke out. When a group of newcomers arrives at one kolkhoz in Aulie-Ata, the peasants and kolkhoz director informed them of their future rank in the local hierarchy. On the day they arrived, "All newcomers were assigned work . . . they worked all day and were supposed to work until the moon came out. They were given food in the evening, but not enough to be full. The night was cold because they literally had no clothes." A few families left the kolkhoz. The others "worked from morning to evening in the beet field, at noon they did not go home to eat, and no food had been organized for them."[335]

Things were no better in the Telestyk kolkhoz in the same district: Newcomers were put into houses without windows and doors and given scant rations although they did hard physical labor. They never saw anything of what had been promised; their families "went half-starved and lived off what their children could scavenge."[336] At another kolkhoz the Russian peasants badgered the aliens persistently and accused them of all kinds of misdoings.[337] As such incidents increased in frequency, party leaders saw themselves compelled to remind regional cadres that caring for the repatriates was one of their most important tasks in their daily work.[338]

In a sense, the famine ended the way it had begun: slowly and gradually. First signs of recovery began emerging in the fall of 1933 and, as 1934 progressed, famine was parried in all regions of Kazakhstan at least to the point that no more died of starvation. Various factors ended the crisis. Overall, there were now fewer people to feed. The immense reduction in population caused by starvation and mass flight heavily reduced the number of Kazakhs. Although we have no reliable numbers, we can assume that by mid-1934 about two million fewer people lived in the Republic of Kazakhstan than three years before. And those who survived were capable of work. Children and the elderly had died in disproportionately high numbers. Those who remained could now fend for themselves.

The decisions of September 1932, especially the resolution to distribute livestock among the kolkhoz farms and the broad exemption of livestock breeding regions from the duty to contribute to the procurement plan for the entire Soviet Union, also helped end starvation by breaking with the rigorous and ruthless policy of exploiting resources. When the new strategy finally began to show some effect, it did lead to a recovery in livestock and helped several thousand people to survive.

Enormous harvest yields in 1934 then further improved conditions. And the strict discipline forced on the rural population, for example, in the form of draconian penalties for grain theft, also began to have an effect. The government did everything in its power to maintain control over the last reserves.

For both state leaders and officials at the local level, decision making oscillated between the two extremes of making concessions and demonstrating relentless severity. Kazakhstan's rural population living in kolkhozes could not escape them. But there they usually had at least minimal resources to share among their members. Famine refugees often got nothing. As disastrous as it was for the impoverished refugees, kolkhoz peasants seem to have accepted it as the only way to secure their own survival and stabilize their existence for the near future.

6

SOVIET NOMADISM

BY THE TIME the crisis ended in 1934 no one seriously questioned the Bolsheviks' claim to power in Kazakhstan. The republic had lost one-fourth of its inhabitants. Many of the networks that had previously woven the fabric of Kazakh society were now nonexistent. The majority of Kazakhs had been forced to settle in misery and destitution, and now lived in poor auls, villages, and kolkhozes on the margin of subsistence, dependent on the caprice of local functionaries. People coped with shortages as well as they could. The old world, the world of their nomadism, was gone.[1]

The famine had not only unraveled Kazakh society, it had torn the steppe economy asunder.[2] Ultimately, Bolshevik leaders came to realize that if they continued their policy of unconditional resource extraction, then even by modest Soviet standards, Kazakhstan would remain a disaster area both economically and socially. What could be done? The party leadership had found a pragmatic solution that Mirzoian presented to the Kazakh Party in June 1934: "Comrade Stalin said that some comrades were quite wrong to think that nomadic animal breeding should be entirely liquidated. He said that on the contrary, Socialism, yes, even Communism does not necessarily exclude nomadic ways of animal husbandry. The most probable solution would be to let certain areas in Kazakhstan and Central Asia return to nomadic livestock traditions."[3] The intent, Mirzoian explained on a different occasion, was to get not just tens of thousands of tons of meat from Kazakhstan, but hundreds of thousands of tons of meat over the coming years.[4] It didn't matter how the target was met. What counted were results. Thus, nomadism remained an option even after 1934.

REVISIONS AND BALANCES

In December 1933, Nikolai Lisitsyn, the RSFSR people's commissar for agriculture, said that poor timing was responsible for the failure of sedentarization policy for Central and Western Kazakhstan in the early 1930s.[5] The drive in the steppe had begun before the Communists had any power there. The oblasts had been basically left to themselves to master "colossal tasks" which they then planned and coordinated poorly. Settlement spots had not reliably documented what they had done with the millions of rubles allotted to them for sedentarization, or even how many buildings they had erected. Doubts arose as to whether the measures made any sense. And this in turn raised the question of the steppe's future. This time, said Lisitsyn, the question should not be answered by ideological principles, but with economic rationality.

First, the situation demanded a survey. In the spring of 1934 the VTsIK sent a commission to Kazakhstan and Kirghizia to investigate sedentarization issues related to the nomadic and seminomadic population. The undertaking was led by Sergei Kiselev, who in 1928 had investigated the Bekker affair in Semipalatinsk.[6] On arriving in Kazakhstan, the members of the commission began culling thousands of documents from which they could glean the details of the disaster.[7] They traveled to all regions of the republic and worked out comprehensive tables, recording not only the state of homes (planned, begun, repaired, completed), but also the number of animals, kinds of construction material, distances between kolkhoz "economic centers" and the next railway stations, the sizes of fields, and much more.[8]

Kiselev also ordered representatives from the nomadic regions to appear in Alma-Ata and answer questions about the steppe. The comrades basically all told the same story. They reported heavy losses in population and herds almost completely vanishing before 1933, but also that gradually things were looking more positive. None tried to conceal that across vast areas of the country conditions were still catastrophic. The men saw sedentarization as a failure. A delegate for Karaganda, declared: "In our oblast sedentarization was never pulled off as planned. . . . Now conditions have changed but people are not returning to nomadism. They can't because they have no means and no goal. Does that mean we have accomplished sedentarization? Never. You say here that we have returned the repatriates to the workforce and provided for them—but that is not true. We have given them shelter. That is all. If you are going to claim that having integrated them into cooperatives means having settled them, I do not agree."[9] The commission issued a crushing verdict on conditions in Kazakhstan. The fatal practice of sedentarization by complete collectivization had become an end in itself, to which everything else had been subordinated. The same could be said for the effort to attract workers to industry and sovkhozes: now animal husbandry lacked workers.[10] Kiselev called the gigantic camps of hundreds of yurts someone's notion of building New Yorks in the mountains and steppe.[11]

In most regions functionaries had filed away the plans for sedentarization. Kiselev detected a "papery-bureaucratic" attitude toward it throughout the entire Kazakh administration.[12] Regional branches of the department

FIGURE 11.   House and yurt of the chairman of the Stalin kolkhoz, district of Kegensk, 1947, Institute for Ethnology and Anthropology, Russian Academy of Sciences

for sedentarization matters at the People's Commissariat for Agriculture, the so-called *osedkomy*, chronically lacked staff and capitulated under the burden of the work. A look at the same department for the region of Alma-Ata illustrated how bad things were—plans issued by the People's Commissariat for Agriculture had been simply filed away and forgotten. Statistics reflected wishful thinking. And no one knew of any progress in surveying the land or erecting buildings. Most of the staff was fully unqualified for the task. Employees included "one drunk, one kulak, and one exiled person." The department had no plan. With few exceptions, the modalities of settling repatriates in kolkhozes had been negotiated with those involved on-site and without involving the osedkom.[13]

Commissioner Sharangovich saw things similarly. In June 1934 he asked that the sedentarization committee be dissolved because neither its current staff nor its organizational skills were adequate for performing its duties while all other organizations that depended on the committee's help with refugee problems simply gave up. The staff's complacency wreaked havoc because, although new plans were devised every year and control figures were estimated for repatriates migrating back to Kazakhstan, no one knew how many households had actually returned and where they were. Sharangovich thought it typical that numerous bais and kulaks were found among the repatriates who had begun to organize vagabonding gangs and new streams of emigration.[14] It was a year before the criticized committees were suspended and their work was handed over to the Narkomzem.[15]

Kiselev and his comrades did not leave it at making critical remarks but instead elaborated recommendations for the organization of future sedentarization that barely deviated from past endeavors. They advised continuing to settle nomads, but to better take local circumstances into account, to do away with purely administrative measures, and to involve the population more in the efforts.[16] They promoted the idea that culturally "civilizing" the Kazakhs and settling them was of the essence for sovietizing the steppe. Their position was supported foremost by the VTsIK's Council on Nationalities Issues that had set up the Kiselev Commission.

The leading thinkers of that largely ineffectual institution made every effort to revitalize and master sedentarization.[17] In September 1935 they held the first nationwide congress on sedentarization. Representatives of all republics and oblasts inhabited by nomads met in Moscow. The council's secretary, Aleksandr Khatskevich, opened a debate by remarking that it was

not advisable to "build Socialism while the population returned to nomadism. . . . What should we do with someone who sits on the hump or the back
of a camel?"[18]

But apparently the nomads' chosen form of transportation no longer
bothered state and party leaders. It was soon clear that none thought of giving sedentarization any priority. It was one of the many Soviet projects about
which one wrote euphonious declarations of intent, but no one was ready
to shoulder the responsibility for implementation, not to mention having no
desire to fund it. And thus the financing of sedentarization was left to the
individual Soviet republics, while the People's Commissariat for Agriculture, despite resolutions and calls to the contrary, symbolically contributed
a mere few hundred thousand rubles a year.

Things looked similar regarding the search for some "strong voice" that
might win consistent attention for the topic at crucial committee meetings.[19]
And ultimately the comrades had to admit that erecting living quarters for
nomads was futile when they continued to inhabit their yurts and "misused"
the buildings as stalls.[20] It was no wonder that local officials steadily lost
interest in sedentarization.[21]

A few months later, in January 1936, the group met again but had no
significant progress to report. Khatskevich complained that "to be frank,
currently all efforts at settling the nomads are stagnant and in a number
of places left to develop as they may."[22] He could have said the same about
the debate that got lost in details. No one had answers for the crucial issues
such as the problem of public water supply that had always been neglected,
either because there were no experts to be had, or because it was easier
to visibly demonstrate "socialist success" by erecting residential buildings and stables, or because fiercely contested investments for irrigation
in Central Asia had not been channeled to the unprofitable steppe, but to
cotton-growing areas instead.[23] Kazakh delegates complained that they had
tried for years to get both People's Commissariats for Agriculture in Moscow interested in the problem of water supply ("at the RSFSR Narkomzen
they said it is not their problem and sent us to the USSR Narkomzen, who
told us to go back to the RSFSR Narkomzen"). To this Khatskevich, unaf-
fected, replied: "Taking a formal approach is never advisable for something
that costs millions and concerns the entire Republic."[24] It was an important point: functionaries who "mechanically" followed standard procedure
through governmental instances thereby demonstrated their disinterest in

the project. Success was had by comrades who favored informal methods and unwritten agreements.[25]

The debate eventually petered out. The data collected by the Kiselev Commission, along with the conclusions drawn from it by Kiselev and others, were sent to the archive. Leaders surrounding Stalin lost interest in sedentarization and few Kazakhs from central steppe regions pushed for settlement, even though it might have been economically reasonable for them to do so. As Kulumbetov remarked: "The majority of the Kazakhs, about 70–80 percent, who had emigrated from livestock breeding regions, have now returned to their old districts, coming back even from places where they had been given work in crop growing. Unfortunately, nomads want to return to their places of origin. These people own one, two, maybe three animals and want to breed them where they themselves were born."[26] Kulumbetov's observation did not lead to any concrete plans for dealing with the matter. Instead, he insisted that "we are absolutely not going to take any measures . . . [for setting up] villages for sedentarization in a number of nomadic districts."[27]

Occasionally a lone state or party official called for more action. In a circular for Kazakhstan's administrative departments, Isaev wrote in June 1936: "Although the present data are incomplete, they do show that this year you have stopped working on the issue of sedentarization and finding accommodations for repatriates. Do you think, perhaps, that the job is done?"[28]

But Isaev's words were far from marking the renaissance of organized sedentarization. Instead, they ushered in a drive that took the shortfalls of sedentarization as a pretense to look more closely at the work of the sedentarization department in the People's Commissariat for Agriculture.[29] The revision found, ruinously enough, that primarily second-rank people had been entrusted with the settling of repatriates from South Kazakhstan and that they had wasted the funds allotted for the purpose.[30] The responsible comrades in Aktiubinsk had no idea where, or under what conditions, repatriates lived.[31] In total, more than 10 percent of all of the money provided for settlement projects went toward bribing kolkhoz directors and other activists to make them accept any new people to the kolkhoz at all. In some places the money went toward building homes for members of the district administration. In the district of Chu the money was spent on gramophones to reward successful kolkhoz directors.[32]

One might possibly curb the waste of funds, but no one knew how to proceed with sedentarization. What was meant to happen next was "totally unclear," wrote Isaev to an official at the People's Commissariat for Nationalities Affairs. The Soviet for Nationalities Affairs "in Moscow" continued to put pressure on him and he therefore wanted some explicit instructions.[33] But other high-ranking cadres "in Moscow" apparently entertained a contrary view. In one remarkable appearance, Mikhail Kalinin, the nominal Soviet head of state, questioned former sedentarization policy and revealed his thoughts on nomadism. With respect to the tuberculosis epidemic in the oblast of Karkaralinsk, he said: "In my opinion, the tuberculosis raging there is a result of sedentarization, moving the people into houses, and damp ones at that. Clearly, [Kazakhs] should live in yurts. . . . We must carefully observe how peasants adjust to sedentary life, because sedentary life influences their physical condition, their health. . . . Of course I support sedentarization, but it must be moderate: Look how difficult it is for the entire population to settle down. They have their own mentality."[34] Other comrades expressed similar views: "The population is losing interest in sedentarization" said one.[35] Another asked himself whether the huge funds "had been spent for naught after a year or two."[36] In 1936 even Stalin said that "livestock-breeding nomads [will] continue their nomadic way of life in individual regions until Socialism and Communism have dawned."[37]

Nomads persisted in the Soviet Union after the mission of Socialism had been announced officially as having been accomplished.[38] This fact was nothing for the Bolsheviks to be particularly proud of but they made no effort to conceal the facts.[39] The premises of Soviet policy on nationalities had changed, no longer emphasizing the constructedness of nations, policy now more emphatically stressed their primordial nature.[40] Although the Bolsheviks never abandoned the idea that one fine day all nationalities would melt together, in the early 1930s they did agree that for a long transitional period some Soviet nations would uphold their own national cultures and traditions.[41]

The time had come to stop talking about superseding nations with Socialism and to begin thinking in terms of a community of many socialist nations united to become one Soviet Union. National peculiarities and customs were to become important resources for mobilizing all peoples.[42] This change, of course, found its outward expression in accentuated esteem for national cultures. Suddenly, customs, traditions, and folklore were no longer components of obsolete backwardness, but an integral part of socialist Soviet culture.[43] Even Stalin presented himself in national garments, and in Moscow

TABLE 3: MEASURES TAKEN BY JANUARY 1, 1937, TOWARD SEDENTARIZING KAZAKHSTAN

Number of nomadic households as of January 1, 1930	564,000
Number thereof settled by January 1, 1937	338,685
Number thereof living in kolkhozes	284,711 (or 83.6%)
Select settling points (places for sedentary centers for living and work)	3354
Newly erected houses for kolkhoz members ready to settle	38,044
Repaired old buildings	86,338
Total of households that received living space	124,382 families of kolkhoz members
Banyas erected in new kolkhozes	248
Land distribution achieved in settlement areas for a total surface of	47,639 hectares
Wells drilled for kolkhozes	2,083
Ponds and other tapped water sources	29
Irrigation	122,249 hectares
The following facilities have been built into kolkhozes ready for settling:	
(a) Stockyards (for animals)	998
(b) Equipment sheds	621
(c) Horse stables	410
(d) Sheep stables	971
(e) Granaries/silos	971
(f) Smithies	499
Schools	160
Agricultural machinery worth	5,305,200 rubles
Government funds (nonrepayable grants)	51,641,300 rubles

Source: GARF, A310-18-204, 69–70.

and other metropolises the best artists from various Soviet republics made public performances.[44] In 1936, Kazakhstan, too, sent its most famous sons and daughters onstage, particularly the aged singer Zhambyl (Dzhambul) Zhabaev, playing his dombra and reciting verses.[45]

The newly adopted schedule for sedentarizing the Kazakhs was relaxed. The Kazakh People's Commissariat for Agriculture planned to erect houses made of locally available building materials in livestock regions for about half of those who lived there (about 60,000 people) by 1942.[46] In reality, in the 1950s large parts of Kazakhstan's population still lived in yurts and makeshift clay huts.[47] The official track record was modest. In 1937, the Russian Narkomzem presented a list of its achievements (see table 3).

On the one hand, this somewhat arbitrary-looking list written up for the Kazakh pavilion at the Central Agricultural Fair in Moscow gives an impression of what officials thought was worth reporting.[48] On the other hand, it shows how little was accomplished in the nomadic and seminomadic regions of Kazakhstan in the seven years since the campaign for sedentarization had begun. A few hundred more buildings for farming now stood in the steppe and slightly more than a third of the Kazakh population now

TABLE 4: NUMBER OF HOUSEHOLDS AFFECTED BY MEASURES TAKEN TOWARD SEDENTARIZATION (AS OF 1937)

YEAR	TOTAL NUMBER OF SETTLED HOUSEHOLDS	IN NOMADIC AND SEMINOMADIC DISTRICTS	IN PREDOMINANTLY GRAIN-GROWING DISTRICTS	IN COTTON-GROWING DISTRICTS	IN PREDOMINANTLY SUGAR BEET-GROWING DISTRICTS
1930	77,400	1,000	76,400	—	—
1931	57,400	22,500	31,800	1,500	1,700
1932	47,700	8,700	34,500	2,000	2,500
1933	111,300	21,000	85,300	4,000	1,000
1934	31,900	5,400	21,400	3,200	1,900
1935	6,000	2,700	—	1,900	1,400
1936	6,900	1,600	1,400	3,500	400
TOTAL	338,700	62,900	250,800	16,100	8,900

Source: TsGARK, 74-11-265, 101.

lived in permanent housing. A closer look at how they arrived at the number of settled households makes the accomplishments look even more paltry.

Table 4 shows that sedentarization did not move forward noticeably until 1933, when large numbers of refugees began returning to Kazakhstan. That year, about one-third of all households was forced to settle. What that meant has been illustrated above. It is not clear how many of the families that had been settled prior to 1933 had in fact remained where they had been placed. But we can say with certainty that tens of thousands of families were forced to settle at least twice, thus making the overall number of settled Kazakhs much lower than a simple addition of (target) figures suggests.[49] It is perhaps more realistic to assume that 200,000 families were affected by the official policy on sedentarization in one form or another. That is the bleak result of a policy that cost more than 1.5 million people their lives.

Communists in Moscow and Alma-Ata now became interested in nomadism as an economic factor. Considerable effort was to be undertaken to make Kazakhstan the Soviet Union's largest meat producer.[50] The Bolsheviks relied on Kazakhstan's nomads for meat.[51] If the nomadic customs of breeding livestock were the most effective and the cheapest way to recover animals, then it was time to tolerate and support it.[52] Interrupting another speaker in January 1935 at an assembly of party secretaries from the nomadic and seminomadic regions, Mirzoian said: "Don't tell us what the nomads are up to, tell us how livestock is faring."[53]

Nomadism continued to be seen as a backward form of culture, unsuitable specifically for the kinds of collectivization that the Bolsheviks had in mind.[54] But grand-scale livestock breeding in the steppe proved to be practical only when herds and drovers remained on the move. This was especially true for the gigantic steppe regions of Central and Western Kazakhstan that had no summer pastures and barely enough water to keep humans and animals alive.[55] The Third Five-Year Plan stated that if the projected growth of herds was to be attained, it would be absolutely necessary "to solve the issue of retrieving former summer pastures and the nomads' routes to them."[56]

A crucial difference from the way things had been prior to the destruction of nomadic culture by famine was that now functionaries tried to guide livestock treks. Drovers were organized in brigades and instructed as to which pastures they would use in the summer and winter. The officials sent expeditions to study nomadic migration routes that would bring the animals to processing centers.[57] And to a limited extent they introduced modern methods of animal husbandry to the steppe. They ignored, and in some cases criminalized, traditional practices of caring for and healing sick animals. By increasingly gaining command of mobile livestock breeding, the officials reduced Kazakh herdsmen to mere rural laborers.[58] They had become nomads to the comrades' liking.

FICTITIOUS KOLKHOZES

Most of the kolkhozes in Kazakhstan were in a desolate condition, especially if they had been run by Kazakhs and had taken in large numbers of repatriates.[59] They were more poorly staffed and equipped than Russian-run collectives, and their performance was noticeably poorer. The difference in productivity was often linked to a lack of knowledge in arable farming, but also to the fact that the machine and tractor stations preferred to lend out their equipment to kolkhozes that seemed more capable of fulfilling the plan.[60] This was exacerbated by the Soviet kolkhoz system's fundamental difficulty with work ethics. Kolkhoz members often had miserable work discipline, their productivity was low, and arbitrary expulsions from the kolkhoz were frequent.[61]

By the end of the 1930s more than half of all Kazakh districts were de facto part of nomadic regions. Most of them were in the steppe regions of Central and Western Kazakhstan. There many of the exemptions arranged in 1932 remained valid and were extended and expanded. For that reason several individual districts tried repeatedly to acquire nomadic status for themselves. When meat procurement drives were gradually reintroduced in 1935, the officials in charge were frustrated. In their opinion it was entirely impossible to fulfill the demands in remote regions that were often hundreds of kilometers away from any railroad.[62]

In those regions kolkhozes were often nothing more than fictitious entities that existed in statistics and plans only. The members of one commission sent in 1939 to the district of Karsakpaisk to examine conditions in kolkhozes found little there to remind them of collectives in other places in the Soviet Union. There a typical kolkhoz consisted of several groups of yurts scattered across several square kilometers, each inhabited by three to five families. "The past distribution of the population across the area determines where the kolkhozes are today and the nature of how land is used in the district." That is why "during the winter the kolkhoz breaks up into several disconnected groups of households." Most of the kolkhozes in the area had no center to speak of and no permanent building.[63] Conditions were similar not only for other nomadic collectives but also for those considered more or less settled.[64]

The worst off were kolkhozes that generally consisted of repatriated famine refugees. In the winter of 1938 the members of the Zhdanov kolkhoz, established two years previously in the district of Kelessk mostly by people who had returned from Uzbekistan, complained that within the past two years their kolkhoz had been ordered to change its location three times. It was impossible for them to erect permanent buildings and their families had no choice but to dwell in earthen huts. Economically, their kolkhoz was a failure.[65]

The description offered by the peasants of Kelessk was not exceptional. And it was not unusual for Soviet authorities to turn down such petitions for support. Due to a lack of economic perspective, kolkhozes in similar predicaments were denied loans everywhere and officials everywhere refused to accept responsibility for the disaster.[66]

One wondered whether any collectives existed in some steppe regions at all. Many peasants refused to work in kolkhozes. In the region of Gur'ev, for example, more than 43 percent of all kolkhoz peasants refused to fulfill even the minimum of the workdays required of them for the year 1939. Theirs was the highest rate of absence across the entire Soviet Union. But there were enormous discrepancies throughout the republic. In the region of Southern Kazakhstan barely 9 percent of all kolkhoz members had not completed the minimum of workdays demanded of them.[67] These differences alone illustrate how much the development in "settled" regions differed from that in the livestock-breeding regions. Kolkhozes in areas inhabited by seminomads were much worse-off than kolkhozes in areas where land was systematically cultivated and technical crops (like cotton) were promoted. There workers had more incentive because they could expect to be paid for their work in some way or another.[68]

While the size of herds did begin to recover from the catastrophic losses of the early 1930s, the compass they had prior to collectivization was not reached again until years after the Second World War. Communists fretted over kolkhoz herd sizes because as the years passed, the growth of herds in the private sector quickly surpassed that of collectivized herds. In 1939 in the district of Zhilokosinsk the kolkhozes looked after only one-fourth of all animals in the district, while kolkhoz members privately owned the greater share of the animals.[69]

In the entire region of Gur'ev kolkhozes controlled just slightly more than 40 percent of the livestock.[70] This resulted in the absurd circumstance that many kolkhozes in livestock-breeding areas had no herds of their own and had become insignificant for the economy.[71]

Then many Kazakhs began growing little crops in the steppe for a bit of additional income.[72] Most part-time kolkhoz farmers kept their animals in pastures near their yurts. Auls that wandered hundreds of kilometers through the steppe were a thing of the past. Most families made the transition to a semi-nomadic way of life, limiting their migration radius to thirty or forty kilometers around the "economic centers" of settled kolkhozes.[73] Relatively small and compact groups of auls that were usually organized by family relations remained isolated from one another. They now no longer had any reason to journey together in the warm months to their summer pasturelands and gather there together with other auls.[74] These weakly connected and economically inefficient groups settled in nomadic regions could hardly be called functioning kolkhozes. They had more similarity to rudimentary forms of nomadic existence, particularly because many of these so-called kolkhozes consisted at core of members of a single clan, just like the family-based Kazakh aul. "Tribal kolkhozes" were a widespread phenomenon; as late as the early 1950s Soviet ethnologists said that most of the Kazakhs in the regions they studied lived in that kind of community.[75] Across the steppe, many of the livestock kolkhozes were ultimately nothing but Potemkin villages.

The Bolsheviks tolerated the practice of nomadic and seminomadic ways of life by part of the Kazakh population and accepted the fact that the people organized themselves according to traditional social customs, as long as the fiction was kept alive that they were organized in kolkhozes. Leading comrades were content with that because their rule rested less on having dedicated followers than it did on maintaining the appearance of that dedication at all times and in all places. Publicly, no one dared express doubt about the beliefs their leaders told them to hold.[76] The state took no action until the decay could no longer be concealed. But when the Great Terror began to rage in Kazakhstan, too, the rules changed entirely.

REPRESSIONS AND CONTROL

"Enemies of the people" had incited kolkhoz peasants to reject kolkhozes and tend solely to personal gain, insisted Mirzoian at a party assembly for the region of Alma-Ata in December 1937.[77] Under the conditions of mass terror looming in 1937 and 1938, such a remark had grave consequences for anyone inculpated in that way. As elsewhere across the Soviet Union, Kazakh Chekists, too, began fabricating conspiracies and detecting alleged networks of enemies, traitors, and spies.[78] Within a few months almost the entire elite of the state and party apparatus had been eliminated by terror. Dangerous times dawned for prominent comrades in Alma-Ata when in the fall of 1937 *Pravda* and the Kazakh newspapers began publishing critical articles on Kazakhstan's party leaders. Mirzoian, who had survived the first wave of repression undamaged but had himself betrayed some of his most loyal comrades, was ousted from his position in May 1938, arrested, and shot for being an enemy of the people.[79] His demise frightened other comrades; a party congress was taking place in Gur'ev when they heard about it. While the delegates were still wrestling for words ("at the moment it is difficult to understand the decision and react to it"), the Soviet secret service NKVD was already taking action. Within a few hours almost the entire ring of the region's party leaders were arrested and exposed as being enemies of the people.[80]

Within a short time, Chekists destroyed the former party boss's real and imaginary networks that Stalin at executive committee meetings in February and March 1937 had already decried as being a particularly negative example of the cronyism so widespread throughout the party.[81] In 1937–38 the Communist Party basically ceased to exist in many regions and had to be built up again.[82] By August 1939 in the district of Narynkol'sk in the region of Alma-Ata, only three members of the district executive committee that had been elected in May 1938 still held their positions; more than 80 percent of the district's Communists (about three hundred in total) had joined the party within the last year. As it turned out, sixty of them had relatives in China, including chairmen and secretaries of local soviets, which made them particularly suspicious in the eyes of the secret police (the NKVD).[83]

In their search for enemies of the people the NKVD looked not only for anyone spreading "anti-Soviet and religious propaganda."[84] They took particular interest in the livestock sector, where (still under Mirzoian's aegis) they expected to identify and expose many enemies.[85] All over the country, Kazakh leaders staged propaganda trials to that end.[86] The comrades pursued the matter with great zeal. Of the approximately 600 trials held all over the Soviet Union by December 1937 for the purpose of "liquidating enemies in the livestock sector," 140 took place in Kazakhstan.[87] The procedure was in line with the unwritten rules of terror: to thoroughly "purge" those realms of every region and institution that the Chekists deemed either particularly significant or particularly problematic.[88]

Half a year after Mirzoian had "revealed" enemies of the people within the livestock sector, his successors accused him of the same. It was, they said, a clear indication of the machinations of the "Trotsky-Bukharin bandits" to incite people to reject kolkhozes and thus ruin them financially.[89]

At the same time that the state began the mass operations of Great Terror, it also went about regaining control over livestock breeding. In the late 1930s, officials used two tools to do so: one was to "strengthen" kolkhozes by returning privately owned animals to collectivized herds. The other was to relocate kolkhozes that lacked any "standard economic center" to specific places such that at least kolkhoz directors and facilities could be found. The implementation of these measures was not restricted to Kazakhstan; animals previously given out to help people survive the famine were now confiscated as common property.[90] Authorities simultaneously made a series of decisions that would prevent any further concentration of livestock in private hands. And once again, this threatened the very foundation of the people's means of existence.

Many Kazakhs tried to prevent the loss of their animals. They complained not only that they had to hand over their livestock but also that the measures taken exhibited the arbitrariness so typical of Soviet campaigns: no one knew exactly just who had to hand over how many animals.[91] Official notices and the press said that the measure involved merely returning to the state the animals that had been "loaned" to people in the early 1930s as compensation for the "excesses" that had taken place at the time.[92] But for most cases no files existed to prove which household had received how many animals during the years of chaos caused by the famine. Many people had moved away and taken their animals with them, and others strictly refused to return the animals.[93] Although some complaints were successful, overall the people of the steppe were expropriated a second time.[94]

Following the collectivization campaign, another broad attempt was made to reorder the steppe that involved, among other things, finding a different way to organize kolkhozes. The majority of them were now integrated into a stronger form of collective economy called artels.[95] Members of artels were to own less livestock in the future. Kolkhozes located in barren, waterless regions were to be relocated to more suitable regions.[96] That step was necessary particularly for Western Kazakhstan. Things there resembled conditions at the Zaburunsk soviet in the district of Dengiz, where in the fall of 1939 the entire population led a seminomadic life and where twenty years of Soviet rule had manifested themselves in "not more than ten old, derelict houses and a few worthless, dilapidated and vacant earthen huts."[97]

Before they could relocate kolkhozes, however, it was necessary first to define just where the "economic centers" for the kolkhozes were to be located.[98] In 1939 and 1940 the nomadic regions of the republic were searched for places appropriate for kolkhoz settlement points.[99] In contrast to the sweeping plans of a decade earlier, this time the desire was only to set up administration buildings and central operations buildings in one specific place.

The establishment of these "economic centers" caused planners the same kinds of problems that had impeded the campaign for sedentarization: a lack of building material, a lack of data on soil and pasture quality, and no knowledge of water sources or wells.[100] Departments at the Kazakh People's Narkomzem in charge of erecting the "economic centers" had no hydrological maps and no idea of where to look for wells and other water sources.[101] "No one in Moscow cares about the questions of Central Kazakhstan" was the well-known complaint of one frustrated comrade from that commissariat in September 1938.[102]

Moscow did not care whether the denizens of the steppe became shining examples of the "New Soviet Man." Loyalty was not asked of them, only compliance and obedience. The Bolsheviks used administrative pressure and repression and continued to overburden the kolkhozes with demands. It was a pragmatic kind of coercion. When criticized for neglecting adult education, one Kazakh kolkhoz chairman justified the shortcoming by saying: "They won't put me on trial for adult education, but they will for not keeping the sowing schedule."[103]

But Moscow had not lost all interest in the Republic of Kazakhstan. On the contrary: along with Siberia, Kazakhstan became one of the most important destinations for mass deportation in the 1930s and 1940s.[104] "Kulaks," "socially alien elements," and entire ethnic groups like Armenians, Koreans, and later also Germans and Chechens populated the "special settlements" and the Kazakh branches of the Gulag, including above all the gigantic Karlag.[105] The more deportees to the steppe, the greater the influence of the NKVD whose mighty planners now competed with Kazakh kolkhoz founders for scarce resources.[106] It was now up to camp inmates and special settlers to fulfill the vision that the Bolsheviks had entertained from the start for the huge territories: Make the steppe arable.[107] In Central Asia the native population no longer played any significant part in the plans for "developing" the "vacant" space there. The Bolsheviks left that up to their prisoners and slave-laborers.[108] The latter were, as Oleg Khlevniuk has put it, the drug that Soviet planners used to dream that they could reach the absurd targets of the Five-Year Plan.[109]

Harsh conditions in the steppe posed an extreme challenge for the deported. In the 1930s many of them feared for their lives because, as one Korean wrote to Molotov in 1937, "We are sedentary people not nomads, we are not accustomed to the climate and living conditions that the local people have known for centuries. . . . We can only expect to die of starvation, both now and in the future."[110] Relations between the native population and their new neighbors were tense. Some of the deported later recalled that at first the Kazakhs had taken them for cannibals and wild bandits.[111]

Many deported people were settled into existing kolkhozes. This gave the repression apparatus an ever greater influence over the Kazakh population and power over the "civic" administrations of the regions in question. Within a few years a dense net of camp territories and special settlements spanned the steppe. The Gulag and its villages and all their headquarters now formed the backbone of Soviet power in Central Kazakhstan.[112]

Kate Brown has argued that the destruction of the steppe by the introduction of camps, fences, and special settlements ended the mobility of the repressed and the "free" people alike.[113] There was no nomadic migration within camp territories and outside their bounds, pastures and migration routes began to vanish, too. After the famine so few Kazakhs still lived in central steppe areas that despite all limitations, the amount of land available would have been sufficient for their needs. Thus the opposite seems true: The immobility forced on a society barricaded by camps and special settlements left the last nomads some kind of existence, albeit a miserable one.[114]

ON THE HOME FRONT

The beginning of the Second World War marked a true renaissance for Kazakhstan's nomadism.[115] Starting in the winter of 1941–42 livestock herds began growing rapidly when hundreds of thousands of animals were evacuated from areas threatened by the German armed forces.[116] Kazakh Bolsheviks wanted to make their republic the most important livestock-breeding base in the country.[117] But they could provide neither stables nor forage for the huge herds. The only way to save the evacuated animals was to drive them to the summer and winter pastures. Even in areas where no noteworthy migration had taken place for years, Kazakhs suddenly reverted to their traditional ways of economy.[118] For the first time since the years of famine, large herds once again traversed the steppe along the old nomadic routes.[119] The number of animals held outdoors year-round increased continually and in 1944–45 constituted almost half of all the livestock in Kazakhstan.[120]

But then a large proportion of the evacuated animals went to waste. Tens of thousands of them froze or starved to death.[121] And many animals perished because kolkhoz workers were unfamiliar with the needs of herds under the conditions of the steppe. According to data from the People's Commissariat, in just the first seven months of 1942, almost 350,000 animals died.[122] Some agronomists considered the cause of such losses the barbarism with which kolkhoz peasants treated animals. They had neither made adequate provisions for the overwinter survival of livestock nor removed the cadavers of dead animals, which then encouraged the spread of disease.[123] But what was more important was the fact that in reviving nomadic ways of animal husbandry those in charge were often faced with structural problems. There was a lack of fundamental prerequisites, such as camels, without which it was extremely difficult to migrate through the steppe. Of the huge camel herds that still existed in the early 1930s, by 1944 only about 90,000 animals were left.[124]

Despite all the problems and setbacks, nomadic and seminomadic forms of animal husbandry continued to get support. The authors of one remarkable document of 1945 discussing economic perspectives for the region of Aktyubinsk explain that the course taken so far, namely, to increase acreage for crop fields, had been wrong. They proposed realigning the economy to concentrate on livestock breeding. The region, they said, had excellent livestock conditions, which had not been exhausted in the least, while crop growing could only be managed with the greatest effort. Over the past three decades they had only had seven "good" harvests. Peasants lived in poverty, and crop acreage, livestock herds, and the population itself were in continual decline.[125]

Something had to be done, and when the war was over, the discussion of nomadism's future gained importance[126] Ethnologists and agronomists debated the advantages of migratory animal husbandry.[127] The former system of pasturing must be revived, wrote one expert, but it would only be successful if a great number of households were to make "year-round livestock pasture grazing" their major form of subsistence and do so "with much larger migration radii."[128] Now it was up to the scientists to secure the knowledge and experience of surviving nomads and make it available for the socialist economy.[129] What fifteen years previously had been seen as the essence of uncivilized life and accepted tacitly, if at all, and that had almost never been publicly discussed as a form of economy, now advanced to become evidence of a superior, "socialistic" means of production and a celebrated contribution to the defense of the fatherland. Even elements of steppe culture that had once been seen as symbols of nomadic "backwardness" were now rehabilitated. "Yurts," wrote Nurtas Undasynov, chairman of the Kazakh Council of the People's Commissioners, in *Pravda* in 1945, "provide the best ... housing for conditions of constant mobility in the steppe."[130]

The Soviet state adapted itself at least partially to the ways of roving nomads. Modest infrastructures consisting of "Red Yurts," boarding schools, and mobile medical teams were set up for the nomads and their families.[131] Experienced nomads were decorated with medals and rewarded with privileges, a clear sign of their now being a part of the apparatus, in other words, a gesture demonstrating that the Kazakhs had finally been successfully Sovietized.[132] Soviet status was no longer bound to a sedentary way of life.[133]

7
LEGACY

I F SOVIETIZATION MEANT subjecting entire collectives to the will of the
state, then famine marked the birth of Soviet Kazakhstan. The years of
famine induced the transition from being a segmented society that took
little notice of the Bolsheviks to becoming an ordered society that could no
longer question Communist authority. The clans that had once given society
its structure soon lost their function and were replaced by the institutions
and administration of the Soviet State, especially that of the kolkhozes.[1]
Kazakhstan's present multiethnic society is largely a product of Stalinism,
forged by the nomads who managed to survive the famine and by the victims
of Stalin's mass deportations who were settled there. Collectivization and
famine left an entire people dependent on the state.

The famine ended when the Bolsheviks sought to limit starvation to villages and auls where food, work animals, and other basic goods were for
the most part subject to the control of local political networks. Survival
was impossible without access to those networks of the party or state. The
catastrophe was split up into countless local conflicts over distribution
that were bitterly fought between the poor and those who owned nothing.
Peasants and nomads fought for reprivatized herds, reductions in taxes and
duties, and food rations. Relief often did not reach those who needed it most
and went instead to whomever could best assert his interests.

Those who survived found themselves subject to Soviet regime standards: only results counted. Moral behavior became perilous during the famine. Many people had no choice but to abet the corrupt system.[2] The distinction between victim and perpetrator was blurred and, even in retrospect, we cannot clearly separate one from the other. A society that deemed the individual worthless and made the collective the greatest good stamped a verdict of guilty on anyone who valued his own life.

Whoever survived the famine thereby also stabilized the Soviet system. The crisis did not erode Soviet structures, it strengthened them by making individual survival almost completely dependent on Soviet mechanisms of order and distribution. Whoever survived the famine did so by the grace of the state that had caused it in the first place.

This resulted in complex processes of adaptation and psychological repression. The destiny of Mukhamet Shaiakhmetov, who has been mentioned several times in this book, was typical in many regards. When the Soviet state set out to destroy nomadic culture in 1928, his family was subject to terror at the hands of local activists. His father, branded a "kulak" and deported, died in exile. The family suffered heavily from the loss and the stigma of having a condemned kulak among themselves. By sheer luck, young Mukhamet, his mother, and his brother survived the years of famine. Countless relatives, friends, and acquaintances perished from exhaustion, disease, and starvation. Shaiakhmetov watched people renounce and exploit one another. As he wrote in his memoirs, when the worst was over, he had but one goal: to go to school and join the Komsomol. As one of the few literate people in his aul he became the right hand of the incompetent local official, not only reading aloud to him and others long articles from *Pravda*, but engaging them all in an effort to interpret what had been published. He fought in Stalingrad and on other fronts during the Second World War. Later he began a career in education and ultimately became a school director. His life was typical for many of his generation. His memoirs offer an explanation for why he uncomplainingly served the very system that had destroyed his family. He wanted to believe that the catastrophe was the fault of individuals and he submitted to "Moscow's will" because he had to believe Communist promises of a better future, or lose all hope. And he was grateful that the Soviet Union had opened doors to opportunities for education and a career.[3]

Many Soviet citizens who had survived hunger, terror, and war, went on to live under the strain and stress of the Soviet system. They learned to cope with the tension and bury the dark sides of their past.[4] The only official part of Soviet history that was permitted commemoration to a certain degree with grief, desperation, and the thought of irretrievable loss was the country's involvement in the Second World War.[5]

The Great Patriotic War, in which victory was eventually won after bitter defeats and painful deprivations, was the most significant feat that the Soviet state had on offer for identification with one's country. It gave suffering a meaning and allowed those who were mourning to partake in the successful community of survivors.[6] That was presumably why the Great Patriotic War blocked the tragedy of famine out of the collective memory of Kazakh society.

After decades, it was finally perestroika that enabled the mention of famine in Kazakhstan. The people of the imploding Soviet empire discovered interest in their own past and published a wealth of literature on the blank spots of history. But due to the challenges of life under ongoing social transformation the topic was soon abandoned. After a short phase of public commemoration and rehabilitation between 1988 and 1993, coming to terms with the past once again became the domain of historians whose findings were barely noticed outside the small world of academic research.[7]

That decline in interest came at the right time for those striving to create a national concept of history for an independent Kazakhstan. Books and textbooks on national history now place more emphasis on a heroic nomadic past, Kazakh national heroes, and the successful processes of modernization and reform from before and after 1991, than on the problems and tragedies suffered by the country during the period of Soviet rule.[8] For the better part of two decades, the famine was not commemorated in any noteworthy way, either in the public spaces of Kazakh cities and villages or in political discourse. Until recently very few monuments have memorialized the famine.[9] For example, a black cube of marble was set up in 1992 in a park in Almaty and was inscribed: "On this site shall stand a monument to the victims of the famine from 1931 to 1933."[10] However, the monument was not completed until 2017.

In 2012 things began to change. In Kazakhstan's capital Astana on May 31, 2012, the Day of Remembrance of the Victims of Political Repressions and Famine, Kazakhstan's president Nursultan Nazarbaev dedicated a Monument to the Victims of Famine. Now, eighty years after the famine, he said, it was important to remember the victims who had a place "in the hearts of

Kazakhs forever." The entity to blame for that "tragedy" was the "inhuman totalitarian system," he continued, and "when contemplating history today we must be wise and not allow this topic to be politicized."[11]

Other cities followed suit and a number of monuments commemorating the famine were erected all over the country. Finally, in 2017 in Almaty the memorial for the victims of the famine was unveiled—just opposite the former KGB headquarters.[12]

The allusion to vehement Ukrainian debates over the famine that took place there shows how much Kazakh leaders feared drawing too much attention in the sphere of public discourse to the famine in their own land. It

FIGURE 12.   Plinth for monument in honor of Kazakh victims of the famine, Wiki Commons

might not only damage Kazakhstan's relations with Russia but also endanger the peace between the country's distinct ethnic groups, which had taken considerable work to achieve. The more the famine is depicted as a Kazakh tragedy, the more urgently a search for those responsible begins, making history an object of reciprocal accusations of guilt. The oasis of stability that the leaders of Kazakhstan like to present may then soon prove to be fictitious.[13]

The Russian position on the famine is crystal clear: it was one of those "tragedies of the people of the Soviet Union." While Stalin and his vassals were no doubt responsible for the famine, they had never intended to destroy entire nations.[14] Starvation was the price they were willing to pay for the push of modernization in the early 1930s. In order not to vex its mighty ally, Kazakhstan had adopted that view itself. But that is presumably not the only and possibly not even the most important reason. Due to the multiethnic structure of its population, Kazakhstan had the reputation of being the "most Soviet" of all Soviet republics. Far into the 1980s it was the sole republic in the Union in which the titular nation was not composed of the majority of the population. According to official statistics, in 1979 slightly more than 5 million Kazakhs and almost 6 million Russians lived in Kazakhstan with

FIGURE 13.   Memorial for the victims of the famine, Astana, photograph
courtesy of Robert Kindler

its total population of 14.7 million inhabitants. In 1989 there were 6.5 million Kazakhs and 6.2 million Russians. The total population at that time numbered 16.5 million people. During the following years the Kazakh headcount kept rising while that of the Russians and other European nationalities dropped rapidly. In 1999 almost 8 million Kazakhs constituted more than half of the 14.9 million people inhabiting Kazakhstan.[15]

This population pattern was a direct consequence of the famine and of settling the "vacant" steppe with special settlers, deported nationalities, and Gulag prisoners. Kazakhstan's multiethnic society is in many ways a product of terror. It combined the survivors of the famine catastrophe with the victims of Stalin's mass deportations. When in the mid-1950s many Europeans followed Nikita Khrushchev's Virgin Lands Campaign and poured into the steppe, the proportions of the various groups shifted definitely in favor of the Europeans. Many of the newcomers were young activists, but a considerable number among them were people with dark pasts who had been lured to Kazakhstan by promises of material gain.[16] The objective was to make a third try at what had not been achieved by nomads or deported people: to make the steppe fit for agricultural cultivation.[17]

Like its forerunners, the Virgin Lands Campaign was an economic failure and caused a gigantic ecological catastrophe, although it did make the region a more thoroughly integrated part of the Soviet Union.[18] Whether or not they had come to the steppe voluntarily, once Stalin's rule of terror was over, people often remained in the region and began to organize their lives in the relative freedom of post-Stalinism. They pursued careers, took up key positions, and forced the Kazakhs increasingly into the margins.[19] In the late phase of the Soviet Union most Kazakhs lived in rural areas while the cities were dominated by Europeans who made up the elite in almost all areas. In the 1980s, Karaganda and Alma-Ata were Russian cities and Russian was spoken in them, whereas one spoke Kazakh mostly in villages and kolkhozes.[20] That did not prevent Soviet officials from presenting the sedentarization of nomads as a successful modernization project.[21]

Russian dominance in the major cities had an effect on the relations between Europeans and Kazakhs throughout Kazakhstan. The Europeans claimed (and some continue to do so today) that they had brought civilization to the backward Kazakhs. Many former Gulag inmates and exiled people can identify with that position if for no other reason than it gives meaning to the lifelong hard work that they were forced to do. Kate Brown has called the phenomenon a transition "from deportee into colonizer."[22] That feeling of superiority changed little during perestroika and the first years of transformation, even as members of the Russian and German minorities left the country in droves.[23]

The long dominance by European elites also left its mark on Kazakhstan's tradition of remembrance. Just as the struggle to understand the country's Stalinist past had begun, the "victims of political repression" were able to make themselves better heard than the Kazakhs because they had privileged access to the media, publishers, and universities. And when after 1991 collectivization, sedentarization, and famine were discussed at all, it was only as the story of the victims of an extremely mighty governmental apparatus, without any personal involvement.

The responsibility for the famine was externalized and seen as the result of abstract entities and a few prominent Bolsheviks.[24] Besides the protagonists Stalin and Goloshchekin, one reads only of a few of their closest vassals who were involved.[25] The fact is that even the most malicious commands and directives could not have been effective without someone to execute them. But investigating that opens up the question of what role Kazakhs themselves played in collectivization and sedentarization. No one holds victims accountable for the events. But when a people is no longer confronted with its past, it begins to forget, and begins writing its own history as a dominant narrative. The memory of famine in Kazakhstan is therefore, above all, the memory of suffering. This holds even for artistic attempts to work out the theme of famine by seeking its heroes among the starving.[26]

The narrative of Kazakh victims impedes the study of the famine in several ways. It ignores the fact that Kazakhs participated and were entangled in radical politics that to a great extent triggered the famine. Until that is discussed and studied, there can be no realistic debate on what conclusions may be drawn from this tragedy. As Aleida Assmann has shown, it also silences those who suffered. The role of the passive, helpless victim is often filled with shame and reluctantly brought to the fore. No one likes to remember experiences of dramatic helplessness and agony. It holds even for the descendants of such "total victims," which the starving Kazakhs appear to have been. Imagined victims and real victims, says Assmann, cannot emerge from their isolation until their suffering is recognized and compensated, at least symbolically. But that would imply a recognition of guilt and responsibility.[27] Before that happens, famine can only be dealt with using abstract and superficial concepts. The narrative of victims thus blocks our view of the local dynamics and processes that are difficult to specify.[28] In the end, the famine as a historical phenomenon will be largely forgotten. What will last is the commemoration of famine as a symbol for human suffering and state terror.

But forgetting a "horrible past" involves more than not admitting unpleasant truths. The historian Christian Meier has pointed out that purposeful oblivion has always been one of the most important human strategies for overcoming crises.[29] Historically, struggling with the causes of wars, crises, catastrophes, and guilt is not the rule, but an exceptional case that emerged essentially from responsibility that the Germans must take for the Holocaust. The unprecedentedness of that crime on humanity, says Meier, demanded a special kind of memory, a culture of remembrance that always speaks of the guilt and responsibility of the perpetrators and their descendants.[30] But we do not know whether the way we deal with one extreme case can be recommended for dealing with other cases of "horrible pasts." If, in other social contexts, there is consensus to "let the past be," says Meier, we have no plausible grounds for forcing others to come to terms with their history.[31]

Coming to terms with the history of the famine in Kazakhstan would involve talking about the problems involved in upholding human solidarity when one is faced with the threat of death by starvation. Keeping silent and not speaking publicly about famine are among the consequences of a Stalinist communication strategy that tied large parts of the population not immediately affected by famine to the regime. It worked because the interests of the rulers and the ruled coincided more than it may at first seem.[32] Where no one spoke of dying and suffering, no one asked about personal responsibility and guilt. Silence held people together. When no one spoke out, it was not only for fear of the regime, it also suppressed awareness of one's own involvement. Excluding the victims meant including everyone else and doing so far beyond the end of the famine itself.

Perhaps we find here an answer to the question of how Soviet society continued to function even in times of extreme crises such as years of famine or during the excesses of terror in 1937 and 1938. It did neither come to a war of each against all, nor did state terror and violence atomize society. Refusing to mention the famine was an offer the dictator made to the people, and it was a threat. The populace understood that they basically had no other choice but to follow the lead of the regime. And the state was the addressee for requests and concerns. Aleksei Tikhomirov has suggested that we think of "forced trust" as a fundamental experience of Soviet existence. Forcing trust from the people was a necessary outcome of the constant mistrust with which the regime beheld its people. It bound leaders and the Soviet citizens together.[33] It was of the essence for each individual to appear absolutely trustworthy and express trust in the leadership and its policies at every opportunity.[34]

Partaking of this system was an important way to prove one's loyalty. Behavior and deeds were not necessarily suitable for proving loyalty because the functioning of the Soviet system, as has been mentioned several times above, rested on the fact that everyone—from the simple kolkhoz peasant to the mighty director of a combine—had to constantly violate plans, norms, and laws, or modify them for their own purposes. It was the only way to keep the planned economy from full chaos. At the same time, all the protagonists found themselves constantly threatened by revisions, controls, and potentially destructive accusations. No one was without flaw. In such circumstances it was rational to use the language prescribed by the regime, or at least to carefully observe taboos. The rules for "successful" communication applied equally to *Pravda*, the village party cell, and the politburo. And the rules prescribed not only what was said, but what remained unsaid, as well.

In light of Kazakh society's instability, was it a rational strategy for coming to terms with the past to ignore the problematic facets of the country's own history? Does it suffice to label the famine a "national tragedy," like a natural disaster, and leave it at that? Or is it time for Kazakhstan to explore its own responsibility for the outbreak of famine? We have no advice to offer. But perhaps Evgenii Dobrenko and Andrei Shcherbenok's analysis of the relationship between power and the past in Russia can be applied to conditions in Kazakhstan. Dobrenko and Shcherbenok write: "The past is the experience of pain, the trauma of experience; history is the anesthesia, the narrative that is produced by power and envelops the pain, thereby creating a nation that can be defined as a community of people united by a shared pain and the contract with the power that plays the role of the anesthesiologist."[35]

Time will tell how the narrative changes. It is clear that famine changed Kazakh society. And there is no way to put that gently.

NOTES

INTRODUCTION

1. Tsentral'nyi Gosudarstvennyi Arkhiv Respubliki Kazakhstan (TsGARK), 1179-5-8, 29ob (report to Karutskii from Evgrashkin, February 25, 1933).

2. For the purpose of this study, the term "Kazakhstan" covers from 1920 to 1925 the Kirghiz Autonomous Soviet Socialist Republic, up to 1936 the Kazakh Autonomous Soviet Socialist Republic (KASSR), and after 1936 the Kazakh Soviet Socialist Republic (KSSR). In *Kazakhs*, Martha Brill Olcott gives an overview of the region's political history.

3. On the scale of the hunger crisis, see Abylkhozhin and Kozybaev, "Kazakhstanskaia tragediia"; Pianciola, "Famine in the Steppe; Pianciola, *Stalinismo di frontiera*; Ohayon, *La sédentarisation*; Kozybaev, *Nasil'stvennaia kollektivizatsiia*; Cameron, "Hungry Steppe"; Mikhailov, *Great Disaster*.

4. For the debate on determining the loss, see Mark, "Die Hungersnot in Kasachstan," 112–30; Alekseenko, "Naselenie Kazakhstana"; Maksudov, "Migratsii v SSSR," 770. On the fate of Kazakhstan's European population, see Maksudov, "Migratsii v SSSR," 774, and Osokina, "Zhertvy goloda 1933 goda."

5. Baberowski, *Scorched Earth*, 4–19; Vert [Werth], *Terror i besporiadok*, 153–54.

6. For the debate on genuine "Communist" modernity, see David-Fox, "Multiple Modernities"; and Arnason, "Communism and Modernity."

7. Khazanov, *Nomads*, 212–21.

8. Weber, *Economy and Society*, 212.

9. Gammer, "Russia and Eurasian Steppe Nomads." For Kazakhstan, see Sokolovskii, *Kazakhskii aul*. Reinhard, *Geschichte des modernen Staates*, 12–14.

10. Taken from Mukhamedina, "Ekonomicheskaia politika," 128.

11. Scott, *Seeing Like a State*, 2–5.

12. Gumppenberg, *Staats- und Nationsbildung*, 48–60.

13. Salzman, *Pastoralists*, 1–9, 122.

14. Riekenberg, *Gewaltsegmente*.

15. "Willing executioner" is an expression borrowed from Goldhagen, who used it in the context of National Socialism. Goldhagen, *Hitler's Willing Executioners*.

16. Blank, "Ethnic and Party Politics"; Koigeldiev, *Stalinizm i repressii*.

17. On the relationship between clans and the Soviet power, see Schatz, *Modern Clan Politics*, 21–27.

18. Shaumian, *Ot kochev'ia*; Tursunbaev, *Kazakhskii aul*; Tursunbaev, *Kollektivizatsiia*.

19. Filipp I. Goloshchekin (1876–1941) was the first party secretary in Kazakhstan from late 1924 until January 1933. For his biography, see Medeubaev, "Palach tsarskoi sem'i." For Goloshchekin as being responsible for the famine, see Mikhailov, *Khronika velikogo dzhuta*.

20. Salzman, "Introduction."

21. Scholz, *Nomadismus*, 149.

22. On practices of mutual encounter, see Fratkin, "Pastoralism"; and Barfield, *Perilous Frontier*. On the influence of indigenous populations, see Malikov, *Tsars, Cossacks, and Nomads*.

23. Cameron, "Kazakh Famine," 117–32.

24. These are some of the core arguments of Ohayon, *La sédentarisation*; Pianciola, "Famine in the Steppe"; Abylkhozhin and Kozybaev, "Kazakhstanskaia tragediia"; and Cameron, "Hungry Steppe."

25. In *La sédentarisation*, Isabelle Ohayon stresses the importance of forced settlement, while Matthew Payne, in "Seeing Like a Soviet State," emphasizes the opposite.

26. In *The Great Disaster*, Valeriy Mikhailov stresses Goloshchekin's role, while M. K. Koigeldiev's approach in *Stalinizm i repressii* is more differentiated.

27. Niccoló Pianciola, in *Stalinismo de frontiera*, and Sarah Cameron, in "Hungry Steppe," call it just that.

28. Benjamin Loring, in "Colonizers with Party Cards," sees Soviet rule in Central Asia as a kind of "internal colonization."

29. Payne, "Seeing Like a Soviet State," 62–65.

30. Zhdanko, "Mezhdunarodnoe znachenie," 5; Ohayon, *La sédentarisation*, 327–43.

31. Martin, *Affirmative Action Empire*, 1–28.

32. Northrop, *Veiled Empire*; Edgar, *Tribal Nation*; Kappeler, *Russland als Vielvoelkerreich*; Slezkine, "USSR as a Communal Apartment"; Roy, *New Central Asia*.

33. Hirsch, *Empire of Nations*. On the problematic role of ethnologists both producing facts and acting as emissaries of Soviet modernity, see Ssorin-Chaikov, "Representing 'Primitive Communists.'"

34. Stalin, "Marxism and the National Question."

35. The following authors stress the major role that Central Asia plays for understanding Russian imperial and Soviet history: Sahadeo, "Home and Away"; Abashin, "Soviet Central Asia on the Periphery"; and Edgar, "Central Asian History."

36. Fedtke, "Wie aus Bucharern," 230–31.

37. See Popitz, *Phänomene der Macht*, 50. Similar contexts have been called "spheres of power." Cf. Schnell, *Räume des Schreckens*, 537–51.

38. Werth, "A State against Its People."

39. For the entire Soviet Union, see Baberowski, *Scorched Earth*.

40. Baberowski, "Auf der Suche nach Eindeutigkeit."

41. Vert, *Terror i besporiadok*, 153–54. Christian Teichmann has suggested that chaos was the fundament of Stalin's power. *Macht der Unordnung*, 240–56.

42. Kassymbekova, "Understanding Stalinism," 1–18, esp. 8–9.

43. Gregory and Markevich, "Creating Soviet Industry," 813.

44. Jakowlew, *Ein Jahrhundert der Gewalt*.

45. Aiagan, *Pravda o golode*, 155–85; Conquest, *Harvest of Sorrow*; Kondrashin, *Golod 1932–1933*; Ivnitskii, *Golod*. For a good review of research on the Kazakh famine, see Grozin, *Golod 1932–1933 godov*.

46. See literature on the Ukrainian *Holodomor*. A model example is "Vernichtung durch Hunger," *Osteuropa* 54, no. 12 (2004).

47. For a differentiated depiction, see Wemheuer, *Der Große Hunger*, 17–23.

48. In contrast to ethnologists and sociologists. See Turnbull, *Mountain People* and Spittler, "Stress, Crisis and Catastrophe."

49. The grave differences in perspective become apparent in carefully argued studies on hunger in Africa. See Keen, *Benefits of Famine* and De Waal, *Famine That Kills*.

50. Aiagan, *Pravda o golode*, 152.

51. Ó Gráda, *Famine.*

52. On the physiology of hunger, see Butterly and Shepherd, *Hunger,* 77–95, 189–225. On distinguishing food shortage crises from famine, see Spittler, "Stress, Crisis and Catastrophe." Devereux, *Theories of Famine,* 16.

53. Collet, "Vulnerabilität," 13.

54. Sen, "Ingredients of Famine Analysis," 460.

55. Watts and Bohle, "Hunger, Famine" and Collet, "Vulnerabilität."

56. Voss, "Vulnerable Can't Speak."

57. Oliver-Smith, "Anthropological Research," 305–9.

58. Spittler, *Handeln in einer Hungerkrise,* 28–32.

59. Bankoff, "Cultures of Disaster."

60. TsGARK, 74-6-63, 67–68 (letter to Kazkraikom from the region of Adai dated June 23, 1927).

61. Tauger, "1932 Harvest" and "Arguing from Errors."

62. Danilov and Zelenin, "Organizovannyi golod."

63. Kindler, "Die Starken."

64. Malysheva and Poznanskii, *Kazakhi*; Kindler, "Auf der Flucht."

65. The term originates in the Russian word for nomad (*kochevnik*) and initially meant nomads who left their own traditional areas (*otkochevali*). During the hunger years from 1931 to 1934 the term began to designate Kazakh famine refugees.

66. Allaniiazov, *Poslednii rubezh*; Omarov, *Rasstrelianaia step'.*

67. Ellman, "Role of Leadership"; Davies and Wheatcroft, "Stalin and the Soviet Famine"; Tauger, "Arguing from Errors"; Ellman, "Stalin and the Soviet Famine."

68. The same holds for the reception of current socioscientific debate on hunger crises. See Devereux, *Theories of Famine,* 5–31.

69. Pianciola, "Famine in the Steppe," 137.

70. Applebaum, *Red Famine*; Kotkin, *Stalin: Waiting for Hitler.*

71. Dietsch, "Politik des Leids." Focusing on the famine in Ukraine, the special issue "Vernichtung durch Hunger," *Osteuropa* 54, no. 12 (2004) shows how widespread the theory of genocide has been: Simon, "Holodomor als Waffe" and Jilge, "Holodomor und Nation." See also Naimark, *Stalin und der Genozid.* For an opposing view see Kondrashin, *Golod 1932–1933,* 10–25. For an attempt to summarize the debate see Kondrashin, *Sovremennaia rossiisko-ukrainskaia istoriografiia.*

72. With one exception: Naimark, *Stalin und der Genozid,* 80–81 See also Simon, *Nationalismus und Nationalitätenpolitik,* 125. In *Golod 1932–1933 godov,* 172–92, Kondrashin tries to show that individual regions along the Middle Volga were as

hit by hunger as was Ukraine. For the extent of hunger throughout the entire Soviet Union, see Kozlov, *Obshchaia tragediia*, 9.

73. Naimark, *Stalin's Genocides*, 70–80.

74. Kindler, "Opfer ohne Täter." On the relationship between victims and aggressors, see Assmann, *Der lange Schatten der Vergangenheit*, 64–84. On Stalinism in general, see Roginskij, "Fragmentierte Erinnerung"; Adler, "Future of the Soviet Past." On historiographical policy in Kazakhstan, see Masanov. Abylkhozhin, and Erofeeva, *Nauchnoe znanie*.

75. Lindner, "What Was a Nomadic Tribe?" 689.

76. In Moscow the Russian State Archive of Socio-Political History (RGASPI) and the State Archive of the Russian Federation (GARF), in Almaty the Archive of the President of the Republic of Kazakhstan (APRK) and the Central State Archive of the Republic of Kazakhstan (TsGARK). RGASPI and APRK are former Soviet Union party and Republic party archives. GARF and TsGARK hold mostly documents from national bureaucratic and governmental departments. Additional documents are from the Russian State Archive of the Economy (RGAE), the Russian State Archive of Contemporary History (RGANI), and the Russian State Military Archive (RGVA).

77. Exceptions are Shayakhmetov, *Silent Steppe*; Chokin, *Chetyre vremeni zhizni*; Nurtazina, "Great Famine." A few fragments from memory have been published, for instance, by Mikhailov in *Khronika velikogo dzhuta*.

78. In 1939 only slightly more than half of the Kazakhs were literate. Bakanov and Zhumashev, "O tempakh," 143.

1. KAZAKH NOMADS AND RUSSIAN COLONIAL POWER

1. Dienes, "Pasturalism in Turkestan," 343. See also Scott, *Seeing Like a State*, 1–5.

2. Barfield, *Perilous Frontier*; Stolberg, "Russland als eurasisches Imperium."

3. Khazanov, *Nomads*, 198.

4. Masanov, *Kochevaia tsivilizatsiia Kazakhov*.

5. Emeljanenko, "Nomadic Year Cycles," 45–49.

6. Sabol, *Russian Colonization*, 22–23.

7. Hudson, *Kazak Social Structure*.

8. This study uses the term "Kazakh" to designate all members of the indigenous population because the sources generally do not reveal any more about the people in question than their (surmised) nationality. For an etymology of the term "kaz-

akh" see Olcott, *Kazakhs*, 4–9. Under the czars the Kazakhs were called "kirgizy" (Kirghiz) and the Kirghiz were called "kara-kirgizy." That did not change during the first years of Soviet rule.

9. Sabol, *Russian Colonization*, 17.

10. Vostrov and Mukanov, *Rodoplemennoi sostav*, 8–10, 248. Thus, for instance, the clan of the Adai, mentioned often in this book, belonged to a tribe of thirteen clans, called a "bajuly," which, in turn, was one of the four lines that constituted the Small Horde.

11. Schatz, *Modern Clan Politics*, 3–11. Esenova, in "Soviet Nationality," does not agree with characterizing the Kazakh nation as an "imaginary community."

12. Abylkhozhin, *Traditsionnaia struktura*, 99–105.

13. Sahadeo, *Russian Colonial Society*, 196.

14. Wendelken, "Russian Immigration," 78–80.

15. In absolute numbers this meant that about 200,000 households were sedentary, about 514,000 households were summer nomads, and about 8,600 were also nomadic during part of the winter. The census concludes that 49,388 households were nomadic throughout the entire year. For the most part, however, these families journeyed at most 50 kilometers between their winter quarters and their summer pasturage. Ohayon, *La sédentarisation*, 371.

16. Atusheva, *Dzhuty v Kazakhstane*. See also Sabol, *Russian Colonization*, 22.

17. For the distinction between "people of Russia" and "Russians," see Torke, *Einführung*, 11–15. The people of Russia includes some who are not necessarily ethnically Russians.

18. Sunderland, *Taming the Wild Field*, 223–28. On the Russian Imperium's treatment of settled and nomadic Muslims see Kappeler, "Die 'vergessenen' Muslime," 35–40.

19. Halperin, *Tartar Yoke*.

20. Khodarkovsky, *Where Two Worlds Met*.

21. Yaroshevski, "Imperial Strategy," 223.

22. For the military conquest, see Becker, "Russia's Central Asian Empire"; Donnely, "Mobile Steppe Frontier." Morrison, "Introduction." For the concept of *inorodtsy*, see Slocum, "Who, and When?" For attempts to settle the nomads, see Sahadeo, "Conquest, Colonialism"; Stolypin and Kriwoschein, *Die Kolonisation Sibiriens*, 111.

23. Sunderland, "Imperial Space," 37.

24. Malikov, *Tsars, Cossacks, and Nomads*, 106–50.

25. Sunderland, "Colonization Question."

26. Erofeeva, "Stolypinskaia agrarnaia reforma."

27. Wendelken, "Russian Immigration." See also Abashin et al., *Tsentral'naia Aziia*, 187–210.

28. For the Kazakh reaction to the statute, see Martin, "Nomadic Land Claims."

29. Happel, *Nomadische Lebenswelten*, 55–90.

30. Bykov, *Istoki modernizatsii Kazakhstana*.

31. Stolypin and Kriwoschein, *Die Kolonisation Sibiriens*, 111.

32. Happel, *Nomadische Lebenswelten*, 60–62; Mark, *Im Schatten*, 78–115.

33. *Materialy po kirgizskomu zemlepol'zovaniiu*, 3.

34. Dingel'shtedt, "Nasha kolonizatsiia," 235.

35. *Materialy po kirgizskomu zemlepol'zovaniiu*, 133–37; Baberowski, *Der Feind*, 71–72.

36. Kendirbay, "Der Kampf um das Land," 390.

37. Pahlen, *Mission to Turkestan*, 18. See also Morrison, "Sowing the Seed," 29.

38. Kappeler, *Russian Empire*, 208.

39. Olcott, "Settlement of the Kazakh Nomads," 21.

40. Pahlen, *Mission to Turkestan*, 174–230. On Russian colonization in Central Asia, see Brower, *Turkestan*. On uprisings, see Malikov, "Kenesary Kasymov Rebellion," and Sabol, "Kazakh Resistance."

41. Crews, *For Prophet and Tsar*, 195.

42. Kuromiya, *Freedom and Terror*.

43. Brower, "Islam and Ethnicity." On adat (customary law), see Martin, *Law and Custom*.

44. Crews, *For Prophet and Tsar*, 199–210.

45. Sabol, *Russian Colonization*.

46. Sabol, *Russian Colonization*, 53–72; Dave, *Kazakhstan*, 33.

47. Kendirbay [Kendirbaeva], "We Are Children of Alash," 6–12.

48. Rottier, "Kazakness of Sedentarization."

49. Amanzholova, *Kazakhskii avtonomizm*. For other regions of Central Asia, see Khalid, *Politics*.

50. Brower, "Kyrgyz Nomads."

51. Happel, *Nomadische Lebenswelten*, 105–21.

52. Happel, *Nomadische Lebenswelten*, 127–46.

53. Mendikulova, *Istoricheskie sud'by*, 82–85.

54. Engelstein, *Russia in Flames*, 348–59.

55. For Turkestan, see Buttino, *Revoliutsiia naoborot*, 21, Khalid, *Making Uzbekistan*, 56–89. For the Caucasus, see Baberowski, *Der Feind*, 109–41. Safarov, *Kolonial'naia revoliutsiia*.

56. Blank, "Ethnic and Party Politics," 2.

57. Abylkhozhin, "Kazakhstan v sovetskom totalitarnom prostranstve," 261.

58. On the fate of members of the Alash Orda, see Koigeldiev, *Stalinizm i repressii,* 17–77.

59. This portrayal follows that of Olcott in *Kazakhs,* 129–56. Research has yet to study the civil war in Central Asia. Its political history can be found in Amanzholova, "Alash, Sovety, Bol'sheviki."

60. The following republics resulted from dividing up Central Asia in 1924–25: Kazakh ASSR, Uzbek SSR, Tadzhik SSR, Turkmen SSR, and the Kara-Kirghiz Autonomous Region, which in 1926 became the Kirghiz ASSR. For more detail on the highly complex division into nations, see Haugen, *Establishment of National Republics.* For a fundamental discussion of the nationalities policy, see Martin, *Affirmative Action Empire.*

2. SOVIET RULE IN THE STEPPE

1. Goloshchekin, "Za sovetizatsiiu aula," 34. See also Isaev, "Natsional'naia politika partii."

2. Rossiiskii Gosudarstvennyi Arkhiv Sotsial'no-Politicheskoi Istorii (RGASPI), 17-6-330, 68 (shorthand note from an Orgu biuro session, n.d. [September 1926]).

3. Thomas, *Kazakh Nomads,* 1–15. For a similar argument with regard to the Russian state in Siberia, see Ssorin-Chaikov, *Social Life,* 4.

4. Baberowski, "Vertrauen durch Anwesenheit," 32. For the Soviet Union, see Schnell, *Räume des Schreckens,* 438–49.

5. The situation was no different in other Central Asian republics. Cf. Edgar, "Genealogy." For Siberia, see Slezkine, *Arctic Mirrors,* 163–83.

6. Easter, *Reconstructing the State*; Hosking, "Patronage"; Baberowski, *Der Feind,* 223–41.

7. Schatz, *Modern Clan Politics,* xvi–xxvi.

8. RGASPI, 17-84-1056, 9 (shorthand note from a meeting at CK RKP[b] of the secretaries of the party organizations in the Turko-Tatar group, January 2, 1926).

9. RGASPI, 17-4-326, 53 top.

10. Arkhiv Prezidenta Respubliki Kazakhstan (APRK), 719-1-1445, 15–15ob (a characterization of the party cells in the district of Alty-Karasuisk, n.d. [1929]).

11. RGASPI, 17-67-82, 136, 138 (report to Stalin from Kauchikovskii, March 12, 1925).

12. Wendelken, "Russian Immigration," 86.

13. Riabokon, "K voprosu o sovetizatsii aula," 42.

14. The infrastructural situation was always a subject of complaints. See Payne, *Stalin's Railroad*.

15. APRK, 141–1–5827, 181–188, found in Degitaeva, *Levon Mirzoian*, 48-49.

16. Riadnin, *Kazakhstan na putiakh*, 44.

17. RGASPI, 17–14–326, 52 (report on the "Red Caravans" dated October 16, 1922). See also Olcott, *Kazakhs*, 207.

18. Feoktistov, "K voprosu ob organizatsii," 24.

19. Feoktistov, "O rabote sredi kirgiz."

20. Gosudarstvennyi Arkhiv Rossiiskoi Federatsii (GARF), 1235–122–318, 11–11ob (excerpt of a complaint from the Department of Syr-Dar'insk, Aul No. 1, n.d. [prior to September 29, 1927]).

21. Otchet Kazakhskoi Kontrol'noi Komissii, 24.

22. RGASPI, 17–67–82, 138.

23. RGASPI, 17–25–146, 67 (shorthand note from the Seventh Zhetysu Government's Conference of the Communist Party [b], January 2–5, 1927).

24. For example, A. Dzhangil'din, one of the few local Communists who took sides with the Bolsheviks during the civil war and survived all purges. Ochak and Takenov, *Internatsional'nyi otriad*. See also Thomas, *Kazakh Nomads*, 46–48.

25. Omarov, *Rasstrelianaia step'*, 10. Al'niiazov's connection to Dzhangil'din had facilitated his placement. See Tlepov, *Stranitsy istorii*, 5–7.

26. APRK, 719–1–1036, 2 ob-3 (report on the Adaevsk region, 1928). On *adat*, the Kazakh customary law, see Martin, *Law and Custom*, 17–34.

27. Aldazhumanov, "Krest'ianskoe dvizhenie," 76.

28. APRK, 719–1–1036, 3.

29. RGASPI, 17–84–586, 47ob (report on the Alash Orda and Kirghiz national groups for the period from January 1–March 1, 1923, dated March 14, 1923).

30. Omarov, *Rasstrelianaia step'*, 12.

31. Ishchenko and Kazbekov, *Osobennosti sel'skogo khoziaistva*, 90–97.

32. According to Omarov, Al'niiazov lost his position in 1922. See Omarov, *Rasstrelianaia step'*, 12. But Aldazhumanov says that Al'niiazov was a member of the KazTsIK until 1925. See Aldazhumanov, "Krest'ianskoe dvizhenie," 78. Perhaps enough material to file charges against him had been gathered by 1924. See APRK, 719–1–1036, 3.

33. Zhanaev, "O chem povedali dokumenty."

34. Eraliev had presumably not been murdered, but had fallen overboard from a ship on the Caspian Sea after a drinking spree. But the local OGPU was less interested in the true circumstances surrounding his death than in deriving some sort of advan-

tage from it. For details, see Aldazhumanov, "Krest'ianskoe dvizhenie," 79; Nabiev, *Stepnaia tragediia*, 257–59.

35. See data in *Materialy k otchetu Kazakhskogo Kraevogo Komiteta*.

36. Goloshchekin, "Ob aul'nom kommuniste." "Face to the aul" was the Kazakh variation of *litsom k derevne* (face to the village), a major Soviet campaign in the countryside. For details, see McDonald, *Face to the Village*.

37. Sokolovskii, *Kazakhskii aul*, 15.

38. For an analysis of the problem and the details of the program, see Goloshchekin, "Za sovetizatsiiu aula," 22–45.

39. Goloshchekin, "Ob aul'nom kommuniste," 88–92.

40. *Otchet Kazakhskoi Kraevoi Kontrol'noi Komissii*, 22–23.

41. *Otchet Kazakhskoi Kraevoi Kontrol'noi Komissii*, 24. Recruiting new cadres was a problem. See APRK 141-1-1045, 57–63, in Kozybaev, *Uraz Dzhandosov*, 1:357–60.

42. APRK, 719-1-1445, 20 (report on the state of the party in the region of Adaevsk, May 1, 1929).

43. RGASPI, 17-85-59, 27 (report on the state of the party in the region of Zhetysu, September 17, 1926).

44. APRK, 719-1-1445, 21. In some places that remained unchanged until the 1930s, see Kozybaev, "Za novuiu zhizn'," 231–32.

45. GARF, 1235-120-106, 20–20ob (message from the RSFSR Department for Court Instruction at the People's Commissariat for Justice, August 13, 1928).

46. Togzhanov, *O kazakhskom aule*, 18–19.

47. Togzhanov, *O kazakhskom aule*, 40–41.

48. Altrichter, *Die Bauern von Tver*, 134–74.

49. Shayakhmetov, *Silent Steppe*, 26.

50. Togzhanov, *O kazakhskom aule*, 19. For similar situations prior to the revolution, see Crews, *For Prophet and Tsar*, 21–30.

51. Togzhanov, *O kazakhskom aule*, 21–27.

52. For similar circumstances in Turkmenistan, see Edgar, *Tribal Nation*, 167–82, in the Caucasus, see Baberowski, *Der Feind*, 478–98, and in Kirghizia, see Loring, "Building Socialism," 97–100.

53. Sokolovskii, *Kazakhskii aul*, 23.

54. RGASPI, 17-85-59, 26 (report on the state of party organization in Zhetysu of September 17, 1926).

55. *Sovetskaia step'*, December 22, 1925, quoted from Sokolovskii, *Kazakhskiii aul*, 24. Similar descriptions can be found in Togzhanov, *O kazakhskom aule*, 19–20.

56. Administrative auls had no names, merely numbers.

57. The entire episode is given in Riabokon, "K voprosu o sovetizatsii aula," 49–51; the quotation is on page 50.

58. For details, see Kotkin, *Magnetic Mountain*, 198–237.

59. Amanzholova, "Kazakhskaia avtonomiia," 140.

60. Sokolovskii, *Kazakhskii aul*, 15.

61. Schatz, *Modern Clan Politics*, xxii.

62. Togzhanov, *O kazakhskom aule*, 62.

63. Togzhanov, *O kazakhskom aule*, 20.

64. Togzhanov, *O kazakhskom aule*, 61.

65. Togzhanov, *O kazakhskom aule*, 62–63.

66. Hausmann, *Gesellschaft als lokale Veranstaltung*, uses the term "local affair."

67. In retrospect, the vision of Soviet ethnographers was restricted to the notion that sedentarization had always been the aim of Soviet policy. See Dakhshleiger, "Iz opyta istorii osedaniia."

68. Thomas, *Kazakh Nomads*, 46–48.

69. Slastukhin, "Sotsialisticheskaia perestroika," 75–77.

70. Stolypin and Kriwoschein, *Die Kolonisation Sibiriens*, 37–40, 111.

71. For Soviet ethnographic views of the essence of nomadism, see Sneath, *Headless State*, 121–56. On interpreting conflict within the aul as class struggle, see Lane, "Ethnic and Class Stratification."

72. Ermikov, "Organizatsiia shkol," 117.

73. Slastukhin, "Sotsialisticheskaia perestroika," 76.

74. Ermikov, "Organizatsiia shkol," 117.

75. Michaels, "Medical Propaganda," 160–61.

76. Michaels, *Curative Powers*, 109–19.

77. On the relation of biomedicine to ethnomedicine, see Michaels, *Curative Powers*, 73–86.

78. For details, see RGASPI, 62-2-975, 14–19 (report on Party Komsomol work at the summering grounds, written before August 2, 1927). Teams like this existed until the 1950s. See Michaels, *Curative Powers*, 170–75.

79. For an overview, see Khalid, *Islam after Communism*, 50–83.

80. Northrop, *Veiled Empire*.

81. RGASPI, 17-10-392, 3–9 (Zhenotdel Meeting for the Government of Semipalatinsk, n.d. [1923]).

82. To use Massel's term; Massel, *Surrogate Proletariat*.

83. For details, see Massell, *Surrogate Proletariat* and Northrop, *Veiled Empire*, 69–101.

84. RGASPI, 17–10–442, 33 (report to the administration of the region of Samarkand, n.d.).

85. On the situation in Turkmenistan, see Edgar, "Emancipation of the Unveiled," 139, and Northrop, *Veiled Empire*, 250, 269–83.

86. Akopov, "Bor'ba s bytovymi prestupleniiami," 62.

87. Baberowski, *Der Feind*, 442–78. See also Michaels, *Curative Powers*, 129–34.

88. RGASPI, 17–10–138 (telegram from Zhetysu dated November 19, 1925) recounts the murder of a Kazakh widow who had refused to marry her deceased husband's brother.

89. RGASPI, 17–10–138, 38 (excerpts from the OGPU's Information Report No. 2 for the period from August 15 to September 1, 1925).

90. RGASPI, 17–10–138, 40 (Report from the Information Department of the OGPU for Kazakstan, n.d. [1925–26]).

91. RGASPI, 17–10–138, 40.

92. Kenzhaliev and Dauletova, *Kazakhskoe obychnoe pravo*, 123.

93. Michaels, *Curative Powers*, 1–4. On continuity and change in the life of Muslim women, see Kamp, *New Woman in Uzbekistan*, 215–23. On conflicts on a local level, see RGASPI, 17–10–138, 15 (report from Uralsk to the party organization, n.d. [1925]).

94. Khrushchev, "Perspektiva." For details, see Payne, *Stalin's Railroad*, 11–38.

95. Payne, "Forge," 231. Railroad advocates saw things differently. See Briskin, *Na Iuzhturksibe*.

96. Payne, "Forge," 237–42.

97. Akiner, *Formation of Kazakh Identity*, 34.

98. Kindler, "New York in der Steppe"; Sneath, *Headless State*, 125–37.

99. Lattimore, *Inner Asian Frontiers*, 522; Golden, "Nomads," 86; Khazanov, *Nomads*.

100. Pianciola, "Famine in the Steppe," 141.

101. Farah and Touati, *Sedentarisierung von Nomaden*, 47.

102. RGASPI, 122–1–156, 1 ob (lecture by Rudzutak, June 16, 1921).

103. Matskevich, "Sravnitel'naia dlina kochevok," 6.

104. Thomas, "Caspian Disputes."

105. APRK, 719–1–1036, 2ob (brief information on the Adaevsk region for the Region Control Commission, 1928).

106. Letter from Dzhanesov in Nabiev, *Stepnaia tragediia*, 360.

107. Chuvelev, "O reorganizatsii," 47.

108. Even Soviet maps indicated this area as no man's land. See Ishchenko and Kazbekov, *Osobennosti sel'skogo khoziaistva*, 90.

109. Chuvelev, "O reorganizatsii," 47.

110. For a history of the concept of dzhut, see Farkas and Kemp, "Reinventing the 'Dzud'" and Atusheva, *Dzhuty v Kazakhstane*. Such extreme events happened regularly. The first decades of the twentieth century saw several such storms with devastating consequences for the regions hit by them: Chuvelev, "O reorganizatsii," 48. Shirin Akiner has said that such events served as anchors for the Kazakhs' collective memory: Akiner, *Formation of Kazakh Identity*, 7. APRK, 141-1-1694, 114–115ob (letter from Ateuliev to Goloshchekin, August 18, 1928). Other areas, such as the region around Semipalatinsk, also experienced great losses due to *dzhuds*. See GARF, 1235-122-304, 7 (letter to SNK RSFSR from Kazakhstan, January 11, 1927) and RGASPI, 17-33-420, 63–64 (report on mass deaths of livestock in the Government of Semipalatinsk, May 8, 1928). See also Kindler, "... es gibt menschliche Opfer," 156–58.

111. Shvetsov, *Kazakhskoe khoziaistvo*, 105.

112. Donich, "Problema," 141. Within a few years both Shvetsov and Donich were branded as vermin for their doubts about sedentarization. See Kurskii, "Kontrrevoliutsionnye urediteli," 24.

113. Donich, "Problema," 142.

114. Sirius, "K voprosu o perspektivakh."

115. Ermikov, "Organizatsiia shkol," 114.

116. Polochanskii, *Za novy aul-kstau*, 10.

117. On insufficient aid for the relevant population, see GARF, 1235-122-304, 5–5ob (letter from Kazakhstan to SNK RSFSR, January 13, 1927 [?]). On possible steps toward improvement, see RGASPI, 17-25-18, 89–91 (resolution regarding the battle against aridity and on preventing dzud, February 1, 1928).

118. Polochanskii, *Za novy aul-kstau*, 12–23.

119. GARF, 393-67-450, 13–14 (SNK RSFSR resolution on increasing animal husbandry in Kazakhstan, n.d. [1927]).

120. On nomadic economy, see Khazanov, *Nomads*, 15–25.

121. Chelintsev, "Perspektiva razvitiia," 3–5; Gromov, "K voprosu."

122. One desiatin equals 2.7 acres.

123. GARF, 393-67-450, 2–12 (report on the development of livestock breeding in Kazakhstan dated January 31, 1927).

124. Togzhanov, "Burzhuaznye i melkoburzhuaznye teorii."

125. Chelintsev, "Perspektiva razvitiia," 5.

126. Donich, "Problema," 141.

127. Brown, "Gridded Lives."

128. Payne, "Seeing Like a Soviet State," 62.

129. RGASPI, 17–14–326, 51 (report on the Red Caravans, October 16, 1922).

130. Donich, "Raionirovanie KSSR," 14.

131. Sokolovskii, *Kazakhskii aul*, 1.

132. Polochanskii, *Za novy aul-kstau.*

133. Sokolovskii, *Kazakhskii aul*, 1.

134. In *Modernity and Ambivalence*, Zygmunt Baumann describes the essence of modernity as an effort to overcome ambivalence.

135. Trotha, "Über den Erfolg," 225–26.

136. On this point their agenda was no different from that of other "modern" states that had nomads living within their territory. See Scott, *Seeing Like a State*, 3–10.

137. Martin, *Affirmative Action Empire*, 59–67.

138. Briskin, *V strane semi rek.* For the region, see *Ocherk o deiatel'nosti*, 6–25.

139. On the 1916 Revolt, see Happel, *Nomadische Lebenswelten.*

140. Buttino, *Revoliutsiia naoborot*, 202–6.

141. Amanzholova, *Alash, Sovety, Bol'sheviki*, 67.

142. Chebotareva, "Problemy russkoi kolonizatsii," 130.

143. Holquist, "To Count," 130.

144. Genis, "Deportatsiia," 44.

145. RGASPI, 85–23–99, 1–2 (report on land distribution in the Turkestan Republic, September 29, 1921). RGASPI, 122–1–131, 1–1ob (edict regarding land distribution, n.d. [1920]).

146. For a different view, see Margulan and Vostrov, *Kul'tura i byt*, 12–13.

147. Genis, "Deportatsiia." See also Pianciola, "Décoloniser l'Asie centrale?"

148. GARF, 393–1a–211, 56 (report from Serafimov to the executive committee of the VTsIK, May 15, 1926).

149. GARF, 393–1a–211, 55. Ryskulov celebrated the land reform as a huge success. Ryskulov, "Dzhetysuiskie voprosy," 7–32.

150. Genis, "Deportatsiia," 46–47.

151. GARF, 3316–64–220, 53 (submitted by farmers from Serafimov, n.d. [1926]).

152. RGASPI, 122–1–156, 3ob (report from Rudzutak, June 14, 1921). For Rudzutak's position on this issue, see Genis, "Deportatsiia," 46.

153. Genis, "Deportatsiia," 45. Serafimov also stresses the element of revenge involved in these events: GARF, 3316–64–220, 12 (Serafimov's report to the executive committee of the VTsIK, May 15, 1926).

154. Genis, "Deportatsiia," 48.

155. Asmis, *Als Wirtschaftspionier*, 202–3.

156. On the escalation of affairs see Genis, "Deportatsiia," 54; RGASPI, 5–2-85, 2, in Amanzholova, *Rossiia i Tsentral'naia Aziia*, 322–23.

157. RGASPI, 558–2-35, 5, in Amanzholova, *Rossiia i Tsentral'naia Aziia*, 326.

158. Genis, "Deportatsiia," 56.

159. RGASPI, 122–1-156, 35–36 (instructions for battling counterrevolutionary, malicious kulaks in traditional relocation villages, n.d. [1922]).

160. GARF, 393–1a-311, 111 (Serafimov's report to the Executive Committee of the VTsIK, before June 4, 1926).

161. Figes, *People's Tragedy*, 617–22.

162. Wehner, *Bauernpolitik*.

163. RGASPI, 122–1-156, 50b and 7 (instructions for fighting counterrevolutionary kulaks in relocation villages, n.d.).

164. Figes, *People's Tragedy*, 775–82; Wehner, *Bauernpolitik*, 59–66.

165. Tsentral'nyi Gosudarstvennyi Arkhiv Respubliki Kazakhstan (TsGARK), 930–1-2, 32, in Karazhanov and Takenov, *Noveishaia istoriia Kazakhstana*, 1:150–52.

166. Masanov, *Istoriia Kazakhstana*, 369. This number coincides with other calculations, for example, in Alekseenko and Alekseenko, *Naselenie Kazakhstana za 100 let*, 43–45.

167. Martin, *Affirmative Action Empire*, 60.

168. On Russian immigration to Xinjiang, see Abdullaev, *Ot Sin'tsziania do Khorasana*, 277–98.

169. For biographical data on Mendeshev (1882–1938), see Medeubaev, "Pervyi vsekazakhstanskii starosta." See also Thomas, *Kazakh Nomads*, 44–46.

170. On relief supplies, see Patenaude, *Big Show*.

171. RGASPI, 558–2-32, 38–39ob, in Amanzhalova, *Rossiia i Tsentral'naia Aziia*, 350–51. For details on relief shipments, see Verkhoturov, "Asharshylyk," 10.

172. Taken from Shakir-zade, *Grundzüge der Nomadenwirtschaft*, 49.

173. Ryskulov, *Revoliutsiia*, 100. For biographical data on Ryskulov (1894–1938), see Akhmetova, Grigor'ev, and Shoikin, "Turar Ryskulov." V. N. Ustinov presents a somewhat more differentiated view in *Turar Ryskulov*.

174. TsGARK, 1145–2-29, 36–41, in Karazhanov and Takenov, *Noveishaia istoriia Kazakhstana*, 155–59. See also Wehner, *Bauernpolitik*, 125–32.

175. For a debate on the New Economic Policy (NEP), see Hildermeier, *Geschichte der Sowjetunion*, 159–61.

176. This fear was expressed by Uraz Dzhandosov: APRK, 1–1-238, 156–157, in Kozybaev, *Uraz Dzhandosov*, 1:159.

177. Ryskulov was against dividing the region into several national republics. See debates, for example, about Tajikistan, in Bergne, *Birth of Tajikistan*, 22, 54.

178. For biographical data on Aytiev (1886–1936), see Zhakypov et al., *Narkomy Kazakhstana*, 46.

179. For biographical data on Struppe (1889–1937), see Zhakypov et al., *Narkomy Kazakhstana*, 320.

180. RGASPI, 558–2–32, 40–44ob (letter from Ryskulov to Stalin on the state of the KASSR, February 20, 1922), in Amanzholova, *Rossiia i Tsentral'naia Aziia*, 348–49.

181. TsGA Respubliki Uzbekistan, R-17–1–734, 37–56ob, in Kozybaev, *Uraz Dzhandosov*, 1:160–70.

182. Dzhandosov, "Stat'ia", in Kozybaev, *Uraz Dzhandosov*, 1:195–209.

183. GARF, 1235–120–178, 72–75ob (letter from Munbaev to the VTsIK, August 11, 1925).

184. Martin, *Affirmative Action Empire*, 61. Agricultural households were granted approximately 120 acres of land, seminomadic households approximately 400 acres, and nomadic households about 1,000 acres of land. See APRK, 141–1–340, 55–65, in Kozybaev, *Uraz Dzhandosov*, 1:309 and Pianciola, "Famine in the Steppe," 145.

185. Chebotareva, "Problemy russkoi kolonizatsii," 88–95.

186. RGASPI, 17–84–949, 18–20, in Gatagova, *TsK RKP(b)*, 1:284–85.

187. In this matter they differed little from representatives of other European colonial powers behaving like members of allegedly superior societies. See Osterhammel, *Colonialism*, 105–12.

188. Regarding what this meant for the native people of Siberia, see Stolberg, *Sibirien*, 168–72.

189. Pahlen, *Mission to Turkestan*, 18–21.

190. Briskin, *V strane semi rek*, 47. On the socialist custom of submitting reports as a means of communication, see Merl, *Politische Kommunikation*, 82–100, and Fitzpatrick, *Stalin's Peasants*, 15–16.

191. GARF, 3316–64–220, 32 (complaint from the official representative of Kaskelensk, n.d. [1926]).

192. GARF, 3316–64–220, 34; quote from 33.

193. GARF, 3316–64–220, 27 (report by farmers from Kazansko-Bogorodskogo to Serafimov, March 11, 1926).

194. GARF, 1235–140–127, 201 (shorthand note from a meeting of the Central Asia Bureau, March 17, 1927).

195. Chebotareva, "Problemy russkoi kolonizatsii," 118.

196. GARF, 1235–121–240, 128 (letter from the village of Obekinsk to the People's Commission for Agriculture in Moscow, n.d. [1924–25]).

197. Martin, *Affirmative Action Empire*, 62.

198. See monthly reports from the OGPU: RGASPI, 17–87, 201 (survey of political conditions in the USSR, January–March 1927). See also RGASPI, 17–87–196, 370–84 (report by the information office of the OGPU, December 29, 1925). Further examples can be found in *Sovershenno sekretno*, vol. 4.2, 104–5 and 928–29.

199. GARF, 1235–140–27, 12 (letter from Smidovich to Zelensky, April 20, 1926). For details on the Central Asian Bureau. see Keller, "Central Asian Bureau."

200. From March to April 1926 alone, more than 1,500 grievances were submitted by European farmers. See GARF, 393–1a-311, 113 (report on creating independent Russian regions in Zhetysu; before June 4, 1926).

201. For exact numbers, see RGASPI, 62–1-42, 106–7 (shorthand note from the Seventh Plenum of the Office for Central Asia, July 3–4, 1925).

202. Amanzholova and Kuleshov, "Istoricheskie sud'by," 71.

203. GARF, 393–1a-311, 114–22.

204. Edgar, *Tribal Nation*, 45.

205. Hirsch, *Empire of Nations*, 165–73.

206. Chebotareva, "Problemy russkoi kolonizatsii," 116.

207. Martin, *Affirmative Action Empire*, 1–27.

208. GARF, 1235–120–178, 91.

209. GARF, 1235–140–127, 5 (letter from Asfendiiarov to Kiselev, April 19, 1926).

210. GARF, 1235–140–127, 215 (shorthand note from the meeting of the Executive Committee of the Central Asian Bureau, March 17, 1927).

211. RGASPI, 62–1-42, 115.

212. GARF, 393–1a-211, 67ob (report on the land issue as dealt with by the Special Committee, May 15, 1926).

213. GARF, 1235–140–127, 193 (proceedings of the Committee for Investigating Complaints, March 15, 1927).

214. RGASPI, 17–84–1056, 33 (shorthand note from a meeting of the secretaries of the national party organizations of the Turko-Tatar group, January 2, 1926).

215. Martin, *Affirmative Action Empire*, 61.

216. GARF, 1235–140–127, 223 (shorthand note from a meeting of the Office for Central Asia, March 17, 1927).

217. Chebotareva, "Problemy russkoi kolonizatsii," 98–111.

218. Koigeldiev, *Stalinizm i repressii*, 329.

219. Martin, *Affirmative Action Empire*, 67.

220. Chelintsev, "Perspektiva razvitiia," 3.

221. Martin, *Affirmative Action Empire*, 67.

222. For population development, see Lariuel' and Peiruz, *Russkii vopros*, 342–43.

223. Amanzholova, "Kazakhskoe obshchestvo," 75.

224. Hirsch, *Empire of Nations*, 94f-8 On Kazakhstan's borders, see Amanzholova, "Kazakhskaia avtonomiia," 120–26.

225. *VII Vsekazakhskaia konferentsiia*, 48–53.

226. Olcott, *Kazakhs*, 209–15. For early forms of the conflict, see Blank, "Ethnic and Party Politics."

227. Buttino, "Politics and Social Conflicts."

228. Trotsky, *Challenges of the Left*, 211. On Trotsky's exile to Alma-Ata, see Service, *Trotsky*, 366–75.

229. APRK, 140-1-121, 1–14, in Karazhanov and Takenov, *Noveishaia istoriia Kazakhstana*, 1:172. Biographical data on Sadvokasov (1900–1933) can be found in Zhakypov et al., *Narkomy Kazakhstana*, 293.

230. On integrating the Alash Orda into the Soviet project, see Gürbüz, "Caught between Nationalism and Socialism," 132–35.

231. Rysakov, "Praktika shovinizma."

232. Fedtke, "Wie aus Bucharern Usbeken." On Stalin's role, see Martin, *Affirmative Action Empire*, 231–32.

233. Martin, *Affirmative Action Empire*, 233.

234. Koigeldiev, *Stalinizm i repressii*.

235. Following a resolution of March 1921 regarding the unity of the party, organizing subgroups and factions was fatal. See Hildermeier, *Geschichte der Sowjetunion*, 161.

236. The chairman of the Kirghiz SNK, Iusup Abdrakhmanov, was deeply frustrated. See Abdrakhmanov, *Izbrannye trudy*, 81–164 and Teichmann, "Arbeiten, Kämpfen, Scheitern."

237. RGASPI, 17-67-87, 163–165 (letter to Rudzutak from Nurmakov, Dzangil'din, and others, May 11, 1924).

238. RGASPI, 17-67-82, 205–11 (letter to Stalin and Kuybyshev from Khodzhanov, April 6, 1925). See also RGASPI, 62-1-42, 17 (shorthand note from the Seventh Plenum of the Office for Central Asia, July 3–4, 1925).

239. That was, for example, Isaak Zelenskii's opinion; RGASPI, 17-84-1056, 35.

240. GARF, 1235-120-178, 17–18 (report from the Kazakh SNK on work during 1924–25); RGASPI, 17-25-146, 35 (shorthand report from the Eighth Zhetysu Government Conference of the VKP(b), January 1–5, 1927).

241. RGASPI, 17-84-1056, 37. This resulted in filling lower positions in the administration with Kazakhs, while in general Europeans filled higher-ranking positions.

242. RGASPI, 17–25–146, 20.

243. Martin, *Affirmative Action Empire*; Hirsch, "Toward an Empire of Nations"; Simon, *Nationalismus und Nationalitätenpolitik*.

244. RGASPI, 17–67–87, 52–53 (letter from Ezhov to the Gubkom RKP(b) in Akmolinsk, December 28, 1924). See also Getty and Naumov, *Yezhov*, 61–63.

245. European comrades thought that the disputes between these groups were mainly conflicts between clans. See RGASPI, 17–67–82, 46–49 (report by I. M. Bekker, secretary of the Aktyubinsk Government Committee, for the period from July to October 1925).

246. APRK, 719–5-5, 71 (report on political groups, n.d. [1925]).

247. On the scandal surrounding this newspaper that caused Stalin to intervene several times, see RGASPI, 558–11–133, 66–67 (letter from Stalin to the Office of the Kirkraikom, May 29, 1925), and 69–71 (the office's reply to Stalin, July 1925).

248. For biographical data on Khodzhanov (1894–1938), see Arapov, "Zapiska," 85.

249. APRK, 719–5-5, 75–77.

250. APRK, 719–1-66, 3, in Kozybaev, *Uraz Dzhandosov*, 1:260-61.

251. Olcott, "Basmachi." On the affair involving Sultan-Galiev, see Baberowski, *Der Feind*, 288–91.

252. Stalin, "Rights and 'Lefts.'" On Ryskulov, see Stalin, *Works*, 5:311–12.

253. RGASPI, 558–11–133, 4 (Stalin's note to Khodzhanov, n.d.).

254. Taken from RGASPI, 17–11–112–566, 16–28, in Gatagova, *TsK RKP(b)*, 1:212. For Khodzhanov's call for a Central Asian federation, see Arapov, "Zapiska," 85–89.

255. Naneishvili (1878–1940) was from Georgia and in office from the autumn of 1924 until the summer of 1925. For Khodzhanov's relationship to these two men, see RGASPI, 17–67–82, 241 (letter from Dzhangil'din to Stalin, n.d. [1925]).

256. He knew with certainty whom he had to thank for his loss of power. See RGASPI, 17–67–82, 23 (letter from Goloshchekin to Stalin, October 25, 1925).

257. Getty and Naumov, *Yezhov*, 65–67. Ezhov later became head of the NKVD.

258. RGASPI, 558–11–133, 88 (Stalin's letter to Goloshchekin, March 9, 1927) and 90–91 (Goloshchekin's letter to Stalin, March 23, 1927).

259. This depiction of events has been taken from APRK, 719–5-5, 11–18 (report on groups in the district of Chelkar, government Aktyubinsk, after May 25, 1927).

260. For biographical data on Almanov (1896–1941), see Zhakypov et al., *Narkomy Kazakhstana*, 52.

261. GASO, 73–1-18, 102, in Amanzholova, *Rossiia i Tsentral'naia Aziia*, 321–22.

262. For more on the methods, see APRK, 719–5-5, 16.

263. APRK, 719–5-5, 14.

264. APRK, 719–5–5, 15–16.

265. Kulumbetov (1891–1938) remained deputy chairman of the Kazakh Sovnarkom until 1935 and was chairman of the KazTsIK from 1935 until his arrest in August 1937. See Zhakypov et al., *Narkomy Kazakhstana*, 214.

266. RGASPI, 17–67–326, 206 (Sadvokasov's letter to Stalin, October 9, 1926).

267. RGASPI, 17–67–326, 206 See also Kozybaev, *Novoe myshlenie*, 64.

268. Goloshchekin, "Za sovetizatsiiu aula," 22–45.

269. Amanzholova and Kuleshov, "Istoricheskie sud'by," 82.

270. Anatolii Al'shanskii (1898–1940) led the government departments of the OGPU in Akmolinsk and Zhetysu until 1927, when he was made a deputy to the commissioned representative of the OGPU in Kazakhstan.

271. APRK, 141–1–1458, 21 (letter to Goloshchekin and Sadvokasov, September 10, 1926).

272. Khodzhanov was of the same mind. RGASPI, 17–67–82, 208 (letter from Khodzhanov to Stalin and Kuybyshev, April 6, 1925).

273. On the fate of those Alash Orda members who joined the Communists, see Koigeldiev, *Stalinizm i represii*, 17–77. Among them was Akhmet Baitursynov (1873–1937), one of Kazakhstan's most prominent intellectuals. See Ashin et al., *Repressirovannaia Tiurkologiia*, 177–95.

274. Kozybaev, "Sud nad pamiat'iu," 139.

275. For example, Mikhailov, *Khronika velikogo dzhuta*.

276. Taken from Koigeldiev, *Stalinizm i repressii*, 323.

277. RGASPI, 17–67–82, 242 (letter from Dzhangil'din to Stalin, n.d. [1925]).

278. Easter, *Reconstructing the State*, 72–88.

279. Mikhailov, *Khronika velikogo dzhuta*, 15–30.

280. The term is modeled after that of the "Team-Stalin" in Wheatcroft, "From Team-Stalin to Degenerate Tyranny."

281. For biographical data on Isaev (1899–1938), see Zhakypov et al., *Narkomy Kazakhstana*, 172. On Kuramysov (1896–1938), 214.

282. Fedtke, "Wie aus Bucharern Usbeken."

283. Stalin, "Foundations of Leninism," 191.

3. COLLECTIVIZATION AND SEDENTARIZATION

1. Olcott, "Collectivization Drive"; Ertz, "Kazakh Catastrophe."

2. Ohayon, *La sédentarisation*, 71–5.

3. Goloshchekin, "Kazakhstan na pod'eme," 19.

4. Fitzpatrick, *Stalin's Peasants*, 4.

5. Stalin, "Year of Great Change." Most current literature uses the phrase "Year of the Great Turn." On the "silencing" of individual peasants, see Merl, *Bauern unter Stalin*. On defining the period covered by measures taken in connection with collectivization see Ivnitskii, *Kollektivizatsiia i raskulachivanie*, 14–16.

6. Hildermeier, *Geschichte der Sowjetunion*, 377–401; Lewin, *Making of the Soviet System*, 91–95.

7. Stalin, "Industrialization," 11:167.

8. Schnell, *Räume des Schreckens*, 465–71.; Viola, *Peasant Rebels*. For a detailed account of how authorities exploited existing conflicts in a Ukrainian village, see Goichenko, *Skvoz' raskulachivanie*, 157–63.

9. Some nomadic regions had no soviets at all until the late 1920s. See Tlepov, *Stranitsy istoriia*.

10. Teichmann, *Macht der Unordnung*, 128–31; Edgar, *Tribal Nation*, 197–220; Kopelev, *Education of a True Believer*, 224–36.

11. Schnell, *Räume des Schreckens*, 402–8.

12. Zulkasheva et al., *Tragediia kazakhskogo aula*, vol. 1.

13. Taken from "Zakliuchenie komissii," 36.

14. Gosudarstvennyi Arkhiv Rossiiskoi Federatsii (GARF), 393–67–449, 4–8ob (report on voluntary bai tributes, before May 31, 1927).

15. GARF, 393–67–449, 9 (NKVD response to the report, n.d.).

16. For exact numbers see Allaniiazov, *Poslednii rubezh*, 104.

17. In 1925 Bekker (1898–1937) was the first party secretary in Aktyubinsk; in 1926 he went to Semipalatinsk where he held the same position.

18. The difference in price that Stalin mentioned was between 12 and 27 kopecks per pood (one pood is a bit more than thirty-six pounds avoirdupois); Rossiiskii Gosudarstvennyi Arkhiv Sotsial'no-Politicheskoi Istorii (RGASPI), 558–11–119, 29 (telegram from Stalin in Novosibirsk to the Central Committee, January 20, 1928).

19. Raiter was probably also ordered to go there; RGASPI, 558–11–119, 35 (telegram from Stalin to Bekker, January 22, 1928). I thank Andreas Oberender for bringing these documents to my attention.

20. Stalin is said to have called the delegates from Semipalatinsk speculators and thrown them off the train. See Platunov, "Stalin na Altae."

21. Quotes taken from Wehner, *Bauernpolitik*, 370. Hughes, "Capturing the Russian Peasantry," 77.

22. For more on Stalin in Siberia, see Hughes, *Stalin, Siberia*, 137–48., Kotkin, *Stalin*, 1:661–91, and Il'inykh, *Khroniki khlebnogo fronta*, 129–43. In February 1928 Golos-

hchekin probably also met with Stalin in Siberian Omsk and received instructions from him on how to execute grain procurement. See Omarbekov, *Golodomor v Kazakhstane*, 10.

23. Dispossession and confiscation were based on Articles 62 and 107 of the RSFSR Penal Code.

24. Arkhiv Prezidenta Respubliki Kazakhstan (APRK), 141–1–1650, 2 (shorthand note from the office of the Kraikom VKP[b] in response to exaggeration regarding the Government of Semipalatinsk, September 9, 1928).

25. RGASPI, 94–1–1, 653 (proceedings no. 48 from a meeting of the VKP[b] faction of the Vserossiiskii tsentral'nyi ispolnitel'nii komitet [VTsIK] executive committee, September 24, 1928).

26. Shayakhmetov, *Silent Steppe*, 13–17.

27. Abylkhozhin and Kozybaev, "Kazakhstanskaia tragediia" and Pianciola, "Famine in the Steppe."

28. Markevich, "Byla li sovetskaia ekonomika planovoi?" See also Edele, *Stalinist Society*, 194–211.

29. RGASPI, 94–1–1, 675.

30. GARF, 1235–140–956, 6–7 (on violating party directives and Soviet laws in Semipalatinsk, n.d. [August 1928].

31. RGASPI, 94–1–1, 677. The number 40,000 resulted when Kiselev rounded the quantity of registered households subjected to repression (8,592) up to 10,000 and then multiplied it by 4 people per household. The number of affected households often found in relevant literature, namely, 17,000, apparently followed from a calculation done by Terry Martin, who added households organized in individual categories to the total of 8,592 registered cases. See Martin, *Affirmative Action Empire*, 67. Pianciola used the same numbers for his work, "Famine in the Steppe," 149.

32. APRK, 141–1–1650, 29.

33. RGASPI, 94–1–1, 647.

34. RGASPI, 17–25–22, 215–216 (proceedings no. 20 from a session of the Kazkraikom, March 19, 1928).

35. GARF, 1235–140–956, 16.

36. RGASPI, 94–1–1, 676. Stalin had registered reserves in Siberia in a similar manner. See Hildermeier, *Geschichte der Sowjetunion*, 379.

37. RGASPI, 94–1–1, 674.

38. GARF, 3316–64–788, 3–8 (Akimov's report to Enukidze, July 28, 1928). GARF, 3316–64–788.

39. RGASPI, 94–1–1, 668.

40. Nurtazina, "Great Famine," 112.

41. Pianciola, "Famine in the Steppe," 149.

42. RGASPI, 94–1–1, 633.

43. Gosudarstvennyi Arkhiv Vostochno-Kazakhstanskoi Oblasti (GAVO), 388p-1–188, 29, taken from Zhandabekova, *Pod grifom sekretnosti*, 14–15. The border guards were not up to the demands of the situation, GAVO, 338p-1–188, 62, Zhandabekova, *Pod grifom sekretnosti*, 15–16. Kazakhs also fled to Siberia. See GARF, 3260–10–3, 16 (resolution by the leaders of the Siberian Regional Executive Committee, October 3, 1928).

44. Aleksei Kiselev (1879–1937) was the secretary of the Executive Committee of the VTsIK from 1924 to 1937 and was assigned several times to investigate matters in Kazakhstan. In the mid-1920s he led a commission for investigating tensions between Kazakhs and Europeans in Zhetysu. In 1934 he chaired the so-called Nomad Commission that dealt with the disastrous consequences of sedentarization policy.

45. APRK, 141–1-1650, 29.

46. RGASPI, 17–3-697, 4 (proceedings no. 35 from the politburo "On Kazakhstan," July 26, 1928).

47. Shorthand note, RGASPI, 94–1-1, 622–82. The commission's report was also debated in the politburo: RGASPI, 17–3-706, 6 (presentation by the Kiselev Commission, September 27, 1928).

48. RGASPI, 94–1-1, 642, 665–66.

49. On the situation of European officials in Central Asia, see Kassymbekova and Teichmann, "Red Man's Burden," 171–73, 182–84.

50. RGASPI, 94–1-1, 636.

51. RGASPI, 94–1-1, 645.

52. RGASPI, 94–1-1, 637.

53. RGASPI, 17–3-706, 6.

54. Bekker died a natural death in 1937. I thank Vitalii Khliupin for details on Bekker's life.

55. Ohayon, *La sédentarisation*, 72–74. On how grain procurement was related to ethnicity in Ukraine, see Martin, *Affirmative Action Empire*, 302–7.

56. On the "paradox of socialist isolation," see Chandler, *Institutions of Isolation*, 3–7. On border populations and nationality policies, see Martin, "Origins," 829–32. On borders in Central Asia, see Shaw, "Friendship."

57. Hildermeier, *Geschichte der Sowjetunion*, 384.

58. GARF, 1235–140-956, 7–16.

59. RGASPI, 17–33–420, 77–78 (addendum to proceedings no. 52 of the Office of the Kraikom, July 19, 1928).

60. For information on Nurmakov (1896–1937), see Zhakypov et al., *Narkomy Kzakhstana*, 258–59.

61. APRK, 141–1–1650, 45–46.

62. Petrov, *Miatezhnoe serdtse Azii*, 329.

63. *Seredniaks* were average-income peasants. RGASPI, 17–33–420, 92–93 (statement by the Information Department of the TsK VKP[b], September 3, 1928).

64. RGASPI, 17–33–420, 95 (Kunaev's letter to the Organizational Department of the TsK VKP[b], December 17, 1928).

65. Schnell, *Räume des Schreckens*, 428–31.

66. Stalin, "Über die rechte Abweichung," 80.

67. For one of Stalin's presumed encounters with peasants, see Hughes, *Stalin*, 144 and Avorkhanov, *Stalin*, 12.

68. "Zakliuchenie komissii." See also Ohayon, *La sédentarisation*, 35–39.

69. Some authors have mistaken one drive for the other. Pianciola writes in detail on debaiization but means only events in Semipalatinsk (Pianciola, "Famine in the Steppe," 148–52). Core elements of *debaiizatsiia* were decided on in March 1928: RGASPI, 17–25–18, 144–47 (resolution passed by the VTsIK on expropriating the wealthiest bais, March 14, 1928).

70. APRK, 141–1–2968, 141–148, taken from Kozybaev, *Nasil'stvennaia kollektivizatsiia*, 34.

71. GARF, 3260–10–3, 80ob (report on the confiscation and eviction of bais, April 22, 1929); this document also includes details on the 4,000 plus more activists involved in the drive. See also Ohayon, *La sédentarisation*, 79.

72. Goloshchekin, *Partiinoe stroitel'stvo*, 72.

73. Goloshchekin coined the term. See Mukhamedina, "Konfiskatsiia baiskikh khoziaistv."

74. RGASPI, 17–25–18, 242–53 (report to the VTsIK on confiscating property from the bais, May 15, 1928).

75. Abdrakhmanov, *Izbrannye trudy*, 94. For biographical data on Abdrakhmanov (1901–38), see Dzhumagaliev and Semenov, "Vernyi syn naroda."

76. APRK, 141–17–255, 59–61, taken from Kozybaev, *Uraz Dzhandosov*, 2:98–99.

77. For the normative principles behind it, see Telitsyn, "Reanimatsiia voennogo kommunizma."

78. Riadnin, *Kazakhstan na putiakh*, 19.

79. GARF, 1235–141–305, 23 (letter from Kazakhstan's chief attorney to the chief

attorney of the RSFSR, May 4, 1929). The case drew much attention: Tsentral'nyi Gosudarstvennyi Arkhiv Respubliki Kazakhstan (TsGARK), 1380-1-3, 98-101, taken from Kozybaev, *Nasil'stvennaia kollektivizatsiia*, 43.

80. GARF, 1235-141-305, 14 (complaint submitted by Zeineb Mametova to the attorney of the republic, January 31, 1929).

81. GARF, 3260-10-3, 13ob.

82. APRK, 141-1-2968, 141-48, taken from Kozybaev, *Nasil'stvennaia kollektivizatsiia*, 35.

83. Ohayon, *La sédentarisation*, 35-39.

84. Pianciola, "Famine in the Steppe," 147. See also Koigeldiev, *Stalinizm i repressii*, 341-50. For attacks on Alash Orda, see Bochagov, *Alash-Orda*.

85. Shayakhmetov, *Silent Steppe*, 55-60.

86. Dmitrii Goichenko from the Ukraine reported how one official destroyed a Ukrainian village from within by offering material incentives and seeming to transfer far-reaching authority to otherwise unimportant people who then followed him as compliant militiamen. See Goichenko, *Skvoz' raskulachivanie*, 157.

87. Nurtazina, "Great Famine," 113.

88. RGASPI, 17-25-159, 213 (shorthand report to the Ninth Regional Party Convention for the region of Alma-Ata, November 10-20, 1928).

89. For the biographical data on Abdrakhmanov (1892-1971), see Zhakypov et al., *Narkomy Kazakhstana*, 36.

90. RGASPI, 17-25-159, 300.

91. RGASPI, 17-25-159, 301. Similar conditions were reported for other regions: Kenzhaliev and Dauletova, *Kazakhskoe obychnoe pravo*, 138.

92. GARF, 3260-10-3, 9.

93. GARF, 3260-10-3, 14ob.

94. Scott, *Weapons of the Weak*.

95. RGASPI, 17-25-159, 91.

96. RGASPI, 17-6-329, 48-49 (information for Stalin, Molotov, Kaganovich, and Kiselev pertaining to confiscation in Aktiubinsk, September 28, 1928).

97. GARF, 3260-10-3, 8ob.

98. RGASPI, 17-6-329, 48.

99. GARF, 1235-141-379, 1-1ob (complaint from Aul No. 12 submitted to the VTsIK, prior to December 28, 1928).

100. GARF, 1235-141-379, 8 (letter from the KazTsIK to the VTsIK, September 2, 1929.

101. GARF, 3260–10–3, 14ob.

102. For biographical data on Mametov (1899–?), see Amanzholova, Asylbekov, and Rysbekova, "Portrety," 98.

103. GARF, 1235–141–305, 13ob-20 (Zeineb Mametova's complaint to a staff member at the office of the district attorney at Katanian, January 31, 1929).

104. GARF, 1235–141–305, 12 (telegram from Zeineb Mametova to Kiselev, before February 18, 1929) and 9–10 (letter from Zeineb Mametova to the chairman of the Executive Committee of the VTsIK, April 13, 1929).

105. GARF, 1235–141–305, 16ob.

106. GARF, 1235–141–305, 21 (letter from the attorney of the Supreme Soviet of the USSR to Kiselev, before February 15, 1929).

107. On Baidil'din (1898–1930), see "Baidil'din, Abdrakhman." http://centrasia.ru/per son2.php?&st=1093493362 (accessed May 18, 2018).

108. APRK, 719–5–45, 1–2 (Kaimulin's complaint to the Central Control Commission, January 31, 1929).

109. APRK, 719–5–45, 11 (letter from Lusubekov to TsKK VKP[b], March 19, 1929).

110. APRK, 719–1–1432, 50 (memorandum containing information on members of Alash Orda, n.d. [1929]).

111. GARF, 1235–140–1218, 7 (letter from Dosov to Kalinin, prior to September 19, 1928).

112. GARF, 3260–1-3, 10ob (report on expropriation and deportation of the bais, April 22, 1929). Over 2,000 complaints were submitted. Ultimately a total of 753 were deemed "true."

113. GARF, 3260–10–3, 8.

114. GARF, 3316–64–788, 5.

115. For a detailed list of confiscations, see Ohayon, *La sédentarisation*.

116. The actual numbers were much higher.

117. APRK, 141–1-2968, 141–48, taken from Kozybaev, *Nasil'stvennaia kollektivizatsiia*, 36; *Itogi konfiskatsii*.

118. RGASPI, 17–25–159, 91.

119. Kuderina, *Genotsid v Kazakhstane*, 18–23.

120. On industrialization, see Davies, "Industry." For the debate on how realistic Soviet plans were, see Lewin, "Disappearance."

121. Baberowski, *Der Rote Terror*, 122. For Kazakhstan see Ertz, "Kazakh Catastrophe."

122. Stalin, *Works*, 12:93.

123. For example, GARF, 1235–141–766, 2–6 (Oblast Executive Committee Pavlodar to

all District Executive Committees, September 26 1929) and 35 (letter from Shefer to the district attorney of Kazakhstan, September 27, 1930).

124. RGASPI, 82–2–60, 157 (Molotov's speech at a meeting of the representatives of national party organizations, February 12, 1930).

125. APRK, 719–1–1436, 1–18 (investigation into the suitability of party organizations for the drive to collectivization, n.d. [1929]).

126. On operations against the kulaks, see Viola, *Unknown Gulag*, 33–53; Baberowski, "Stalinismus von oben"; "Postanovlenie politburo"; RGASPI, 82–2–60, 163, 166.

127. Wehner, *Bauernpolitik*, 291–98. For tangible examples, see Altrichter, *Die Bauern von Tver*, 95–101.

128. For the numbers for Kazakhstan, see Kozybaev, "Klassovy 'natisk,'" 175.

129. Wehner, *Bauernpolitik*, 296.

130. See Kopelev, *Education of a True Believer*, 228–236.

131. Scott, *Weapons of the Weak*, 28–47.

132. GARF, 1235–141–766, 73.

133. A "nagants" is a Russian revolver carried by the Chekists. APRK, 141–1–5208, 67 (report on the relationship of OGPU district organizations and the District Committee of the VKP[b], n.d. [late 1931]).

134. Mikhailov, *Great Disaster*, 275.

135. Abylkhozhin, Kozybaev, and Tatimov, "Novoe o kollektivizatsii," 203.

136. GARF, 1235–141–766, 74ob (report on excesses during the economic-political campaigns in the KASSR, December 4, 1930).

137. GARF, 1235–141–766, 74.

138. TsGARK, 74–11–54, 2 (report on sedentarization in the district of Enbekshil'dersk, n.d. [1932]).

139. GARF, 1235–141–766, 72.

140. Rossiiskii Gosudarstvennyi Arkhiv Ekonomiki (RGAE), 7486–37–49, 86 (report on the seed campaign and collectivization in the districts of Zatobol'sk and Borovsk, April 19, 1930). For other oblasts, see Merridale, *Night of Stone*, 167–75; and Teichmann, "Kollektivierung tatarisch."

141. GARF, 1235–141–766, 76.

142. Schnell, *Räume des Schreckens*, 454–64.

143. GARF, 1235–141–766, 73–73ob.

144. GARF, 1235–141–766, 77ob. See also Solomon, *Soviet Criminal Justice*, 111–52.

145. Viola, *Unknown Gulag*, 2. See also Baberowski, "Stalinismus von oben." For conditions in Kazakhstan, see Kozybaev, "Klassovy 'natisk,'" 177–79.

146. On districts and oblasts subject to dekulakization and the corresponding target numbers, see APRK, 141-1-2969, 4 and 14–17, in Kozybaev, *Nasil'stvennaia kollektivizatsiia*, 54–55, 59–62.

147. In February 1931 the politburo decided to relocate 200,000 to 300,000 kulak families in Kazakhstan. See Khaustov, Maumov, and Plotnikova, *Lubianka*, 254.

148. RGAE, 7486-37-200, 3 (report on hydrological conditions in the oblast Akmolinsk, March 15, 1931).

149. On the economic efficiency of the Gulag in general, see Ertz, *Zwangsarbeit*. On the expansion of the Gulag to include Kazakhstan, see Hedeler and Stark, *Das Grab*.

150. GARF, 9414-1-1943, 6–48 in Tsarevskaia-Diakina et al. *Istoriia stalinskogo gulaga*, 5:113. From 1930 to 1931, 44,000 families were deported to Kazakhstan from other parts of the Soviet Union. In early 1932, more than 180,000 special settlers were registered there. Zemskov, *Spetsposelentsy*, 17–24.

151. APRK, 141-1-2969, 14–17. Taken from Kozybaev, *Nasil'stvennaia kollektivizatsiia*, 61. In *Cannibal Island*, Werth describes a particularly dramatic instance from Siberia.

152. APRK, 141-1-5006, 128 (telegram from Gur'ev, n.d. [September 1931]).

153. Werth, *A State against Its People*, 146 [translation revised].

154. RGASPI, 82-2-653, 48 (statistics on collectivization in the USSR, December 15, 1929).

155. For biographical data on Dzhanaidar Sadvakasov (1898–1938), see Zhakypov et al., *Narkomy Kazakhstana*, 292.

156. GARF, 1235-141-766, 30 (telegram from Sadvakasov to the district attorney in Pavlodar, November 4, 1929).

157. RGAE, 7486-37-49, 86 (letter from mobilized soviet workers in the district of Kustanai, n.d. [early 1930]).

158. GARF, 1235-141-766, 74.

159. GARF, 1235-141-766, 72. Some years later, cities and oblasts all over the Soviet Union strove to attain "regime status" because it permitted them to turn away undesired migrants. See Shearer, *Policing Stalin's Socialism*, 258–59.

160. Viola, *Unknown Gulag*, 13.

161. For instance, Hildermeier, *Geschichte der Sowjetunion*, 370–74.

162. Viola, *Peasant Rebels*, 21–23.

163. Lewin, "On Soviet Industrialization," 272–84.

164. Neutatz, "Die Suggestion."

165. Viola, *Peasant Rebels*, 100–101.

166. Kopelev, *Education of a True Believer*.

167. RGASPI, 17-165-15, 18–19 (shorthand note from the Assembly of Representatives

from the National Republics and Oblasts at the TsK VKP[b] on the matter collectivization, February 11, 1930).

168. Stalin, "Concerning the Policy."

169. On the relentless demand for grain supply from starving regions, see RGASPI, 558–11–740, 69–72, in Khlevniuk et al., *Stalin i Kaganovich*, 179–80.

170. RGASPI, 558–11–45, 45 (Stalin's telegram to Goloshchekin and Isaev, November 21, 1932).

171. Goloshchekin, *Na poroge*, 34.

172. APRK, 141–1–2968, 137–39 (report on collectivization in the district of Chelkar, March 23, 1930).

173. Nurtazina, "Great Famine," 113; APRK, 141–17–465, 2–3 (report on soviet and party organs in the borderland, April 9, 1930).

174. Kassymbekova, "Helpless Imperialists."

175. Chokin, *Chetyre vremeni zhizni*, 24–41. For similar narrations from other parts of the Soviet Union, see Goichenko, *Skvoz' raskulachivanie* and Kopelev, *Education of a True Believer*, 224–86.

176. For the year 1930 the OGPU counted about two hundred such incidents; see Eisener, *Konterrevolution*, 79.

177. Stalin, "Dizzy with Success."

178. Simon, *Nationalism and Policy*, 108.

179. GARF, 1235–141–766, 75ob, 74.

180. APRK, 141–1–2954, 20–21 (telegram from the Kazkraikom to the party's regional committee, April 6, 1930).

181. RGASPI, 62–2–2143, 11–14 (Kisliakov's report of April 5, 1930). All quotations in this and the next two paragraphs were taken from his report. The report was also sent to Danilovskii and Zelenskii, permanent representatives of the OGPU in Kazakhstan. RGASPI, 62–2–2143, 10 (report from Volynskii, April 19, 1930).

182. APRK, 141–1–4577 (government commission material on the district of Chubartavsk, May 5, 1931).

183. APRK, 8–1–28, 26 (Davletbekov's report to Kuramysov, September 30, 1932). Another commissioner said he would not collect grain for the state "over the [dead] bones" of the kolkhoz peasants. See Verkhoturov, "Asharshylyk," 175.

184. Kopelev, *Education of a True Believer*, 230.

185. Viola, *Best Sons*. Over 1,200 were sent to Kazakhstan. See Abuseitova et al., *Istoriia Kazakhstana*, 480.

186. RGAE, 7486–37–49, 83.

187. GARF, 1235–141–1092, 42–43 (report by David N. Tsirkovich, one of the 25,000, June 27, 1931).

188. Kuderina, *Genotsid v Kazakhstane*, 14.

189. APRK, 141–1–3297, 109–11 (Ernazarov's report to Goloshchekin on the revolt in Balkhash, April 21, 1930).

190. APRK, 141–1–2968, 137–39.

191. Olcott, *Kazakhs*, 20–21.

192. GARF, 6985–1–6, 223 (report on the settlement of the nomadic and seminomadic population, n.d. [fall 1934]) and RGASPI, 82–2–665, 1–11 (Balitskii's letter to Molotov regarding livestock procurement, May 20, 1932).

193. GARF, 1235–141–1007, 5 (Kiselev's report on the state of livestock breeding in Kazakhstan, November 28, 1931). For an overview, see Davies and Wheatcroft, *Years of Hunger*, 312–13.

194. RGASPI, 17–165–25, 110.

195. RGAE, 7486–37–49, 124–27 (circular on the procurement and contracting of cattle, horses, and sheep in private households, n.d.); RGAE, 7486–37–49, 129–129ob (Grin'ko's letter to Iakovlev, March 15, 1930).

196. APRK, 141–1–5059, 7 (report on the krai kontor "Soiumiaso" for meat procurement and delivery, January 15, 1931).

197. APRK, 141–1–5059, 9.

198. RGASPI, 558–11–40, 100a (Stalin and Molotov's telegram to Goloshchekin, Roshal, Isaev, and Eliaev, February 26, 1931).

199. APRK, 719–3–217, 22–25 (Mironov's letter to Kuramysov, November 12, 1931).

200. RGAE, 7486–37–193, 33 (report on meat procurement in West Kazakhstan as of February 1, 1931).

201. GARF, 1235–141–1092, 41 (authorized TO OGPU at the station of Nurinsk, n.d. [spring 1931]).

202. GARF, 1235–141–1092, 41ob.

203. GARF, 1235–141–1092, 41ob.

204. GARF, 1235–141–766, 75.

205. GARF, 1235–141–766, 75.

206. GARF, 1235–141–1092, 41ob.

207. GARF, 1235–141–1007, 4.

208. RGASPI, 17–165–25, 13–19.

209. Abylkhozhin, Kozybaev, and Tatimov, "Novoe o kollektivizatsii," 200. For early fundamental skepticism of the value of kolkhoz livestock farms, see Schiller, *Die Kollektivbewegung*, 68–69.

210. Cairns, *Soviet Famine*, 10.

211. Goloshchekin, "Kazakhstan na pod'eme," 19; Ohayon, *La sédentarisation*, 157–60; Thomas, "Kazakh Nomads," 201–20.

212. Kuramysov, "K voprosu," 14, 16.

213. Zveriakov, *Ot kochevaniia k sotsializmu*.

214. TsGARK, 74–11–11, 2–3 (Isaev's report on settling nomadic and seminomadic households in the Kazakh ASSR, n.d. [prior to April 16, 1930]).

215. TsGARK, 74–11–11, 1 (Isaev's letter to Syrgabekov, April 20, 1930). For the resolutions, see Shaumian, *Ot kochev'ia*, 93–95.

216. Kamenskii, "Piatliletnii plan," 49.

217. Distributed across individual years, this meant the settlement of 84,400 households in 1929–30, 211,800 households in 1930–31, 116,000 households in 1931–32, 42,000 in 1932, and 72,000 households in 1933. TsGARK, 74–11–11, 4.

218. On Soviet statistics, see Davies and Wheatcroft, "Crooked Mirror."

219. RGASPI, 17–3–755, 5 (proceedings from the politburo meeting on June 29, 1929).

220. TsGARK, 74–11–11, 12.

221. RGAE, 7486–19–10, 64ob (conclusions drawn from the Five-Year Plan for Kazakhstan's agriculture, prior to April 14, 1930).

222. During the 1920s Grigorii Fedorovich Grin'ko (1890–1938) worked first in the Ukrainian and later in the Soviet Gosplan (soviet office for Five-Year Plans).

223. RGAE, 7486–19–10, 18–20ob (report on the development of agriculture in Kazakhstan, n.d. [spring 1930]), quotation on 19ob. See also GARF, 5446–13a-2451, 6 (letter to Molotov from the People's Commissariat for Finances, February 23, 1932).

224. RGAE, 7486–19–10, 14–15 (financing Kazakhstan's agriculture, n.d.).

225. RGAE, 7486–19–10, 1–10 (perspectives for Kazakhstan's agriculture, n.d. [spring 1930]).

226. TsGARK, 1179-1-3, 15 (minutes from the first meeting on sedentarization, November 9–10, 1930).

227. S.M., "Osedanie," 34.

228. Levin, "Agrarnaia politika Kazakhstana," 13.

229. APRK, 719-4-70, 6 (report on the emigration of people from Kazakhstan, June 15, 1932).

230. TsGARK, 1179-1-3, 7.

231. TsGARK, 1179-1-3, 28.

232. GARF, 6985-1-5, 13–13ob (proceedings no. 22 from the executive committee of the KazTsIK, November 2, 1931); GARF, 6985-1-5, 11–12 (proceedings no. 50 of the SNK KASSR, October 7, 1931).

233. TsGARK, 1179-3-39, 54 (letter from the chairman of the Kazakh Office for Water Management to the district's executive committee, December 7, 1930).

234. TsGARK, 1179-3-39, 163 (letter from the district executive committee to the settlement sector, n.d. [April 1931]).

235. TsGARK, 74-11-11, 3.

236. GARF, 6985-1-2, 288ob.

237. GARF, 5446-12-667, 3-6 (Goloshchekin's telegram to Stalin and Molotov, perhaps of March 7, 1931).

238. TsGARK, 1179-1-3, 40.

239. TsGARK, 1179-1-3, 80.

240. TsGARK, 1179-1-3, 39.

241. Ryskulov, "Vnimanie skotovodstvu."

242. TsGARK, 1179-1-3, 47.

243. APRK, 719-4-69, 86 (report from the OGPU on sedentarization, May 15, 1932). For similar opinions, see APRK 141-17-675, 9 (shorthand note from the meeting of a committee for settlement, n.d. [early 1932]).

244. For examples, see *Materialy k otchetu Krai*, 29–35.

245. TsGARK, 1179-3-39, 111 (statement on the settlement sport of the village of Asubai, n.d. [prior to June 4, 1931]).

246. APRK, 141-17-675, 14. For Kazakh customs regarding the dead and the importance of graves, see Bacon, *Central Asians*, 43.

247. GARF, 6985-1-5, 200b (conclusions drawn regarding Soviet development of the KASSR, August 31, 1930).

248. GARF, 6985-1-3, 30 (shorthand note from a meeting of party workers, June 18, 1934).

249. APRK, 141-17-675, 53 (shorthand note from a meeting of the Committee for Settlement Issues, n.d. [late 1931 or early 1932]).

250. APRK, 719-4-69, 84. For a large number of similar cases, see 80.

251. GARF, 6985-1-5, 20.

252. GARF, 6985-1-7, 147 (report from the VTsIK Nationalities Department on the status of sedentarization and future tasks, n.d. [1933–34]).

253. APRK, 719-4-69, 78 (report on settling the nomadic and seminomadic population of Kazakhstan, written after May 15, 1933).

254. APRK, 719-4-69, 85–87.

255. Resolution of December 25, 1931: Zveriakov, *Ot kochevaniia k sotsializmu*, 128–32. For the debate among the People's Commissariats involved, see GARF, 5446-13-2451 (On the Sedentarization Plan for the Years 1932–33). See also Goloshchekin, "Iz tsarskoi kolonii."

256. GARF, 5446–13–2451, 29.

257. An overview is given in Leonov and Semevskii, "Uroki pervogo goda," 16.

258. APRK, 719–4-69, 87–88 (both quotations).

259. Ashimbaev and Khliupin, *Kazakhstan*, 343.

260. GARF, 6985–1-7, 60 (building material supply, 1931–33, n.d.).

261. TsGARK, 1179–1-3, 46.

262. TsGARK, 1179–1-3, 104.

263. GARF, 6985–1-5, 200b. The People's Commissariat for Agriculture declared in February 1932 that the plans for house construction were not financeable. See GARF, 5446–13a-2451, 7–70b (letter from the Narkomzem SSSR, February 25, 1932).

264. Goloshchekin, "Puti sotsialisticheskaia nastupleniia."

265. For biographical data on Jakov Petrovich Belikov (1893–1958), see Zhakypov et al., *Narkomy Kazakhstana*, 86.

266. APRK, 141–17–675, 54. For biographical data on Nikokai Zalogin (1892–?), see Zhakypov et al., *Narkomy Kazakhstana*, 163.

267. Kosokov, "Itogi planovogo osedaniia," 71.

268. Shayakhmetov, *Silent Steppe*, 234–39.

269. GARF, 6985–1-8, 43–45 (report on construction in the KASSR, July 10, 1934).

270. GARF, 6985–1-8, 41.

271. GARF, 6985–1-2, 290 (shorthand note from a meeting of the Commission for Sedentarization, July 8, 1934).

272. The same was true even two decades later: see Sabitov, "Kul'tura i byta," 55. It was also true of Kirghizia: see Abramzon, "V kirgizskikh kolkhozakh," 65, and Bacon, *Central Asians*, 120.

273. GARF, 6985–1-2, 277 (shorthand note from a meeting of the Commission for Sedentarization, July 8, 1934).

274. For the Kazakh leaders' thoughts on this, see GARF, 5446–13a-2451, 31 (Isaev's letter to Molotov prior to February 10, 1932). Regarding the practice, see GARF, 1235–141–1359, 13 (report to Kiselev, May 10, 1932). For criticism of the practice, see GARF, 6985–1-7, 147, and on gigantomania in setting up kolkhozes, see Merl, "Bilanz der Unterwerfung," 141. For a description of those sites, see Abuseitova et al., *Istoriia Kazakhstana*, 480; APRK, 141–1-2986, 11.1–30b (report from Asylbekov to the Kazkraikom, April 26, 1930), in Gribanov et al., *Iz istorii deportatsii*, 255.

275. GARF, 6985–1-3, 13–39 (shorthand note from a meeting between Kiselev and comrades from nomadic districts of the KASSR, June 18, 1934).

276. Mikhailov, *Great Disaster*, 338.

277. Kotkin, *Magnetic Mountain*.

278. GARF, 5446–13–2451, 102–7.

279. GARF, 5446–13a-2451, 22 (calculating the number of Kazakh households, n.d. [1932]). Isaev's argument that in addition to the 50,000 households that had been settled in 1930 and 1931, another 114,000 households had been assigned land resulted in a total of 164,000 households that had been settled during the first two years of the campaign. GARF, 5446–13a-2451, 6–6ob (letter to Molotov, February 23, 1932); GARF, 6985–1-5, 19–18ob (report on fulfilling the resolution of February 6, 1931, n.d. [early 1931]).

280. For a contrary opinion, see Scholz, *Nomadismus*, 148.

281. Brown, *Biography*, 173–86; Payne, "Seeing Like a Soviet State"; Gribanova, *Iz istorii deportatsii*, 23–26.

282. RGAE, 7486–37–200, 17 (Mikshis's report to the Central Administration of the Militia, March 10, 1931).

283. Hedeler and Stark, *Das Grab*, 18.

4. CIVIL WAR AND FLIGHT

1. Tarkhova, *Krasnaia Armiia*, 143–45.

2. RGASPI, 74-2-99, 68ob (report from Duganov and Bazilevich to Voroshilov, April 18, 1930). An unknown person added in handwriting "except in larger towns."

3. Ishchenko and Kazbekov, *Osobennosti sel'skogo khoziaistva*, 90. This convergence had been in the making since 1927 when the Adai migrated south because of the frost and cold that killed many animals. See Tsentral'nyi Gosudarstvennyi Arkhiv Respubliki Kazakhstan (TsGARK), 74–6-63, 102 (letter from the chairman of the regional executive committee to the Kazakhiskii Tsentral'nii Ispolnitel'nii Komitet [KazTsIK], November 9, 1927).

4. Allaniiazov, *Krasnye Karakumy*.

5. RGASPI, 613-3-80, 6 (Popkov's letter to Iaroslavskii, prior to August 7, 1931).

6. RGASPI, 62-2-2546, 185 (Matson's report to Gorbunov, August 3, 1931). For a detailed overview of the revolt by the Adai, see Omarov, *Rasstreliannaia step'*; Nabiev, *Stepnaia tragediia*, 11–14.

7. Rossiiskii Gosudarstvennyi Arkhiv Sotsial'no-Politicheskoi Istorii (RGASPI), 613-3-80, 6. For biographical data on Iaroslavskii (1878–1943), see Dahlke, *Individuum und Herrschaft*.

8. Kulumbetov's letter to Danilovskii and Isaev, August 5, 1931, taken from Nabiev, *Stepnaia tragediia*, 371.

9. Gratsiosi, *Velikaia krest'ianskaia voina*, 45–47; Viola, *Peasant Rebels*; Fitzpatrick, *Stalin's Peasants*, 48–79.

10. On armed struggles in Turkmenistan see Allaniiazov, *Krasnye Karakumy*; Poliakov, "Karakumskaia operatsiia"; Edgar, *Tribal Nation*, 197–212. For Kirghizia, see Loring, "Building Socialism," 300, 319–28, and Loring, "Rural Dynamics." For the Caucasus, see Baberowski, *Der Feind*, 691–721. For Ukraine, see Schnell, *Räume des Schreckens*, 454–83.

11. For various interpretations, see Allaniiazov, "Protestnye dvizheniia."

12. Wieviorka, *Violence*, 27–31

13. Kalyvas, *Logic of Violence*. On the dynamics of violence in civil wars, see Waldmann, "Gesellschaften im Bürgerkrieg," 353–68.

14. Studies for other regions of the Soviet Union come to similar conclusions. See Schnell, *Räume des Schreckens*.

15. Gerlach, *Extrem gewalttätige Gesellschaften*, 383.

16. In nomadic society it was tradition to turn to wealthy authorities in times of trouble. See Abylkhozhin, "Konfiskatsiia skota," 21–22.

17. For biographical data on Bak (1902–40), see Petrov, *Kto rukovodil NKVD*, 98.

18. RGASPI, 82-2-904, 1–2ob (from Bak to Iagoda, May 27, 1929). For biographical data on Yagoda (1891–1938), see Petrov, *Kto rukovodil NVKD*, 459.

19. J. Arch Getty incorrectly attributes fear of their own shadows to the Bolsheviks: Getty, "Afraid of Their Shadows." I have discussed this elsewhere: Kindler, "New York in der Steppe," 48.

20. Stalin, "Concerning the Policy," 189.

21. Viola, *Peasant Rebels*, 38–44.

22. RGASPI, 17-165-15, 18–19 (shorthand note from the Assembly of the Representatives of the National Republics and Oblasts at TsK TsKP[b] on the matter of collectivization, February 11, 1930).

23. Koigeldiev, *Stalinizm i repressii*, 238.

24. Rossiiskii Gosudarstvennyi Voennyi Arkhiv (RGVA), 25895-1-711, 169–71 (Kurmangaliev's telegram to the Red Army Staff in Moscow, prior to September 2, 1930).

25. RGVA, 25895-1-711, 229 (extra report on the situation in Kazakhstan, after September 12, 1930). "Dzhigit," a word of Turkic origin, describes a skillful equestrian or a brave person.

26. RGVA, 25895-1-711, 229.

27. RGASPI, 62-2-2203, 163–164ob (message from Danilovskii to the OGPU in Moscow, April 25, 1930).

28. For the OGPU's logic of action, see Hagenloh, *Stalin's Police*, 48–53.

29. Helbling, "Etwas Kritik."

30. Waldmann, "Zur Asymmetrie," 256–57.

31. Baecker, *Form und Formen*, 171.

32. Sperling, *Der Aufbruch*, 351–57.

33. For example, in Kirghizia: RGASPI, 62-2-2136, 211 (conversation between Polno-mochnii Predstavitel' OGPU [PP OGPU] in Tashkent and Kirotdel OGPU, Frunze, April 13, 1930).

34. Viola, *Peasant Rebels*, 45–47.

35. Riekenberg, "Zur Anthropologie," 213.

36. Arkhiv Prezidenta Respubliki Kazakhstan (APRK), 141-1-464, 4 (telegram to Goloshchekin, March 9, 1930).

37. The autonomous region of Karakalpakstan (Karakalpakskaia AO) belonged to the KASSR from 1924 until July 1930. Thereafter it belonged to the RSFSR. In 1932 it gained the status of an autonomous Soviet republic, at first within the RSFSR and from 1936 until 1991 within the Uzbek SSR.

38. RGASPI, 62-2-2203, 40. For details on the envoy, see Allaniiazov, *"Kontrrevoliut-siia" v Kazakhstane*, 57.

39. Dhzunaid-khan's actual name was Mukhammed-Kurban Serdar (1857–1938). He ruled in Khiva from 1918 until 1920 after murdering the last khan. See Kozlovskii, *Krasnaia Armiia*, 62–68; Keller, "Central Asian Bureau," 285–86, 292. In the 1920s Dhzunaid-khan organized resistance to the Bolsheviks. For the fight against his group of rebels in 1927, see Borisov, *Pokhod konnoi gruppy*, 24, 59–61.

40. The OGPU was also interested in the connections to Dhzunaid-khan: Tsentral'nyi Arkhiv Federal'noi Sluzhby Bezopasnosti Rossiiskoi Federatsii (TsA FSB RF), 2-8-23, 2–13, taken from *Sovetskaia derevnia glazami*, vol. 3, bk. 1, 150.

41. Allaniiazov, *"Kontrrevoliutsiia" v Kazakhstane*, 64.

42. RGASPI, 62-2-2203, 38–40.

43. Arkhiv Zhokargy Kenesa Respubliki Karakalpakstan (AZhKRK), 1-2-66, 83–85ob, taken from Allaniiazov, *"Konterrevoliutsia" v Kazakhstane*, 155–57.

44. Allaniiazov, *"Konterrevoliutsiia" v Kazakhstane*, 61.

45. RGASPI, 62-2-2203, 39 (operative report to Zelenskii regarding gangs, January 23, 1930). On trials and punishment, see Allaniiazov, *Poslednii rubezh*, 274.

46. Allaniiazov, *"Konterrevoliutsia" v Kazakhstane*, 96–98.

47. AZhKRK, 1-2-753, 1–46, in Allaniiazov, *"Konterrevoliutsia" v Kazakhstane*, 186–190.

48. Allaniiazov, *"Konterrevoliutsia" v Kazakhstane*, 196–200.

49. Allaniiazov, *"Konterrevoliutsia" v Kazakhstane*, 207.

50. Goloshchekin believed it to the bitter end. See Koigeldiev, *Stalinizm i repressii,* 249.

51. Asadulla Ibrahim (1880–1930) was apparently Persian and had come to Tashkent via Baku during the civil war and lived in the district of Suzak since 1920. See Kozybaev, *Nasil'stvennaia kollektivizatsiia,* 62n.

52. Aldazhumanov, "Krest'ianskoe dvizhenie," 70.

53. For an overview of the history of the uprising, see Pianciola, "Interpreting an Insurgency," 297–340.

54. Sultanbek Sholakov (about 1880–1930) had held the office of community elder prior to the revolution. See Arkhiv Komitet Natsional'noi bezopasnosti Respubliki Kazakhstan KNB RK, 189–2–39, 358–358ob, taken from Kozybaev, *Nasil'stvennaia kollektivizatsiia,* 63n.

55. APRK, 141–1–2968, 141–43, in Kozybaev, *Nasil'stvennaia kollektivizatsiia,* 69.

56. RGASPI, 62–2–2203, 65 (report on the liquidation of the uprising in the district of Suzak, March 2, 1930).

57. APRK, 141–1–2968, 141–43, taken from Kozybaev, *Nasil'stvennaia kollektivizatsiia,* 69–70.

58. Arkniv KNB RK, 189–2–39, 258–258ob, taken from Kozybaev, *Nasil'stvennaia kollektivizatsiia,* 62.

59. Aldazhumanov, "Krest'ianskoe dvizhenie," 70.

60. RGASPI, 62–2–2203, 56ob (Karutskii's report to Shubrikov, February 14, 1930).

61. Happel, *Nomadische Lebenswelten,* 74–75.

62. RGASPI, 62–2–2203, 67.

63. RGASPI, 62–2–2203, 64.

64. RGVA, 8296–1–35, 49 (operative report by the 84th Cavalry Division on events in Suzak, n.d.).

65. RGASPI, 62–2–2203, 65. See also Sakharov, Zemskov, and Serdiuk, *Tashkentskoe Krasnozamennoe.*

66. APRK, 141–1–2922, 1–4 (letter from the Kazkraikom to all district committees in nomadic and seminomadic districts, n.d. [1930]).

67. RGASPI, 62–2–2203, 117 (Mironov's letter to the commander of the SAVO, Dybenko, and to Shubrikov, April 11, 1930).

68. Popov, "Kak prokhodila kollektivizatsiia."

69. APRK, 141–1–2966, 9 (Goloshchekin's letter to the Kazkraikom, n.d. [1930]).

70. APRK, 141–17–464, 115 (telegram to Stalin from Roshal', March 18, 1930).

71. RGASPI, 613–3–80, 6.

72. APRK, 141–17–464, 5 (Dzhusupov's letter to Goloshchekin, October 7, 1930).

73. APRK, 141–17–464, 4.

74. RGASPI, 74-2-99, 71. RGVA, 8296-1-35, 33 (troop identification for airplanes, n.d.).

75. Allaniiazov, *Poslednii rubezh*, 350.

76. Allaniiazov, *Poslednii rubezh*, 351.

77. Allaniiazov, *Poslednii rubezh*, 340–41.

78. Allaniiazov, *Krasnye Karakumy*, 133–58; Sakharov, Zemskov, and Serdiuk, *Tashkentskoe Krasnoznamenoe*, ch. 2.

79. Omarov, *Rasstreliannaia step'*, 37.

80. Allaniiazov, *Krasnye Karakumy*, 158–81.

81. Popov, "Pokhody dalekikh dnei," 40.

82. RGASPI, 62–2–2203, 124 (OGPU report from Aralskoe more [Aral Sea], after April 14, 1930).

83. RGASPI, 74-2-99, 69ob.

84. RGASPI, 613–3–80, 6 (Popkov's letter to Jaroslavsky, prior to August 7, 1931).

85. The most commonly mentioned number of 80,000 people involved in various uprisings is a rather conservative estimate. See, for example, Aldazhumanov, "Krest'ianskoe dvizhenie," 13. Turganbek Allaniiazov assumes that Kazakhstan had a total of 397 "massive peasant uprisings" and 25 "armed uprisings," most of which happened in 1930. See Allaniiazov, *Poslednii rubezh*, 175; and for debate on the numbers, 162–65.

86. RGASPI, 74-2-99, 70ob.

87. RGASPI, 62–2–2546, 27 (report by Kinderli, June 29, 1931). Years later Fetisov's death was still seen as evidence of the insurgents' cruelty. See Popov, "Pokhody dalekikh dnei," 42.

88. Allaniiazov and Taukenov, *Shetskaia tragediia*, 68–72.

89. Allaniiazov and Taukenov, *Shetskaia tragediia*, 76–77.

90. Shaltai batyr's group operated between summer 1929 and January 1930 in the region of Tashauzk in Karakalpakstan. He died there in January 1930. See Zevelev, Poliakov, and Chugunov, *Basmachestvo*, 170; Borisov, *Pokhod konnoi gruppy*, 24.

91. RGVA, 8296-1-35, 25, taken from Allaniiazov, *Poslednii rubezh*, 405–6.

92. For details on Ibrahim Bek (1889–1931), see Abdullaev, *Ot Sin'tsziana do Khorasana*, 343-5. On his situation in Afghanistan, see Boiko, "Sredneaziatskaia emigratsiia" and Ritter, "Final Phase."

93. Canetti, *Crowds and Power*, 163–65.

94. Riekenberg, "Zur Anthropologie," 213.

95. APRK, 719–4-70, 2 (report on the exodus from Mironov to Fekhter, June 15, 1932). For biographical data on Mironov (1894–1940), see Petrov, *Kto rukovodil NKVD*, 310–11.

96. APRK, 141–1-4577, 13 (material on the exodus, n.d. [early 1931]).

97. Omarov, *Rasstreliannaia step'*, 35.

98. Omarov, *Rasstreliannaia step'*, 35.

99. Genschel and Schlichte, "Wenn Kriege chronisch werden," 503.

100. Neitzel and Welzer, *Soldiers*, 327–29.

101. Arkhiv Zhezkazganskogo UVD, 1–8737-2, 698–700, taken from Allaniiazov, "K zachistke bandelementa," 149.

102. Allaniiazov and Taukenov, *Shetskaia tragediia*, 82.

103. Arkhiv Zhezkazganskogo UVD, 1–8737-2, 693, taken from Allaniiazov, *K zachistke bandelementa*, 146–47.

104. RGVA, 25895–1-869, 35–36 (interrogation record Mukan Kevilev, June 16, 1931).

105. RGASPI, 62–2-2546, 107–8 (operative report to SAVO and PP OGPU in Central Asia, June 30, 1931).

106. RGASPI, 62–2-2546, 107–8

107. Allaniiazov, *"Kontrrevoliutsiia" v Kazakhstane*, 109–11.

108. Hedeler and Stark, *Das Grab*, 33–34.

109. For the uprising in Western Kazakhstan, see Omarov, *Rasstreliannaia step'*.

110. For the concept of "borderland," see, in general, Newman, "Boundary Geopolitics."

111. Forbes, *Warlords*, 71–72.

112. APRK, 141–17-465, 84 (report from Ernazarov on emigration to China, February 16, 1931).

113. Lattimore, "Chinese Turkestan," 190.

114. Concerning nomadic cultures and national borders, see Barfield, *Perilous Frontier*. With respect to Russia, see Gammer, "Russia and the Eurasian Steppe" and Stolberg, "Russland als eurasisches Imperium."

115. On trade between the Soviet Union and Xinjiang, see Barmin, *Sovetskii Soiuz*.

116. APRK, 141–1-4577, 21 (material on emigration, n.d. [1930]).

117. APRK, 141–17-465, 64–65 (report on the situation in the border regions and emigration, n.d. [1930]).

118. Svanberg, "Nomadism," 114; Happel, *Nomadische Lebenswelten*, 153–60. For family memoirs from that period, see Nurtazina, "Great Famine," 112.

119. Cameron, "Violence"; Thomas, "Kazakh Nomads," 122–27. For a similar situation on the Soviet-Afghanistan border, see Edgar, *Tribal Nation*, 213–20.

120. On Soviet border policy in general, see Chandler, *Institutions of Isolation*; Nekh,

Istoriia sovetskoi pogranichnoi politiki. For Soviet borders in Central Asia, see Shaw, "Friendship."

121. Martin, *Affirmative Action Empire*, 314.

122. Martin, *Affirmative Action Empire*, 315; see also Martin, "Origins."

123. Chandler, *Institutions of Isolation.* In the second half of the 1930s the Bolsheviks purged the Soviet border regions of "unreliable" populations. See Polian, *Against Their Will*, 95–100.

124. RGASPI, 62–2–2209, 20ob (report on the situation in Xinjiang, December 4, 1930).

125. RGASPI, 62–2–2209, vol. 2 (letter to Zelensky from the People's Commissariat for Foreign Affairs in Uzbekistan, January 25, 1930).

126. Nurtazina, "Great Famine," 115.

127. APRK, 141–1–5076, 20 (report on emigration in 1930, February 28, 1931).

128. APRK, 141–1–4577, 1 (report from Kolosov, Soviet consul in Ghulja [Yining], to the People's Commissariat for Foreign Affairs, January 1, 1931).

129. Gosudarstvennyi Arkhiv Vostochno-Kazakhstanskoi Oblasti (GAVO), 788–1–35, 107–16, taken from Zhandabekova, *Pod grifom sekretnosti*, 31. For attacks on Soviet territory, see Forbes, *Warlords*, 71–72.

130. GAVO, 788–1–35, 107–16, taken from Zhandabekova, *Pod grifom sekretnosti*, 24.

131. APRK, 141–1–4577, 1.

132. RGVA, 25895–1–711, 389 (administration report on PP OGPU border troops in Kazakhstan, December 3, 1930).

133. RGVA, 25895–1–711, 390–93.

134. RGVA, 25895–1–711, 394.

135. RGVA, 25895–1–711, 395.

136. RGVA, 25895–1–711, 396.

137. RGVA, 38333–1–24, 138 (command from Yagoda, February 3, 1933).

138. RGASPI, 17–162–8, 94–101, taken from Danilov and Manning, *Tragediia sovetskoi derevni*, 3:253.

139. GAVO, 788–1–38a, 13, taken from Zhandabekova, *Pod grifom sekretnosti*, 23–24.

140. RGASPI, 17–162–11, 74 (minutes no. 78 from the politburo; resolution on guarding Soviet state borders in Kazakhstan, Central Asia, and the Far East, November 26, 1931).

141. APRK, 141–1–5076, 24.

142. TsA FSB RF, 2–8–743, 542, taken from Kondrashin ed., *Golod v SSSR*, vol. 1, pt. 1, 206. The list mentions that it was not possible to say how many had been taken prisoners.

143. APRK, 141–1–4577, 2.

144. APRK, 141–1-4577, 2.

145. APRK, 141–1-5057, 1–14, taken from Kondrashin et al., *Golod v SSSR*, vol. 1, pt. 2, 126.

146. Nurtazina, "Great Famine," 118–19.

147. Nazemtseva, "Aktivizatsiia."

148. Petrov, *Miatezhnoe serdtsa*, 333.

149. APRK, 141–17–465, 88 (Ernazarov's report on emigration to China, February 16, 1931).

150. Millward, *Eurasian Crossroads*, 198–234; Forbes, *Warlords*, 97.

151. GAVO, 269–2-407, 4–6ob, taken from Zhandabekova, *Pod grifom sekretnosti*, 73–74.

152. APRK, 141–1-4577, 5–7 (letter to Kolosov, the Soviet consul in Ghulja, n.d. [1930]).

153. APRK, 141–1-4577, 8.

154. APRK, 141–1-4577, 3.

155. APRK, 141–1-4577, 2.

156. Abdrakhmanov, *Izbrannye trudy*, 123.

157. RGASPI, 62–2-2203, 45–47 (Postnikov's letter to Tsukerman, January 25, 1930).

158. GAVO, 788–1-35, 107–116, taken from Zhandabekova, *Pod grifom sekretnosti*, 31.

159. RGVA, 25895–1-726, 48 (operative report on border troops, January 31, 1931).

160. RGVA, 25895–1-726, 125 (operative report on border troops, February 28, 1931).

161. GAVO, 788–1-35, 107–116, taken from Zhandabekova, *Pod grifom sekretnosti*, 31.

162. Occasionally Soviet and Chinese troops cooperated in the fight against Kazakh and Kirghiz "gangs" in the borderland; see Forbes, *Warlords*, 71–72.

163. Svanberg, *Nomadism of Orta Zhuz Kazaks*, 114–25.

164. APRK, 719–4-70, 5.

165. Quotation taken from Gosudarstvennyi Arkhiv Rossiiskoi Federatsii (GARF), 1235–141–1371, 267 (letter from Pershin, n.d. [August 1932]).

166. GARF, 1235–141–1371, 267.

167. See Tsentr dokumentatsii po noveishei istorii Orenburgskoi obl., 267–3-48, 11–12, taken from Kondrashin et al., *Golod v SSSR*, vol. 1/2, 133.

168. For an overview, see Baigisieva, "Zemledel'cheskie i osedlye raiony," 112–24.

169. Kozybaev, Abylkhozhin, and Aldazhumanov, *Kollektivizatsiia*, 30.

170. TsGARK, 30–6-207, 21 (shorthand note of the Ryskulov Commission, February 22, 1933).

171. For details on the numbers see Malysheva and Poznanskii, *Kazakhi*, 254–58.

172. APRK, 141–1-5192, 107, taken from Kozybaev, *Nasil'stvennaia kollektivizatsiia*, 123.

173. APRK, 141–1-5057, taken from Kondrashin et al., *Golod v SSSR*, vol. 1/2, 125.

174. APRK, 141–17–465, 52–54 (letter from Mangistau to the secretary of Turkmenian district party leaders, December 4, 1930).

175. TsGARK, 30–6–28, 87 (report from Kul'dzhanov, March 9, 1930).

176. Edgar, *Tribal Nation*.

177. APRK, 719-4-70, 14.

178. APRK, 141–17–465, 41 (letter from Al'shanskii to Goloshchekin, November 25, 1930).

179. RGASPI, 62–2–2176, 64–69 (telegrams from Roshal' to Zelenskii and the Uzbek Party Leaders, August 11–15, 1930).

180. RGASPI, 62–2–2201, 242–244 (letter from the PP OGPU to the Central Asian Bureau, August 18, 1930).

181. APRK, 719–4–70, 17.

182. RGASPI, 62–2–3135, 43 (letter to Ermukhamedov, prior to July 5, 1933).

183. RGASPI, 17–120–106, 20–20ob (Umarov's letter to Goloshchekin, March 18, 1932).

184. Malysheva and Poznanskii, *Kazakhi*.

185. APRK, 141–1–5192, 21, taken from Kozybaev, *Nasil'stvennaia kollektivizatsiia*, 110.

186. Cairns, "Soviet Famine," 10.

187. APRK, 141–1–5192, 21, taken from Kozybaev, *Nasil'stvennaia kollektivizatsiia*, 110.

188. RGAE, 7486–37–154, 158, taken from Kondrashin et al. *Golod v SSSR*, vol. 1/2, 132.

189. Malysheva and Poznanskii, *Kazakhi*, 200–211. See also Kessler, "1932–1933 Crisis."

190. Malysheva and Poznanskii, *Kazakhi*, 303.

191. TsGARK, 30–7–108, 58–60ob, taken from Kozybaev, *Nasil'stvennaia kollektivizatsiia*, 127. See also Malysheva and Poznanskii, *Kazakhi*, 297–98. For the role played by livestock theft in Kazakh culture, see Martin, "Barimta," 260–70. For examples of organized horse theft, see TsGARK, 30–7–108, 58–60ob, taken from Kozybaev, *Nasil'stvennaia kollektivizatsiia*, 128.

192. Quotations taken from Malysheva and Poznanskii, *Kazakhi*, 299.

193. TsGARK, 30–7–108, 58–60ob, taken from Kozybaev, *Nasil'stvennaia kollektivizatsiia*, 129.

194. GARF, 1235–141–1448, 4 (letter from M. A. Kalnin to Kalinin, May 4, 1932).

195. GARF, 1235–141–1448, 1 (letter to the executive committee of the VTsIK, July 15, 1932).

196. TsA FSB RF, 3–11–1449, 106–18, taken from Danilov and Manning *Tragediia sovetskoi derevni*, 3:427.

197. Tsentr dokumentatsii po noveishei istorii Orenburgskoi obl., 267–3–48, 11–12.

Taken from Kondrashin et al., *Golod v SSSR*, vol. 1/2, 133. See also Rittersporn, "Soviet Citizens," 141.

198. Partiinii Arkhiv Novosibirskogo Obkoma KPSS (PANO), 3-6-67, 40, taken from Poznanskii, *Gonimye golodom*, 3:16.

199. TsGARK, 1179-1-103, 194 (report on the *otkochevniki* in the Middle Volga region, prior to April 21, 1931).

200. TsGARK, 1179, op. 5-4, 138 (report by the chairman of Orenburg's soviet, November 20, 1932).

201. Kessler, "1932–1933 Crisis," 256.

202. Malysheva and Poznanskii, *Kazakhi*, 360–64.

203. GARF, 1235-141-1371, 246–47 (Umurgalii Aukeev's petition to the TsIK and Central Committee, n.d.). GARF, 1235-141-1380, 257–257ob can be used to date the letter as being from July 4, 1932.

204. Malysheva and Poznanskii, *Kazakhi*, 345–47.

205. For details, see Malysheva and Poznanskii, *Kazakhi*, 342–45.

206. APRK, 141-1-5192, 42–43, taken from Kozybaev, *Nasil'stvennaia kollektivizatsiia*, 117. Party leaders from Western Kazakhstan expressed similar complaints: TsGARK, 1179-5-4, 27–28 (letter from Kashanbaev to the chairman of the executive committee for the Middle Volga region, December 14, 1932).

207. PANO, 3-6-67, 25–26, taken from Poznanskii, *Gonimye golodom*, 3:7–9.

208. PANO, 3-6-67, 121–24, taken from Poznanskii, *Gonimye golodom*, 3:23–28.

209. PANO, 3-6-67, 1–6, taken from Poznanskii, *Gonimye golodom*, 3:52–57.

210. It was true even for the largest part of Moscow. Hoffmann, *Peasant Metropolis*, 127–57.

5. FAMINE

1. The number of victims varies widely from source to source. Documented calculations estimate between 5.5 million and 6.5 million deaths. By far the most people died in Ukraine (around 3.5 million). See Davies and Wheatcroft, *Years of Hunger*, 401.

2. On the erosion of social values, see Kenzhaliev and Dauletova, *Kazakhskoe obychnoe pravo*, 137–41.

3. Edele, *Stalinist Society*, 196.

4. Ohayon, *La sédentarisation*, 230–35.

5. Tsentral'nyi Gosudarstvennyi Arkhiv Respubliki Kazakhstan (TsGARK), 30-6-28,

71 (letter from Goloshchekin and Isaev to Anastas Mikoyan, December 29, 1929). See also Kindler, " . . . es gibt menschliche Opfer," 153–57.

6. TsGARK, 30–6-86 (report by the Pavlodar Oblast Committee, February 27, 1930).

7. Rossiiskii Gosudarstvennyi Arkhiv Ekonomiki (RGAE), 7486–37–132, 107–9 (special report no. 15 on supply complications, July 14, 1930).

8. Arkhiv Prezidenta Respubliki Kazakhstan (APRK), 719–2-125, 139 (letter from Al'shanskii to Roshal', July 12, 1930).

9. TsGARK, 30–6-86, 52 (telegram from Isaev to Kuramysov, April 22, 1930).

10. TsGARK, 30–6-28, 65 (SNK KASSR resolution of January 13, 1930).

11. APRK, 719–2-125, 140 (letter from Al'shanskii to the Kraikom, June 17, 1930).

12. For details see Davies, "Soviet Famine," and Kondrashin, Golod 1932–1933 godov, 66–93.

13. Payne, "Seeing Like a Soviet State," 72.

14. Kozybaev, Abylkhozhin, and Aldazhumanov, Kollektivizatsiia, 18.

15. Rossiiskii Gosudarstvennyi Arkhiv Sotsial'no-Politicheskoi Istorii (RGASPI), 631–5-75, 33–35, taken from Kondrashin, Golod v SSSR, vol. 1/2, 129-30.

16. Davies and Wheatcroft, Years of Hunger, 230.

17. On Zhana-Arinsk, see APRK, 719–4-68, 8 (report on emigration and the sedentarization of returning households, November 20, 1932). On Turgai, see APRK, 719–4-73, 224 (OGPU report on supply problems in villages and auls, October 10, 1932). On Chubartavsk, see APRK, 719–4-667, 1 (report on conditions in the district of Chubartavsk, January 1, 1933).

18. APRK, 141–1-5827, 32, taken from Degitaeva, Levon Mirzoian, 31–35.

19. TsGARK, 1179–1-17, 36–37 (report fom Rozykulov, n.d. [July 1932]).

20. In contrast, in the Middle Volga region, even at the peak of the famine, cases and causes of death were recorded with care: Kondrashin, Golod 1932–1933 godov, 237–48, 515–16.

21. APRK, 719–4-73, 220 (report on supply problems in auls and villages, October 10, 1932).

22. For calculations, see: Maksudov, "Migratsii v SSSR"; Asylbekov and Galiev, Sotsial'no-demograficheskie protsessy; Alekseenko and Alekseenko, Naselenie Kazakhstana; Kozuybaev, "Demograficheskie issledovaniia"; Kozybaev, Abylkhozhin, and Aldazhumanov, Kollektivizatsiia, 28–29. The following sources estimate a total of about 1.5 million deaths by starvation: Pianciola, "Famine in the Steppe"; Ohayon, La sédentarisation, 264–67; Omarbekov, Golodomor v Kazakhstane, 5. Historians among the Russian diaspora in Kazakhstan find the numbers exaggerated. See

Khliupin and Puzanov, "Obratnaia storona elity," 92–95. For interpretations of the numbers of victims and the significance of calculations produced by Kazakh nationalists that deviate considerably in terms of total numbers, see Mark, "Die Hungersnot." For the census of 1937, see Schlögel, *Moscow 1937*, 109–24. For criticism of census taking in Kazakhstan, see RGASPI 82–2–537, 96–123 (report on the census for Kazakhstan, n.d. [1937]).

23. Gangrade and Dhadda, *Challenge and Response*, 18.

24. Reemtsma, *Trust and Violence*, 12–17.

25. For instance, in Turnbull, *Mountain People*. In "Social Responses," Dirks also argues that societies did not totally disintegrate under such conditions.

26. Gosudarstvennyi Arkhiv Rossiiskoi Federatsii (GARF), 1235–141–766, 54 (file from an investigative committee in the Petropavlovsk oblast, May 12, 1930).

27. For the district of Zhana-Arinsk, see APRK, 719–4–68, 4 (report on the district of Zhana-Arinsk, n.d. [December 1932]). See also APRK, 719–5–169, 3–3ob (letter from Chagirov to Fekter, August 21, 1932).

28. Mikhailov, *Great Disaster*, 9.

29. Canetti, *Crowds and Power*, 60–62.

30. Sofsky, *Zeiten des Schreckens*, 123 and *Traktat über die Gewalt*, 166–72.

31. Sofsky, *Zeiten des Schreckens*, 124.

32. One example for the disintegration of a "mass of fleeing people" is the plight of Napoleon's Grande Armée in 1812. See Zamoyski, *1812*, 539–60.

33. Dirks, "Social Responses," 30.

34. Spittler, "Handeln in einer Hungerkrise," 32–37.

35. Shayakhmetov, *Silent Steppe*, 186–89.

36. TsGARK, 509–1–178, 240 (report from Karutskii and Skomorkhov, October 27, 1932).

37. GARF, 6985–1–6, 28–34 (report on children's homes in the KASSR, n.d. [mid-1934]).

38. TsGARK, 509–1–78, 241.

39. Ó Gráda, *Famine*, 61.

40. Taken from Kirchner, "Zur Bildhaftigkeit."

41. On the problem of child abandonment, see Rahmato, *Famine*, 185–92 and Panter-Brick, "Nobody's Children?" The latter suggests that the emotional charge attached to the notion of the abandoned child is considerably shaped by Western ideas of the family and childhood.

42. Mikhailov, *Great Disaster*, 325.

43. Mikhailov, *Great Disaster*, 142–43.

44. TsGARK, 509–1-78, 60 (letter from the *detkomissiia* in Semipalatinsk to Alma-Ata, March 3, 1932).

45. TsGARK, 509–1-78, 28 (file about one orphanage in Semipalatinsk, July 8, 1932).

46. GARF, 6985–1-22, 101–3 (file on the children's work commune in Tobodinsk, June 12, 1934).

47. TsGARK, 509–1-178, 78 (report on the Children's Commission for the region of Eastern Kazakhstan, July 29, 1932).

48. APRK, 141–1-5233, 8–9, taken from Kozybaev, *Nasil'stvennaia kollektivizatsiia*, 108.

49. TsGARK, 509–1-178, 80.

50. TsGARK, 509–1-78 (file on the inspection of the children's town in Steklianskoe, July 6, 1932).

51. APRK, 141–1-5894, 26 (shorthand note from an assembly of functionaries from nomadic and seminomadic districts, November 6, 1933).

52. Conditions were similar in other regions gripped by famine: Falk, *Sowjetische Städte*, 299–305.

53. On gangs of this nature, see Galley, "Wir schlagen," 26–53.

54. See United Nations Refugee Agency, "Kazakhstan."

55. APRK, 719–4-719, 276 (special report from Mironov on food supply problems, April 10, 1933).

56. APRK, 719–4-719, 271.

57. Mikhailov, *Great Disaster*, 14.

58. Mikhailov, *Great Disaster*, 354.

59. APRK, 719–4-673, 19–20 (GPU report on murder and cannibalism in the region of Alma-Ata, March 16, 1933).

60. This holds for practically all human societies. See Arens, *Man-Eating Myth*.

61. Kindler, "Die Starken," 72–73.

62. APRK, 719–4-719, 115 (OGPU report on food supply problems in the KASSR, April 1, 1933).

63. APRK, 719–4-719, 275f; APRK, 719–4-673, 18–20; APRK, 719–4-675, 11–12 (report on cannibalism in the village of Trakhtobrod, May 11, 1933).

64. APRK, 719–4-675, 11–12.

65. TsGARK, 1179–5-8, 33–43 (letter from Kunashchaev to Isaev, February 20, 1933).

66. Many examples can be found in Mikhailov, *Great Disaster*.

67. TsGARK, 1179–5-8, 29ob.

68. GARF, 6985–1-27, 115.

69. GARF, 1235–141–1371, 48ob (report from M. Pershin on the conditions in Kazakhstan, n.d. [summer 1932]).

70. Mikhailov, *Great Disaster*, 14–16.

71. GARF, 6985–1–27, 115 (report on the district of Chubartavsk, September 9, 1933).

72. RGASPI, 17–120–80, 84 (letter from Aronshtam to Stalin, Kaganovich, Postyshev, and Rudzutak, August 20, 1932).

73. APRK, 141–1–6403, 254 (report to Mirzoian, n.d. [spring 1933]).

74. APRK, 719–4–68, 8.

75. Shayakhmetov, *Silent Steppe*, 85–90.

76. For stages of malnutrition and the related physical and psychological effects, see Dirks, "Social Responses," 23–24; and Butterly and Shepherd, *Hunger*, 55–60. Franklin et al., "Observations"; Helweg-Larsen et al., "Die Hungerkrankheit," 170–71.

77. Turnbull, *Mountain People*. Sorokin, *Man and Society*, 82. Examples can also be found in Reid, *Blokada*, 279–87.

78. Agamben, *Remnants*, 52, 55. See also Ryn and Klodzinski, "An der Grenze."

79. Shayakhmetov, *Silent Steppe*, 137.

80. Ikramov, *Delo moego otsa*, 97. Akmal Ikramov lived from 1898 to 1938.

81. Cameron, "Hungry Steppe," 281–82. Nikolai Bukharin, too, was shocked when he traveled through Kazakhstan. See Abylkhozhin, Kozybaev, and Tatimov, "Novoe o kollektivizatsii," 217.

82. RGASPI, 82–2–148, 192–93 (letter from Vasil'ev to Molotov, n.d. [September 1932]).

83. RGASPI, 82–2–148, 193.

84. Iakovenko, *Agnessa*, 56–57.

85. Maillart, *Turkestan Solo*, 24.

86. Maillart, *Turkestan Solo*, 243.

87. APRK, 141–1–5774, 8 (report from Volodzh'ko on the otkochevniki in Karaganda, January 2, 1933).

88. These purges happened at the same time and were done by the same methods as the drive to purge cities from "marginalized elements." Shearer, *Policing Stalin's Socialism*, 181–82.

89. APRK, 719–4–719, 279 (OGPU report to Gusev and Egorov, prior to May 7, 1933). Mikhailov depicts a similar scene at the market of Akmolinsk (*Great Disaster*, 335).

90. On the role of the refugee, see Bauman, *Modernity and Ambivalence*, 56–65, and Bauman, *Wasted Lives*, 73–80.

91. Groebner, *Ungestalten*, 171.

92. For the significance of visual representations of famines, see Edkins, *Whose Hunger?* 3–6.

93. Patenaude, *Big Show.*

94. Interestingly, reports on famine in Ukraine for the years 1932–33 are often illustrated with photographs that have been proved to show conditions during the famine of 1921–22 on the Volga. On the role of silence in Soviet society, see Kindler, "Famines and Political Communication."

95. On how difficult it is to communicate pain, see Scarry, *Body in Pain*, 3–11; Trotha, "Zur Soziologie," 29–30.

96. Kindler, "Die Starken," 69.

97. Any mention of the starving population was at least not included in the published version of the plenum's minutes. See *Shestoi plenum.*

98. *Shestoi plenum*, 184. For biographical data on Nurmukhamedov (1900–1938), see Zhakypov et al., *Narkomy Kazakhstana*, 259–60.

99. *Shestoi plenum*, 209.

100. Mikhailov, *Great Disaster*, 209.

101. APRK, 141–1-6403, 254 (letter to Mirzoian).

102. APRK, 141–1-6403, 254.

103. APRK, 719–4-673, 7–8 (report on otkochevniki in Aulie-Ata, March 8, 1933).

104. For similar practices in Ukraine, see Werth, "A State against Its People," 162–64.

105. See Werth, *Cannibal Island*, 170.

106. APRK, 141–1-7372, 52–53 (minutes of a session of the City Party Committee of the Communist All-Union Party of the Bolsheviks, Aktyubinsk, April 15, 1934).

107. TsGARK, 1179–1-17, 21–23 (letter from the administration of the militia to Isaev and Mironov, June 17, 1932).

108. APRK, 719–4-19, 331 (OGPU report on emigration in Kazakhstan, July 22, 1933).

109. For example, in Karaganda: APRK, 719–4-675, 2–3 (GPU report, after April 11, 1933).

110. TsGARK, 44–14-871, 36–37 (report on inspection of Barracks No. 6, March 5, 1933).

111. GARF, 6985–1-41, 74–75 (report on conditions in the district of Chu, December 4, 1933).

112. TsGARK, 509–1-229, 9ob (file from Semenov in the district of Merke, January 27, 1933).

113. The officials held responsible claimed that not a single person there had died of hunger. TsGARK, 1179–5-8, 141 (minutes of the operative troika, January 28, 1933).

114. TsGARK, 1179–5-7, 25–27.

115. APRK, 141-1-6017, 26 (report on otkochevniki at the Merke Sovkhoz's Sugar Trust, July 7, 1933). Another report on this same event says that the children were brought to Kirghizia and left to their fate there: TsGARK, 44-14-869, 151. As punishment for these activities, several comrades were excluded from the party and put on trial.

116. APRK, 141-1-5774, 9 (letter from Volod'sko about the otkochevniki in Karaganda, January 2, 1933).

117. TsGARK, 1179-5-8, 300.

118. APRK, 719-4-69, 87.

119. RGASPI, 17-120-80, 88.

120. Pianciola, "Famine in the Steppe."

121. APRK, 141-1-5984, 40.

122. GARF, 6985-1-27, 145 (letter from Bokhov to Tabolov and Tulepov, August 28, 1933).

123. GARF, 6985-1-27, 144.

124. APRK, 141-1-6403, 255.

125. GARF, 6985-1-27, 143.

126. GARF, 6985-1-27, 142, and APRK, 141-1-6403, 256.

127. APRK, 719-4-68, 12 (report on emigration and returnees to the KASSR, November 20, 1932).

128. TsGARK, 30-6-226, 6.

129. APRK, 719-4-674, 66-85 (report on the cereal harvest, harvest surveillance, and produce delivery, July 20, 1933).

130. APRK, 719-4-674, 86-88 (supplement to the report on the cereal harvest, based on data from July 21, 1933). See also APRK, 141-1-5775, 44 (information on supervising the harvest in the region of Aktiubinsk, n.d. [summer 1933]).

131. APRK, 719-4-667, 67 (GPU report on a counterrevolutionary-chauvinist group in the village of Khriachevka, region of Karaganda, March 22, 1933). See also TsGARK 44-4-869, 149 (report on phenomena of Great Power chauvinism, n.d. [fall 1933]).

132. APRK, 719-4-675, 158-60 (report on Great Power chauvinism and *samosud* in the district of Bulaevsk, August 28, 1933).

133. McDonald, *Face to the Village*, 236-37; Frank, *Crime, Cultural Conflict*, 245-75.

134. APRK, 141-1-6403, 257.

135. Aronshtam (1893-1938) was Turkmenistan's first party secretary from 1928 to 1930. For more on Aronshtam and Soviet policy on nationalities, see Edgar, *Tribal Nation*, 86-87, 114, 118n. Quote from RGASPI, 17-120-80, 84, 85ob.

136. APRK, 141-1-6403, 256.

137. For a systematic study, see Kassymbekova, *Despite Cultures*,199–204.

138. Kassymbekova and Teichmann, "Red Man's Burden," 165, 185–86.

139. Baron, "Stalinist Planning."

140. Merl, *Politische Kommunikation*, 105.

141. Ledeneva, *Russia's Economy*, 83–85.

142. Merl, *Politische Kommunikation*, 108–9.

143. For networks inside the party, see Easter, *Reconstructing the State*. On the relationship of Stalinist leadership and local interests, see Harris, *Great Urals*.

144. Fitzpatrick, *Everyday Stalinism*, 109–14; Ledeneva, *Russia's Economy*, 84.

145. Fitzpatrick, "Blat," 178.

146. Ledeneva, *Russia's Economy*, 76–78; Rittersporn, "Omnipresent Conspiracy," 262.

147. Siegelbaum, "Dear Comrade," 231–32.

148. See, for example, Allaniiazov, *Kollektivizatsiia*, 62–63.

149. Shayakhmetov, *Silent Steppe*, 183–88. On the correlation of group cohesion and chances of survival, see Ó Gráda, *Famine*, 45–46, 90–91.

150. TsGARK, 74–11–168, 135–36 (report from Uravov and Akzhanov to Isaev, October 2, 1934). This was also true of networks within cadre hierarchies that had different kinds of access to supplies. See Osokina, *Our Daily Bread*, 61–81.

151. Tsentral'nyi Arkhiv Federal'noi Sluzhby Bezopasnosti Rossiiskoi Federatsii (TsA FSB RF), 2–11–47, 209–11, taken from Kondrashin et al., *Golod v SSSR*, 2:636; Gosudarstvennyi Arkhiv Zapadno-Kazakhstanskoi obl. RK, 580–1-6, 18–19, taken from from Kondrashin et al., *Golod v SSSR*, 2:631.

152. APRK, 141-1-6017, 22 (excerpts from reports on nomadic oblasts, n.d. [summer/early fall 1933]).

153. TsGARK, 1179-5-1, 208 (letter from Gataulin to Golodov, Isaev, and Kulumbetov, March 13, 1933).

154. GARF, 1235–141–1371, 269.

155. TsA FSB RF 2–11–1449, 106–18, taken from Danilov and Manning, *Tragediia sovetskoi derevni*, 3:427.

156. APRK, 141-1-5775, 5–6 (report on a counterrevolutionary group at the May Day kolkhoz in the district of Akbulak, Aktiubinsk oblast, March 9, 1933).

157. Ashimbaev and Khliupin, *Kazakhstan*, 341–42.

158. APRK, 141-1-6107, 4–4ob (report on the district of Aralsk, February 6, 1933).

159. GARF, 6985-1-27, 112 (report on the district of Chubartavsk, September 9, 1933).

160. GARF, 6985-1-27, 115.

161. APRK, 719-4-675, 9 (report on criminal actions by officials in the district of Mangistau, May 5, 1933).

162. APRK, 719-4-675, 9.

163. Plaggenborg, "Staatlichkeit als Gewaltroutine."

164. Holquist, "State Violence."

165. Trotha, "Über den Erfolg," 227.

166. For this kind of Bolshevik, see Baberowski, *Der Rote Terror*, 88. An example of a Bolshevist problem solver can be found in Wheatcroft, "Agency and Terror."

167. On using physical violence to intimidate the weak, see Schnell, *Räume des Schreckens*, 344-48; and on using violence as a means of communication, see p. 359. On using violence as a message for third parties, see Reemtsma, *Trust and Violence*, 266-74.

168. Reemtsma, *Trust and Violence*, 21-24.

169. Kenzhaliev and Dauletova, *Kazakhskoe obychnoe pravo*, 137-42.

170. APRK, 719-4-675, 69-70 (report on officials beating kolkhoz peasants in the aul soviet of Akir-Tiubinsk, August 26, 1933).

171. APRK, 719-4-675, 42 (report on the apparatus in the district of Iany-Kurgan, August 17, 1933).

172. APRK, 719-4-675, 43.

173. TsGARK, 1179-5-8, 299.

174. APRK, 719-4-672, 7 (minutes no. 25 from the party troika of the Control Commission for the region of Alma-Ata, August 1-2, 1933).

175. APRK, 719-4-675, 49-53 (report on the soviet apparatus in the district of Bostandyk, August 17, 1933).

176. On the widespread practice of offering "honored guests" one's own wife or daughter for the purpose of sexual intercourse, see Kenzahaliev and Dauletova, *Kazakhskoe obychnoe pravo*, 138.

177. APRK, 141-1-5774, 92-94 (special report on the criminal activity of the militia organ in the district of Zharminsk, February 20, 1933).

178. This practice reached its zenith in the Great Terror. See, for example, Vatlin, *Terror raionnogo masshtaba*.

179. APRK, 141-1-5287, 17-22, taken from Degitaeva, *Levon Mirzoian*, 25. In his speech at a famous plenum of February-March 1937, Stalin picked out Mirzoian from among all the leaders of the republics as an especially striking paragon of nepotism and clientelism.

180. See, for instance, Isaev's speech, in which he sought to liberate himself from Goloshchekin: *Shestoi plenum*, 153-55.

181. See, for example, "Ob oshibkakh starogo rukovodstva"; "Opportunicheskaia bezdeiatel'nost.'" Stalin authorized the publication of selected verdicts: RGASPI, 558-11-46, 51 (Stalin's telegram to Mirzoian, March 14, 1933).

182. Bogdanov, "Chistka partii."

183. TsGARK, 30-6-227, 31-32 (Tashtitov's letter to Mirzoian and Isaev, April 11, 1933).

184. GARF, 6985-1-27, 145.

185. On the distribution of food in the Soviet Union, see Falk, *Sowjetische Städte*, 141–43; Kondrat'eva, *Kormit' i pravit'*, 94–95.

186. Werth, "A State against Its People," 167. See also Lih, Naumow, and Chlewnyuk, *Stalin*, 251.

187. That was not only the opinion of contemporary propaganda and Soviet historians, but also essentially the opinion of Western historians: Baishev, *Pobeda sotsializma*, 198; Ohayon, *La sédentarisation*; Pianciola, *Stalinismo di frontiera*; Cameron, "Hungry Steppe."

188. RGASPI, 17-162-13, 116–17, taken from Danilov and Manning, *Tragediia sovetskoi derevni*, 3:483–84; Akhmetova, Grigor'ev, and Shoikin, "Turar Ryskulov," 190.

189. "Artel" was short for *selsko-khoziaistvennii artel'*, that is, kolkhoz; Olcott, *Kazakhs*, 319.

The collective nature of the TOZ was limited to labor cooperation. The means of production (i.e., livestock) was to remain the private property of peasants and nomads. See Merl, *Bauern unter Stalin*, 207. For its normative principles see *Primernyi ustav*.

190. On private operations and the reforms of the year 1933, see Merl, *Bauern unter Stalin*, 257–80.

191. Hildermeier, *Geschichte der Sowjetunion*, 536–38.

192. For debates, see Zelenin, "Byl li kolkhoznyi neonep?"

193. Solomon, *Soviet Criminal Justice*, 113–18. For Stalin's justification, see Khlevniuk et al., *Stalin i Kaganovich*, 240–41.

194. Kondrashin, *Golod 1932–1933 godov*, 285.

195. APRK, 141-17-607, 1–14 taken from Abdirainymov, Bukhonova, and Gribanova, *Golod*, 140–51.

196. Goloshchekin, *Na poroge*, 34.

197. RGASPI, 17-3-914, 9 (politburo minutes no. 129 of February 3, 1933, resolution concerning Goloshchekin dated January 21, 1933). Until his arrest in 1939, Goloshchekin was called on to act as a national arbitrator: RGASPI, 558-11-81, 86 (telegram to Stalin from Kaganovich and Molotov, October 2, 1933), 84 (telegram from Stalin to Kaganovich and Molotov, October 3, 1933). For details on Mirzoian's biography (1869–1939), see Khurshudian, "Slovo o Mirzoiane."

198. For example, Batchaev, "Protiv iskazhenii postanovleniia"; Brainin, Shafiro, and Timofeev, "Ob oshibkakh"; Varlamov and Savinskii, "My otvechaem."

199. *Shestoi plenum*, 187. Later, in his famous "Secret Speech" given at the Twentieth Party Congress of the CPSU, Nikita Khrushchev accused Stalin of the same behavior. After his return from Siberia he had never again visited a Russian village. Talbott, *Khrushchev Remembers*, 610.

200. RGASPI, 81-3-419, 55–59, taken from *Sovetskoe rukovodstvo*, 245–49, 258.

201. Koigeldiev, *Stalinizm i repressii*, 248–49.

202. APRK, 141-1-5287, 17–22, taken from Degitaeva, *Levon Mirzoian*, 22.

203. In early 1933 Alma-Ata had no direct telephone or telegraph line to Moscow. In the republic's interior things were even worse. APRK, 141-1-5287, 32, taken from Degitaeva, *Levon Mirzoian*, 31–35.

204. APRK, 141-1-5287, taken from Degitaeva, *Levon Mirzoian*, 47. At the time, the authorities estimated that population to consist of about 800,000.

205. Concerning that Party Congress, see Hildermeier, *Geschichte der Sowjetunion*, 446. For Mirzoian's speech, see Mirzoian, "Rech'."

206. See, for example, Khurshudian, *Slovo o Mirzoiane*. For a critical assessment, see Abylkhozhin, "Inertsiia," 251–52.

207. APRK, 141-1-5827, 33–38, taken from Omarbekov, *Golodomor v Kazakhstane*, 194.

208. APRK, 141-1-5828, 81–85, taken from Degitaeva, *Levon Mirzoian*, 62. For more detail on livestock from China, see GARF, 5446-14a-313, 5–6 (letter to Stalin and Molotov from Kulumbetov, April 28, 1933); RGASPI, 17-162-14, 160–61 (TsK politburo resolution of June 15, 1933); APRK, 719-4-672, 73–81 (report on the purchase of livestock in West China, October 1, 1933).

209. For numerous examples, see APRK, 719-4-672, 37–42 (report on aid for households without livestock, October 21, 1933).

210. Batchaev, "Protiv iskazhenii postanovleniia," 62.

211. APRK, 141-1-5894 (shorthand note from an assembly of officials from nomadic and seminomadic districts, November 6, 1933).

212. TsGARK, 1179-5-8, 296 (Abdrakhmanov's report on the resolutions of September 17 and December 20, 1932, dated January 31, 1933).

213. APRK, 141-1-7415, 53 (report on the district of Kounradsk, September 6, 1934).

214. APRK, 141-1-5894, 34.

215. APRK, 141-1-5894, 86; emphasis added.

216. Fitzpatrick, "Blat," 170.

217. APRK, 719-4-672, 42.

218. APRK, 141-1-6017, 22 (report on the region of Turgai and the decision of September 17, 1932, n.d. [fall 1933]).

219. APRK, 141.1.5894, 12 (assembly of party secretaries for nomadic and seminomadic districts, November 6, 1933).

220. RGASPI, 17–2-525, 86 (shorthand note from the TsK VKP[b] plenum, June–July 1934).

221. For a survey of the disputes, see Khalidullin, "Agrarnaia politika," 198.

222. APRK, 719–4-70, 19.

223. Ohayon, *La sédentarisation*, 279–97.

224. APRK, 141–1-5192, 17–20, taken from Kondrashin et al., *Golod v SSSR*, vol. 1/2, 272.

225. APRK, 141–1-5192, 42–43, taken from Kozybaev, *Nasil'stvennaia kollektivizatsiia*, 117–18.

226. Kozybaev, *Nasil'stvennaia kollektivizatsiia*, 133.

227. GARF, 1235–141–1371, 246.

228. TsGARK, 30–7-108, 58–60ob, taken from Kozybaev, *Nasil'stvennaia kollektivizatsiia*, 131.

229. TsGARK, 30–6-207, 1 (shorthand note from the Ryskulov Commission, February 22, 1933).

230. Kondrashin, *Golod 1932–33 godov*, 172–92.

231. RGASPI, 558–11–45, 109–1090b, taken from Danilov and Manning, *Tragediia sovetskoi derevni*, 3:634–35.

232. For details, see Werth, *Cannibal Island*, 59–85.

233. Khlevniuk et al., *Stalin i Kaganovich*, 260.

234. APRK, 141–1-5774, 37 (special notice on emigration from the southern regions of Kazakhstan, January 15, 1933).

235. As late as March 1933, he still tried to keep them out, as attested by a letter to Stalin and Molotov. APRK, 141–1-5827, 33–38, taken from Omarbekov, *Golodomor v Kazakhstane*, 195.

236. Ryskulov's report of September 29, 1932 (APRK, 141–1-6403, 13–16) was published in Ryskulov, *Sobranie sochinenii*, 3:304–16; his letter of March 1933 (GARF, 5446–27–23) was published in *Sovetskoe rukovodstvo*, 204–24.

237. Abylkhozhin, Kozybaev, and Tatimov, "Novoe o kollektivizatsii."

238. Baberowski, *Der Rote Terror*, 124. For less prominent attempts to get Stalin's attention, see Aibasov, *Odin iz pervykh*, 3–5, 66–69.

239. TsGARK, 30–6-207, 27–30 (letter from "Karim" to Isaev, February 25, 1933).

240. TsGARK, 30–6-207, 4 (shorthand note from the Ryskulov Commission, February 22, 1933).

241. TsGARK, 30–6-207, 14.

242. TsGARK, 30–6-207, 16.

243. TsGARK, 30–6–207, 14.

244. TsGARK, 30–6–207, 22.

245. Ryskulov, *Sobranie sochinenii*, 3:352.

246. RGASPI, 62–2–3135, 38 (SNK KSSR resolution of February 25, 1933). Quotation, 37 (letter from Arsen'ev to TsKK TsKP[b], n.d. [after February 25, 1933]).

247. TsGARK, 1179–5–7, 36–38 (minutes no. 70 taken at from a meeting of central committee secretaries of the Communist Party [Bolshevist] of Uzbekistan, February 28, 1933).

248. GARF, A-259–16–31, 66–67 (central executive committee resolution of March 10, 1932).

249. GARF, A-259–16–31, 20 (SNK RSFSR resolution of February 2, 1933).

250. GARF, A-259–16–31, 16 (Ryskulov's letter to Bykin, chairman of the Bashkir Regional Committee, September 21, 1933).

251. GARF, A-259–16–31, 10–14 (Kal'metev's letter to Ryskulov, October 15, 1933). For more on this affair, see Ryskulov, *Sobranie sochinenii*, 3:351–52.

252. On the competition between oblasts, which were always struggles between personal networks, see Easter, *Reconstructing the State*, 109–10.

253. Fedtke, "Wie aus Bucharern," 230–31.

254. During the final years of Stalin's life this was also true of those closest to him. See Baberowski, *Scorched Earth*, 411–22.

255. GARF, 5446–14a-409, 7 (Ryskulov's letter to Kuybyshev, March 29, 1933). Statisticians calculated that by allotting rations of 250 grams per day per person this amount would feed 67,000 people for two months.

256. Later the SNK SSSR issued the corresponding resolution. GARF, 5446–14a-409, 4 (SNK SSSR resolution of April 15, 1933).

257. GARF, 5446–14a-409, 20–22ob (SNK RSFSR resolution of March 13, 1933).

258. GARF, 5446–14a-409, 19 (Sulimov's letter to Kuybyshev, April 15, 1933).

259. GARF, 5446–14a-13, 2–3 (Isaev's telegram to Molotov, May 5, 1933).

260. GARF, 5446–14a-13, 1 (SNK telegram reply to Isaev, May 25, 1933).

261. APRK, 141–1–5828, 22–26, taken from Degitaeva, *Levon Mirzoian*, 53.

262. Nurtazina, "Great Famine," 120.

263. Shaumian, *Ot kochev'ia*, 157–59.

264. TsGARK, 1179–5–7, 3–4, taken from Kozybaev, *Nasil'stvennaia kollektivizatsiia*, 223–24.

265. Abdrakhmanov, *Izbrannye trudy*, 160.

266. Ryskulov, *Sobranie sochinenii*, 3:348–50.

267. Dzhumagaliev and Semenov, "Vernyi syn naroda," 41.

268. Dzhumagaliev and Semenov, "Vernyi syn naroda," 41. For more on Abdrakhmanov,

see Teichmann, "Arbeiten, Kämpfen, Scheitern." Differences in developments in Kazakhstan and Kirghizia have been investigated by Pianciola, "Stalinist Spatial Hierarchies."

269. TsGARK, 509–1–229, 14 (Semenov's letter to Kurmagaliev, February 6, 1933).

270. For a summary, see RGASPI, 62–2–3135, 66–68ob (Telegin's report on the situation of otkochevniki in Karakalpak, November 14, 1933).

271. TsGARK, 44–14–872, 31 (telegram from Aralskoe More, September 1933).

272. GARF, 5446–15a–307, 12–17 (Loginov and Aliev's report to Zhdanov and Ryskulov on otkochevniki in Karakalpak ASSR, before May 25, 1934); RGASPI, 17–163–1042, 156–59, taken from Gatagova, *TsK VKP(b)*, 2:76–80.

273. GARF, 5446–15a–307, 4 (resolution passed by Truda i Oborony soviet, June 16, 1934); and 8 (Pakhomov's letter to Kuybyshev, June 11, 1934).

274. GARF, 5446–15a–307, 3 (Isaev's letter to Molotov, July 4, 1934).

275. GARF, 5446–15a–316, 6 (Kaganovich and Molotov's telegram to Isaev, n.d. [summer 1934]).

276. On "national kolkhozes" in West Siberia, see Gosudarstvennyi Arkhiv Novosibirskoi Oblasti (GANO), 47–1–2192, 111–17, in Poznanskii, *Gonimye golodom*, 3:59–62.

277. For details, see Viola, *Unknown Gulag*, 33–53.

278. Werth, *Cannibal Island*.

279. RGASPI, 17–2–525, 17, taken from Danilov and Manning *Tragediia sovetskoi derevni*, 4:163.

280. RGASPI, 17–2–518, 185.

281. RGASPI, 17–2–525, 17, taken from Danilov and Manning, *Tragediia sovetskoi derevni*, 4:165. On the role of jokes in inner circles of power, see Schilling, "Mächtige Signale," 334.

282. Adams, "Reemigration." A large part of the refugees stayed in Xinjiang. See Medikulova, *Kazakhskaia diaspora*; Benson and Svanberg, *China's Last Nomads*. Large numbers did not return to Kazakhstan until 1991. See Diener, *One Homeland or Two?* 244–53.

283. APRK, 141–1–5775, 60–66 (report to Mirzoian from the PP OGPU in Kazakhstan, December 6, 1934).

284. Alma-Ata was assigned 10,000 households; South Kazakhstan, 8,000; Karaganda, 8,000; East Kazakhstan, 7,000; and West Kazakhstan, 4,000.

285. Shaumian, *Ot kochev'ia*, 162.

286. RGASPI, 17–25–76, 83 (Kraikom resolution on "Measures for Accommodating the Otkochevniki," March 31, 1933).

287. APRK, 725–1–196, 43–45 (report on relocations to sugar beet regions of Kazakh-

stan, after August 5, 1934); APRK, 725-1-222, 3 (SNK KASSR resolution of May 23, 1934); TsGARK, 74-11-264, 31; TsGARK 74-11-265, 100 (report on sedentarization in Kazakhstan, 1930-37, n.d. [1937]); APRK, 719-4-73, 203-10 (report on the cotton harvest in South Kazakhstan, October 28, 1932).

288. RGASPI, 17-2-525, 17, taken from Danilov and Manning, *Tragediia sovetskoi derevni*, 4:163.

289. APRK, 141-1-7372, 117 (survey of otkochevniki who returned between June 15, 1933, and May 1, 1934, n.d. [after May 1, 1934]).

290. Shayakhmetov, *Silent Steppe*, 207-20.

291. APRK, 141-1-7372, 73.

292. TsGARK, 74-11-270, 51 (number of returning households, n.d. [summer 1936]).

293. Kulumbetov, "Reshenie TsK VKP(b)."

294. TsGARK, 1179-5-3, 44 (Kazkraikom Bureau resolution of February 24, 1933).

295. TsGARK, 1179-5-3, 64 (Kazkraikom resolution of March 26, 1933).

296. TsGARK, 1179-5-9, 1 (Egorov's letter to Regional Executive Committees, April 3, 1933).

297. Ellman, "Stalin," 689.

298. Kessler, "Origins," 67-71; Shearer, "Elements."

299. Kessler, "Passport System," 478.

300. For a particularly dramatic example, see Werth, *Cannibal Island*.

301. TsGARK, 1179-5-3, 44 (Kazpromkom Bureau resolution of February 24, 1933).

302. APRK, 141-1-7372, 52 (minutes of a meeting of the Office of the Aktyubinsk Party Committee, April 15, 1934).

303. APRK, 141-1-7372, 52 A resolution from Petropavlovsk was similar, see Rossiiskii Gosudarstvennyi Arkhiv Noveishei Istorii (RGANI), 6-1-43, 88-89 (resolution of the KPK Bureau at the TsK VKP[b] regarding violations of revolutionary law in the region of Karaganda, January 13, 1935).

304. For example, RGASPI, 17-25-76, 59 (telegram to the District Committee in Uilsk, February 1933).

305. APRK, 8-1-105, 15 (conversation between Moldazhanov and Ospanov, February 12, 1933). For biographical details on Maldazhanov, see Zhakypov et al., *Narkomy Kazakhstana*, 242.

306. TsGARK, 74-11-264, 30 (report on settling the nomadic population, n.d. [mid-1937]).

307. APRK, 141-1-7284, 121-22, taken from Degitaeva, *Levon Mirzoian*, 66. The Kraikom decision was dated March 25, 1933. It included a discussion on closing food supply centers.

308. TsGARK, 1179–5-1, 1–4 (report on the distribution of food, April 17, 1933).

309. TsGARK, 1179–5-8, 301.

310. In this context, "handed out" means only that the grain was delivered to auls and kolkhozes. The statistics say nothing about who had access to those resources.

311. The detailed list is found in TsGARK, 30–6-226, 55–61 (food relief and food loans based on data provided by Zagotzerno on October 1, 1932 and December 4, 1932).

312. TsGARK, 44–16–603, 35 (Karutskii's letter to Goloshchekin and Isaev, December 10, 1932).

313. TsGARK, 1380–2-483, 83 (state prosecutor's report on struggling with crime in agriculture, December 21, 1933). According to official data, in 1933 a total of 4,167 hundredweights of food relief were wasted and another 4,467 hundredweights were not used for the intended purpose.

314. TsGARK, 44–14–869, 31–31ob (Chagirov's letter to Fekter, August 21, 1932); APRK, 719–4-719, 112 (report on difficulties in food provision for the KASSR, April 1, 1933).

315. Batchaev, "Protiv iskazhenii postanovleniia," 72.

316. APRK 141–1-7372, 18–19ob (insert to the minutes of the Bureau of the Org Committee, February 5, 1934).

317. APRK 141–1-7372, 306.

318. APRK, 725–1-206, 16–36 (report on the use of state relief, April 26, 1934).

319. TsGARK 30–6-299, 16 (situational report on the region of Aktiubinsk, March 29, 1933).

320. APRK, 141–1-7372, 65–66 (Borev's report to Mirzoian and Stakun, March 31, 1934).

321. APRK, 141–1-5894, 82. See also Payne, "Seeing Like a Soviet State," 78.

322. For details on the Party Control Commission, see Getty, *Pragmatists and Puritans*.

323. APRK, 725–1-206, 53 (Sharangovich's report to Stalin and Kaganovich on relief for Kazakhstan, June 7, 1934).

324. APRK, 725–1-206, 17.

325. APRK, 725–1-206, 55.

326. APRK, 725–1-206, 65.

327. APRK, 725–1-206, 10–11 (Mirzoian and Sharangovich's telegram to all regional party secretaries, n.d. [after June 7, 1934]).

328. RGASPI, 17–3-929, 9 (TsK VKP[b] resolution regarding kolkhoz funds for providing for otkochevniki in Kazakhstan, August 29, 1933).

329. GAVO, 139–1-140, 218, taken from Zhandabekova, *Pod grifom sekretnosti*, 67.

330. TsGARK, 44–14–872, 13–15 (report on conditions in the district of Urdzharsk, n.d. [late 1933]).

331. GARF, 6985–1-1, 219 (Takoev's letter to Kiselev, May 27, 1934).

332. GARF, 6985–1-2, 235 (shorthand note from the governing commission's session of the VTsIK, July 8, 1934).

333. APRK, 141–1-5894, 82.

334. RGASPI, 17–25–77, 85 (Kazkraikom resolution on tasks related to settling the otkochevniki, November 29, 1933).

335. TsGARK, 74–11–168, 137.

336. TsGARK, 74–11–168, 135ob.

337. GARF, 6985–1-40, 4 (material related to the investigation of the Iaroslavskii kolkhoz, n.d. [summer–fall 1933]).

338. "Ob osedanii," 264.

6. SOVIET NOMADISM

1. Ohayon, *La sédentarisation,* 327–34.

2. Karagizova, "Likvidatsiia posledstvii," 111–12.

3. Mirzoian, "Ob itogakh."

4. Gosudarstvennyi Arkhiv Rossiiskoi Federatsii (GARF), 6985–1-9, 132 (Mirzoian's presentation of results at the November meeting of the Central Committee of the VKP[b], December 20, 1934).

5. GARF, 6985–1-5, 160 (Lisitsyn at a VTsIK executive committee meeting, December 1, 1933).

6. For a list of commission members, see GARF, 6985–1-1, 1 (VTsIK executive committee resolution of April 20, 1934).

7. For the work accomplished by this commission, see Pianciola, "Famine in the Steppe," 178–82.

8. GARF, 6985–1-43. For detailed reports on individual kolkhozes, see GARF, 6985–1-46.

9. GARF, 6985–1-3, 21–22.

10. GARF, 6985–1-7, 149–46.

11. Pianciola, "Famine in the Steppe," 164.

12. GARF, 6985–1-6, 224 (report on sedentarizing the nomadic and seminomadic population of the RSFSR, n.d. [1934]).

13. Tsentral'nyi Gosudarstvennyi Arkhiv Respubliki Kazakhstan (TsGARK), 1179–1-98, 2–5 (Faizov and Karataev's report to Karibaev, n.d. [December 1934]).

14. Arkhiv Prezidenta Respubliki Kazakhstan (APRK), 725–1-206, 64–66 (Sharangovich's report to Stalin and Kaganovich, June 7, 1934).

15. GARF, 6985-1-6, 249 (TsIK SSSR's Nationalities Soviet executive committee resolution of October 4, 1935).

16. GARF, 6985-1-2, 74–101 (findings and suggestions of the governmental commission of the VTsIK with respect to settling nomads and seminomads in the KASSR, n.d. [summer 1934]); TsGARK, 1179-1-102, 1–25 (on the same topic).

17. Martin, "Interpreting," 114–15.

18. GARF, 3316-28-802, 42 (Assembly of the Nationalities Soviet of the TsIK, September 20, 1935).

19. GARF, 3316-28-802, 30–31.

20. GARF, 3316-28-802, 32.

21. "Soveshchanie po voprosam."

22. GARF, 3316-28-802, 75 (shorthand note from the assembly of the Nationalities Soviet of the TsIK SSSR on settling the nomadic and seminomadic population, January 19, 1936).

23. On irrigation see Teichmann, "Canals."

24. GARF, 3316-28-802, 126.

25. Merl, *Politische Kommunikation*, 109.

26. GARF, 3316-28-802, 132.

27. GARF, 3316-28-802, 135.

28. TsGARK, 30-5-553, 4 (Isaev's letter to Varov, June 26, 1936).

29. TsGARK, 30-5-530, 30 (SNK KASSR resolution on the investigation of work in the agrarian sector, July 21, 1936).

30. TsGARK, 30-5-530, 107 (SNK KASSR resolution concerning the revision results for the agrarian sector, October 22, 1936).

31. TsGARK, 30-5-474, 25 (report on sedentarizing nomads in the region of Akmolinsk, n.d. [1936]).

32. TsGARK, 74-11-187, 8–10 (revision report on money spent on repatriation in 1936, n.d. [April 1937]).

33. TsGARK, 74-11-264, 1 (Isaev's letter to Pankratov, February 4, 1937).

34. GARF, 1235-141-1682, 15–17 (Kalinin's speech at a session of the executive committee of the TsIK, August 20, 1935).

35. GARF, 6895-1-3, 27.

36. GARF, 6985-1-2, 243ob.

37. GARF, 3316-28-802, 82.

38. In 1936 on the occasion of adopting the new Soviet Constitution, Stalin announced "Socialism's Victory." See Hildermeier, *Geschichte der Sowjetunion*, 437.

39. Bacon, *Central Asians*, 120–23. By then nomads made up only a very small part of

the population. According to official statistics, in 1942 just 24,000 people trekked with their households all year through the steppe. Full-time nomads had thus permanently become a rarity. Ohayon, *La sédentarisation*, 336.

40. Martin, "Modernization?" 354. For a contrary view, see Hirsch, *Empire of Nations*, 268. A line similar to Martin's is suggested by Slezkine, "USSR as a Communal Apartment," 442–52.

41. Winner, "Some Problems," part 1, 256–59.

42. Ree, "Heroes and Merchants," 45.

43. Hirsch, *Empire of Nations*, 266–70.

44. Baldauf, "Tradition," 108–10.

45. It is a matter of some controversy whether Zhambyl wrote his own poems or sang what others wrote for him. See Volkow, *Die Memoiren*, 265–68; Kumanbaev, "800 millionov tenge."

46. TsGARK, 74–11–264, 20–21.

47. Kor'be, "Kul'tura i byt"; Sabitov, "Rabota."

48. TsGARK, 74–11–265, 63 (letter from the RSFSR Narkomzem to the KSSR Narkomzem, November 20, 1937). It is unknown whether sedentarization was actually a topic of discussion there. It does not turn up in the guide to the fair. See Pospelov et al., *Vsesoiuznaia Sel'skokhoziaistvennaia Vystavka*, 182–86, 331–33.

49. The (allegedly achieved) number of 77,400 sedentarized households, as shown in the table for 1930, was the same number targeted by the original plans.

50. This was to be done without losing sight of the country's grain production and industrial development. See Samatov, "Zhivotnovodstvo Kazakhstana," 62–63; Burkhanov, "Gosudarstvennyi plan." See also Mirzoian's speech on the state of agriculture in *VIII Kraevaia konferentsiia*, 37.

51. Winner, "Some Problems," part 1, 257.

52. Filatov, "Itogi i perspektivy"; Letunovskii, "Itogi zimovki"; Samatov and Kavaraiskii, "Zhivotnovodstvo Kazakhstana." Western observers reported on finding "functional nomadism" in the steppe. See Dunn and Dunn, "Soviet Regime," 160; Bacon, *Central Asians*, 120–26.

53. APRK, 141–1–9572, 17 (shorthand note from a meeting of party secretaries from nomadic and seminomadic regions, January 10, 1935).

54. Pogorel'skii, "Osedanie kochevykh i polukochevykh khoziaistv," 38.

55. Zenkovich, "Kochevye rajony," 51.

56. TsGARK, 74–11–264, 62 (measures for setting up nomadic households in livestock breeding regions of the KSSR, n.d. [1936]).

57. Ohayon, *La sédentarisation*, 330–31.

58. Ohayon, *La sédentarisation*, 332.

59. These conditions were true of almost all regions of the Soviet Union. See Fitzpatrick, *Stalin's Peasants*, 128–51; Rittersporn, "Das kollektivierte Dorf."

60. APRK, 141-1-7415, 46–46ob (letter from Riadnin, head of the polit-department at the MTS of Kulashansk, to Mirzoian, prior to August 7, 1934).

61. In general, see Merl, *Bauern unter Stalin*, 463–69. For practical examples, see TsGARK, 1137-3-504, 152 (report on regions proposed for a change of status, prior to June 14, 1939); TsGARK, 1137-1-726, 66–67 (letter to Isaev from Western Kazakhstan, June 15, 1937).

62. TsGARK, 1140-1-153, 23–24 (letter on meat procurement in formerly nomadic regions, March 28, 1935).

63. TsGARK, 1208-1-31, 81–85 (report from Karsakpaisk to the relocation authorities, n.d. [1939]).

64. TsGARK, 1137-3-848a, 250 (report on economic and cultural conditions in the district of Zhilokosinsk, n.d. [1939]).

65. TsGARK, 1208-1-31, 40 (letter from members of the Zhdanov kolkhoz to Stalin, December 23, 1938).

66. TsGARK, 1208-1-31, 54–55 (protest from the Kazakh People's Commissariat for Agriculture, n.d. [1939].

67. Rossiiskii Gosudarstvennyi Arkhiv Ekonomiki (RGAE), 4372-38-68, 30–40, taken from Danilov and Manning, *Tragediia sovetskoi derevni,* vol. 5/2, 494.

68. On remuneration for kolkhoz workers, see Merl, *Bauern unter Stalin*, 360–70.

69. TsGARK, 1137-3-848a, 233.

70. TsGARK, 1137-3-848a, 1 (resolution concerning the economic and cultural situation of the Gur'ev oblast, n.d. [September 1939]).

71. TsGARK, 1137-3-504, 151.

72. GARF, 6985-1-2, 274.

73. Shaumian, *Ot kochev'ia*, 157–60.

74. TsGARK, 74-11-264, 4–8.

75. Kor'be, "Kult'tura i byt," 71; Winner, "Some Problems," part 2, 356–57.

76. Merl, *Politische Kommunikation*, 101–10.

77. APRK, 8-1-610, 311–29, taken from Degitaeva, *Levon Mirzoian*, 216.

78. For an impressive study on how they devised conspiracies, see Zhdanova, *Massovye repressii*, 54–58.

79. See, for example, Rossiiskii Gosudarstvennyi Arkhiv Noveishei Istorii (RGANI), 89-48-10, 1 (Mirzoian's telegram to Stalin, July 27, 1937). Rossiiskii Gosudarstven-

nyi Arkhiv Sotsial'no-Politicheskoi Istorii (RGASPI), 17–12–1349, 70 (Kazkraikom minutes of May 15, 1938). Shortly thereafter, Isaev met the same fate. RGASPI, 17–12–1349, 74 (Kazkraikom minutes of May 25, 1938). For a vivid depiction of these events, see Shreider, *NKVD iznutri*, 109–15. For the resolution, see RGASPI, 17–21–1349, 70 (minutes of a meeting of the bureau of the VKP[b]'s central committee, May 16, 1938).

80. RGASPI, 17–21–1548, 194 (shorthand note from the First Regional Party Congress for the region of Gur'ev, May 15–23, 1938).

81. RGASPI, 17–2–607, 251–54 (Stalin's speech at the executive committee meeting in February–March, March 5, 1937).

82. For the mass operations in Kazakhstan, see Koigeldiev, *Stalinizim i repressii*. For terror used against the party elite, see Shreider, *NKVD iznutri*, 109–11.

83. APRK, 8–1–1016, 60–65 (Beliakov's report on the district of Narynkol'sk, August 10, 1939).

84. Koigeldiev, *Stalinizm i repressii*, 376–84.

85. RGASPI, 17–42–231, 39, taken from Danilov and Manning, *Tragediia sovetskoi derevni*, 5:487.

86. APRK, 708–1–53, taken from Degitaeva, *Politicheskie repressii*, 195–96. See also RGANI, 89–48–20, 1–2 (Stalin and Molotov's directive regarding enemies in animal husbandry, October 2, 1937).

87. The unique cluster of 120 trials took place in the region of Eastern Kazakhstan alone. Arkhiv Prezidenta Rossiiskoi Federatsii (APRF), 3–58–389, 89–93, taken from Danilov and Manning, *Tragediia sovetskoi derevni*, 5:512–16, esp. 513–14.

88. Binner, Bonwetsch, and Junge, "Der operative Befehl," 38–39.

89. RGASPI, 17–21–1331, 255 (shorthand note from the Second Congress of the Communist Party of Kazakhstan, vol. 4, July 4, 1938).

90. APRK, 8–1–1006, 143 (shorthand note from a meeting of district party secretaries and delegates from the land administration, November 28, 1939). For the overall situation in the Soviet Union, see Merl, *Bauern unter Stalin*, 158–64.

91. TsGARK, 1137–3–738, 23 (kolkhoz and peasants' complaints concerning livestock breeding, January 21–June 27, 1939).

92. TsGARK, 1137–3–305, 27–28 (SNK KSSR resolution regarding the return of livestock that had been given to kolkhoz peasants during the period from 1933 to 1935 as a form of loan, n.d. [May 1939]). On the execution of the measure, see RGANI, 6–6–294, 28–31 (report by Fedorenko from the KPK in Kazakhstan, April 11, 1940).

93. For a discussion among officials on this matter, see APRK, 8–1–1006, 143–47.

94. Merl, "Why Did the Attempt?" 209–11.

95. For details, see *Primernyi ustav.*

96. TsGARK, 1208-1-31, 65–66 (resolution concerning the situation of kolkhozes that have no economic center of their own, Kzyl-Orda, February 3–4, 1940).

97. TsGARK, 1137-3-848a, 128 (material on economic and cultural conditions at the Zaburunsk selsoviet, July 29–August 7, 1939). Conditions in the district of Zhilokosinsk were similar. TsGARK, 1137-3-848a, 258 (report on economic and cultural conditions in the district of Zhilokosinsk, n.d. [1939]).

98. TsGARK, 1208-1-31, 84.

99. TsGARK, 1208-1-1, 34–36 (report on relocation measures for the region of Western Kazakhstan for the year 1941, October 30, 1940).

100. TsGARK, 1208-1-31, 15–16 (report on kolkhozes having no standard economic center, n.d. [early 1940]).

101. TsGARK, 1137-2-1512, 45 (shorthand note from an assembly of the Council of People's Commissars, June 11, 1938).

102. TsGARK, 1137-2-1512, 45

103. GARF, 8131-14-31, 8.

104. Polian, *Against Their Will*, 95–114.

105. Brown, *Biography*, 176–92. On the Karlag, see Hedeler and Stark, *Das Grab* and Barnes, *Death and Redemption*, 28–77. On the deportation of Germans to the Kazakh steppe during the Second World War, see Dalos, *Geschichte*, 172–218.

106. TsGARK, 1137-2-1512, 46.

107. Hedeler and Stark, *Das Grab*, 31–42.

108. For the extent of deportation, see Pohl, *Ethnic Cleansing.* For individual groups in Kazakhstan, see contributions to Anes, *Deportirovannye v Kazakhstan narody.*

109. Khlevnjuk [Khlevniuk], "Economy," 65.

110. GARF, 5446-29-49, 7–8, taken from Tsarevskaia-Diakina, *Istoriia stalinskogo gulaga*, 5:239.

111. Kim, "Eshelon-58," 72; Aidamirov, "Pokhozhdenie."

112. Bachmann, *Memories of Kazakhstan*, 33–79.

113. Brown, *Biography*, 189.

114. Omarov, *Rasstreliannaia step'*, 4–5.

115. On Kazakhstan as an "Arsenal for the Front," see Kozybaev, *Kazakhstan—arsenal fronta.*

116. Winner, "Some Problems," part 1, 257; Manley, *To the Tashkent Station*; Balakaev, *Kolkhoznoe krest'ianstovo*, 134–47.

117. Undasynov, "Vazhneishaia zhivotnovodcheskaia baza."

118. Balakaev, *Kolkhoznoe krest'ianstvo*, 160.; on nomadic livestock breeding during the war, see Chulanov, *Ocherki istorii*, 3:207–18; Ohayon, *La sédentarisation*, 333.

119. See the map in Pogorel'skii, *Osedanie kochevnikov*, 130.

120. Balakaev, *Kolkhoznoe krest'ianstvo*, 165.

121. GARF, 8131–22–280, 1–14 (correspondence concerning 10,000 goats that froze to death at a meat combine in Semipalatinsk, December 1944).

122. RGASPI, 17–21–165, 85 (Kobulov's letter to Andreev, August 9, 1942).

123. GARF, A310–1–2524, 12 (Viazmin and Khokhul'nikov reporting on their inspection trip to Western Kazakhstan, n.d. [after May 9, 1943]). Losses remained high throughout the war. See RGANI, 6–6–305, 209–15 (Kanareikin's report to Andreev and Borkov, July 27, 1945).

124. RGASPI, 17–21–284, 4 (Andreev's letter to Stalin and Malenkov, May 15, 1944).

125. RGAE, 7486–14–334, 1–8 (information on the state of agriculture in the region of Aktyubinsk, n.d. [early 1945]). In 1944 and 1945 the population in vast parts of Kazakhstan went hungry. See RGASPI, 82–2, 904, 101–6 (Bogdanov's report to Beriia on the district of Suzak, June 12, 1944). On famine, see also Zhanguttin, "Golod voennogo vremeni." On providing for animals and drovers, see Krivitskii, "Legkomyslennoe otnoshenie."

126. RGANI, 6–6–310, 128–41 (report on serious deficiencies in the development of animal husbandry in the kolkhozes of the Kazakh SSR, May 18, 1946).

127. Chbyshev, "Perspektivy razvitiia otgonnogo zhivotnovodstva."

128. Chbyshev, "Perspektivy razvitiia i organizatsionnye formy," 58, 60.

129. Kor'be, "Kult'tura i byt"; Sabitov, "Rabota."

130. Undasynov, "Chemu uchit opyt." For biographical details on Undasynov (1904–89), see Zhakypov et al., *Narkomy Kazakhstana*, 342.

131. Ohayon, *La sédentarisation*, 335–41; Michaels, *Curative Powers*, 153–64.

132. RGANI, 6–6–310, 32–34 (report on the violation of the resolution for rewarding workers in agriculture and livestock breeding by the party regional committee for the region of Gur'ev, n.d. [after June 20, 1946]).

133. Bacon, *Central Asians*, 119; Pogorel'skii, *Osedanie kochevnikov*, 144. See also Abylkhozhin, *Traditsionnaia struktura*, 232–35. and Winner, "Some Problems," part 1, 257–58.

7. LEGACY

1. Schatz, *Modern Clan Politics*, 58–59.

2. Kindler, "Opfer ohne Täter."

3. Shayakhmetov, *Silent Steppe*, 212, and *Kazakh Teacher's Story*.

4. Figes, *Whisperers*, 597–608, 629–44.

5. On the ambivalence of (post) Soviet commemoration of the Great Patriotic War, see Etkind, *Warped Mourning*.

6. Merridale, *Ivan's War*, 321–36.

7. Narodetskii, "Golodomor." For an evaluation of debate in Kazakhstan, see Mark, "Die Hungersnot." For a more recent take, see Grozin, *Golod 1932–1933*, 121–68. For the basically very different situation in Ukraine, see Jilge, "Die 'Große Hungersnot'" and Dietsch, "Politik des Leids." For work on the differences in traditions of commemoration, see Kindler, "Opfer ohne Täter."

8. Aiagan et al., *Sovremennaia istoriia Kazakhstana*. More than three hundred of over four hundred pages of this book are dedicated to Kazakhstan's recent history since gaining independence. The region's historical development from first traces of humankind there up to the year 1991 are rushed through quickly in about one hundred pages.

9. A recent publication on historic sites in Kazakhstan does not mention any famine monument at all. Bonora, *Guide to Kazakhstan*.

10. Sindelar, "Vyzhivshee pokolenie." See also Cameron, "Hungry Steppe," 286–92.

11. [Nazarbayev], "Vystulplenie prezidenta," 8.

12. Trochev, "Transitional Justice," 95.

13. Dave, *Kazakhstan*, 140–45.

14. See, among others, Kozlov, "Obshchaia tragediia."

15. Lariuel' and Peiruz, *"Russkii vopros,"* 342.

16. On the newcomers and the conflicts that resulted from their settlement, see Pohl, "Planet," 245–50.

17. For an overview, see Olcott, *Kazakhs*, 224–46. Contemporary criticism can be found in Durgin, "Virgin Lands Programme."

18. Pohl, "Planet," 37–40.

19. Laird and Chappell, "Kazakhstan," 333–34.

20. Dave, *Kazakhstan*, 50–54.

21. Soviet scientists and officials presented their experience with sedentarization at international conferences as a model for developing countries. Zhdanko, "Mezhdunarodnoe znachenie."

22. Brown, *Biography*, 173–92. On the self-perception of former forced-laborers as contributors to civilization, 188. See also Figes, *Whisperers*, 638–44.

23. Khliupin and Puzanov, "Obratnaia storona elity." On the situation of Russians in

Kazakhstan in general, see Lariuel' and Peiruz, *"Russkii vopros."* On the German emigration, see Dalos, *Geschichte*, 256–90.

24. This was similar for Ukraine. Dietsch, "Politik des Leids," 348–50.

25. Mark, "Die Hungersnot," 124. It has become a constitutive element of the narrative that all the "guilty parties" came from outside of Kazakhstan. See, for example, Verkhoturov, "Asharshylyk," 3.

26. For example, Zhubanyshuly, *Sred' bela dnia.*

27. Assmann, *Shadows of Trauma*, 53.

28. There have been some exceptions, for example, work by Turganbek Allaniiazov, who has presented a series of local studies. But such investigations are not viewed favorably, as he says.

29. Meier, *Das Gebot*, 44.

30. Meier, *Das Gebot*, 89.

31. This position has been criticized by König in "Paradoxien der Erinnerung."

32. Kindler, "Famines and Political Communication," 255–58.

33. Tikhomirov, "Regime of Forced Trust," 80–87.

34. Hosking, "Trust and Distrust."

35. Dobrenko and Shcherbenok, "Between History and the Past," 77–78.

GLOSSARY

ALASH ORDA	Kazakh party. Collective movement of the national Kazakh intelligence.
AUL	Group consisting of several families (households) that migrate together. Several auls were combined to become "administrative auls" that represented the lowest level of administration in Soviet Kazakhstan.
BAI	Wealthy livestock owner, head of smaller tribal groups; the Bolsheviks considered the bais the Central Asian version of "kulaks." The word itself means "elder."
BATRAK	Rural worker.
BEDNIAK	Poor peasant.
DESIATIN	2.7 acres or 1.1 hectares.
DZHUT	Mass livestock destruction due to frost and cold, particularly late winter thaw followed by heavy frost that left the steppe covered with a thick layer of ice that animals could not break through with their hooves to find food.
GOSPLAN	Soviet authority responsible for the Five-Year Plan.
GULAG	Government agency in charge of the Soviet camp system. The term refers also to any forced-labor camp.
KAZKRAIKOM	Central committee of the Kazakh party organization.

KIRKRAIKOM Central committee of the Kirghiz party organization; predecessor of the Kazkraikom.

KOMSOMOL Communist Youth Organization

KRAIOSEDKOM Kazakh committee for sedentarization.

KULAK Wealthy peasant. The Bolsheviks turned the term into one of political struggle.

NARKOMZEM People's Commissariat for Agriculture.

OTKOCHEVNIKI Term for Kazakh famine refugees, derived from the Russian word for nomad (*kochevnik*).

POOD Russian weight measure; 1 pood = 16.38 kilograms or slightly over 36 pounds avoirdupois.

SEREDNIAK Average-income peasant.

SOVNARKOM Council of People's Commissars.

BIBLIOGRAPHY

UNPUBLISHED SOURCES

ARKHIV PREZIDENTA RESPUBLIKI KAZAKHSTAN (APRK)

f. 8 Alma-Atinskii oblastnoi komitet Kommunisticheskoi partii Kazakhstana

f. 141 Kazakhskii Kraevoi Komitet Vsesoiuznoi Kommunisticheskoi partii (bol'she-vikov)—Kazkraikom VKP(b)

f. 708 Tsentral'nyi Komitet Kommunisticheskoi partii Kazakhstana (TsK KP Kazakh-stana)

f. 719 Kazakhskaia kraevaia kontrol'naia komissiia Vsesoiuznoi Kommunisticheskoi partii (bol'shevikov)—Narodnyi komissariat raboche-krest'ianskoi inspektsii KASSR

f. 725 Upolnomochennyi Komissii partiinogo kontrolia pri Tsentral'nom Komitete Vse-soiuznoi Kommunisticheskoi partii (bol'shevikov) po Kazakhstanu

GOSUDARSTVENNYI ARKHIV ROSSIISKOI FEDERATSII (GARF)

f. 393 Narodnyi komissariat vnutrennykh del RSFSR

f. 1235 Vserossiiskii tsentral'nyi ispolnitel'nyi komitet RSFSR

f. 3260 Federal'nyi komitet po zemel'nomu delu pri prezidiume VTsIK

f. 3316 Tsentral'nyi Ispolnitel'nyi komitet sovetov rabochikh, krest'ianskikh i krasnoarmeiskikh deputatov SSSR (TsIK SSSR)

f. 5446 Sovet Narodnykh Komissarov SSR

f. 6985 Komissiia VtsIK po voprosam osedaniia kochevogo i polukochevogo naseleniia

f. 8131 Prokuratura SSSR

f. A-259 Sovet Ministrov RSFSR

f. A-310 Ministerstvo sel'skogo khoziaistva RSFSR

ROSSIISKII GOSUDARSTVENNYI ARKHIV EKONOMIKI (RGAE)

f. 7486 Ministerstvo sel'skogo khoziistva SSSR

ROSSIISKII GOSUDARSTVENNYI ARKHIV NOVEISHII ISTORII (RGANI)

f. 6 Komitet partiinogo kontrolia pri TsK KPSS

f. 89 Dokumenty, rassekrechennye spetsial'noi komissiei po arkhivam pri prezidente RF v 1992–1994 gg.

ROSSIISKII GOSUDARSTVENNYI ARKHIV SOTSIAL'NO-POLITICHESKOI ISTORII (RGASPI)

f. 17 Tsentral'nyi komitet KPSS (TsK KPSS)

f. 62 Sredneaziatskoe Biuro TsK VKP(b) (Sredazbiuro)

f. 74 Voroshilov, Kliment Efremovich (1881–1969)

f. 82 Molotov, Viacheslav Mikhailovich (1890–1986)

f. 85 Ordzhonikidze, Grigorii Konstantinovich (1886–1937)

f. 94 Fraktsii RKP(b), VKP(b) na vserossiiskikh (vsesoiuznykh) s"ezdakh sovetov, vo vserossiiskom tsentral'nom ispolnitel'nom komitete, v Prezidiume TsIK SSSR

f. 122 Komissiia VTsIK i SNK RSFSR po delam Turkestana

f. 558 Stalin, Iosif Vissarionovich (1878–1953)

f. 613 Tsentral'naia kontrol'naia komissiia VKP (b)

ROSSIISKII GOSUDARSTVENNYI VOENNYI ARKHIV (RGVA)

f. 8296 84. Kavaleriiskii polk, 8-oi otedel'nyi Turkmenskoi kavallereiskoi brigade

f. 25895 Sredne-Aziatskii Voennyi Okrug (SAVO)

f. 38333

TSENTRAL'NYI GOSUDARSTVENNYI ARKHIV RESPUBLIKI KAZAKHSTAN (TSGARK)

f. 30 Sovet Narodnykh Komissarov Kazakhskoi ASSR (Sovnarkom KASSR)

f. 44 Narodnyi komissariat raboche-krest'ianskoi inspektsii Kazakhskoi ASSR

f. 74 Narodnyi komissariat zemledeliia Kazakhskoi ASSR (Narkomzem KASSR)

f. 509 Tsentral'naia detskaia komissiia po uluchsheniiu zhizni detei pri TsIK Kazakhskoi ASSR (Kazdetkomissiia)

f. 1137 Sovet Narodnykh Komissarov Kazakhskoi ASSR

f. 1179 Komitet po osedaniiu kochevogo i polukochevogo naseleniia Kazakhstana

f. 1208 Pereselencheskii otdel pri SNK

f. 1380 Narodnyi komissariat iustitsii Kazakhskoi ASSR

PUBLISHED SOURCES

Abashin, S. N. "Soviet Central Asia on the Periphery." *Kritika* 16, no. 2 (2015), 359–74.

Abashin, S. N., ed. *Tsentral'naia Aziia v sostave rossiiskoi imperii.* Moscow, 2008.

Abdirainymov, S., I. N. Bukhonova, and N. R. Gribanova, eds. *Golod v kazakhskoi stepi: pis'ma trevogi i boli.* Alma-Ata, 1991.

Abdrakhmanov, Jusup. *Izbrannye trudy.* Bishkek, 2001.

Abdullaev, Kamoludin. *Ot Sin'tsziania do Khorasana: iz istorii sredneaziatskoi emigratsii XX veka.* Dushanbe, 2009.

Aben, E., E. Aryn, and I. Tasmagambetov, eds. *Pervye litsa gosudarstva: politicheskie portrety: s tochki zreniia istorii i sovremennosti.* Almaty, 1998.

Abramzon, S. M. "V kirgizskikh kolkhozakh Tian'-Shana." *Sovetskaia Etnografiia,* no. 4 (1949), 55–74.

Abuseitova, M. Ch., et al., eds. *Istoriia Kazakhstana i tsentral'noi Azii.* Almaty, 2001.

Abylkhozhin, Zh. B. "Inertsiia mifotvorchestva v osveshchenii sovetskoi i postsovetskoi istorii Kazakhstana." In *Nauchnoe znanie i mifotvorchestvo v sovremennoi istoriografii Kazakhstana,* edited by Nurbulat Masanov, 225–91. Almaty, 2007.

Abylkhozhin, Zh. B. "Kazakhstan v sovetskom totalitarnom prostranstve: istoricheskaia dinamika." In *Istoriia Kazakhstana: narody i kul'tury,* edited by N. E. Masanov, 257–366. Almaty, 2001.

Abylkhozhin, Zh. B. "Konfiskatsiia skota 20-kh godov: udar po sisteme zhizneobespechenie etnosa." In *Narod ne bezmolvstvuet,* edited by M. I. Ponomarev, 21–22. Almaty, 1996.

Abylkhozhin, Zh. B. *Traditsionnaia struktura Kazakhstana: sotsial'no-ekonomicheski aspekty funktsionirovaniia i transformatsii (1920–1930-e gg.)*. Alma-Ata, 1991.

Abylkhozhin, Zh. B., and M. K. Kozybaev. "Kazakhstanskaia tragediia." *Voprosy istorii*, no. 7 (1989), 53–71.

Abylkhozhin, Zh. B., M. K. Kozybaev, and M. B. Tatimov. "Novoe o kollektivizatsii v Kazakhstane." In *Istoriia Kazakhstana: belye piatna*, edited by Zh. B. Abylkhozhin, 183–217. Alma-Ata, 1991.

Adams, Bruce. "Reemigration from Western China to the USSR, 1954–1962." In *Migration, Homeland, and Belonging in Eurasia*, edited by Cynthia J. Buckley and Blair A. Ruble, 183–202. Washington, 2008.

Adler, Nanci. "The Future of the Soviet Past remains Unpredictable: The Resurrection of Stalinist Symbols Amidst the Exhumation of Mass Graves." *Europe-Asia Studies* 57, no. 8 (2008), 1093–119.

Agamben, Giorgio. *Remnants of Auschwitz: The Witness and the Archive*. New York, 2002.

Aiagan, B. G., ed. *Pravda o golode 1932–1933 godov*. Almaty, 2012.

Aiagan, B. G. et al., eds. *Sovremennaia istoriia Kazakhstana*. Almaty, 2010.

Aibasov, Erken. *Odin iz pervykh: dokumental'naia povest'*. Almaty, 2005.

Aidamirov, Musa. "Pokhozhdenie volkogo potomka." http://deport-chr.ru/index.php/rem/75-musaaydamirov-3 (accessed October 2, 2013).

Akhmetova, A. S., V. K. Grigor'ev, and G. N. Shoikin. "Turar Ryskulov: iarkii politik sovetskogo vostoka." In *Alikhan Bukeikhanov, Akhmet Baitursynov, Turar Ryskulov: Kazakhstan Pervye litsa strany XX veka*, edited by A. S. Akhmetova, 119–98. Astana, 2008.

Akiner, Shirin. *The Formation of Kazakh Identity: From Tribe to Nation-State*. London, 1995.

Akopov, S. "Bor'ba s bytovymi prestupleniiami." *Revoliutsiia i natsional'nosti* 1, no. 4/5 (1930), 58–69.

Aldazhumanov, Kaidar. "Krest'ianskoe dvizhenie soprotivleniia." In Anes, *Deportirovannye v Kazakhstan*, 66–93.

Aldazhumanov, Kaidar. "Krest'ianskoe dvizhenie soprotivleniia kollektivizatsii i politicheskie repressii v Kazakhstane." In *Narod ne bezmolvstvuet*, edited by M. I. Ponomarev, 12–20. Almaty, 1996.

Alekseenko, A. N. "Naselenie Kazakhstana v 1926–1939gg." In *Komp'iuter i istoricheskaia demografiia*, edited by V. N. Vladimirov, 9–26. Barnaul, 2000.

Alekseenko, N. V., and A. N. Alekseenko. *Naselenie Kazakhstana za 100 let (1897–1997gg.)*. Ust-Kamenogorsk, 1999.

Allaniiazov, Turganbek. "'K zachistke bandelementa pristupit' nemedlenno . . .' dokumenty Semipalatinskogo OGPU 1931g." *Istoricheskii arkhiv* 11, no. 3 (2003), 137–54.

Allaniiazov, Turganbek. *Kollektivizatsiia po-karsakpaiski, 1928–1933 gg.* Almaty, 2001.

Allaniiazov, Turganbek. *Krasnye Karakumy: ocherki istorii bor'by s antisovetskim povstancheskim dvizheniem v Turkmenistane (mart–oktiabr 1931 goda).* Almaty, 2006.

Allaniiazov, Turganbek. *"KontrRevoliutsiia" v Kazakhstane: Chimbaiskii variant.* Almaty, 1999.

Allaniiazov, Turganbek. *Poslednii rubezh zashchitnikov nomadizma: istoriia vooruzhennykh vystuplenii i povstancheskikh dvizhenii v Kazakhstane (1929–1931gg.).* Almaty, 2009.

Allaniiazov, Turganbek. "Protestnye dvizheniia v Srednei Azii i Kazakhstane 1920–1930-kh godov v otsenkakh zapadnoi, sovetskoi i natsional'nykh (Rossiia, Kazakhstan, Uzbekistan) istoriografii: Traditsii i inovatsii." *International Newsletter of Communist Studies Online* 16 (2010), 89–96.

Allaniiazov, Turganbek, and Amangel'dy Taukenov. *Shetskaia tragediia: iz istorii antisovetskikh vooruzhennykh vystuplenii v Tsentral'nom Kazakhstane v 1930–1931gg.* Almaty, 2000.

Allen, Naomi, and George Saunders, eds. *Leon Trotsky: The Challenge of the Left Opposition (1926–1927).* New York, 1980.

Altrichter, Helmut. *Die Bauern von Tver: Vom Leben auf dem russischen Dorf zwischen Revolution und Kollektivierung.* Munich, 1984.

Amanzholova, D. A. "Alash, Sovety, Bol'sheviki." *Otechestvennaia istoriia,* no. 1 (1994), 57–73.

Amanzholova, D. A. "Kazakhskaia avtonomiia: ot zamysla natsionalov k samoopredeleniiu po-sovetski." *Acta Slavica Iaponica* 21 (2004), 115–43.

Amanzholova, D. A. *Kazakhskii avtonomizm i Rossiia: istoriia dvizheniia Alash.* Moscow, 1994.

Amanzholova, D. A. "Kazakhskoe obshchestvo v 1-i chetverti XX veka: problemy etnoidentifikatsii." In *Rossiia i Kazakhstan: problemy istorii (XX–nachalo XXI v.),* edited by N. F. Bugai, 14–83. Moscow, 2006.

Amanzholova, D. A., ed. *Rossiia i Tsentral'naia Aziia, 1905–1925 gg.: Sbornik Dokumentov.* Karagandy, 2005.

Amanzholova, D. A., M. Ch. Asylbekov, and S. T. Rysbekova. "Portrety na fone epokhi: k 90-letiiu dvizheniia Alash." *Istoricheskii Arkhiv* 17, no. 1 (2009), 90–99.

Amanzholova, D. A., and S. V. Kuleshov. "Istoricheskie sud'by 'natsional'nogo nepa.'" In *Rossiia nepovskaia,* edited by A. N. Iakovlev, 58–94. Moscow, 2002.

Anes, Garifulla, ed. *Deportirovannye v Kazakhstan narody: vremia i sud'by*. Almaty, 1998.

Appelbaum, Anne. *Red Famine: Stalin's War on Ukraine*. New York, 2017.

Arapov, D. Iu. "Zapiska Sultanbeka Khodzhanova v TsK RKP(b) 1924g." *Istoricheskii Arkhiv* 17, no. 1 (2009), 85–89.

Arens, William. *The Man-Eating Myth: Anthropology and Anthrophagy*. Oxford, 1979.

Arnason, Johann P. "Communism and Modernity." *Daedalus* 129, no. 1 (2000), 61–90.

Ashimbaev, Daniiar, and Vitalii Khliupin. *Kazakhstan: istoriia vlasti. Opyt rekonstrukt-sii*. Almaty, 2008.

Ashin, F. D., ed. *Repressirovannaia Tiurkologiia*. Moscow, 2002.

Asmis, Rudolf. *Als Wirtschaftspionier in Russisch-Asien: Tagebuchblätter*. Berlin, 1926.

Assmann, Aleida. *Der lange Schatten der Vergangenheit: Erinnerungskultur und Geschichtspolitik*. Munich, 2006.

Assmann, Aleida. *Shadows of Trauma: Memory and the Politics of Postwar Identity*. New York, 2016.

Asylbekov, M. Ch., and A. B. Galiev. *Sotsial'no-demograficheskie protsessy v Kazakhstane (1917–1980 gg.)* Alma-Ata, 1991.

Atusheva, S. B. *Dzhuty v Kazakhstane v kontse XIX–nachale XX vv*. Almaty, 2000.

Avorkhanov, Abdurakhman. *Stalin and the Soviet Communist Party*. New York, 1959.

Baberowski, Jörg. "Auf der Suche nach Eindeutigkeit. Kolonialismus und zivilisatorische Mission im Zarenreich und in der frühen Sowjetunion." *Jahrbücher für Geschichte Osteuropas* 47 (1999), 482–504.

Baberowski, Jörg. *Der Feind ist überall: Stalinismus im Kaukasus*. Munich, 2003.

Baberowski, Jörg. *Der Rote Terror: Die Geschichte des Stalinismus*. Frankfurt am Main, 2007.

Baberowski, Jörg. *Scorched Earth: Stalin's Reign of Terror*. New Haven, 2016.

Baberowski, Jörg. "Stalinismus von oben, Kulakendeportationen in der Sowjetunion 1929–1933." *Jahrbücher für Geschichte Osteuropas* 46 (1998), 572–95.

Baberowski, Jörg. "Vertrauen durch Anwesenheit. Vormoderne Herrschaft im späten Zarenreich." In *Imperiale Herrschaft in der Provinz. Repräsentationen politischer Macht im späten Zarenreich*, edited by Jörg Baberowski, Christoph Gumb, and David Feest, 17–37. Frankfurt am Main, 2008.

Bachmann, Berta. *Memories of Kazakhstan: A Report on the Life Experiences of a German Woman in Russia*. Lincoln, NE, 1983.

Bacon, Elizabeth E. *Central Asians under Russian Rule: A Study in Cultural Change (1966)*. Ithaca, 1980.

Baecker, Dirk. *Form und Formen der Kommunikation*. Frankfurt am Main, 2005.

"Baidil'din, Abdrakhman." http://centrasia.ru/person2.php?&st=1093493362 (accessed May 18, 2018).

Baigisieva, Z. M. "Zemledel'cheskie i osedlye raiony Kazakhstana v usloviiakh nasil'st-vennogo razvertyvaniia kolkhoznogo dvizheniia: osobennosti i tragicheskie itogi (1929–1935)." PhD diss. Almaty, 2001.

Baishev, S. B. *Pobeda sotsializma v Kazakhstane (ocherki po teorii i istorii voprosa).* Alma-Ata, 1961.

Bakanov, S. A., and R. M. Zhumašev. "O tempakh likvidatsii negramotnosti v Kazakhstane v 1926–1939 godach." *Voprosy istorii*, no. 8 (2002), 142–45.

Balakaev, T. B. *Kolkhoznoe krest'ianstvo Kazakhstana v gody velikoi otechestvennoi voiny, 1941–1945.* Alma-Ata, 1971.

Baldauf, Ingeborg. "Tradition, Revolution, Adaption: Die kulturelle Sowjetisierung Zentralasiens." *Osteuropa* 57, no. 8/9 (2007), 99–120.

Bankoff, Greg. "Cultures of Disaster, Cultures of Coping: Hazard as a Frequent Life Experience in the Phillipines." In *Natural Disasters, Cultural Responses: Case Studies towards a Global Environmental History*, edited by Christof Mauch and Christian Pfister, 265–84. Lanham, 2009.

Barfield, Thomas J. *The Perilious Frontier: Nomadic Empires and China.* Oxford, 1989.

Barmin, V. A. *Sovetskii Soiuz i Sin'tszian 1918–1941gg.: regional'nyi faktor vo vneshnei politike Sovetskogo Soiuza.* Barnaul, 1999.

Barnes, Steven A. *Death and Redemption: The Gulag and the Shaping of Soviet Society.* Princeton, 2011.

Baron, Nick. "Stalinist Planning as Political Practice: Control and Repression on the Soviet Periphery, 1935–1938." *Europe-Asia Studies* 56, no. 3 (2004), 439–62.

Batchaev, M. "Protiv iskazhenii postanovleniia TsK ot 17 sentiabria." *Bol'shevik Kazakhstana*, no. 7 (1933), 61–74.

Bauman, Zygmunt. *Modernity and Ambivalence.* Cambridge, 1991.

Bauman, Zygmunt. *Wasted Lives: Modernity and Its Outcasts.* Cambridge, 2004.

Becker, Seymour. "Russia's Central Asian Empire, 1885–1917." In *Russian Colonial Expansion to 1917*, edited by Michael Rywkin, 235–56. London, 1988.

Benson, Linda, and Ingmar Svanberg. *China's Last Nomads: The History and Culture of China's Kazaks.* Armonk, NY, 1998.

Bergne, Paul. *The Birth of Tajikistan: National Identity and the Origins of the Republic.* London, 2007.

Beyrau, Dietrich. "Der Erste Weltkrieg als Bewährungsprobe: Bolschewistische Lernprozesse aus dem 'imperialistischen Krieg.'" *Journal of Modern European History* 1, no. 1 (2003), 96–123.

Binner, Rolf, Bernd Bonwetsch, and Marc Junge. "Der operative Befehl Nr. 00447. Sein Schicksal in der Provinz." In *Stalinismus in der sowjetischen Provinz: Die Massenaktion aufgrund des operativen Befehls Nr. 00447*, edited by Rolf Binner, 9–51. Berlin, 2010.

Blank, Stephen. "Ethnic and Party Politics in Soviet Kazakstan, 1920–1924." *Central Asian Survey* 10, no. 3 (1991), 1–19.

Bochagov, A. K. *Alash-Orda: kratkii istoricheskii ocherk o natsional'no-burzhuaznom dvizheniem v Kazakhstane perioda 1917–19 gg.* Kzyl-Orda, 1927.

Bogdanov, A. "Chistka partii i zadachi partorganizatsii natsional'nykh respublik." *Revoliutsiia i natsional'nosti* 4, no. 2 (1933), 27–32.

Boiko, V. S. "Sredneaziatskaia emigratsiia na zakliuchitel'nom etape grazhdanskoi voiny v Afganistane (1930–1931 gg.)." In *Vostokovednye issledovaniia na Altae*, vypusk III, edited by V. A. Moisev, 226–35. Barnaul, 2003.

Bonora, Gian Luca. *Guide to Kazakhstan: Sites of Faith, Sites of History*. Turin, 2010.

Borisov, A. B. *Pokhod konnoi gruppy 8-i kavbrigady v kara-kumskuiu pustyniu v 1927 godu*. Moscow, 1932.

Brainin, S., Sh. Shafiro, and N. Timofeev. "Ob oshibkakh kazakhstanskoi partorganizatsii v rukovodstve sel'skim khoziaistvom." *Bol'shevik Kazakhstana*, no. 7 (1933), 46–60.

Briskin, A. *Na Iuzhturksibe (ocherki Turksiba)*. Alma-Ata, 1930.

Briskin, A. *V strane semi rek: ocherki sovremennogo Semirech'ia*. Moscow, 1926.

Brower, Daniel. "Islam and Ethnicity: Russian Colonial Policy in Turkestan." In Brower and Lazzerini, *Russia's Orient*, 115–35.

Brower, Daniel. "Kyrgyz Nomads and Russian Pioneers: Colonization and Ethnic Conflict in the Turkestan Revolt of 1916." *Jahrbücher für Geschichte Osteuropas* 46, no. 1 (1996), 41–53.

Brower, Daniel. *Turkestan and the Fate of the Russian Empire*. London, 2003.

Brower, Daniel, and Edward J. Lazzerini, eds. *Russia's Orient: Imperial Borderlands and Peoples, 1700–1917*. Bloomington, 1997.

Brown, Kate. *A Biography of No Place: From Ethnic Borderland to Soviet Heartland*. Cambridge, MA, 2004.

Brown, Kate. "Gridded Lives: Why Kazakhstan and Montana Are Nearly the Same Place." *American Historical Review* 106 (2001), 17–48.

Burbank, Jane, Mark von Hagen, and Anatolyi Remnev, eds. *Russian Empire: Space, People, Power, 1700–1930*. Bloomington, 2007

Burkhanov, A. "Gosudarstvennyi plan razvitiia zhivotnovodstva." *Revoliutsiia i natsional'nosti* 6, no. 7 (1935), 31–36.

Butterly, John R., and Jack Shepherd. *Hunger: The Biology and Politics of Starvation.* Hanover, NH, 2010.

Buttino, Marco. "Politics and Social Conflicts during a Famine: Turkestan Immediately after the Revolution." In *In a Collapsing Empire: Underdevelopement, Ethnic Conflicts and Nationalism in the Soviet Union,* edited by Marco Buttino, 257–77. Milan, 1993.

Buttino, Marko [Marco]. *Revoliutsiia naoborot: Sredniaia Aziia mezhdu padeniem tsarskoi imperii i obrazovaniem SSSR.* Moscow, 2007.

Bykov, A. Iu. *Istoki modernizatsii Kazakhstana: problema sedentarizatsii v rossiiskoi politike XVIII–nachala XX veka.* Barnaul, 2003.

Cairns, Andrew. *The Soviet Famine 1932–33: An Eye-Witness Account of Conditions in the Spring and Summer of 1932 by Andrew Cairns.* Edmonton, 1989.

Cameron, Sarah. "The Hungry Steppe: Soviet Kazakhstan and the Kazakh Famine, 1921–1934." PhD diss., Yale University, 2010.

Cameron, Sarah. "The Kazakh Famine of 1930–1933: Current Research and New Directions." *East/West: Journal of Ukrainian Studies* 2 (2016), 117–32.

Cameron, Sarah. "Violence, Flight, and Hunger: The Sino-Kazakh Border and the Kazakh Famine." In *Stalin and Europe: Imitation and Domination, 1928–1953,* edited by Timothy Snyder and Ray Brandon, 44–72. New York, 2014.

Canetti, Elias. *Crowds and Power.* New York, 1981.

Chandler, Andrea. *Institutions of Isolation: Border Controls in the Soviet Union and Its Successor States, 1917–1993.* Montreal, 1998.

Chbyshev, M. V. "Perspektivy razvitiia i organizatsionnye formy zhivotnovostva v nizovykh reki Ili." *Vestnik Akademii Nauk Kazakhskoi SSR,* no. 65 (1950), 55–62.

Chbyshev, M. V. "Perspektivy razvitiia otgonnogo zhivotnovodstva v tsentral'nom Kazakhstane." *Vestnik Akademii Nauk Kazakhskoi SSR,* no. 53 (1949), 29–37.

Chebotareva, V. G. "Problemy russkoi kolonizatsii: byla li Rossiia 'tiur'moi narodov?'" In *Rossiia i Kazakhstan: problemy istorii (XX–nachalo XXI v.),* edited by N. F. Bugai, 83–132. Moscow, 2006.

Chelintsev, A. N. "Perspektiva razvitiia sel'skogo khoziaistva Kazakhstana." *Narodnoe khoziaistvo Kazackhstana* 3, no. 4/5 (1928), 1–39.

Chirov, D. "Karagandinskie spetspereselentsy: kak eto bylo?" In *Istoriia Kazakhstana: belye piatna,* edited by Zh. B. Abylkhozhin, 223–29. Alma-Ata, 1991.

Chokin, Shafik. *Chetyre vremeni zhizni: vospominaniia i razmyshleniia.* Almaty, 1998.

Chruščev [Khrushchev], Nikita. *Chruschtschow erinnert sich,* edited by Strobe Talbott. Reinbek, 1971.

Chulanov, G. Ch., ed. *Ocherki istorii narodnogo khoziaistva Kazakhskoi SSR*. vol. 3. Alma-Ata, 1963.

Chuvelev, K. A. "O reorganizatsii kochevogo i polukochevogo khoziaistva." *Narodnoe khoziaistvo Kazakhstana* 3, no. 2/3 (1928), 43–58.

Collet, Dominik. "'Vulnerabilität' als Brückenkonzept der Hungerforschung." In Collet, Lassen, and Schanbacher, *Handeln in Hungerkrisen*, 13–26.

Collet, Dominik, Thore Lassen, and Ansgar Schanbacher, eds. *Handeln in Hungerkrisen: Neue Perspektiven auf soziale und klimatische Vulnerabilität*. Göttingen, 2012.

Conquest, Robert. *The Harvest of Sorrow: Soviet Collectivization and the Terror-Famine*. Oxford, 1987.

Crews, Robert. *For Prophet and Tsar: Islam and Empire in Russia and Central Asia*. Cambridge, MA, 2006.

Dahlke, Sandra. *Individuum und Herrschaft im Stalinismus: Emel'jan Jaroslavskij (1878–1943)*. Munich, 2010.

Dakhshleiger, G. F. "Iz opyta istorii osedaniia kazakhskikh kochevykh i polukochevykh khoziaistv (do massovoi kollektivizatsii sel'skogo khoziaistva). *Sovetskaia etnografiia*, no. 4 (1966), 3–23.

Dalos, György. *Geschichte der Russlanddeutschen: Von Katharina der Großen bis zur Gegenwart*. Munich, 2014.

Danilov, V. P., and I. E. Zelenin. "Organizovannyi golod: k 70-letiiu obshchekrest'ianskoi tragedii." *Otechestvennaia istoriia*, no. 5 (2004), 97–111.

Danilov, Viktor, and Roberta T. Manning, eds. *Tragediia sovetskoi derevni: kollektivizatsiia i raskulachivanie*. Dokumenty i materialy v 5 tomakh, 1927–1939. 5 vols. Moscow, 1999–2006.

Dave, Bhavna. *Kazakhstan: Ethnicity, Language and Power*. London, 2007.

David-Fox, Michael. "Multiple Modernities vs. Neo-Traditionalism: On Recent Debates in Russian and Soviet History." *Jahrbücher für Geschichte Osteuropas* 54, no. 4 (2006), 535–55.

Davies, Robert W., and Stephen Wheatcroft. "The Crooked Mirror of Soviet Economic Statistics." In Davies, Harrison, and Wheatcroft, *Economic Transformation of the Soviet Union*, 24–37.

Davies, Robert W. "Industry." In Davies, Harrison, and Wheatcroft, *Economic Transformation of the Soviet Union*, 131–51.

Davies, Robert W. "The Soviet Famine of 1932–33 and the Crisis of Agriculture." In *Challenging Traditional Views of Russian History*, edited by Stephen G. Wheatcroft, 69–91. Houndmills, 2002.

Davies, Robert, W. Mark Harrison, and Stephen G. Wheatcroft, eds. *The Economic Transformation of the Soviet Union, 1913–1945.* Cambridge, 1994.

Davies, Robert W., and Stephen G. Wheatcroft. *The Years of Hunger: Soviet Agriculture, 1931–1933.* Houndmills, 2004.

Davies, Robert W., and Stephen G. Wheatcroft. "Stalin and the Soviet Famine of 1932–33: A Reply to Ellman." *Europe-Asia Studies* 58, no. 4 (2006), 625–33.

De Waal, Alex. *Famine That Kills: Darfur, Sudan, 1984–1985.* Oxford, 1989.

Degitaeva, L. D., ed. *Levon Mirzoian v Kazakhstane: sbornik dokumentov i materialov (1933–1938gg.).* Almaty, 2001.

Degitaeva, L.D., ed. *Politicheskie repressii v Kazakhstane v 1937–1938gg.: sbornik dokumentov.* Almaty, 1998.

Devereux, Stephen. *Theories of Famine.* New York, 1993.

Diener, Alex C. *One Homeland or Two? The Nationalization and Transnationalization of Mongolia's Kazakhs.* Washington, DC, 2009.

Dienes, Leslie. "Pasturalism in Turkestan: Its Decline and Persistence." *Soviet Studies* 27, no. 3 (1975), 343–65.

Dietsch, Johan. "Politik des Leids: Der Hunger in der Ukraine 1932/33 und das Paradigma des Vorsatzes." In *Hunger, Ernährung und Rationierungssysteme unter dem Staatssozialismus (1917–2006),* edited by Matthias Middell and Felix Wemheuer, 327–50. Frankfurt am Main, 2011.

Dingel'stedt, N. "Nasha kolonizatsiia Srednei Azii: russkie poselki v Turkestane." *Vestnik Evropy* 27, no. 11 (1892), 231–57.

Dirks, Robert. "Social Responses during Severe Food Shortages and Famine." *Current Anthropology* 21, no. 1 (1980), 21–44.

Dobrenko, Evgeny, and Andrey Shcherbenok. "Between History and the Past: The Soviet Legacy as a Traumatic Object of Contemporary Russian Culture." *Slavonica,* no. 2 (2011), 77–84.

Donich, A. N. "Problema 'novogo kazakhskogo aula.'" *Narodnoe khoziaistvo Kazakhstana* 3, no. 4/5 (1928), 141–68.

Donich, A. N. "Raionirovanie KSSR i ego ocherednye zadachi." *Narodnoe khoziaistvo Kazakhstana* 3, no. 2/3 (1928), 11–24.

Donnely, Alton. "The Mobile Steppe Frontier: The Russian Conquest and Colonization of Bashkiria and Kazakhstan to 1850." In *Russian Colonial Expansion to 1917,* edited by Michael Rywkin, 189–207. London, 1988.

Dunn, Stephen P., and Ethel Dunn. "Soviet Regime and Native Culture in Central Asia and Kazakhstan: The Major Peoples." In *Current Anthropology* 8, no. 3 (1967), 147–208.

Durgin, Frank A. Jr. "The Virgin Lands Programme 1954–1960." *Soviet Studies* 13, no. 3 (1962), 255–80.

Dzhumagaliev, D., and I. E. Semenov. "Vernyi syn naroda." In Abdrakhmanov, *Izbrannye trudy*, 7–80.

Easter, Gerald. *Reconstructing the State: Personal Networks and Elite Identity in Soviet Russia.* Cambridge, 2000.

Edele, Mark. *Stalinist Society, 1928–1953.* Oxford, 2011.

Edgar, Adrienne Lynn. "Central Asian History as Soviet History." *Kritika* 17, no. 3 (2016), 621–29.

Edgar, Adrienne Lynn. "Emancipation of the Unveiled: Turkmen Women under Soviet Rule, 1924–29." *Russian Review* 62, no. 1 (2003), 132–49.

Edgar, Adrienne Lynn. "Genealogy, Class, and 'Tribal Policy' in Soviet Turkmenistan, 1924–1934." *Slavic Review* 60, no. 2 (2001), 266–88.

Edgar, Adrienne Lynn. *Tribal Nation: The Making of Soviet Turkmenistan.* Princeton, 2004.

Edkins, Jenny. *Whose Hunger? Concepts of Famine, Practices of Aid.* Minneapolis, 2000.

VIII Kraevaia konferentsiia VKP(b), 8–16 ianvaria 1934 g. Stenograficheskii otchet. Alma-Ata, 1935.

Eisener, Reinhard. *"Konterrevolution auf dem Lande": Zur inneren Sicherheitslage in Mittelasien 1929/30 aus Sicht der OGPU.* Berlin, 1999.

Ellman, Michael. "The Role of Leadership Perceptions and of Intent in the Soviet Famine of 1931–1934." *Europe-Asia Studies* 57, no. 6 (2005), 823–41.

Ellman, Michael. "Stalin and the Soviet Famine of 1932–33 Revisited." *Europe-Asia Studies* 59, no. 4 (2007), 663–93.

Emeljanenko, Tatjana. "Nomadic Year Cycles and Cultural Life of Central Asian Livestock-breeders before the 20th Century." In *Nomads in Central Asia: Animal Husbandry and Culture in Transition (19th–20th Century),* edited by Carel van Leeuwen, 37–68. Amsterdam, 1994.

Engelstein, Laura. *Russia in Flames: War, Revolution, Civil War, 1914–1921.* New York, 2018.

Ermikov, A. A. "Organizatsiia shkol sredi kazakhskogo naseleniia." *Narodnoe khoziaistvo Kazakhstana* 1, no. 1 (1926), 113–24.

Erofeeva, I. V. "Stolypinskaia agrarnaia reforma i massovoe pereselenie slavianskogo i nemetskogo krest'ianstva (1900–1917)." In Masanov, *Istoriia Kazakhstana,* 244–56.

Ertz, Simon. "The Kazakh Catastrophe and Stalin's Order of Priorities, 1929–1933: Evidence from the Soviet Secret Archives." *Zhe: Stanford's Student Journal of Russian, East European, and Eurasian Studies* 1 (2005), 1–14.

Ertz, Simon. *Zwangsarbeit im stalinistischen Lagersystem: Eine Untersuchung ihrer Methoden, Strategien und Ziele ihrer Ausnutzung am Beispiel Noril'sk, 1935–1953.* Berlin, 2006.

Esenova, S. "Soviet Nationality, Identity, and Ethnicity in Central Asia: Historic Narratives and Kazakh Ethnic Identity." *Journal of Muslim Minority Affairs* 22, no. 1 (2002), 11–38.

Etkind, Alexander. *Warped Mourning: Stories of the Undead in the Land of the Unburied.* Stanford, 2013.

Falk, Barbara. *Sowjetische Städte in der Hungersnot 1932/33: Staatliche Ernährungspolitik und städtisches Alltagsleben.* Cologne, 2005.

Farah, Mohamed I., and Jasmin Touati. *Sedentarisierung von Nomaden: Chancen und Gefahren einer Entwicklungsstrategie am Beispiel Somalias.* Bielefeld, 1991.

Farkas, Otto, and Béla Kemp. "Reinventing the 'Dzud': Livestock Famine in Twenty-First-Century Mongolia." In *Continuity and Change in Central and Inner Asia: Papers Presented at the Central and Inner Asia Seminar. University of Toronto, 24/25 March 2001 and 4/5 May 2001,* edited by Michael Gervers and Wayne Schlepp, 127–59. Toronto, 2002.

Fedtke, Gero. "Wie aus Bucharern Usbeken und Tadschiken wurden: Sowjetische Nationalitätenpolitik im Lichte einer persönlichen Rivalität." *Zeitschrift für Geschichtswissenschaft* 54, no. 3 (2006), 214–31.

Feoktistov, N. "K voprosu ob organizatsii krasnykh agit-propagandistkikh karavanov." *Kommunist* 1, no. 4 (1923), 23–26.

Feoktistov, N. "O rabote sredi kirgiz." *Kommunist* 1, no. 1 (1923), 92–95.

Figes, Orlando. *A People's Tragedy: The Russian Revolution 1891–1924.* London, 1996.

Figes, Orlando. *The Whisperers: Private Life in Stalin's Russia.* New York, 2007.

Filatov, N. P. "Itogi i perspektivy razvitiia kolkhoznogo zhivotnovodstva." *Narodnoe khoziaistvo Kazakhstana* 11, no. 7/8 (1939), 24–38.

Fitzpatrick, Sheila. "Blat in Stalin's Times." In *Bribery and Blat in Russia: Negotiating Reciprocity from the Middle Ages to the 1990s,* edited by Stephen Lovell and Alena V. Ledeneva, 166–82. Basingstoke, 2000.

Fitzpatrick, Sheila. *Everyday Stalinism: Ordinary Life in Extraordinary Times: Soviet Russia in the 1930s.* New York, 1999.

Fitzpatrick, Sheila. *Stalin's Peasants: Resistance and Survival in the Russian Village after Collectivization.* Oxford, 1994.

Fitzpatrick, Sheila, ed. *Stalinism: New Directions.* London, 2000.

Forbes, Andrew. *Warlords and Muslims in Chinese Central Asia: A Political History of Republican Sinkiang, 1911–1949.* Cambridge, 1986.

Frank, Stephen P. *Crime, Cultural Conflict, and Justice in Rural Russia, 1856–1914.* Berkeley, 1999.

Franklin, Joseph C., ed. "Observations on Human Behavior in Experimental Semistarvation and Rehabilitation." *Journal of Clinical Psychology* 4, no. 1 (1948), 28–45.

Fratkin, Elliot. "Pastoralism: Governance and Development Issues." *Annual Review of Anthropology* 26 (1997), 235–61.

Galley, Mirjam. "Wir schlagen wie eine Faust: Straßenkinder, Gangs und Staatsgewalt in Stalins Sowjetunion." *Jahrbücher für Geschichte Osteuropas*, 64, no. 1 (2016), 26–53.

Gammer, Moshe. "Russia and the Eurasian Steppe Nomads: An Overview." In *Mongols, Turks, and Others*, edited by Reuven Amitai and Michel Biran, 483–502. Leiden, 2005.

Gangrade, K. D., and S. Dhadda. *Challenge and Response: A Study of Famines in India.* Delhi, 1973.

Gatagova, L. S., ed. *TsK RKP(b)—VKP(b) i natsional'nyi vopros.* 2 vols. Moscow, 2005–9.

Genis, Vladimir Leonidovich. "Deportatsiia russkikh iz Turkestana v 1921 godu ('Delo Safarova')." *Voprosy istorii*, no. 1 (1998), 44–58.

Genschel, Philipp, and Klaus Schlichte. "Wenn Kriege chronisch werden: Der Bürgerkrieg." *Leviathan: Zeitschrift für Sozialwissenschaft* 25, no. 4 (1997), 501–17.

Gerlach, Christian. *Extrem gewalttätige Gesellschaften: Massengewalt im 20. Jahrhundert.* Munich, 2010.

Getty, J. Arch. "Afraid of Their Shadows: The Bolshevik Recourse to Terror, 1932–1938." In *Stalinismus vor dem Zweiten Weltkrieg: Neue Wege der Forschung*, edited by Manfred Hildermeier, 169–91. Munich, 1998.

Getty, J. Arch. *Pragmatists and Puritans: The Rise and the Fall of the Party Control Commission.* The Carl Beck Papers in Russian and East European Studies, vol. 1208. Pittsburgh, 1997.

Getty, J. Arch, and Oleg V. Naumov. *Yezhov: The Rise of Stalin's "Iron Fist."* New Haven, 2008.

Goichenko, Dmitrii D. *Skvoz' raskulachivanie i golodomor: svidetel'stvo ochevidtsa.* Moscow, 2006.

Golden, Peter B. "Nomads and Sedentary Societies in Eurasia." In *Agricultural and Pastoral Societies in Ancient and Classical History*, edited by Michael Adas, 71–115. Philadelphia, 2001.

Goldhagen, Daniel Jonah. *Hitler's Willing Executioners: Ordinary Germans and the Holocaust.* New York, 1966.

Goloshchekin, F. I. "Iz tsarskoi kolonii—v peredovye riady stroitelei sotsializma." *Pravda*, February 5, 1932.

Goloshchekin, F. I. "Kazakhstan na pod'eme." *Narodnoe khoziaistvo Kazakhstana* 5, no. 5/6 (1930), 18–22.

Goloshchekin, F. I. *Na poroge vtoroi piatiletki: rech' na V plenume Kazkraikoma VKP(b) 16 dekabria 1932 goda.* Alma-Ata, 1933.

Goloshchekin, F. I. "Ob aul'nom kommuniste: stat'ia v zhurnale 'Kzyl-Kazakstan' 1926 g." In Goloshchekin, *Partiinoe stroitel'stvo v Kazakhstane*, 88–92.

Goloshchekin, F. I. *Ocherednye zadachi VKP(b) v Kazakhstane.* Kzyl-Orda, 1926.

Goloshchekin, F. I. *Partiinoe stroitel'stvo v Kazakhstane: sbornik rechei i statei.* Moscow, 1930.

Goloshchekin, F. I. "Puti sotsialisticheskogo nastupleniia v Kazakhstane i osedanie kazakhskogo naseleniia." In Goloshchekin, *Desiat' let proidennykh i prestoiashchie zadachi*, 45–49. Alma-Ata, 1930.

Goloshchekin, F. I. "Za sovetizatsiiu aula: doklad na V kraevoi partkonferentsii o rabote kraikoma VKP(b) 1925." In Goloshchekin, *Partiinoe stroitel'stvo v Kazakhstane*, 22–45.

Gratsiotsi [Graziosi], Andrea. *Velikaia krest'ianskaia voina v SSSR: Bol'sheviki i krest'iane, 1917–1933.* Moscow, 2001.

Gregory, Paul R., and Andrei Markevich. "Creating Soviet Industry: The House That Stalin Built." *Slavic Review* 61, no. 4 (2002), 787–814.

Gribanov, N. R. et al. *Iz istorii deportatsii: Kazakhstan 1930–1955 gg. Sbornik dokumentov.* Almaty, 2012.

Groebner, Valentin. *Ungestalten: Die visuelle Kultur der Gewalt im Mittelalter.* Munich, 2003.

Gromov, E. "K voprosu o rassolenii krest'ianstva v Kazakhstane." *Revoliutsionnyi vostok*, no. 3 (1928), 168–87.

Grozin, A. V. *Golod 1932–1933 godov i politika pamiati v Respublike Kazakhstan.* Moscow, 2014.

Gumppenberg, Marie-Carin von. *Staats- und Nationsbildung in Kazakhstan.* Opladen, 2002.

Gürbüz, Yunus Emre. "Caught between Nationalism and Socialism: The Kazak Alash Orda Movement in Continuity." PhD diss., Ankara, 2007.

Hagenloh, Paul. *Stalin's Police: Public Order and Mass Repression in the USSR, 1926–1941.* Washington, DC, 2009.

Halperin, Charles J. *The Tatar Yoke: The Image of Mongols in Medieval Russia.* Bloomington, 2009.

Happel, Jörn. *Nomadische Lebenswelten und zarische Politik: Der Aufstand in Zentralasien 1916.* Stuttgart, 2010.

Harris, James R. *The Great Urals: Regionalism and the Evolution of the Soviet System.* Ithaca, 1999.

Haugen, Arne. *The Establishment of National Republics in Central Asia.* Basingstoke, 2003.

Hausmann, Guido, ed. *Gesellschaft als lokale Veranstaltung: Selbstverwaltung, Assoziierung und Geselligkeit in den Städten des ausgehenden Zarenreiches.* Göttingen, 2002.

Hedeler, Wladislaw, and Meinhard Stark. *Das Grab in der Steppe: Leben im Gulag: Die Geschichte eines sowjetischen Zwangsarbeitslagers, 1930–1959.* Paderborn, 2007.

Helbling, Jürg. "Etwas Kritik und noch eine Theorie des Krieges." *Zeitschrift für Ethnologie* 121 (1996), 55–67.

Helweg-Larsen, Per, ed. "Die Hungerkrankheit in den deutschen Konzentrationslagern." In *Gesundheitsschäden durch Verfolgung und Gefangenschaft und ihre Spätfolgen. Zusammenstellung der Referate und Ergebnisse der Internationalen Sozialmedizinischen Konferenz über die Pathologie der ehemaligen Deportierten und Internierten, 5.-7. Juni 1954 in Kopenhagen und ergänzender Referate und Ergebnisse einschl. 1955,* edited by Max Michel, 148–71. Frankfurt am Main, 1955.

Hildermeier, Manfred. *Geschichte der Sowjetunion 1917–1991: Entstehung und Niedergang des ersten sozialistischen Staates.* Munich, 1998.

Hirsch, Francine. *Empire of Nations: Ethnographic Knowledge and the Making of the Soviet Union.* Ithaca, 2005.

Hirsch, Francine. "The Soviet-Union as a Work-in-Progress: Ethnographers and the Category Nationality in the 1926, 1937, and 1939 Censuses." *Slavic Review* 56, no. 2 (1997), 251–78.

Hirsch, Francine. "Toward an Empire of Nations, Border-Making and the Formation of Soviet National Identities."*Russian Review* 59, no. 2 (2000), 201–26.

Hoffmann, David L. *Peasant Metropolis: Social Identities in Moscow, 1929–1941.* Ithaca, 1994.

Holquist, Peter. "State Violence as Technique: The Logic of Violence in Soviet Totalitarianism." In *Landscaping the Human Garden: Twentieth-Century Population Management in a Comparative Framework,* edited by Amir Weiner, 19–45. Stanford, 2003.

Holquist, Peter. "To Count, to Extract, and to Exterminate. Population Statistics and Population Politics in Late Imperial and Soviet Russia." In Suny and Martin, *State of Nations,* 111–44.

Holquist, Peter. "Violent Russia, Deadly Marxism? Russia in the Epoch of Violence, 1905–1921." *Kritika* 4, no. 3 (2003), 627–52.

Hosking, Geoffrey. "Patronage and the Russian State." *Slavonic and East European Review* 78, no. 2 (2000), 301–20.

Hosking, Geoffrey. "Trust and Distrust in the USSR: An Overview." *Slavonic and East European Review* 91, no. 1 (2013), 1–25.

Hudson, Alfred E. *Kazak Social Structure.* New Haven, 1964 [1938].

Hughes, James. "Capturing the Russian Peasantry: Stalinist Grain Procurement and the 'Ural-Siberian Method.'" *Slavic Review* 53, no. 1 (1994), 76–103.

Hughes, James. *Stalin, Siberia and the Crisis of the New Economic Policy.* Cambridge, 1991.

Iakovenko, M. M. *Agnessa: ustnye rasskazy Agnessy Ivanovy Mironovoi-Korol' o ee iunosti, o schast'e i gorestiakh trekh ee zamuzhestv, ob ogromnoi liubvi k znamenitomu stalinskomu chekistu Sergeiu Naumovi Mironovu, o shikarnykh kurortakh, priemakh v Kremle i . . . o tiur'makh, etapakh, lageriakh—o zhizni, prozhitok na kacheliakh sovetskoi istorii.* Moscow, 1997.

Ikramov, Kamil. *Delo moego otsa: Roman-khronika.* Moscow, 1991.

Il'inykh, Vladimir. *Khroniki khlebnogo fronta: zagotovitel'nye kampanii kontsa 1920-kh gg. v Sibiri.* Moscow, 2010.

Isaev, U. D. "Natsional'naia politika partii v Kazakhstane." *Narodnoe khoziaistvo Kazakhstana* 5, no. 5/6 (1930), 23–26.

Ishchenko, M. M. and I. S. Kazbekov. *Osobennosti sel'skogo khoziaistva adaevskogo uezda: otchet rabotakh pochvenno-botanicheskogo otriada.* Leningrad, 1928.

"Itogi konfiskatsii: Rezoliuciia plenuma, 2–7 dek. 1928." In *Kommunisticheskaia partiia Kazakhstana v rezoliutsiiakh i resheniiakh s"ezdov, konferentsii i plenumov,* vol. 2: 1928–1937, 28–38. Alma-Ata, 1981.

Ivnitskii, Nikolai. *Golod 1932–1933 godov v SSSR: Ukraina, Kazakhstan, Severnyi Kavkaz, Povolzh'e, Tsentral'no-Chernozemnaia oblast', Zapadnaia Sibir', Ural.* Moscow, 2009.

Ivnitskii, Nikolai. *Kollektivizatsiia i raskulachivanie (nachalo 30-kh gg.).* Moscow, 1996.

Jakowlew, Alexander. *Ein Jahrhundert der Gewalt in Sowjetrussland.* Berlin, 2004.

Jilge, Wilfried. "Die 'Große Hungersnot' in Geschichte und Erinnerungskultur der Ukraine." In *Erinnerungsorte an den Holodomor 1932/33 in der Ukraine,* edited by Anna Kaminsky, 11–24. Leipzig, 2008.

Jilge, Wilfried. "Holodomor und Nation: Der Hunger im ukrainischen Geschichtsbild." *Osteuropa* 54, no. 12 (2004), 147–64.

Kalyvas, Stathis N. *The Logic of Violence in Civil War.* Cambridge, 2008.

Kamenskii, K. P. "Piatiletnii plan razvitiia i rekonstruktsii sel'skogo khoziaistva Kazakhstana." *Narodnoe khoziaistvo Kazakhstana* 5, no. 5/6 (1930), 42–57.

Kamp, Marianne. *The New Woman in Uzbekistan: Islam, Modernity, and Unveiling under Communism.* Seattle, 2006.

Kappeler, Andreas. "Die 'vergessenen' Muslime: Russland und die islamischen Völker seines Imperiums." *Saeculum* 55, no. 1 (2004), 19–47.

Kappeler, Andreas. *The Russian Empire: A Multiethnic History.* London, 2001.

Kappeler, Andreas. *Russland als Vielvoelkerreich: Entstehung, Geschichte, Zerfall.* Munich, 2001.

Karagizova, G. B. "Likvidatsiia posledstvii nasil'stvennoi kollektivizatsii i problemy sotsial'no-ekonomicheskogo razvitiia aula i sela v Kazakhstane (1933–1940 gg.)." PhD diss., Astana, 2002.

Karazhanov, K., and A. Takenov, eds. *Noveishaia istoriia Kazakhstana: sbornik dokumentov i materialov. Vol. 1: 1917–1939.* Almaty, 1998.

Kassymbekova, Botakoz. *Despite Cultures: Early Soviet Rule in Tajikistan.* Pittsburgh, 2016.

Kassymbekova, Botakoz. "Helpless Imperialists: European State Workers in Soviet Central Asia in the 1920s and 1930s." *Central Asian Survey* 30, no. 1 (2011), 21–37.

Kassymbekova, Botakoz. "Understanding Stalinism in, from, and of Central Asia: Beyond Failure, Peripherality, and Otherness." *Central Asian Survey* 36, no. 1 (2017), 1–18.

Kassymbekova, Botakoz, and Christian Teichmann. "The Red Man's Burden: Soviet European Officials in Central Asia in the 1920s and 1930s." In *Helpless Imperialists: Imperial Failure, Fear and Radicalization,* edited by Maurus Reinkowski and Gregor Thum, 163–86. Göttingen, 2013.

Keen, David. *The Benefits of Famine: A Political Economy of Famine and Relief in Southwestern Sudan, 1983–1989.* Oxford, 2008.

Keller, Shoshana. "The Central Asian Bureau: An Essential Tool in Governing Soviet Turkestan." *Central Asian Survey* 22, no. 2/3 (2003), 281–97.

Kendirbaeva, Gulnar. "'We Are Children of Alash . . .': The Kazakh Intelligentsia at the Beginning of the 20th Century in Search of National Identity and Prospects of the Cultural Survival of the Kazakh People." *Central Asian Survey* 18, no. 1 (1999), 5–36.

Kendirbay [Kendirbaeva], Gulnar. "Der Kampf um das Land in der Kazakhischen Steppe am Anfang des 20. Jahrhunderts." *Jahrbücher für Geschichte Osteuropas* 47, no. 3 (1999), 381–95.

Kenzhaliev, Z. Zh., and S. O. Dauletova. *Kazakhskoe obychnoe pravo v usloviiakh sovetskoi vlasti (1917–1937 gg.).* Almaty, 1993.

Kessler, Gijs. "The 1932–1933 Crisis and Its Aftermath beyond the Epicentre of Famine: The Urals Region." *Harvard Ukrainian Studies* 25, no. 3/4 (2001), 253–65.

Kessler, Gijs. "The Origins of Soviet Internal-Migration Policy: Industrialization and the 1930s Rural Exodus." In *Russia in Motion: Cultures of Human Mobility since 1850*, edited by John Randolph and Eugene M. Avrutin, 63–79. Urbana, 2012.

Kessler, Gijs. "The Passport System and State Control over Population Flows in the Soviet Union, 1932–1940." *Cahiers du monde russe* 22, no. 2/3/4 (2001), 477–504.

Khalid, Adeeb. *Islam after Communism: Religion and Politics in Central Asia*. Berkeley, 2007.

Khalid, Adeeb. *Making Uzbekistan: Nation, Empire, and Revolution in the Early USSR*. Ithaca, 2015.

Khalid, Adeeb. *The Politics of Muslim Cultural Reform: Jadidism in Tsarist Central Asia*. Madison, 1993.

Khalidullin, G. "Agrarnaia politika sovetskoi vlasti v Kazakhstane v 1917–1940 gg." PhD diss., Almaty, 2001.

Khaustov, V. N., V. P. Naumov, and N. S. Plotnikova, eds. *Lubianka: Stalin i VChK-GPU-OGPU-NKVD, ianvar' 1922–dekabr' 1936*. Moscow, 2003.

Khazanov, Anatoly M. *Nomads and the Outside World*. Madison, 1994.

Khlevniuk, O. V. et al., eds. *Stalin i Kaganovich: perepiska, 1931–1936 gg*. Moscow, 2001.

Khlevnyuk [Khlevniuk], Oleg. "The Economy of the OGPU, NKVD, and MVD of the USSR, 1930–1953: The Scale, Structure, and Trends of Development." In *The Economics of Forced Labor: The Soviet Gulag*, edited by Paul Gregory and Valery Lazarev, 43–66. Stanford, 2003.

Khliupin, V. N., and V. I. Puzanov. "Obratnaia storona èlity." In *Genotsid Russkie v Kazakhstane: Tragicheskaia sud'ba*, edited by V. N. Khliupin, 82–108. Moscow, 2011.

Khodarkovsky, Michael. *Where Two Worlds Met: The Russian State and the Kalmyk Nomads, 1600–1771*. Ithaca, 1992.

Khrushchev, F. Ia. "Perspektiva sveklosakharnoi promyshlennosti v Dzhetysuiskoi gubernii." *Narodnoe khoziaistvo Kazakhstana* 1, no. 1 (1926), 43–50.

Khurshudian, Eduard. "Slovo o Mirzoiane." In Degitaeva, *Levon Mirzoian*, 3–13.

Kim, Vladimir. "Eshelon-58." In *Dorogoi gor'kikh ispytanii: K 60-letiiu deportatsii koreitsev Rossii*, edited by V. V. Tian, 69–81. Moscow, 1997.

Kindler, Robert. "Auf der Flucht—Die kasachischen Nomaden und die Hungersnot von 1930–1934." In *Hunger, Ernährung und Rationierungssysteme unter dem Staatssozialismus (1917–2006)*, edited by Matthias Middell and Felix Wemheuer, 35–57. Frankfurt am Main, 2011.

Kindler, Robert. "Die Starken und die Schwachen: Zur Bedeutung physischer Gewalt während der Hungersnot in Kasachstan." *Jahrbücher für Geschichte Osteuropas* 59, no. 1 (2011) 51–78.

Kindler, Robert. "' . . . es gibt menschliche Opfer': Hungerkrise und Herrschafts-durchsetzung in Westkasachstan, 1927–1934." In Collet, Lassen, and Schanbacher, *Handeln in Hungerkrisen*, 151–69.

Kindler, Robert. "Famines and Political Communication in Stalinism: Possibilities and Limits of the Sayable." *Jahrbücher für Geschichte Osteuropas* 62, no. 2 (2014), 255–72.

Kindler, Robert. "'New York in der Steppe': Die Sesshaftmachung der kasachischen Nomaden." *Jahrbuch für historische Kommunismusforschung* (2012), 47–62.

Kindler, Robert. "Opfer ohne Täter: Kasachische und ukrainische Erinnerung an den Hunger 1932/33." *Osteuropa* 62, no. 3 (2012), 105–20.

Kirchner, Mark. "Zur Bildhaftigkeit im kasachischen Sprichwort." *Oriens* 34 (1994), 459–69.

Koigeldiev, M. K. *Stalinizm i repressii v Kazakhstane 1920–1940-kh godov*. Almaty, 2009.

Kondrashin, Viktor. *Golod 1932–1933 godov: tragediia rossiiskoi derevni*. Moscow, 2008.

Kondrashin, Viktor, ed. *Golod v SSSR: 1929–1934*. Dokumenty v 3 tomakh. Moscow, 2011–12.

Kondrashin, Viktor, ed. *Sovremennaia rossiisko-ukrainskaia istoriografiia goloda 1932–1933 gg. v SSSR*. Moscow, 2011.

Kondrat'eva, Tamara. *Kormit' i pravit': o vlasti v Rossii XVI–XX vv*. Moscow, 2009.

König, Helmut. "Paradoxien der Erinnerung: Über Wissen und Vergessen." *Osteuropa* 61, no. 4 (2011), 43–54.

Kopelev, Lev. *The Education of a True Believer*. New York, 1978.

Kopelew, Lew [Kopelev, Lev]. *Und schuf mir einen Götzen: Lehrjahre eines Kommunisten*. Munich, 1981.

Kor'be, O. A. "Kul'tura i byt kazakhskogo kolkhoznogo aula." *Sovetskaia etnografiia* 4 (1950), 67–91.

Kosokov, I. "Itogi planovogo osedaniia i prakticheskie zadachi." *Revoliutsiia i natsional'nosti*, no. 5/6 (1933), 67–73.

Kotkin, Stephen. *Magnetic Mountain: Stalinism as a Civilization*. Berkeley, 1995.

Kotkin, Stephen. *Stalin, vol.1: Paradoxes of Power, 1878–1928*. New York, 2014.

Kotkin, Stephen. *Stalin, vol. 2: Waiting for Hitler, 1929–1941*. New York, 2017.

Kozlov, V. P. "Obshchaia tragediia narodov SSSR." In *Golod v SSSR: 1929–1934: dokumenty v 3 tomakh*, 1:5–9. Moscow, 2011.

Kozlovskii, E. *Krasnaia Armiia v Srednei Azii: voenno-istoricheskii ocherk*. Tashkent, 1928.

Kozybaev, K. "Za novuiu zhizn'." In *Gody muzhaniia: vospominaniia uchastnikov sotsialisticheskogo stroitel'stva v Kazakhstane*, edited by P. M. Pakhmurnyi. Alma-Ata 1969.

Kozybaev, M. K. "Demograficheskie issledovaniia v Kazakhstane: itogi i perspektivy." In Kozybaev, *Kazakhstan na rubezhe vekov*, 348–57.

Kozybaev, M. K. *Kazakhstan—arsenal fronta*. Alma-Ata, 1970.

Kozybaev, M. K. *Kazakhstan na rubezhe vekov: razmyshleniia i poiski. Sotsializm. Nesby-vshiesia nadezhdy*, vol. 2. Almaty, 2000.

Kozybaev, M. K. "'Klassovyi' natisk." In Kozybaev, *Kazakhstan na rubezhe vekov*, 172–83.

Kozybaev, M. K., ed. *Nasil'stvennaia kollektivizatsiia i golod v Kazakhstan: 1931–1933gg. Sbornik dokumentov*. Almaty, 1998.

Kozybaev, M. K. "Novoe myshlenie i nekotorye problemy istorii kollektivizatsii." In Kozybaev, *Kazakhstan na rubezhe vekov*, 52–70.

Kozybaev, M. K. "Sud nad pamiat'iu." In Kozybaev, *Kazakhstan na rubezhe vekov*, 134–51.

Kozybaev, M. K. *Uraz Dzhandosov: Dokumenty i publitsistika (1918–1937gg.)*. 2 vols. Almaty, 1999.

Kozybaev, M. K., Zh. B. Abylkhozhin, and K. S. Aldazhumanov. *Kollektivizatsiia v Kazakhstane: tragediia krest'ianstva*. Alma-Ata, 1992.

Krivitskii, A. "Legkomyslennoe otnoshenie k otgonnomu zhivotnovodstvu." *Pravda*, January 11, 1945.

Kuderina, L. D. *Genotsid v Kazakhstane*. Moscow, 1994.

Kulumbetov, U. D. "Reshenie TsK VKP(b) i SNK SSSR o Kazakhstane." *Revoliutsiia i natsional'nosti* 5 (1935), 18–24.

Kumanbaev, Erbol. "800 millionov tenge za stat'iu." *Svoboda slova*, June 15, 2007.

Kuramysov, I. "K voprosu o sotsialisticheskoi rekonstruktsii s/kh v Kazakhstane." In Kuramysov, *Za leninskuiu natsional'nuiu politiku v Kazakhstane: sbornik rechei i statei, 1928–1932*, 13–21. Alma-Ata, 1932.

Kuromiya, Hiroaki. *Freedom and Terror in the Donbass: A Russian-Ukrainian Border-land, 1870s–1990s*. Cambridge, 1998.

Kurskii, A. "Kontrrevoliutsionnye vrediteli sel'skogo khoziaistva v Kazakhstane." In *Kondrat'evshchina v planirovanii narodnogo khoziaistva Kazakhstana: sbornik statei*, edited by A. Kurskii, 21–51. Alma-Ata, 1931.

Laird, Roy D., and John E. Chappell. "Kazakhstan: Russia's Agricultural Crutch." *Russian Review* 20, no. 4 (1961), 326–43.

Lane, David. "Ethnic and Class Stratification in Soviet Kazakhstan, 1917–39." *Comparative Studies in Society and History* 17, no. 2 (1975), 165–89.

Lariuel', Marlen, and Sebast'ian Peiruz [Laruelle, Marlène, and Sèbastien Peyrouse]. *"Russkii vopros" v nezavisimom Kazakhstane: istoriia, politika, identichnost'*. Moscow, 2007.

Lattimore, Owen. "Chinese Turkestan." In *Studies in Frontier History: Collected Papers 1928–1958*, edited by Owen Lattimore, 183–99. Paris, 1962.

Lattimore, Owen. *Inner Asian Frontiers of China*. New York, 1962.

Ledeneva, Alena V. *Russia's Economy of Favours: Blat, Networking and Informal Exchange*. Cambridge, 1998.

Leonov, A., and B. N. Semevskii. "Uroki pervogo goda osedaniia." *Narodnoe khoziaistvo Kazakhstana* 5, no. 7/8 (1930), 16–22.

Letunovskii, A. "Itogi zimovki 1934–1935 goda i ocherednye zadachi zhivotnovod-cheskikh sovkhozov Kazakhstana." *Narodnoe khoziaistvo Kazakhstana* 7, no. 5/6 (1935), 38–42.

Levin, A. A. "Agrarnaia politika Kazakhstana v period sotsialisticheskoi rekonstruktsii." *Narodnoe khoziaistvo Kazakhstana* 5, no. 9/10 (1930), 11–23.

Lewin, Moshe. "The Disappearance of Planning in the Plan." *Slavic Review* 32, no. 2 (1973), 171–87.

Lewin, Moshe. *The Making of the Soviet System: Essays in the Social History of Interwar Russia*. London, 1985.

Lewin, Moshe. "On Soviet Industrialization." In *Social Dimensions of Soviet Industrialization*, edited by William G. Rosenberg and Lewis H. Siegelbaum, 272–84. Bloomington, 1993.

Lih, Lars T., Oleg Naumow, and Oleg Chlewnjuk, eds. *Stalin: Briefe an Molotow, 1925–1936*. Berlin, 1996.

Lindner, Rudi Paul. "What Was a Nomadic Tribe?" *Comparative Studies in Society and History* 24, no. 4 (1982), 689–711.

Loring, Benjamin H. "Building Socialism in Kyrgyzstan: Nation-Making, Rural Development, and Social Change, 1921–1932." PhD diss., Brandeis University, 2008.

Loring, Benjamin H. "Colonizers with Party Cards: Soviet Internal Colonization in Central Asia, 1917–1939." *Kritika* 15, no. 1 (2014), 77–103.

Loring, Benjamin H. "Rural Dynamics and Peasant Resistance in Southern Kyrgyzstan, 1929–1930." *Cahiers du monde russe* 49, no. 1 (2008), 183–210.

Maillart, Ella. *Turkestan Solo: One Woman's Expedition from the Tien Shan to the Kizil Kum*. New York, 1935.

Maksudov, Sergei. "Migratsii v SSSR v 1926–1939 godakh." *Cahiers du monde russe* 40, no. 4 (1999), 763–96.

Malikov, Yuriy. "The Kenesary Kasymov Rebellion (1837–1847): A National-liberation Movement or 'a Protest of Restoration?'" *Nationalities Papers* 33, no. 4 (2005), 569–97.

Malikov, Yuriy. *Tsars, Cossacks, and Nomads: The Formation of a Borderland Culture in Northern Kazakhstan in the Eighteenth and Nineteenth Centuries*. Berlin, 2011.

Malysheva, M. P., and V. S. Poznanskii. *Kazakhi—bezhentsy ot goloda v zapadnoi Sibiri (1931–1934 gg.)*. Almaty, 1999.

Manley, Rebecca. *To the Tashkent Station: Evacuation and Survival in the Soviet Union at War.* Ithaca, 2009.

Margulan, A., and V. V. Vostrov. *Kul'tura i byt Kazakhskogo kolkhoznogo aula.* Alma-Ata, 1967.

Mark, Rudolf A. "Die Hungersnot in Kasachstan: Aufarbeitung der stalinistischen Verbrechen." *Osteuropa* 57, no. 8/9 (2007), 571–88.

Mark, Rudolf A. "Die Hungersnot in Kazachstan: Historiographische Aufarbeitung im Wandel." *Osteuropa* 54, no. 12 (2004), 112–30.

Mark, Rudolf A. *Im Schatten des "Great Game": Deutsche "Weltpolitik" und russischer Imperialismus in Zentralasien, 1871–1914.* Paderborn, 2012.

Markevich, A. M. "Byla li sovetskaia ekonomika planovoi? Planirovanie v narkomatakh v 1930-e gg." In *Ekonomicheskaia istoriia: ezhegodnik 2003,* 20–54. Moscow, 2004.

Martin, Terry. *The Affirmative Action Empire: Nations and Nationalism in the Soviet Union, 1923–1939.* Ithaca, 2001.

Martin, Terry. "Interpreting the New Archival Signals: Nationalities Policy and the Nature of the Soviet Bureaucracy." *Cahiers du monde russe* 40, no. 1/2 (1999), 113–24.

Martin, Terry. "Modernization or No-Traditionalism? Ascribed Nationality and Soviet Primordalism." In Fitzpatrick, *Stalinism,* 348–67.

Martin, Terry. "The Origins of Soviet Ethnic Cleansing." *Journal of Modern History* 70, no. 4 (1998), 813–61.

Martin, Virginia. "Barimta: Nomadic Custom, Imperial Crime." In Brower and Lazzerini, *Russia's Orient,* 249–70.

Martin, Virginia. *Law and Custom in the Steppe: The Kazakhs of the Middle Horde and Russian Colonialism in the Nineteenth Century.* Richmond, 2001.

Martin, Virginia. "Nomadic Land Claims in the Colonized Kazakh Steppe." *Mitteilungen des SFB 586 "Differenz und Integration"* 1, no. 2 (2002), 65–74.

Masanov, N., Zh. B. Abylkhozhin, and I. V. Erofeeva, eds. *Nauchnoe znanie i mifotvorchestvo v sovremennoi istoriografii Kazakhstana.* Almaty, 2007.

Masanov, Nurbulat, ed. *Istoriia Kazakhstana: narody i kul'tury.* Almaty, 2001.

Masanov, Nurbulat. *Kochevaia tsivilizatsiia Kazakhov.* Almaty, 1995.

Massell, Gregory J. *The Surrogate Proletariat: Moslem Women and Revolutionary Strategies in Central Asia, 1919–1929.* Princeton, 1974.

Materialy k otchetu Kazakhskogo Kraevogo Komiteta VKP(b) na VI kraevoi partiinoi konferentsii. Kzyl-Orda, 1927.

Materialy k otchetu Krai KK-NK RKI KASSR vos'moi Kraevoi Partiinoi Konferentsii. Alma-Ata, 1934.

Materialy po kirgizskomu zemlepol'zovaniiu: sobrannye i razrabotannye ekspeditsiei po isledovaniiu stepnykh oblastei. Akmolinskaia oblast'. Vol. 1: *Kokchetavskii uezd.* Voronezh, 1898.

Matskevich, N. N. "Sravnitel'naia dlina kochevok kazakhskogo naseleniia b. Semipalatinskoi gubernii." In *Zapiski semipalatinskogo otdela obshchestva izucheniia Kazakhstana,* vol. 1, 1–33. Semipalatinsk, 1929.

McDonald, Tracy. *Face to the Village: The Riazan Countryside under Soviet Rule, 1921–1930.* Toronto, 2011.

Medeubaev, Erlan. "Palach tsarskoi sem'i i avtor 'Malogo Oktiabria': F. I. Goloshchekin (1925–1933)." In Aben, Aryn, and Tasmagambetov, *Pervye litsa gosudarstva,* 231–45.

Medeubaev, Erlan. "Pervyi vse Kazakhstanskii starosta: S. Mendeshev (1920–1925)." In Aben, Aryn, and Tasmagambetov, *Pervye litsa gosudarstva,* 219–30.

Meier, Christian. *Das Gebot zu vergessen und die Unabweisbarkeit des Erinnerns: Vom öffentlichen Umgang mit schlimmer Vergangenheit.* Munich, 2010.

Mendikulova, G. M. *Istoricheskie sud'by Kazakhskoi diaspory: proizkhozhdenie i razvitie.* Almaty, 1997.

Mendikulova, G. M. *Kazakhskaia diaspora: istoriia i sovremennost'.* Almaty, 2006.

Merl, Stefan. *Bauern unter Stalin: Die Formierung des sowjetischen Kolchossystems 1930–1941.* Berlin, 1990.

Merl, Stefan. "Bilanz der Unterwerfung—die soziale und ökonomische Reorganisation des Dorfes." In *Stalinismus vor dem Zweiten Weltkrieg: Neue Wege der Forschung,* edited by Manfred Hildermeier, 119–46. Munich, 1998.

Merl, Stefan. *Politische Kommunikation in der Diktatur: Deutschland und die Sowjetunion im Vergleich.* Göttingen, 2012.

Merl, Stefan. "Why Did the Attempt under Stalin to Increase Agricultural Productivity Prove to Be Such a Fundamental Failure?" *Cahiers du Monde Russe* 57, no. 1 (2016), 191–220.

Merridale, Catherine. *Ivan's War: The Red Army 1939–45.* London, 2005.

Merridale, Catherine. *Night of Stone: Death and Memory in Twentieth-Century Russia.* New York, 2000.

Michaels, Paula. *Curative Powers: Medicine and Empire in Stalin's Central Asia.* Pittsburgh, 2003.

Michaels, Paula. "Medical Propaganda and Cultural Revolution in Soviet Kazakhstan, 1928–1941." *Russian Review* 59, no. 2 (2000), 159–78.

Mikhailov, Valeriy. *Khronika Velikogo Dzhuta.* Almaty, 1996.

Mikhailov, Valeriy. *The Great Disaster: Genocide of the Kazakhs.* London, 2014.

Millward, James A. *Eurasian Crossroads: A History of Xinjiang.* New York, 2007.

Mirzoian, L. I. "Ob itogakh posevnoi i uborochnoi 1934 g." *Narodnoe khoziaistvo Kazakhstana* 6, no. 6 (1934), 18–19.

Mirzoian, L. I. "Rech' na XVII s"ezde partii." *Bol'shevik Kazakhstana*, no. 3/4 (1934), 1–4.

Morrison, Alexander. "Introduction: Killing the Cotton Canard and getting rid of the Great Game: Rewriting the Russian Conquest of Central Asia, 1814–1895." *Central Asian Survey* 33, no. 2 (2014), 131–42.

Morrison, Alexander. "Sowing the Seed of National Strife in This Alien Region: The Pahlen Report and Pereselenie in Turkestan, 1908–1910." *Acta Slavonica Iaponica* 31 (2012), 1–29.

Mukhamedina, Sh. "Ekonomicheskaia politika sovetskoi vlasti v kazakhstanskom regione 1917–1926." *Voprosy istorii*, no. 6 (1997), 125–32.

Mukhamedina, Sh. "Konfiskatsiia baiskikh khoziaistv v Kazakhstane." *Voprosy istorii*, no. 4 (2002), 136–42.

Nabiev, Zhaugashty. *Stepnaia tragediia: adaiskoe vosstanie 1929–1931gg.* Almaty, 2010.

Naimark, Norman. *Stalin's Genocides.* Princeton, 2010.

Naimark, Norman. *Stalin und der Genozid.* Berlin 2010.

Narodetskii, Aleksandr. "Golodomor ne puskaiut v Kazakhstan." http://www.respublika-kz.info/news/politics/18997/ (accessed October 2, 2013).

[Nazarbayev, Nursultan]. "Vystuplenie prezidenta Respubliki Kazakhstan N. A. Nazarbaeva na otkrytii Monumenta pamiati zhertv goloda 1932–1933gg." In *Golod v Kazakhstane: tragediia naroda i uroki istorii: sbornik materialov*, edited by B. G. Aiagan, 6–10. Astana, 2012.

Nazemtseva, E. N. "Aktivizatsiia antisovetskoi deiatel'nosti beloi emigratsii v Sin'tsziane v 1927–1930gg." In *Vostokovednye issledovaniia na Altae*, Vyp. IV, edited by V. A. Moisev, 133–43. Barnaul, 2004.

Neitzel, Sönke, and Harald Welzer. *Soldiers: German POWs on Fighting, Killing, and Dying.* New York, 2012.

Nekh, V. F. *Istoriia sovetskoi pogranichnoi politiki, 1917–1941.* Moscow, 2008.

Neutatz, Dietmar. "Die Suggestion der 'Front': Überlegungen zu Wahrnehmungen und Verhaltensweisen im Stalinismus." In *Stalinistische Subjekte: Individuum und System in der Sowjetunion und der Komintern, 1929–1953*, edited by Brigitte Studer and Heiko Haumann, 67–80. Zurich, 2006.

Newman, David. "Boundary Geopolitics: Towards a Theory of Territorial Lines?" In *Routing Borders between Territories: Discourses and Practices*, edited by Eiki Berg and Henk van Houtum, 227–91. Aldershot, 2003.

Northrop, Douglas. *Veiled Empire: Gender and Power in Stalinist Central Asia.* Ithaca, 2004.

Nurtazina, Nazira. "Great Famine of 1931–1933 in Kazakhstan: A Contemporary's Reminiscences." *Acta Slavonica Iaponica* 32 (2012), 105–29.

Ó Gráda, Cormac. *Famine: A Short History*. Princeton, 2009.

Ochak, I., and A. Takenov. *Internatsional'nyi otriad: k istorii ekspeditsii A. Dzhangil'dina*. Alma-Ata, 1974.

Ocherk o deiatel'nosti dzhetysuiskogo oblastnogo ekonomicheskogo soveshchaniia za 1921–1922 khoziaistvennyi god. Alma-Ata, 1923.

Ohayon, Isabelle. *La sédentarisation des Kazakhs dans l'URRS de Stalin: collectivisation et changement social, 1928–1945*. Paris, 2006.

Olcott, Martha Brill. "The Basmachi or Freemen's Revolt in Turkestan 1918–24." *Soviet Studies* 33, no. 3 (1981), 352–69.

Olcott, Martha Brill. "The Collectivization Drive in Kazakhstan." *Russian Review* 40, no. 2 (1981), 122–42.

Olcott, Martha Brill. *The Kazakhs*. Stanford, 1988.

Olcott, Martha Brill. "The Settlement of the Kazakh Nomads." *Newsletter of the Commission on Nomadic Peoples*, no. 8 (1981), 12–23.

Oliver-Smith, Anthony. "Anthropolgical Research on Hazards and Disasters." *Annual Review of Anthropology* 25 (1996), 303–28.

Omarbekov, Talas. *Golodomor v Kazakhstane: prichiny, masshtaby i itogi (1930–1933 gg.)* Almaty, 2009.

Omarov, M. *Rasstrelianaia step': dokumental'noe povestvovanie*. Almaty, 1994.

Osokina, Elena. *Our Daily Bread: Socialist Distribution and the Art of Survival in Stalin's Russia, 1927–1941*. New York, 2001.

Osokina, Elena. "Zhertvy goloda 1933 goda: skol'ko ikh? (Analiz demograficheskoi statistiki TsGANKh SSSR)." *Istoriia SSSR*, no. 5 (1991), 18–26.

Osterhammel, Jürgen. *Colonialism: A Theoretical Overview*. Princeton, 2005.

Otchet Kazakskoi Kraevoi Kontrol'noi Komissii VKP(b) i Narodnogo Komissariata Raboche-Krest'ianskoi Inspektsii k 6-oi Kazakskoi Partkonferentsii (Za vremia s 1-go ianvaria 1926 g. po 1-oe oktiabria 1927 g.). Kzyl-Orda, 1927.

Pahlen, Constantin. *Mission to Turkestan: Being the Memoirs of Count K. K. Pahlen*. Edited by Richard A. Pierce. Oxford, 1964.

Panter-Brick, Catherine. "Nobody's Children? A Reconsideration of Child Abandonment." In *Abandoned Children*, edited by Catherine Panter-Brick and Malcolm T. Smith, 1–26. Cambridge, 2000.

Patenaude, Bertrand M. *The Big Show in Bololand: The American Relief Expedition to Soviet Russia*. Stanford, 2002.

Payne, Matthew. "The Forge of the Kazakh Proletariat? The Turksib, Nativization, and

Industrialization during Stalin's First Five-Year Plan." In Suny and Martin, *State of Nations*, 223–52.

Payne, Matthew. "Seeing Like a Soviet State: Settlement of the Nomadic Kazakhs, 1928–1934." In *Writing the Stalin Era: Sheila Fitzpatrick and Soviet Historiography*, edited by Golfo Alexopoulos, Julie Hessler, and Kiril Tomoff, 59–86. Houndmills, 2011.

Payne, Matthew. *Stalin's Railroad: Turksib and the Building of Socialism*. Pittsburgh, 2001.

Petrov, Nikita, ed. *Kto rukovodil NKVD 1934–1941: spravochnik*. Moscow, 1999.

Petrov, V. I. *Miatezhnoe serdtse Azii: Sin'tszian. Kratkaia istoriia narodnykh dvizhenii i vospominaniia*. Moscow, 2003.

Pianciola, Niccoló. "Décoloniser l'Asie centrale?" *Cahiers du monde russe* 49, no. 1 (2008), 101–44.

Pianciola, Niccoló. "Famine in the Steppe: The Collectivization of Agriculture and the Kazak Herdsmen, 1928–1934." *Cahiers du monde russe* 45, no. 1/2 (2004), 137–92.

Pianciola, Niccoló. "Interpreting an Insurgency in Soviet Kazakhstan: The OGPU, Islam and Qazaq 'Clans' in Suzak, 1930." In Pianciola and Sartori, *Islam, Society and States*, 297–340.

Pianciola, Niccoló. "Stalinist Spatial Hierarchies: Placing the Kazakhs and Kyrgyz in Soviet Economic Regionalization." *Central Asian Survey* 36, no. 1 (2017), 73–92.

Pianciola, Niccoló. *Stalinismo di frontiera: Colonizzazione agricola, sterminio dei nomadi e costruzione statale in Asia centrale (1905–1936)*. Rome, 2009.

Pianciola, Niccoló, and P. Sartori, eds. *Islam, Society and States across the Qazaq Steppe (18th–Early 20th Centuries)*. Vienna, 2013.

Plaggenborg, Stefan. "Die Organisation des Sowjetstaates." In *Handbuch der Geschichte Russlands, vol. 3: 1856–1945. Von den autokratischen Reformen zum Sowjetstaat*, 2nd half volume, edited by Gottfried Schramm, 1413–525. Stuttgart, 1992.

Plaggenborg, Stefan. "Staatlichkeit als Gewaltroutine: Sowjetische Geschichte und das Problem des Ausnahmezustands." In *Staats-Gewalt, Ausnahmezustand und Sicherheitsregimes: Historische Perspektiven*, edited by Alf Lüdtke and Michael Wildt, 117–44. Göttingen, 2008.

Platunov, Evgenii. "Stalin na Altae." http://komsomol.ucoz.kz/publ/19-1-0-361 (accessed March 20, 2013).

Pogorel'skii, P. *Osedanie kochevnikov i razvitie zhivotnovdstva*. Alma-Ata, 1949.

Pogorel'skii, P. "Osedanie kochevykh i polukochevykh khoziaistv." In *Osedanie kochevykh i polukochevykh khoziaistv Kirgizii*, edited by P. Pogorel'skii, 7–41. Moscow, 1934.

Pohl, Michaela. "The 'Planet of One Hundred Languages': Ethnic Relations and Soviet Identity in the Virgin Lands." In *Peopling the Russian Periphery: Borderland Colo-*

nization in Eurasian History, edited by Nicholas B. Breyfogle, Abby Schrader, and Willard Sunderland, 237–61. London, 2007.

Pohl, Otto J. *Ethnic Cleansing in the USSR, 1937–1949*. Westport, 1999.

Poliakov, Iu. A. "Karakumskaia operatsiia 1931 goda." *Otechestvennaia istoriia*, no. 4 (2007), 164–71.

Polian, Pavel. *Against Their Will: The History and Geography of Forced Migrations in the USSR*. Budapest, 2004.

Polochanskii, E. *Za novyi aul-kstau*. Moscow, 1926.

Popitz, Heinrich. *Phänomene der Macht*. Tübingen, 1992.

Popov, Iu. "Kak prokhodila kollektivizatsii i bor'ba s nei v Kazakhstanskoi Sary-Arke (istoriia)." http://www.centrasia.ru/newsA.php?st=1265753520 (accessed May 18, 2018).

Popov, V. "Pokhody dalekikh dnei." In *Chekisty Kazakhstana*, edited by N. I. Milovanov and A. F. Minaichev, 37–62. Alma-Ata, 1971.

Pospelov, P. I., ed. *Vsesoiuznaia Sel'skokhoziaistvennaia Vystavka 1939*. Moscow, 1939.

"Postanovlenie politbiuro TsK VKP(b) 'O meropriatiiakh po likvidatsii kulatskikh khoziaistv v raionakh sploshnoi kollektivizatsii,' 30 ianvaria 1930." *Istoricheskii arkhiv*, no. 4 (1994), 147–52.

Poznanskii, V. S., ed. *Gonimye golodom: Dokumenty o sud'be desiatkov tysiach kazakhov, bezhavshikh v Sibir' v nachale 30-kh godov*. 4 vols. Almaty, 1995.

Primernyi ustav sel'skokhoziaistvennoi arteli: Priniat Vtorym Vsesoiuznom s"ezdom kolkhoznikov-udarnikov i utverzhden Sovetom Narodnykh Komissarov SSSR i Tsentral'nym Komitetom VKP(b) 17 fevralia 1935. Moscow, 1950.

Rahmato, Dessalegn. *Famine and Survival Strategies: A Case Study from Northeast Ethopia*. Uddevalla, 1991.

Rakisheva, Botagoz. *Deportatsiia narodov v Kazakhstan v 1930–1950gg.: obshchnost' istorii (interv'iu s postradavshim ot deportatsii v 1930–50 gody v Kazakhstan)*. Astana 2013.

Ree, Eric van. "Heroes and Merchants: Stalin's Understanding of National Character." *Kritika* 8, no. 1 (2007), 41–65.

Reemtsma, Jan Phillip. *Trust and Violence: An Essay on a Modern Relationship*. Princeton, 2012.

Reid, Anna. *Blokada: Die Belagerung von Leningrad 1941–1944*. Berlin, 2011.

Reinhard, Wolfgang. *Geschichte des modernen Staates*. Munich, 2007.

Riabokon, V. "K voprosu o sovetizatsii aula." *Krasnyi Kazakhstan* 1, no. 1 (1926), 35–62.

Riadnin, M. *Kazakhstan na putiakh k sotsialisticheskomu stroitel'stvu: otvet na vystupleniia oppozitsii po natsional'nomu voprosu*. Kzyl-Orda, 1928.

Riekenberg, Michael. *Gewaltsegmente: Über einen Ausschnitt der Gewalt in Lateinamerika*. Leipzig, 2003.

Riekenberg, Michael. "Zur Anthropologie des Krieges in Lateinamerika im 19. Jahrhundert." In *Formen des Krieges: Von der Antike bis zur Gegenwart*, edited by Dietrich Beyrau, Michael Hochgeschwender, and Dieter Langewiesche, 197–221. Paderborn, 1997.

Ritter, William S. "The Final Phase in the Liquidation of Anti-Soviet Resistance in Tadzhikistan. Ibrahim Bek and the Basmachi, 1924–1931." *Soviet Studies* 37, no. 4 (1985), 484–93.

Rittersporn, Gábor T. "Das kollektivierte Dorf in der bäuerlichen Gegenkultur." In *Stalinismus vor dem Zweiten Weltkrieg: Neue Wege der Forschung*, edited by Manfred Hildermeier, 147–67. Munich, 1998.

Rittersporn, Gábor T. "The Omnipresent Conspiracy: On Soviet Imagery of Politics and Social Relations in the 1930s." In *The Stalinist Dictatorship*, edited by Chris Ward, 260–77. London, 1998.

Rittersporn, Gábor T. "Soviet Citizens between Indignation and Resignation: Loyalty and Lost Hope in the USSR." *Telos* 2005, no. 131 (Summer 2005), 104–25.

Roginskij, Arsenij. "Fragmentierte Erinnerung: Stalin und der Stalinismus im heutigen Russland." *Osteuropa* 59, no. 1 (2009), 37–44.

Rottier, Peter. "The Kazakness of Sedentarization: Promoting Progress as Tradition in Response to the Land Problem." *Central Asian Survey* 22, no. 1 (2003), 67–81.

Roy, Oliver. *The New Central Asia: The Creation of Nations*. New York, 2000.

Rudenko, S. I. *Ukraintsy—pereselentsy semipalatinskoi Gubernii*. Leningrad, 1930.

Ryn, Zdzisław, and Stanisław Kłodziński. "An der Grenze zwischen Leben und Tod: Eine Studie über die Erscheinung des 'Muselmanns' im Konzentrationslager." In *Die Auschwitz-Hefte: Texte der polnischen Zeitschrift "Przeglad lekarski" über historische, psychische und medizinische Aspekte des Lebens und Sterbens in Auschwitz*, vol. 1, edited by Jochen August, 89–154. Hamburg, 1995.

Rysakov, P. "Praktika shovinizma i mestnogo natsionalizma." *Revoliutsiia i natsional'nosti* 1, no. 8/9 (1930), 25–34.

Ryskulov, Turar. "Dzhetysuiskie voprosy." In *Sobranie sochinenii*, 2:7–32.

Ryskulov, Turar. *Revoliutsiia i korennoe naselenie Turkestana*. Tashkent, 1925.

Ryskulov, Turar. *Sobranie sochinenii v trekh tomakh*. Almaty, 1997.

Ryskulov, Turar. "Vnimanie skotovodstvu v kochevykh i polukochevykh raionakh." In *Sobranie sochinenii*, 3:298–304.

S. M. "Osedanie—vazhneishii etap likvidatsii natsional'nogo neravenstva." *Revoliutsiia i natsional'nosti*, no. 7 (1932), 33–39.

Sabitov, N. S. "Kul'tura i byta Kazakhskogo kolkhoznogo aula." *Vestnik Akademii Nauk Kazakhskoi SSR*, no. 10 (1950), 51–60.

Sabitov, N. S. "Rabota po izucheniiu kul'tury i byt kazakhskogo kolkhoznogo aula (obzor materialov etnograficheskikh ekspeditsii za 1946–1951 gody)." *Vestnik Akademii Nauk Kazakhskoi SSR* (1952), 89–94.

Sabol, Steven. "Kazakh Resistance to Russian Colonization: Interpreting the Kenesary Kasymov Revolt, 1837–1845." *Central Asian Survey* 22, no. 2/3 (2003), 231–52.

Sabol, Steven. *Russian Colonization and the Genesis of Kazak National Consciousness*. Basingstoke, 2003.

Safarov, G. *Kolonial'naia revoliutsiia: opyt Turkestana*. Moscow, 1921.

Sahadeo, Jeff. "Conquest, Colonialism, and Nomadism on the Eurasian Steppe." *Kritika* 4, no. 4 (2003), 942–54.

Sahadeo, Jeff. "Home and Away: Why the Asian Periphery Matters in Russian History." *Kritika* 16, no. 2 (2015), 375–88.

Sahadeo, Jeff. *Russian Colonial Society in Tashkent, 1865–1923*. Bloomington, 2007.

Sakharov, V., E. Zemskov, and K. Serdiuk. *Tashkentskoe Krasnoznamennoe: ocherki istorii tashkentskogo vysshego obshchevoiskogo kommandnogo krasnoznamennogo ordena Krasnoi Zvezdy uchilishcha imeni V. I. Lenina*. Tashkent, 1988.

Sakovskii, K. K., ed. *Materialy ekspeditsii sredneaziatskogo gosudarstvennogo univer-siteta po obsledovaniiu zhivotnovodstva v dzhetysuiskoi gubernii i karakulevodstva v kara-kalpakskoi avtonomnoi oblasti v 1927 godu*. Tashkent, 1930.

Salzman, Philip C. "Introduction: Processes of Sedentarization as Adaptation and Response." In *When Nomads Settle: Processes of Sedentarization as Adaptation and Response*, edited by Philip C. Salzman, 1–19. New York, 1980.

Salzman, Philip C. *Pastoralists: Equality, Hierarchy, and the State*. Boulder, 2004.

Samatov, M. "Zhivotnovodstvo Kazakhstana na pod'eme." *Bol'shevik Kazakhstana*, no. 7 (1935), 49–63.

Samatov, M., and V. Kavraiskii. "Zhivotnovodstvo Kazakhstana na pod'eme: itogi perepiski skota na 1-e ianvaria 1936 goda." *Narodnoe khoziaistvo Kazakhstana* 8, no. 3/4 (1936), 57–77.

Scarry, Elaine. *The Body in Pain: The Making and Unmaking of the World*. New York, 1985.

Schatz, Edward. *Modern Clan Politics: The Power of "Blood" in Kazakhstan and Beyond*. Seattle, 2004.

Schiller, Otto. *Die Kollektivbewegung in der Sowjetunion: Ein Beitrag zu den Gegenwarts-fragen der russischen Landwirtschaft*. Berlin, 1931.

Schilling, Tadzio. "Mächtige Signale: Informelle Kommunikation und Herrschaft an Stalins Hof, 1927–1940." *Journal of Modern European History* 10, no. 3 (2012), 320–40.

Schlögel, Karl. *Moscow 1937*. Cambridge, 2012.

Schnell, Felix. *Räume des Schreckens: Gewalt und Gruppenmilitanz in der Ukraine 1905–1933*. Hamburg, 2012.

Scholz, Fred. *Nomadismus: Theorie und Wandel einer sozio-ökologischen Kulturweise*. Stuttgart, 1995.

Scott, James. *Seeing Like a State: How Certain Schemes to Improve the Human Condition Have Failed*. New Haven, 1998.

Scott, James. *Weapons of the Weak: Everyday Forms of Peasant Resistance*. New Haven, 1987.

Sen, Amartya. "Ingredients of Famine Analysis, Availability and Entitlements." *Quarterly Journal of Economics* 96, no. 3 (1981), 433–64.

Service, Robert. *Trotsky: A Biography*. London, 2009.

VII Vsekazakhskaia konferentsiia VKP(b): stenograficheskii otchet. Alma-Ata, 1930.

Shakir-zade, Tahir. *Grundzüge der Nomadenwirtschaft: Betrachtung des Wirtschaftslebens der sibirisch-centralasiatischen Nomadenvölker*. Bruchsal, 1931.

Shaumian, M. *Ot kochev'ia k sotsializmu*. Alma-Ata, 1967.

Shaw, Charles. "Friendship under Lock and Key: The Soviet Central Asian Border, 1918–1934." *Central Asian Survey* 30, no. 3/4 (2011), 331–48.

Shayakhmetov, Mukhamet. *A Kazakh Teacher's Story: Surviving the Silent Steppe*. London, 2012.

Shayakhmetov, Mukhamet. *The Silent Steppe: The Story of a Kazakh Nomad under Stalin*. London, 2006.

Shearer, David. "Elements Near and Alien. Passportization, Policing, and Identity in the Stalinist State, 1932–1953." *Journal of Modern History* 76, no. 4 (2004), 835–81.

Shearer, David. *Policing Stalin's Socialism: Repression and Social Order in the Soviet Union, 1924–1953*. New Haven, 2009.

Shestoi plenum Kazakhskogo Kraevogo Komiteta VKP(b), 10.–16. iiulia 1933g. Stenograficheskii otchet. Alma-Ata, 1936.

Shreider, Mikhail. *NKVD iznutri: zapiski chekista*. Moscow, 1995.

Shvetsov, S. P. *Kazakhskoe khoziaistvo v ego estestvenno-istoricheskikh i bytovykh usloviiakh: materialy k vyrabotke norm zemel'nogo ustroistva v Kazakhskoi Avton. Sovetskoi Sotsialisticheskoi Respublike*. Leningrad, 1926.

Siegelbaum, Lewis H. "'Dear Comrade, You Ask What We Need': Socialist Paternalism and Soviet Rural 'Notables' in the mid-1930s." In Fitzpatrick, *Stalinism*, 231–55.

Simon, Gerhard. "Holodomor als Waffe: Stalinismus, Hunger und der ukrainische Nationalismus." *Osteuropa* 54, no. 12 (2004), 37–56.

Simon, Gerhard. *Nationalism and Policy toward the Nationalities in the Soviet Union: From Totalitarian Dictatorship to Post-Stalinst Society.* Boulder, 1991.

Simon, Gerhard. *Nationalismus und Nationalitätenpolitik in der Sowjetunion: Von der totalitären Diktatur zur nachstalinschen Gesellschaft.* Baden-Baden, 1988.

Sindelar, Daisy. "Vyzhivshee pokolenie nazyvaet Golod 'zabytym genotsidom.'" http://rus.azattyq.org/content/article/1357667.html (accessed May 18, 2018).

Sirius, M. G. "K voprosu o perspektivakh skotovodstva v Kazakhstane." *Narodnoe khoziaistvo Kazakhstana* 1, no. 1 (1926), 26–30.

Slastuchin, F. "Sotsialisticheskaia perestroika kochevogo kazakhskogo aula." *Sovetskaia etnografiia,* no. 1 (1933), 68–97.

Slezkine, Yuri. *Arctic Mirrors: Russia and the Small Peoples of the North.* Ithaca, 1994.

Slezkine, Yuri. "The USSR as a Communal Apartment, or How a Socialist State Promoted Ethnic Particularism." *Slavic Review* 53, no. 2 (1994), 414–52.

Slocum, John W. "Who, and When, Were the Inorodtsy? The Evolution of the Category of 'Aliens' in Imperial Russia." *Russian Review* 57 (1998), 173–90.

Sneath, David. *The Headless State: Aristocratic Orders, Kinship Society, and Misrepresentations of Nomadic Inner Asia.* New York, 2007.

Sofsky, Wolfgang. *Traktat über die Gewalt.* Frankfurt am Main, 1996.

Sofsky, Wolfgang. *Zeiten des Schreckens: Amok, Terror, Krieg.* Frankfurt am Main, 2002.

Sokolovskii, V. G. *Kazakhskii aul: k voprosu o metodakh ego izucheniia gosudarstvennoi statistiki na osnove reshenii V-i Vsekazakskoi Partkonferentsii i 2-go Plenuma Kazkraikoma VKP(b).* Tashkent, 1926.

Solomon, Peter. *Soviet Criminal Justice under Stalin.* Cambridge, 1996.

Sorokin, Pitirim. *Man and Society in Calamity: The Effects of War, Revolution, Famine, Pestilence upon Human Mind, Behaviour, Social Organization and Cultural Life.* New York, 1942.

"Sovershenno sekretno": Lubianka—Stalinu o polozhenie v strane (1922–1934gg.). 10 vols. Moscow, 2001–4.

"Soveshchanie po voprosam osedaniia kochevykh khoziaistv i zemleustroistva kolkhozov natsional'nykh respublik i oblastei." *Revoliutsiia i natsional'nosti* 6, no. 10 (1935), 83–89.

Sovetskaia derevnia glazami VChK—OGPU—NKVD: Dokumenty i materialy v 4 tomakh. 4 vols. Moscow, 1998–2005.

Sovetskoe rukovodstvo: perepiska 1928–1941, edited by A. V. Kvashonkin et al. Moscow, 1999.

Sperling, Walter. *Der Aufbruch der Provinz: Die Eisenbahn und die Neuordnung der Räume im Zarenreich.* Frankfurt am Main, 2011.

Spittler, Gerd. "Handeln in einer Hungerkrise: Das Beispiel der Kel Ewey Tuareg." In Collet, Lassen, and Schanbacher, *Handeln in Hungerkrisen,* 27–44.

Spittler, Gerd. *Handeln in einer Hungerkrise: Tuaregnomaden und die große Dürre von 1984.* Opladen, 1989.

Spittler, Gerd. "Stress, Crisis and Catastrophe: Communication and Survival Strategies of Tuareg Nomads during a Famine." In *Food Security and Nutrition: The Global Challenge,* edited by Uwe Kracht and Manfred Schulz, 157–68. New York, 1993.

Ssorin-Chaikov, Nikolai. "Representing 'Primitive Communists': Ethnographic and Political Authority in Early Soviet Siberia." In Burbank, von Hagen, and Remnev, *Russian Empire,* 268–92.

Ssorin-Chaikov, Nikolai. *The Social Life of the State in Subarctic Siberia.* Stanford, 2003.

Stalin, J. W. [Stalin, Iossif Vissarionovich]. "Das Jahr des großen Umschwungs: Zum 12. Jahrestag des Oktober." In Stalin, *Werke,* 12:105–20.

Stalin, J. W. "Marxismus und nationale Frage." In Stalin, *Der Marxismus und die nationale und koloniale Frage,* 26–93. Berlin, 1952.

Stalin, J. W. "Über die Grundlagen des Leninismus: Vorlesungen an der Swerdlow-Universität. Die Partei." In Stalin, *Werke,* 6:62–166.

Stalin, J. W. "Über die Industrialisierung und das Getreideproblem: Rede am 9. Juli 1928." In Stalin, *Werke,* 11:139–66.

Stalin, J. W. "Über die rechte Abweichung in der KPdSU(B): Rede auf dem Plenum des ZK und der ZKK der KPdSU (B) im April 1929 (Stenographisches Protokoll)." In Stalin, *Werke,* 12:1–95.

Stalin, J. W. "Über die Rechten und 'Linken' in den nationalen Republiken und Gebieten: Rede zum ersten Tagesordnungspunkt der Beratung, 'Der Fall Sultan-Galiev,' 10. Juni." In Stalin, *Werke,* 5:264–73.

Stalin, J. W. "Vor Erfolgen von Schwindel befallen: Zu den Fragen der kollektivwirtschaftlichen Bewegung, 2. March 1930." In Stalin, *Werke,* 12:168–75.

Stalin, Joseph. "A Year of Great Change: On the Occasion of the Twelfth Anniversary of the October Revolution." In Stalin, *Works,* 12:124–41.

Stalin, J. W. "Zur Frage der Politik der Liquidierung des Kulakentums als Klasse." In Stalin, *Werke,* 12:157–61.

Stalin, Joseph. "Concerning the Policy of Eliminating the Kulaks as a Class." In Stalin, *Works,* 12:184–89.

Stalin, Joseph. "Dizzy with Success: Concerning Questions of the Collective-Farm Movement." In Stalin, *Works,* 12:197–205.

Stalin, Joseph. "Foundations of Leninism: Lectures Delivered at the Sverdlov University." In Stalin, *Works*, 6:71–196.

Stalin, Joseph. "Industrialization and the Grain Problem: Speech Delivered on July 9, 1928." In Stalin, *Works*, 11:165–96.

Stalin, Joseph. "Marxism and the National Question." In Stalin, *Works*, 2:300–382.

Stalin, Joseph. "The Right Deviation in the C.P.S.U.(B): Speech delivered at the plenum of the Central Committee and Central Control Commission of the C.P.S.U.(B) in April 1929 (verbatim report)." In Stalin, *Works*, 12:1–113.

Stalin, Joseph. "Rights and Lefts in the National Republics and Regions: Speech on the First Item of the Conference Agenda: The Sultan Galiev Case, June 10." In Stalin, *Works*, 5:308–19.

Stalin, Joseph. *Works*. 13 vols. Moscow, 1954.

Stolberg, Eva-Maria. "Russland als eurasisches Imperium: Grenzregime und Grenzgesellschaft von der Neuzeit bis zum 20. Jahrhundert." *Comparativ. Zeitschrift für Globalgeschichte und vergleichende Gesellschaftsforschung* 17, no. 4 (2007), 37–55.

Stolberg, Eva-Maria. *Sibirien. Russlands "Wilder Osten": Mythos und soziale Realität im 19. und 20. Jahrhundert*. Stuttgart, 2009.

Stolypin, P. A., and Kriwoschein, A. W. *Die Kolonisation Sibiriens: Eine Denkschrift*. Berlin, 1912.

Sunderland, Willard. "The 'Colonization Question': Visions of Colonization in Later Imperial Russia." *Jahrbücher für Geschichte Osteuropas* 48, no. 2 (2000), 210–32.

Sunderland, Willard. "Imperial Space: Territorial Thought and Practice in the Eighteenth Century." In Burbank, von Hagen, and Remnev, *Russian Empire*, 33–66.

Sunderland, Willard. *Taming the Wild Field: Colonization and Empire on the Russian Steppe*. Ithaca, 2004.

Suny, Ronald G., and Terry Martin, eds. *A State of Nations: Empire and Nation-Making in the Age of Lenin and Stalin*. Oxford, 2001.

Svanberg, Ingvar. "The Nomadism of Orta Zhuz Kazaks in Xinjiang 1911–1949." In *The Kazaks of China: Essays on an Ethnic Minority*, edited by Linda Benson and Ingmar Svanberg, 107–40. Uppsala, 1988.

Talbot, Strobe, ed. *Khrushchev Remembers*. Boston, 1970.

Tarkhova, Nonna. *Krasnaia Armiia i stalinskaia kollektivizatsiia, 1928–1933 gg.* Moscow, 2010.

Tauger, Mark. "Arguing from Errors: On Certain Issues in Robert Davies' and Stephen Wheatcroft's Analysis of the 1932 Soviet Grain Harvest and the Great Soviet Famine of 1931–1933." *Europe-Asia Studies* 58, no. 6 (2006), 973–84.

Tauger, Mark. "The 1932 Harvest and the Famine of 1933." *Slavic Review* 50, no. 1 (1991), 70–89.

Teichmann, Christian. "Arbeiten, Kämpfen, Scheitern: Ein kirgisisches Funktionärstagebuch aus der Stalinzeit." *Osteuropa* 62, no. 3 (2012), 121–36.

Teichmann, Christian. "Canals, Cotton, and the Limits of De-colonization in Soviet Uzbekistan, 1924–1941." *Central Asian Survey* 26, no. 4 (2007), 499–519.

Teichmann, Christian. "Kollektivierung tatarisch: Asekeevo, Mittlere Wolga 1929–1930." In *Neuordnungen von Lebenswelten? Studien zur Gestaltung muslimischer Lebenswelten in der frühen Sowjetunion und in ihren Nachfolgestaaten*, edited by Andreas Frings, 99–125. Münster, 2006.

Teichmann, Christian. *Macht der Unordnung: Stalins Herschaft in Zentralasien.* Hamburg, 2016.

Telitsyn, V. L. "Reanimatsiia voennogo kommunizma v derevne." In *Rossiia Nepovskaia,* edited by S. A. Pavliuchenko, 419–40. Moscow, 2002.

Thomas, Alun. "The Caspian Disputes: Nationalism and Nomadism in Early Soviet Central Asia." *Russian Review* 76, no. 3 (2017), 502–25.

Thomas, Alun. "Kazakh Nomads and the New Soviet State, 1919–1934." PhD diss., University of Sheffield, 2017.

Tikhomirov, Alexey. "The Regime of Forced Trust: Making and Breaking Emotional Bonds between People and State in Soviet Russia, 1917–1941." *Slavonic and East European Review* 91, no. 1 (2013), 78–118.

Tlepov, S. T. *Stranitsy istorii Mangyshlaka.* Alma-Ata, 1980.

Togzhanov, G. "Burzhuaznye i melkoburzhuaznye 'teorii' ob aule." *Narodnoe khoziaistvo Kazakhstana* 6, no. 5 (1931), 21–34.

Togzhanov, G. *O kazakhskom aule.* Kzyl-Orda, 1927.

Torke, Hans-Joachim. *Einführung in die Geschichte Rußlands.* Munich, 1997.

Trochev, Alexei. "Transitional Justice Attempts in Kazakhstan." In *Transitional Justice and the Former Soviet Union: Reviewing the Past, Looking Toward the Future*, edited by Cynthia M. Horne and Lavinia Stan, 88–108. New York, 2018.

Trotha, Trutz von. "Über den Erfolg und die Brüchigkeit der Utopie staatlicher Herrschaft: Herrschaftssoziologische Betrachtungen über den kolonialen und nachkolonialen Staat in Westafrika." In *Verstaatlichung der Welt? Europäische Staatsmodelle und außereuropäische Machtprozesse*, edited by Wolfgang Reinhard, 223–52. Munich, 1999.

Trotha, Trutz von. "Zur Soziologie der Gewalt." *Kölner Zeitschrift für Soziologie und Sozialpsychologie* 57 (1997), 9–56.

Trotsky, Leon. "National Aspects of Politics in Kazakhstan, March 11, 1927." In *Leon Trotsky: The Challenges of the Left Opposition (1926–1927)*, edited by Naomi Allen and George Sanders, 210–13. New York, 1980.

Tsarevskaia-Diakina, T. V., ed. *Istoriia stalinskogo gulaga: konets 1920-kh–pervaia polovina 1950-kh godov*. Sobranie dokumentov v semi tomakh. 7 vols. Moscow, 2004.

Turnbull, Collin. *The Mountain People*. New York, 1987.

Tursunbaev, A. B. *Kazakhskii aul v trekh revoliutsiiakh*. Alma-Ata, 1967.

Tursunbaev, A. B., ed. *Kollektivizatsiia sel'skogo khoziaistva Kazakhstana (1926– iiun' 1941)*. Alma-Ata, 1967.

Undasynov, N. "Chemu uchit opyt otgonnogo zhivotnovodstva v Kazakhstane." *Pravda*, November 16, 1945.

Undasynov, N. "Vazhneishaia zhivotnovodcheskaia baza strany." *Pravda*, April 25, 1942.

United Nations Refugee Agency. "Kazakhstan: The Forgotten Famine." December 2007, p. 28. http://www.refworld.org/docid/4783869028.html (accessed May 18, 2018).

Ustinov, V. N. *Turar Ryskulov: ocherki politicheskoi biografii*. Almaty, 1996.

Varlamov, A., and F. Savinskii. "My otvechaem za nedostatki raboty v aule i derevne." *Bol'shevik Kazakhstana*, no. 3 (1933), 37–44.

Vatlin, Aleksandr. *Terror raionnogo masshtaba: "Massovye operatsii" NKVD v kuntsevskom raione moskovskoi oblasti 1937–1938gg*. Moscow, 2004.

Verkhoturov, D.N. *Asharshylyk: velikii golod v Kazakhstane, 1932–1933 godov*. N. p., 2013. http://1916.kg/sites/default/files/library/nid_376/verkhoturov_d_n_asharshylyk_ velikiy_golod_v_kazakhstane.pdf (accessed February 6, 2018).

Vert, Nikola [Werth, Nicolas]. *Terror i besporiadok: Stalinizm kak sistema*. Moscow, 2010.

Viola, Lynne. *The Best Sons of the Fatherland: Workers in the Vanguard of Soviet Collectivization*. New York, 1989.

Viola, Lynne. *Peasant Rebels under Stalin: Collectivization and the Culture of Peasant Resistance*. New York, 1996.

Viola, Lynne. *The Unknown Gulag: The Lost World of Stalin's Special Settlers*. Oxford, 2007.

Volkow, Solomon, ed. *Die Memoiren des Dmitrij Schostakowitsch: Aufgezeichnet und herausgegeben von Solomon Volkow*. Munich, 1979.

Voss, Martin. "The Vulnerable Can't Speak: An Integrative Vulnerability Approach to Disaster and Climate Change Research." *Behemoth: A Journal on Civilization* 1, no. 3 (2008), 39–59.

Vostrov, V. V., and M. S. Mukanov. *Rodoplemennoi sostav i rasselenie Kazakhov (konets XIX–nachalo XX v.)*. Alma-Ata, 1968.

Waldmann, Peter. "Gesellschaften im Bürgerkrieg: Zur Eigendynamik entfesselter Gewalt." *Zeitschrift für Politik* 42, no. 4 (1995), 343–68.

Waldmann, Peter. "Zur Asymmetrie von Gewaltdynamik und Friedensdynamik am Beispiel von Bürgerkriegen und bürgerkriegsähnlichen Konflikten." In *Gewalt: Entwicklungen, Strukturen, Analyseprobleme*, edited by Wilhelm Heitmeyer and Hans-Georg Soeffner, 246–65. Frankfurt am Main, 2004.

Watts, Michael J., and Hans G. Bohle. "Hunger, Famine, and the Space of Vulnerability." *GeoJournal* 30, no. 2 (1993), 117–25.

Weber, Max. *Economy and Society: An Outline of Interpretative Sociology.* Berkeley, 1978.

Wehner, Markus. *Bauernpolitik im proletarischen Staat: Die Bauernfrage als zentrales Problem der sowjetischen Innenpolitik 1921–1928.* Cologne, 1998.

Wemheuer, Felix. *Der Große Hunger: Hungersnöte unter Stalin und Mao.* Berlin, 2012.

Wendelken, Rebecca W. "Russian Immigration and Its Effect on the Kazakh Steppes (1552–1965)." In *The Role of Migration in the History of the Eurasian Steppe: Sedentary Civilization vs. "Barbarian" Nomads*, edited by Andrew Fell-Bialkoff, 71–97. Basingstoke, 2000.

Werth, Nicolas. *Cannibal Island: Death in a Siberian Gulag.* Princeton, 2007.

Werth, Nicolas. *Ein Staat gegen sein Volk: Das Schwarzbuch des Kommunismus. Sowjetunion.* Munich, 2002.

Werth, Nicolas. "A State against Its People: Violence, Repression, and Teror in the Soviet Union." In *The Black Book of Communism: Crimes, Terror, Repression*, edited by Stéphane Courtois et al., 33–268, Cambridge, MA, 1999.

Wheatcroft, Stephen G. "Agency and Terror: Evdokimov and Mass Killing in Stalin's Great Terror." *Australian Journal of Politics and History* 53, no. 1 (2007), 20–43.

Wheatcroft, Stephen G. "From Team-Stalin to Degenerate Tyranny." In *The Nature of Stalin's Dictatorship: The Politburo, 1924–1953*, edited by E. A. Rees, 79–107. Basingstoke, 2004.

Wieviorka, Michel. *Violence: A New Approach.* London, 2009.

Winner, Irene. "Some Problems of Nomadism and Social Organization among the Recently Settled Kazakhs." *Central Asian Review* 11 (part 1), no. 3 (1963), 246–67, and (part 2), no. 4, 355–73.

Yakovlev, Alexander N. *A Century of Violence in Soviet Russia.* New Haven, 2002.

Yaroshevski, D. B. "Imperial Strategy in the Kirghiz Steppe in the Eighteenth Century." *Jahrbücher für Geschichte Osteuropas* 39, no. 2 (1991), 221–24.

"Zakliuchenie komissii Prezidiuma Verkhovnogo Soveta Respublik Kazakhstana po izucheniiu postanovlenii KazTsIK I SNK KASSR ot 27 avgusta 1928 goda 'O kon-

fiskatsii baiskikh khoziaistv' ot 13 sentiabria 1928 goda 'Ob ugolovnoi otvetstven-
nosti za protivodeistvie konfiskatsii i vyseleniiu krupneishego i polufeodal'nogo
baistva' ot 19 fevralia 1930 goda 'O meropriiatiiakh po ukrepleniiu sotsialisticheskogo pereustroistva sel'skogo khoziaistva v raionakh sploshnoi kollektivizatsii i
po bor'be s kulachestvom i baistvom.'" In Kozybaev, *Kazakhstan na rubezhe vekov*,
2:35–51.

Zamoyski, Adam. *1812: Napoleons Feldzug in Russland*. Munich, 2012.

Zelenin, I. E. "Byl li kolkhoznyi neonep?" *Otechestvennaia istoriia*, no. 2 (1994), 105–21.

Zemskov, V. N. *Spetsposelentsy v SSSR 1930–1960*. Moscow, 2005.

Zenkovich, F. I. "Kochevye raiony Kazakhstana i osnovnye linii ikh razvitiia." *Narodnoe
khoziaistvo Kazakhstana*, no. 9/10 (1936), 45–55.

Zevelev, A. I., Iu. A. Poliakov, and A. I. Chugunov. *Basmachestvo: voznikovenie, sushch-
nost,' krakh*. Moscow, 1981.

Zhakypov, M. Kh. et al., eds. *Narkomy Kazakhstana: 1920–1946 gg.: biograficheskii spravochnik*. Almaty, 2007.

Zhanaev, Bolat. "O chem povedali dokumenty: k 120-letniiu Tobaniiaza Allaniiazova." In
Nabiev, *Stepnaia tragediia*, 418–25.

Zhandabekova, O. V. *Pod grifom sekretnosti: otkochevki kazakhov v Kitai v period kollektivizatsii. Reemigratsiia, 1928–1957gg. Sbornik dokumentov*. Ust'-Kamenogorsk,
1998.

Zhanguttin, V. O. "Golod voennogo vremeni v Kazakhstane: dokladnye zapiski narkoma
NKVD Kazakhskoi ASSR N. K. Bogdanova—narkomu NKVD SSSR L.P. Berii 1944g."
Istoricheskii arkhiv 17, no. 1 (2009), 44–55.

Zhdanko, T. A. "Mezhdunarodnoe znachenie istoricheskogo opyta perekhoda
kochevnikov na osedlost' v Srednei Azii i Kazakhstane." *Sovetskaia etnografiia*, no.
4 (1967), 3–24.

Zhdanova, G. D., ed. *Massovye repressii v altaiskom krae 1937–1938 gg.: Prikaz Nr. 00447*.
Moscow, 2010.

Zhubanyshuly, Makan. *Sred' bela dnia: roman*. Astana, 2005.

Zulkasheva, A. A. et al., eds. *Tragediia kazakhskogo aula, 1928–1934: sbornik dokumentov, vol. 1: 1928–aprel' 1929*. Almaty, 2013.

Zveriakov, I. A. *Ot kochevaniia k sotsializmu*. Alma-Ata, 1932.

INDEX